CH

D1008714

MUSIC

THE BUSINESS

THE
ESSENTIAL
GUIDE TO THE
LAW AND
THE DEALS

7TH EDITION

MUSIC
THE BUSINESS

FULLY REVISED AND UPDATED

ANN HARRISON

The law in this book is correct to the best of my knowledge as of 31 December 2016, but the views I expound are mine alone. Although I have tried to give practical examples throughout the book, everyone's circumstances are different, as are the facts of every case. The book is not a substitute for independent legal advice given to you personally. No liability can be accepted by me or Virgin Books for anything in reliance on the matters referred to in this book.

Ann Harrison

3 5 7 9 10 8 6 4 2

Virgin Books, an imprint of Ebury Publishing,
20 Vauxhall Bridge Road,
London SW1V 2SA

Virgin Books is part of the Penguin Random House group of companies whose addresses can be found at global.penguinrandomhouse.com

Penguin
Random House
UK

First published in the United Kingdom by Virgin Books in 2000
This edition published 2017

www.penguin.co.uk

A CIP catalogue record for this book is available from the British Library

ISBN 9780753548202

Printed and bound in Great Britain by Clays Ltd, St Ives PLC

Penguin Random House is committed to a sustainable future for our business, our readers and our planet. This book is made from Forest Stewardship Council® certified paper.

MIX
Paper from
responsible sources
FSC
www.fsc.org   FSC® C018179

Contents

Introduction

When I started work in the music business I had very little idea how it worked. Record and publishing companies were a mystery to me. I looked for books that might help me but there weren't many around. Those were mostly out of date or applied to the US and not to the UK music business. I had to learn from my colleagues as I went along. I was lucky in that they were very knowledgeable and very generous with their time.

Now there are many more sources of information available on the UK music business and there are many good full- and part-time media and law courses available to give you a head start. To accompany these I felt we needed an easy-to-read guide to how the business works from a legal viewpoint – one that explains what a publisher does, for example, and what copyright is. Many of the books on the business are written from the US perspective. I wanted to write one based on the UK music industry which could be read as a road map through the industry. Where I've used technical expressions I have tried to give a non-technical explanation alongside. This book is not, however, intended to be a substitute for legal textbooks on copyright, other intellectual property rights or contract. There are many good examples of these sorts of books around.

The music business is a dynamic one and each new edition involves a reworking of most of the chapters. This latest edition was no different. In particular, anything to do with new media is difficult to keep up to date. The chapter on digital uses has been completely rewritten, with a greater emphasis on streaming.

The state of the recording industry is looked at in some detail as part of an overview of the industry generally and there have been changes in the live industry, on secondary ticketing in particular. The chapter on publishing has seen major re-writing as a result of some interesting new cases and legal developments particularly in the US and in relation to parody and fair dealing. The usually arcane world of collection societies has also undergone significant changes reflected in a rewrite of much of that chapter.

Wherever possible, I have tried to illustrate points with practical examples. I have to add a health warning that the examples produced and the guidelines given are mine alone and others may not agree or may have had different experiences.

We've all been fascinated by newspaper reports of artists in court over disputes with their ex-managers, record companies or even other members of the band. Are these reports accurate? Do these cases have any long-term effect? Do they matter? The facts of some of the more important cases have been highlighted, what was decided and the effects of these decisions on the music business. I've included several new cases throughout this edition, particularly in the area of sampling and band name disputes.

What I've tried to do is to let you in to some of the things I have learned over the last 34 years in the music business. There is, however, no substitute for legal advice on the particular facts of your case. Chapter 1 deals with choosing your advisers. Please read it. Good advisers will help to save you from what can be expensive mistakes. Most artists only have one chance of a successful career in this business – make sure you don't lose it through poor advice.

In writing this book I hope I will be able to convey some of the excitement of the music business to you. I have used 'he' throughout. This is just convention and is not intended as a slur on female artists or on the many excellent women working at all levels in the music business. The law is correct to the best of my ability as at 31 December 2016.

Chapter 1

Getting Started

INTRODUCTION

How do you get into the music business as a performing artist or songwriter? How do you get your foot in the door and how and when do you start gathering your team of advisers around you?

Maybe you want to be a manager or wish to adopt the DIY approach and set up your own record label or publishing company. This book is all about understanding the music business, the deals and how you get started.

CREATING A BUZZ

How do you get your work noticed? The idea is to create interest, a 'buzz' by whatever means you can. We'll see later that lawyers and accountants can help you to get noticed but you also need to work out your own plan and make it unique to you. 'Discoverability' is the new word for it, but it means 'how to rise above the noise'.

You can play as many gigs as you can and hope to be recognised by a scout on the lookout for a record company or music publisher or you can make a demo of your performances or songs and post it on a website like SoundCloud for peer review. You might also submit it to an A&R person direct or send him a link to your website. However, many companies, particularly the bigger ones, the 'majors', are refusing to accept unsolicited demos and many now only accept demos from a tried and tested or well-known source. Most companies also now ask for digital submissions or links to music. Check out their websites for their specific requirements.

There's no guarantee of success. No one is 'owed' a living in this business. You have to earn it, often through sheer hard slog.

Many try to improve their chances by coming up with a previously untried marketing ploy. Nowadays, these seem to focus on viral online marketing strategies but anything which is newsworthy and creates media interest will do. As we'll see later unusual crowd-funding ideas can also raise profile but I'd say that more than ever it is important to have good contacts and a good team of people to help you if you are looking for commercial success.

You can also shamelessly exploit any and all contacts you have with anyone who has even the remotest connection with the music business. You can pester these hapless souls to 'get their mate to the next gig' or to listen to your demo or visit your Facebook or YouTube page. This can improve your chances of at least getting your work listened to, but still isn't any guarantee it will lead to a record or publishing deal.

The live side of the industry is increasingly important as traditional record sales have declined. Record and publishing companies send scouts out to find undiscovered talent playing in out-of-the-way pubs. Posting details of up-coming gigs on your website or a good quality videoclip of you performing live up on YouTube could greatly improve your chances of someone deciding to come out and see you live. Supporting a band already on the A&R radar will also help.

A&R people live a precarious existence. They are only as good as their last successful signing. So they tend to like to have their hunches about an artist confirmed by someone else whose opinion they respect. This could be someone in their own company but, somewhat surprisingly, they will often talk to A&R people from rival companies. You would think that if they found someone they thought was good they would keep it to themselves until the deal was done. Some do, but many seem to need to be convinced that they have got it right by talking to friends at other companies, even if this pushes up the cost of the deal when the rival company joins in the race to sign the same artist. For the artist this may be a dream come true. He can choose the company that works best for him, and his lawyer will negotiate between the companies to get a better deal. This is what we call using your bargaining power. The more bargaining power you have, the better your overall deal is likely to be. In the last couple of years, the trend has been for several successful artists to make their mark elsewhere before becoming big with a major record company. Keane were signed to BMG Music Publishing for two years before they got major record company interest in their brand of music. London Grammar with Ministry of Sound's Metal & Dust Recordings label and Arctic Monkeys with Domino Records are other good examples of independent labels punching above their weight. Increasingly, A&R people largely adopt a cautious approach and want actual evidence of an artist's ability to complete recording of an album and being able to promote it before they come on board. This can be a depressing thought for an artist just starting out, but it could also be seen as an opportunity to create and develop your own style on a smaller independent label first or DIY self-release. Indeed, one of the biggest growth areas of the business is that of independent labels making their own story and either feeding artists into the bigger labels or releasing records themselves before the acts are picked up by the bigger labels. An example of an artist who has made it big independently without being picked up by a major is Passenger who has released his records on a network of independent labels achieving Number 1 album status across Europe and now also beginning to break the US market.

THE ARTIST NAME

The name an artist chooses is a vital part of his identity, his brand. It's a very difficult thing to get right and it's quite common for artists to go through various name changes before they settle on one they're happy with. It should be memorable, because if you combine a good name with a clever logo, design or idea then you are already halfway to having the basis of a good marketing campaign. If it's a name that you can do some wordplay with, so much the better.

Finding a good name is easier said than done. I'm sure you've sat around at some time in the pub after a beer or three and tried to come up with good band names. Despite all my advice on branding, I suspect that most artists choose their name for much more down-to-earth reasons, like it sounds cool, or it is the only one they can think of that is not naff and that no one else has already nabbed. Raiding books, old films and song titles are other good sources, for example, All About Eve, His Latest Flame and Janus Stark (from a comic). History is also a fertile source, The Levellers, Franz Ferdinand and The Boxer Rebellion being good examples.

You might decide on a name not knowing that anyone else has already claimed it. You may then invest a lot of time and maybe some money in starting to develop a reputation in that name. You're not going to be very happy if you then find out that someone else has the same name.

So how do you check if someone else is already using a band name? There are a couple of easy and cheap means of doing this.

Use the Internet to make your search as wide as possible, using a good search engine to check if the name you've chosen appears and not just in relation to the UK but also worldwide.

You could apply to register a domain name and see if anyone has claimed any of the main top-line domain categories for that name. If it is available do register it quickly, but also think about your logo as increasingly Apps are replacing domains as the place to go for information.

There are companies who advertise online that they can protect your band name but often these are adverts for trade mark agents so be careful that you know what you are being offered and if there are any charges before using their services. A listing on a band register database doesn't of itself give you special protection. If the same band name comes up on your online search that also doesn't mean that the other band will automatically succeed in stopping you from using the same name. You have to also look at whether they have an existing name or reputation, whether they have registered a trade mark or a domain name, and whether the other band has a reputation in the same area of the business as you.

If you choose a name and another artist objects to you continuing to use it because it is the same as one they have been using for a while, they may sue you. This could be for a breach of their trade mark (see Chapter 8) but, if they haven't registered a trade mark, they would have to argue that they had a reputation in the same area of music, in the same country as you and that you were creating confusion in the mind of the public and trading on their reputation. This is called 'passing off' (see Chapter 8). If they can establish these things (and that is not always easy to do) and they can also show that they are losing or are likely to lose out financially as a result, then they can ask the court to order you to stop using the name and also to award them financial compensation (damages) against you. They would have to establish a number of things, including an existing reputation. Just because a band has done a gig or two under the same name as you doesn't necessarily mean that they have a reputation or that they can satisfy the other tests of 'passing off'. You may have the greater reputation or the greater bargaining power; the other band may have split up or be about to do so. If you've already got a record deal or are about to release a single or album under that name, you may be able to persuade the other band that they are, in fact, trading on your reputation and that they should stop using the name. A word of warning, though, if you have a US label or intend to license recordings for sale in the US, it is quite likely that the US company will be unhappy at the existence of another artist with the same or a very similar name. They may well put considerable pressure on you either to change the name or to do a deal whereby you can definitely get the rights to use that name from the other artist. US labels, particularly majors, tend to be risk adverse and a potential threat to stop their sales will have them running scared.

In the US, the record company often makes it a condition of the record deal that it runs a trade mark search and charges you for it by adding the cost on to your account. If the search reveals another band or artist with the same name has already registered a trade mark, the record company will usually insist on you changing your name.

If you do find another artist with the same name, then you could do a deal with them to buy the right to use the name from them. You pay them an agreed sum and they stop using it, allowing you to carry on. If you're going to do these sorts of deals you should also make sure that you get from them any domain name that they have registered in the band name and, if they have a trade mark, an agreement to assign the trade mark registration and any ongoing applications to you. Take specialist advice.

The law can be somewhat confusing on this question of band names as highlighted by these two band name cases.

The Liberty X Case (Keith Floyd Sutherland v. V2 Music and others, [2002] Chancery Div)
V2 Music, had an exclusive recording contract with the members of Liberty and was preparing to release and promote their first album. The claimant was a member of a funk band formed in the late 1980s who also went by the name Liberty. This band had had a lot of publicity and played a number of live concerts up to 1996 but never got a record contract. Their 3 independent releases made between 1992 and 1995 sold only a few thousand copies. The public interest in them had become virtually non-existent by the mid-1990s, although they kept going in the business, where they were known and respected, and appeared as session musicians on other people's work. But did they have sufficient residual goodwill left to be entitled to be protected against passing off?

The pop group Liberty argued that even if there was residual goodwill their activities could not be seen to interfere with the old Liberty as they were in different areas of music.

The Judge decided that on the facts, while it was 'very close to the borderline', there was a small residual goodwill that deserved protection. He granted an injunction against the new Liberty band's continued use of the name. The band renamed itself Liberty X .

The Blue Case

In complete contrast, in June 2003 a case brought by the original band Blue – a Scottish rock group – came before the courts. Their last hit was in 1977 when a single by them reached number 18 in the charts. They had had a long career spanning 16 singles and 7 albums. They had a fan base and nowadays sold records mostly by mail order or over the Internet. The new Blue was a boy band formed in 2000 who had had 3 number one singles. The old Blue sued new Blue and its record company EMI/Virgin for substantial damages for passing off. The case came before Judge Laddie, who made it very clear at the beginning of the case that he found these claims somewhat dubious. He is quoted as saying, 'Are you seriously saying that fans of one group would mistake one for the other?' 'One is aged like you and me, the other is a boy band.' These are comments that could just as easily have been made in the Liberty case but different times, different outcomes. In this case, the early indication of the Judge's view led to the two sides reaching an out-of-court settlement. Both bands were to be permitted to continue to use the same name.

One Direction reached an agreement with a US band of the same name. The US band claimed that they had formed in 2009 and released several albums together. The claim stated that Syco and Sony were made aware of the confusion in 2011, but chose to ignore the claimants. The UK band were sued for over $1m in damages and faced claims for a further three times the profits they had made. The UK group countersued, claiming that they owned the name. The agreement reached by the groups allows them both to continue using the One Direction name.

SHOWCASING YOUR TALENT

Let's assume you've got a name, can legitimately use it and are getting some interest from the business. Record companies have in the past had their fingers burned by signing artists for large sums of money that they haven't seen perform and then discovering that they can't play or sing at all. So most record companies will insist on seeing you play live. If you are already playing the club circuit they may just turn up to a gig. If you aren't then they may pay for the hire of a venue or more likely ask you to arrange one. This is called a showcase. The venue is likely to be either a club or a rehearsal studio. These showcases may be open to the public but more often they will be by invitation only. It might pay for you to get at least some of your mates/fans along so there are a few friendly faces there as an industry showcase can be a daunting affair.

You could hire a venue yourself and send invitations out to all the record companies. However, just because you've invited them doesn't mean they'll come. Don't be at all surprised if they say they're coming and then don't show up. It's a very fickle business. They probably got a better offer on the day. The more of a 'buzz' there is about you the more likely it is that they will turn up, as they won't want to miss out on what could be 'the next big thing'.

I once asked the MD of a major record company why he was paying for an artist to do a showcase which would be open to the public when he knew that the artist would then be seen by the A&R people from rival record companies. His answer was quite revealing. He said that he knew how far he was prepared to go on the deal and so was not worried that it would be hyped up. He felt that if this artist really wanted to be with his record company he wouldn't be influenced by the interest from other companies. Confidence indeed. In fact, the artist did sign to his company and remained on the label for a number of albums.

If you are working with an independent label or production company it is likely that they will set up the showcases and invite along either a broad selection of bigger labels or only those with whom they have a special relationship, maybe ones for whom they already act as a talent out-source.

PRESENTING YOURSELF WELL

Here are some tips that may help you showcase your talents successfully. First, do your homework. Read the music press. Find out the current 'happening' venues, the places that regularly get written up in the music press. Pester that venue to give you a spot, even if it's the opening spot, and get all your mates to come along so that it looks like you've already got a loyal following. You may need to start out in the clubs outside the main circuit and work your way in.

You should also find out what nights the venue features your kind of music. If you play radio-friendly, commercial pop you don't want to get a gig on a heavy metal night.

Make sure the songs you play (your set) are a good cross-section of what you do. What goes down well with your mates in the local pub may not work for a more urban audience (but you'll want to play one or two of the firm favourites to give you a confidence boost).

Be professional. Rehearse, rehearse, rehearse. Think about your image and style. Don't send mixed messages. Think about your relationship with the audience. If yours is the 'say nothing, the music will speak for itself' style, that's fine – but make sure you're sending that message clearly to your audience. We all like a 'personality'. If your band has one, make sure you use him or her to your best advantage.

Always tell your audience who you are at the beginning and end of your set. You'd think this was obvious but you'd be surprised how many gigs I've been to where it's been impossible to tell who the artist is unless you've seen them before. The line-up of the bands on the night can change and no gig ever starts at the time it's supposed to, so you can't even make an intelligent guess. Make life easier for us – tell us clearly who you are, this is not the time for a shoe-gazing mumble.

Try to get your local press behind you. I know of one Nottingham band that did this very successfully. They made a fan of a local arts reporter who wrote a popular blog and kept him up to date on what they were up to and when they were playing. This made sure they got good reviews. A scout read the blog and went to the next gig, which was on the outer-London circuit. He liked what he saw and at the next gig the band took 'rent-a-crowd' with them and was spotted by an A&R man tipped off by the scout. A record deal followed. The local blogger was the first one they told – after their mums, of course. Followers of artists on Twitter have been alerted to gigs through Tweets. Also, no self-respecting artist these days is without a Facebook page with gig details on it or their own website and maybe also a blog, a SoundCloud, WeTransfer or Dropbox presence and plenty of shots on Instagram. They are actively posting details of their activities online, often via their own YouTube channel. If they have got mates who are good with a camera they are also putting video clips with their music on YouTube but more of this later in Chapter 7.

SHORT CUTS

It's a long haul and it needs determination and dedication to plug away on the gig circuit like this. Are there any short cuts? Yes, there are some. There are 'battle of the bands' competitions. If you get through to the final three or even win, then that will give you valuable exposure and should ensure a number of follow-up gigs in the local area and some useful publicity. They don't often lead directly to deals, although, if you win, you may get free studio time to make a demo (see below). But there are also a number of less scrupulous operators out there who promise a recording or management contract if you win. There is often an entry fee and you may well find that the deal you are offered is either worthless or on such poor terms that it isn't worth looking at. Remember if it seems too good to be true it probably is. Glastonbury has an Emerging Performers Competition for bands to play on one of its main stages. She Drew the Gun won in 2016. This initiative has helped artists like Charlene Soraia and Stornoway come to a wider audience. It's open to UK and Irish acts and there is a fee for entry. In June 2016 Gilles Peterson launched a regional initiative to discover new acts called 'Future Bubblers'. It's aimed at discovering ten of the next generation of innovative, 'outside the box' musicians who might be excluded from the networks and opportunities of London.

Then, of course, there are online band competitions – such as those promoted by the web-based unsignedonly.com or the International Songwriting Competition, which features a special category for unpublished writers. There are also 'open mike' evenings at clubs, when anyone can turn up and ask to play one or two numbers. Tony Moore's unsigned-acts nights at The Bedford pub in Balham, South London are a regular stopping-off spot for scouts. Tony Moore has also opened an additional live acoustic venue, The Regal Room, based at The Distillers in Fulham Palace Road, Hammersmith. Outside London, Night and Day, in Manchester, has regular local band showcases. The industry's trade paper, *Music Week*, runs a showcase for the best unsigned and just-signed talent to be held four times a year at the venue 'Under The Bridge' in Chelsea. Use Your Ears also acts as a music industry advice portal, including lists of places holding open mic nights or check out http://openmicfinder.com/UK/ for a venue near you. A web search may well turn up others.

Music industry organisations such as the Performing Right Society Limited (PRS) or its US equivalents, The American Society of Composers and Publishers (ASCAP), or Broadcast Music, Inc. (BMI), sometimes arrange nights at a Central London venue to showcase two or three acts who are either unsigned or have signed a record deal but not a publishing deal (or vice versa). ASCAP Presents helps showcase unsigned acts around industry events in the US like SXSW in Austin Texas. More recently PRS has offered grants (Momentum) to help take artists to the next level, see prsformusic.com for more details and in late 2016 announced a tie-in with performing right society Public Performance Limited. Also in 2016 the Government committed to hand over up to £2.8m in grants to independent UK music companies until 2020 through a re-launch of the Music Export Growth Scheme. Sums of between £5,000 and £50,000 will be paid out to qualifying labels, management companies, distributors and artists.

This is a good result for the lobbying efforts by the UK recorded music industry, led by the BPI. Artists successfully supported to date include 2016 BRIT Awards winners, Catfish and the Bottlemen, Mercury Prize shortlisted act Eska and 2014 Mercury Prize winners Young Fathers.

There are also annual UK music industry conventions such as Liverpool Sound City and The Great Escape (Brighton) and the spin-off launched in 2016 – First Fifty. Attached to them are a series of showcases for unsigned acts. An armband system allows you to pay a fixed fee to see all the bands performing at the various venues. You could get lucky and meet one or two A&R people and get your demo to them. Remember, however, that they get given many promo CDs, often late at night and possibly after several pints of beer, and they will probably need to be reminded who you are in a follow-up call or email a few days later. If you want to get on a showcase then you need to follow the submissions policy on their websites. Interestingly the criteria for what The Great Escape is looking for in a potential artist include 'a strong online presence', 'an original and accessible sound' as well as a 'sense of excitement around the band' in the lead-up to the performance. High standards indeed.

If you're chosen for one of the unsigned showcases, it should guarantee that at least one A&R person will be at your gig. The Great Escape saw an early performance by Adele in 2007. The now defunct In The City showcase helped break acts like Suede, Oasis and Muse.

Liverpool Sound City has been an early launchpad for acts as diverse as Grimes and Ed Sheeran and its overseas made missions help emerging artists access other markets.

THE DEMO RECORDING

For most people, making progress in the music business means having a demo recording of your work. This is your calling card, your way of introducing people to your work. It should be recorded to the best standard you can. A home studio recorded track, or one made on college facilities, may be fine if you are skilled enough in recording techniques and can play all the instruments but many people end up trying to get some time in a commercial studio.

STUDIO DEALS

How do you afford to make a recording in a commercial studio if you haven't any money? One way is to beg 'down time' from your local recording studio. This is time when the studio is not being hired out commercially. It may be at really unsociable hours such as 2 a.m. to 8 a.m. But who needs sleep when you've got a record deal to get?

The studio may give you the time cheaply or even free, but they may let you have the time in return for promises of what they will get when you get your first deal. The studio owner may want some of the income (the royalty) you earn from the sale of your records. This is sometimes called an override royalty. This is fair if you get a deal using recordings made at the studio, but take care that the studio is not asking for too much. A 1–1.5% override royalty is usually enough. By that I mean that if you are offered an 18% royalty you have to give 1–1.5% to the studio owner, leaving you with 16.5–17%. Some studios try to get royalties on your second and third album too. They argue that you wouldn't have got your chance to record at all without their generosity. This is true, but there comes a time when your success has nothing to do with that original generosity. One album is plenty in most cases or if it goes beyond that then the royalty percentage should reduce to say 0.5–0.75%.

The studio may also want a guarantee that you use their facilities when you make your album. Or the studio owner may want to produce your first commercial album. You should be careful about agreeing to these types of conditions. Record companies don't usually like these kinds of package deals on studio and producer. They like to have some say on these things themselves. If the producer is a proven talent they may be less concerned but you should try and build in flexibility.

The demo should feature a good cross-section of your work. Most people think that it should contain no more than three or four different pieces, with your best one first, your second-best one last and contrasting style pieces in the middle, but be careful of sending a confusing message by mixing too many different styles on one recording. The opening number should have immediate impact in case the listener fast-forwards it before you've got into your stride. Many A&R people listen to demos in their car or on their laptop. If you don't grab their attention, they'll move on to the next track or to another artist altogether. If you are sending a CD, then the case and the CD itself should both contain details of who you are, the names of the pieces, who wrote them and, most importantly, a contact number, otherwise, when, inevitably, the case gets separated from the CD, there is no way of telling who the band are and how to get hold of them. Most submissions are by MP3 or an online link to a service like Dropbox or SoundCloud and there it is important that the file name is distinctive and that the metatags on the recording itself identify the artist and the name of the tracks. If you can include an email or webpage contact address so much the better. Make yourself as easy as possible to find. When websites like MySpace, Facebook, SoundCloud and YouTube first began to offer new music they were such a novelty that it was an easy place to get yourself noticed and A&R people used them as a convenient place to talent search. Now practically every artist on these sites has a track to sell or download and rising above the rest is now a serious challenge. Online music sharing sites have become the convenient way for A&R people to hear new tracks and find out more about an artist before deciding whether or not to attend a gig but they are no longer such an easy place to get spotted in the first place. A video as opposed to still photographs is now becoming a 'must-have', with as good a quality as you can make and also some social networking 'likes', 'plays', 'streams' or real 'followers'.

FINDER'S AGREEMENT

These kinds of deals go in and out of popularity. They have largely been overtaken by the production deal, but they are still used where someone just wants to find a deal and not be further involved at any level. A studio owner, producer, manager or an established writer that you may be working with may like what they hear but may not have the resources or the inclination to sign you up to a record deal themselves. They may also not wish to become involved in your career longer term as a manager, but might spot an opportunity to use their contacts to further your and their own prospects. Such people might offer to find a deal for you and, if you agree in principle, they may then want you to sign a finder's agreement.

This is usually a short document where you appoint them for a period of time to get you a record or publishing deal. The period varies from six months up to eighteen months and may be non-exclusive, in which case the period is of less concern, or exclusive, in which case you might want to keep the period quite short. On an exclusive deal you pass through any interest you get to the finder who is in overall charge. If it's non-exclusive you and others can go on looking for a deal but you need to have a mechanism for how to tell who actually made the successful introduction. This is why most finders favour an exclusive arrangement.

If the finder gets a deal within the agreed time span that usually ends the ongoing relationship between you and the finder. Occasionally, however, it changes into a different type of deal such as that of artist/manager, artist/producer or co-writer.

The fee that the finder gets varies. It may be a percentage of what you get on signing the deal, a percentage of all monies paid you in the first contract period of the deal, or a share of these monies and of future royalties. The percentage is usually somewhere between 5% and 10%, but higher figures are possible depending on the services they are providing. Sometimes the finder argues for a percentage of monies beyond the initial contract period. This is less usual and I would want to see strong reasons to justify that and even then might well argue for the percentage to be reduced to say 2.5–5%.

Demo Deal

If an A&R man gets to hear your music through a demo or indeed at a live gig and has a good initial impression, he will undoubtedly want to hear more.

If this is not a situation where there is an existing production company with access to studio facilities, the A&R man may pay for some studio time for you to record more material, or to try out different versions of what you've already recorded on your demo, or work with selected producers or writers. In which case he may offer you a demo deal. This has to be distinguished from a development deal of which more in Chapter 3.

The deal will usually guarantee you a certain amount of time in a professional or in-house recording studio. Some record and publishing companies have their own studio facilities, which they may offer to make available. Perhaps you shouldn't look a gift horse in the mouth, but if the studio doesn't have the equipment you need to show yourself off to best advantage you should say so, and either ask for that equipment to be hired in or ask to go into a commercial studio. Cheeky, yes, but you can do it politely – it's your chance, so don't blow it.

The record or publishing company will probably expect to own the copyright in what you record (see Chapter 4) and to have the right to control what happens to the recording. However, some major record labels offer more flexible arrangements whereby in certain circumstances you get to regain ownership of the recordings. A record company will not usually expect to own rights in the song but a music publisher might. Try to take advice before you agree to give away rights in the song. At the very least they shouldn't own the song unless they offer you a proper publishing deal (see Chapter 4). The company offering you the deal will also usually want to own the physical recording or 'master'. This is fine as long as they don't stop you recording the same song for someone else if they don't want to take things further. They should also agree that they won't do anything with the master without first getting your permission. This is important. When you finally sign your record deal, you will be asked to confirm that no one else has the right to release recordings of your performances. Your record company will not find it funny if a rival company releases the very track that they had planned as your first single. The company who paid for the demo will usually agree that you can play it to other companies if they decide not to offer you a deal within a reasonable period of time.

The record or publishing company will normally want some exclusivity in return for the studio time they are giving you. They may want you to agree not to make demos for anyone else or not to negotiate with another company for a period of time.

They may be slightly more flexible and want the right of first negotiation or refusal. This means that they will want either to have the first chance to try to negotiate a deal with you or they will want to have the right to say yes or no first before you sign to another company. This is a difficult call. You will no doubt be excited and perhaps desperate not to risk losing the deal but, before agreeing to exclusivity or these negotiating options, you need to be sure that the exclusive time period is not too long. If they tie you up for months you may miss your moment. If they have first negotiating or rejection rights, then they should tell you as soon as possible where you stand. If they're not interested, then you need to move on as quickly as possible.

Bear in mind, though, that the record company has to go through a number of stages before they can make a decision. They have to listen to the recording, probably then discuss it at an A&R meeting and then maybe also with their immediate bosses or even overseas colleagues. All this takes time and they may not want to risk losing you to a rival company. So you need to get a balance between the needs of the two sides.

Don't be surprised or depressed if, after you make the demo, the company decides not to offer you a deal. I know several artists who got demo time from two or three record companies and ended up with an excellent set of demos that they took to another company who then signed them up. What you don't want to happen is for people to feel that you've been around for a while and are sounding a bit stale. This is a difficult balance to strike.

On a more positive note, the first company may love what you've recorded. The demos may confirm the A&R man's faith in your abilities and he may be ready to do a deal with you. You've passed go and, once you've read the rest of this chapter on getting yourself some good advisers, you should go straight to Chapter 3 (What Is A Good Record Deal?).

GETTING HELP AND PUTTING TOGETHER YOUR TEAM

All of this may seem a bit daunting. Don't worry about negotiating or signing a studio or demo deal. There are people that you can turn to for help. You should be looking to put your team of advisers in place as soon as you start to get a bit of a 'buzz' about you so that you are ready to move quickly.

THE LAWYER

A good lawyer with experience of the business can be of enormous help to you. So where do you find one and what can they do for you?

FINDING A LAWYER

General
You can ask the Law Society for their suggestions. They have entertainment firms on their referral lists but make no judgement on the quality of the advice.

Many law firms have their own websites, which will tell you a bit about the firm and its areas of expertise. It will usually contain an email address, so you could try sending them a message asking for further information.

Some websites contain details of the last big deals the firm did and, where their clients allow them to, list the names of some of their clients. It is not necessarily a bad thing if there aren't many clients mentioned. Professional rules mean they have to keep client information confidential and not even say that someone is a client without the client's permission or unless it is public knowledge. If a client is kind enough to give me a credit on his album artwork, I take it that he's happy for people to know I'm his lawyer, but if in doubt I have to ask.

Other sources could be the Musicians' Union and the Music Managers Forum. The PRS runs a legal referral scheme where firms of music lawyers agree to see you for up to an hour free. Similar schemes are run by BASCA and AIM.

Directories

You could also look in the two main directories listing UK legal firms – *Chambers* and *Legal 500*. The guides are both available online. Both have a similar approach, breaking down the lists into areas of the country and particular specialisations. Most UK music lawyers are based in London, but there are one or two in places like Cheltenham, Manchester, Liverpool and Glasgow. The directories have short pieces on those it thinks are the leading players in a particular field and operate on a league principle. The search facility enables you to get more in-depth profiles of individuals and firms.

In addition to these general legal guides, the *Music Week Directory* also lists UK law firms and is a good first stop for an overview of lawyers who claim to have expertise in the music business. *Music Week* is the leading trade journal for the music industry in the UK. You need to take out a subscription to get the directory and online access but you may find it in bigger reference libraries or a contact in the business might lend you a copy. As with the more general guides, an entry in a directory is not any guarantee that they are any good.

Managers and accountants

If you already have a manager or an accountant, they may be able to recommend a lawyer to you. You should check if your manager has the same lawyer. Most managers realise that for some things (for example, negotiating the management contract) you have to have a separate lawyer. There is a conflict in the interests of the two of you that means you must be separately advised. Where there is no conflict of interest, there is usually nothing wrong in you and your manager having the same lawyer. You may, however, still feel more comfortable having your own lawyer on board.

Other bands

Other bands or contacts in the business may be able to recommend someone to you. This may be their own lawyer or someone they have heard others say is good. We lawyers love personal recommendations as a source of new work. It means we must be doing something right.

How do you go about choosing and employing a lawyer?
Occasionally, lawyers are in the public eye because of a particularly high-profile piece of work they have done and everyone wants to have them as their lawyer. You must, however, try to find out whether the lawyer is experienced and not a one-hit wonder. How do you do that? Ideally, you should have two or three names on your list, possibly gathered from a variety of sources. You should call them, tell them you are looking for a lawyer and ask to meet with them. Be wary of lawyers who promise the earth. We don't have all the answers. Before you meet up with the lawyers, have some questions ready for them. Ask how long they've been doing this and who their main clients are. They may be a bit reluctant to do this because of their duty to keep clients and their business confidential. Ask them how their firm is structured. Will they be doing the work for you or will it be handed over to a more junior person? Can you call up the lawyer you are meeting at any time to discuss your case or are you expected to work with the junior person?

You should also ask the lawyers the all-important questions of what they charge, when they expect to send you a bill and when they expect it to be paid. Will they accept payment in instalments and, if so, do they charge interest on the balance like you would on a credit card bill that you were paying off monthly? Can you pay by credit card? Beware of a lawyer who is reluctant to discuss his costs. If he tells you what he charges by the hour, you may get a bit of a shock as it sounds like a lot of money. But quoting hourly rates doesn't really help you to compare two firms, as one lawyer may work faster than the other. A better way to do it is to ask them to give you a ballpark figure for what it usually costs for them to do a record or publishing deal. If you ask each lawyer the same question, you'll have a better basis for a comparison. Don't necessarily go for the lowest price. It may be that the deal gets done more cheaply but it's a short-term view. Where the lawyer really comes into his own is when something goes wrong in six months' or a year's time. Then the thoroughness with which he has done his job in protecting your interests really gets put to the test. Some lawyers will agree to do a piece of work for a fixed price. I usually work in that way when I can as it gives the client certainty, but as with any job of work if it turns out to be far more complicated than it appeared at first I reserve the right to revisit that fixed fee.

The lawyer you finally choose should send you a letter setting out the basis on which he is going to work for you, including details of what he expects to charge and who you should complain to if you have a problem. Your lawyer is a fundamental part of your team. Take your time in choosing one and don't be afraid to say if you are not happy with a piece of work, including voting with your feet and changing lawyers if it doesn't work out, although you may want to give the lawyer the chance to explain his position before you leave. As a last resort, you can sue but this is all very negative. In the majority of cases, there isn't a problem that can't be sorted out with a phone call.

Conflicts of interest

There are firms of lawyers that work mostly for record and publishing companies and others that work for what we call the 'talent' (the creative end of the business). It is important to know this. If the record label interested in you uses the same firm for their own legal advice, there may well be a conflict of interest at some point that will make it difficult for that lawyer to work for you if you're ever in a dispute with the record company. Some say it's possible to build Chinese Walls (artificial barriers where, in theory, one lawyer within a firm knows nothing about what another is doing, so can't be influenced in any negotiation). When things are going well, this can work, provided everyone knows it is happening and the proper procedures are followed. When things aren't going so well, will you feel confident that your lawyer is looking after your interests?

Beauty parades

When you go to meet lawyers, it's only fair that you tell them that you're seeing lawyers from other firms. Lawyers call these meetings 'beauty parades' – when we set out to impress you. There's nothing worse than spending an hour giving advice to someone you think has already chosen you as their lawyer only to be told as they walk out of the door, 'Thanks for that, I'll get back to you when I've seen the other firms on my list.'

If you're asked what other firms you've seen, you don't have to say, but if you do it helps that lawyer, who then knows who he is in competition with and can adjust his 'sales pitch' accordingly.

When you've decided who you want to work with, you should tell the others who've given up an hour or more of their valuable time that they are out of luck. You never know, you may want to change lawyers at some point and there's no harm in keeping things civil.

What does your lawyer do for you?
A trite answer may be to say whatever you instruct him to do (provided it is legal). We do work 'on instructions' from you, but that's really not a true picture of all that we can do for you. We're there to advise you, to help you decide what the best deal is for you. We give you the benefit of our experience of similar situations. We know who's doing what deals and how much would be a good deal.

If you want, we can help you to target companies that our experience tells us should be interested in your type of music. This can help you to be more focused. This doesn't mean to say that we act as A&R people, although I have come across one or two lawyers who do think they are and indeed there are some law firms that employ young lawyers as quasi-scouts looking for up-and-coming artists who might be future clients. The type of music you're into shouldn't influence your lawyer, who should be able to represent you whatever style of music you make, provided it's not so far out of his area of expertise that he doesn't have the necessary experience or commercial knowledge of whether the deal is good, bad or indifferent.

There's also a growing band of lawyers who, following the American trend, are acting as quasi-managers, only taking on clients who they think they can get a deal for. Managers seem a little uncomfortable about this, as it blurs the edges between their respective roles. It also means that the lawyer is making a judgement call, and those who really need advice may be losing out. With this breed of lawyer you need to be very clear what they are expecting to charge you. Is it their normal rate or is there a premium for this service? Are they charging a percentage of the deal they get for you? If so, does that mean that they only focus on getting the most money and to hell with the small print?

Your lawyer's role can be as wide or as narrow as you want it to be. If you are already clued-up on the type of deal you want, or have a manager who is, then you won't need that sort of advice. If you're quite happy about negotiating a deal direct with the record or publishing company, then you can bring your lawyer in later when the commercial terms are agreed and you need to get the legal contract in place. On the other hand, if you are new to the business and aren't confident enough to negotiate commercial terms, you'll want to involve your lawyer at a much earlier stage.

I work differently with different types of clients. If it's a new artist who either doesn't have a manager or has a manager who isn't very experienced, I run with things right from the beginning when a record company says it wants to do a deal. I contact the record company, get its deal proposal and, after talking to the client, I go back to the record company with any counter-proposals, continuing this process until the deal is in its final form. I then get the draft contract, check it, make any necessary changes, and negotiate those with the company until the contract is ready for me to recommend to the client for signature.

With other clients there may be an experienced manager on board who knows exactly what his bargaining power is and what sort of deal he would ideally like to end up with. My role at the beginning is more that of an adviser or sounding board. The manager will usually make sure I get a copy of the proposal and any counter-proposals, but won't want to involve me directly in the negotiations. He may contact me from time to time to ask if I think company X can do better than what they are offering. I'll tell him what I think based on other deals I have done with that company. I keep the names of the clients confidential, but I can say whether I know they can do better on a particular point or not. Once this type of client is happy with the commercial terms, I'm then brought in to do the negotiation of the contract itself.

You should establish with your lawyer what kind of relationship you want to have. This may well change from deal to deal as you grow in experience.

I like to take an interest in my clients' work. I'm delighted to be sent a copy of the new album or single. It helps to cement the relationship between us. I also like to go and see my clients play live. I have to admit, though, that when I'm in the middle of a very long week at work and a client rings up and says, 'Hi, I'm on stage tonight at the Laughing Cow at 10.30 p.m.' (which means 11 p.m. at the earliest) then my wish to support the client is tested to the full.

What you don't want to happen is for your advisers to embarrass you. And yes, it does happen. I can still remember a gig a few years ago when four members of a top entertainment accountancy firm were standing proudly in the front row wearing the band's T-shirt over their work suits.

Legal or business affairs consultants

There is another type of legal adviser in the UK. These are lawyers, usually, but not always, qualified solicitors or barristers, who, for one business reason or another, have decided not to practise as solicitors and be regulated by the

Solicitors Regulatory Authority (SRA). Instead, they practise as business affairs consultants. In practice, you will probably not notice any difference. In theory, because they are not bound by the SRA's rules, they can be more flexible in how they get paid for their work, for example, working on a percentage of your advances or royalties. They are more restricted in that they cannot, for example, do contentious work involving representing you in court. However, most legal consultants have arrangements in place to refer such work to lawyers who do contentious work, and as it is a specialist field even if you were using a solicitor they would probably also refer you to a colleague if it became litigious. Of course, because they are not regulated by the SRA, you couldn't complain to the SRA about them. But they are still open to being sued by you if they screw up and most of them carry professional indemnity insurance as an additional protection for you if they make a mistake.

When should you get a lawyer?
There are a number of different views on this. Some say that there's no need to get a lawyer until you've a contract in front of you. I think you should get a lawyer earlier than this. The whole process of getting a deal is so much of a lottery that anything you can do to reduce the odds must be worth doing. Most of us are happy to give initial advice and guidance for free, or only charge you when your first deal is in place. Just be careful and check this before going ahead.

ACCOUNTANTS

At some stage, you are also going to need a good accountant. How do you find one and what can they do for you?

The Institutes
The Institutes of Chartered Accountants in England & Wales, Scotland or Northern Ireland and the Association of Chartered and Certified Accountants can recommend firms to you. It's important that the accountant is qualified, preferably a chartered or certified accountant. Anyone can set up in business giving financial advice, so you should check that they're properly regulated. You shouldn't allow them to keep your money in an account to which they can have access without your knowledge. If they are to have signing rights on the bank account make sure there are sufficient controls in place.

Directories

There isn't any general guide similar to the legal directories. The accountancy profession is broken down into the big international firms like Ernst & Young and Deloitte, medium-sized national firms with international networks like BDO Stoy Hayward, and smaller local firms.

The *Music Week Directory* has a section on accountants. Inclusion in the directory is not a recommendation that they're any good, but it is a good starting point.

Music Managers Forum (MMF)

The MMF can give you recommendations for accountants as well as for lawyers. They have firms of accountants who are corporate members as well as individual accountants who provide business or quasimanagement services.

Lawyers

Your lawyer should have had dealings with a number of accountants and should be able to recommend two or three to you that they know have experience in the music business.

Other sources of information

Your A&R or other record or publishing company contacts or friends in the music business may be able to suggest some names. It's always good to get a recommendation from someone who rates a particular accountant highly. The Musician's Union, AIM, FAC and BASCA may also be able to provide contacts or recommendations.

How to choose an accountant

As I suggested when choosing your lawyer, you should see more than one accountant. You should ask them the type of work they can do for you. Some are strong on tour accounting or in auditing (checking) the books and records of companies. They may also do general bookkeeping and tax advice, but they may not, so ask.

If you expect to do a lot of touring, it's worth having an accountant who's experienced in putting together tour accounts and is familiar with tour budgets and all the necessary arrangements to deal with VAT on overseas tours and taxes on overseas income (see Chapter 10).

It's less important that your accountant's offices are in the same city as the record and publishing companies. The main thing is that they are familiar with the music business and how it works. They must know the sources of income and how and when it's paid, including potential new revenue sources like neighbouring rights and YouTube or Google Ad Partners. They need to know how to read and understand a royalty statement. These things are often, literally, written in code. You need to know what country A is and what the code for CD sales is. Your local family accountant can, of course, do the basic accounting work, but this probably isn't enough once you start getting deals. Just as you need a lawyer with specialised music business knowledge, so you need the same expertise from your accountant if he's to be able to look after your interests properly. The basic accountancy and tax rules do, of course, apply to artists and songwriters, but there are an increasing number of specialised rules and regulations aimed at them. Your accountant must be up to date on these rules.

Some accountants don't claim to be experts in tax planning or advice and, if that is an area that you need to have covered, you would be best advised to go to an accountant that can provide that and then get a specialist accountant in to do the tour accounting or auditing.

As your accountant will have intimate knowledge of your finances and may have some control over your bank account, it is vitally important that you trust them, that they have a good reputation and that there are suitable checks and balances in place to protect you and your money. They should be fully integrated into your team alongside your lawyer and manager.

Increasingly, accountants act as quasi-financial directors running payroll and managing cashflow.

Business managers

There is another breed of accountant that could provide the sort of services you are looking for, and that is a business manager. This is a term that has come across from the US, where they are quite common. In the US, they generally act as business and financial advisers alongside a personal manager who looks after the day-to-day and creative aspects of the artist's career (see Chapter 2). In the UK, they provide day-to-day business advice and book-keeping services. They'll do your VAT and tax returns for you. They can provide business plans and advice and some also do tour accounts. Most don't provide international tax planning or audits. Their argument is that this makes them more cost-effective as you are not paying for a full tax planning and audit service when you don't need it. This means they can charge less than the bigger firms of accountants do. When specialist tax or international advice is required, they have relationships with more than one of the bigger accountancy firms and other financial advisers and can refer you to the right company for you, to get the advice you need when you need it.

How do accountants charge?

Accountants usually charge fees rather than commission. They may quote you a rate per annum for advising you. Some of the bigger accountancy firms run special schemes where the first year's work for you is done at a special, discounted rate. You don't have to stay with them after the first year. If you are tempted by these schemes, you should ask what exactly is covered by the discount rate. It's likely that you won't get the same service as the full-price one. You should also ask what the non-discounted rate would be after the first year so that you can decide whether you think you'd be able to stay with them afterwards or will have to start the search for a new accountant, which could be disruptive.

You should ask them what their experience is and who will be doing the work. Often you find that the person who sees you and does the hard sell is the partner or even the marketing person. Someone quite different and possibly much less experienced may be doing the work. This sort of thing is more likely to happen in the bigger firms, particularly those that are offering a discount rate. You can be reasonably sure that it will not be a partner that will be doing the cut-price work.

What does an accountant do?

Accountants can do a number of things for you. They do the accounts books for you, advise and help you to complete your tax return. They register you for VAT, if necessary, and can do your quarterly VAT returns. Depending on your accountant, they may also do your tour accounts and help prepare a tour budget. Your accountant will advise you on whether you should be a sole trader, in partnership or a limited company or limited liability partnership (see Chapter 11). He can prepare partnership or company accounts. Some accountants can also act as the auditor of your company books; many can also act as the company secretary and can arrange for the company's registered office to be at their offices.

Your accountant can act as your financial adviser, telling you where is the best place to invest your money. Because this area is very closely regulated, not all accountants are authorised to provide financial services advice. You should ask if your accountant is. If he isn't you will need a separate financial adviser should the need arise.

Your accountant can be your tax adviser and help plan with you things such as whether you could consider putting your income in an offshore tax haven or, indeed, if you could, or should, become a tax exile or non-domiciled. The Government has tightened up on the tax benefits of being non-domiciled so this may not be an attractive option. Tax laws change frequently and it is important your accountant is up to speed on those which affect your business.

Can your accountant help you get a record deal?
Yes, he can. You can use accountants in the same way as lawyers. Use their contacts and pick their brains for information on companies and A&R people. Some accountants also send out selected demos or email their contacts directly on behalf of artists and songwriters.

If your accountant does find you a deal, then he shouldn't charge you a commission for doing so. He should just charge for any accountancy advice that he gives you on that deal. If your accountant offers to get you a deal, ask him on what basis he is doing it before you give him the go-ahead.

The accountant should be able to work as part of the team with you, your manager and your lawyer. It's important that you keep your accountant in the loop about the deal so that he can advise how it can be structured as tax-effectively as possible before you sign anything.

All accountants should give you a letter of engagement, setting out the basis on which they will work for you and how they will charge. They should give you the name of someone in their firm that you can complain to if you've a problem with your accountant. If the complaint is about fees, you can ask for a breakdown of the bill. The professional body that your accountant belongs to is the first port of call for complaints about your accountant. If they don't deal with the complaint to your satisfaction, you can take it to court. This is of course looking at the negative side and most relationships proceed smoothly.

An accountant can have conflict of interest just as your lawyer can. If your accountant acts for one of the major record or publishing companies, and you then want to do a deal with that company, the conflict may or may not arise at that stage. However, if later on you aren't sure whether the company is accounting to you properly and you want to send someone in to look at (audit) the books, then your accountant will have a conflict of interest and you will probably have to take that work elsewhere. There are, in fact, specialist firms of accountants who only do audits. Sometimes it's best to use their specialised knowledge even if there isn't a conflict of interest with your own accountant.

So now you've got your lawyer and your accountant lined up. You have two members of your team, getting a manager could be the critical third stage. I'll deal with this in the next chapter.

CONCLUSIONS

- If you hope to get noticed through doing live work, do your homework first.
- Investigate your venues and rehearse thoroughly. Tailor your material to your audience and tell your audience who you are.
- Consider short cuts like industry-organised showcases, open mic evenings or music conventions as well as competitions.
- Make sure your demo is the best quality that you can afford and that it has a good cross-section of your work. Put your name and contact number on the CD as well as the packaging or make sure they have your email on any MP3 submission.
- If you do a deal with a studio for studio time, make sure it's for no more than 1–1.5% royalty and don't agree that they can be the producer of your first album unless there are excellent reasons to do so.
- If you do a demo deal, keep the exclusive period as short as possible and make sure that no one can do anything with the recordings without your agreement.
- If you do a finder's deal, keep the percentages to no more than 5–10% and for as short a period as you reasonably can get away with.
- When picking a lawyer or accountant, arrange to see two or three different firms and ask them for estimates of their charges for a particular piece of work. Find out their expertise and, if possible, who their clients are.
- When you appoint a lawyer or accountant, get written confirmation from them of their charges.
- Your accountant and lawyer are vital members of your team – take your time to choose the right ones.

Chapter 2

Management Deals

INTRODUCTION

In this chapter I'm going to look at how to find a good manager, what to expect from a manager, and what you have to think about when entering into a management contract. I'm going to look at it from the artist's point of view, but when we get to the section on contracts I'm also going to put the manager's side of the argument. The section on what to expect from a manager should also be useful to managers. It'll give them an idea of what might be expected from them.

It's great to see the right manager team up with the right artist; it's like watching a well-oiled machine going into action. It's also great to work with a good artist/manager team, as everyone's pulling in the same direction.

HOW TO FIND A MANAGER

Directories

One of the main music business directories in the UK is the *Music Week Directory*. It lists managers and the acts they manage. Directories can be an excellent starting point for finding a manager who looks after artists who are similar to you or who share a particular musical genre.

The drawback with all directories, however, is that they don't give you any clues as to whether the managers listed are any good. The information you get from them needs to be backed up from other sources.

Music Managers Forum (MMF)

One such source is the MMF. The MMF was formed in 1992 by a group of like-minded managers who felt that they could achieve more, both for their artists and for themselves, if they grouped together. They act as a lobbying group on behalf of their members in relation to national and international issues facing the music industry. In recent years, they have become much more politically active and have also tried to use their collective muscle to negotiate better deals for their members with retailers and to open up the doors to potential alternative sources of investment. The MMF has affiliations with other manager organisations worldwide. It doesn't act as a dating agency for setting managers up with artists. It does, however, publish a directory of its members and is helpful in putting you in contact with individual managers. It currently (in December 2016) costs £100 per year to join.

Membership of the MMF is not a recommendation that a manager is any good but, if a manager is a member, it shows that he is interested in talking to other managers and in keeping up to date with what is going on in the outside world that can affect the music business and his or your livelihood. The MMF also runs training courses for wannabe managers, mostly in London, but occasionally regional courses or ones in conjunction with other organisations such as the Featured Artist Coalition (FAC) and usually at quite reasonable rates.

Recommendations

You may by now have quite a lot of information about various managers, but you still may not know if they're any good or even if they're looking for new artists to manage. What you need are personal recommendations (references, if you like) from people who have worked with a particular manager or know him by reputation. Where do you get these? You can ask around among other bands to see if they have any good or bad experiences of particular managers. Bad reports can be as useful to you as good ones. At the end of the day, you'll have to make up your own mind whether to trust a particular manager, but, if people who know him keep saying bad things about him, you can't say you weren't warned.

Lawyers and accountants

If you've already found yourself a lawyer or accountant, then they should be able to tell you what sort of reputation a particular manager has. They are also good sources of contacts and can put you in touch with managers that you may not have discovered on your own. They may know that a particular manager is looking for more acts to manage or, conversely, is too busy to devote the necessary time to a new artist.

As with all major decisions, you shouldn't rush into anything. In particular, if a lawyer or accountant has recommended someone, you should try to find out what the relationship is with that manager. If, for example, they get most of their work from that manager, how independent are they and is there any conflict of interest? They can't advise you independently if the rest of the time they are advising the manager. This doesn't mean to say that just because a lawyer recommends a manager who they regularly work with there is necessarily a conflict of interest. You just have to be clear who is looking after your interests. If there is a conflict of interest but you still want to work with that manager, you can appoint a different lawyer.

Surgeries

The Performing Right Society Limited (PRS) and the songwriter's body, BASCA, as well as AIM and FAC, hold occasional 'surgeries'. These are meetings where music business professionals such as lawyers, managers and A&R people discuss particular topics and answer your questions. They are sociable events, often held in a pub or club, and are a good place to meet other music business people. Details of their meetings are given in the PRS Newsletter or direct from their websites. Sign up to mailing lists, blogs and follow on Twitter and Facebook for up-to-date information.

A&R contacts

Record or publishing company scouts or A&R people can be an excellent source of information on managers and whether a particular manager is looking for new artists to manage. They can put you in contact with managers. In fact, they may try to insist on you getting a manager before they are prepared to discuss a possible deal with you, because they're happier dealing with a middleman (and preferably someone with a track record).

Managers

A manager may approach you direct. They may have heard about you from an A&R man, a lawyer or accountant, or they may have seen you play live or spotted you on YouTube, Facebook, SoundCloud or another online forum. It's not unheard of for a manager to come up to you after a gig to say that he wants to manage you. A word of warning – just because a manager approaches you doesn't mean they're any good, nor does it mean that you have to leap at the chance of being managed by anyone regardless of who they are. You still have to do your homework and make as sure as you can that this is the right manager for you.

TRIAL PERIOD

You should always think about asking for a trial period to make sure that the relationship is working. It takes time to build up the necessary trust between you. Three to six months is a reasonable trial period, but it can be shorter or longer depending on the circumstances. The manager should agree to that, but he will be looking for commitment from you before he spends any significant amounts of his own time or money on you. He'll be looking for you to confirm that you want him to manage you before he approaches record and publishing companies on your behalf. If he's prepared to commit time and spend money on you, then it's reasonable to expect some commitment from you in return. Sometimes managers ask you to sign a short agreement to cover their expenses and any deals they may get for you during the short trial period. As with any legal agreement, if in doubt get it checked out by a lawyer.

THE LEGAL PRINCIPLES

Having discussed how to find managers, we should now look at one or two of the principles behind the artist/manager relationship. Many of these principles have been developed and applied to management contracts through a series of cases involving some of the leading players of the time.

The first thing you have to understand is that it's a relationship based on trust. If the trust is lost then there's little hope for the relationship. The contract won't hold you together if the trust isn't there. All that a management contract will then do is tell you what your rights are and what happens if you part company.

This loss of trust has led to many disputes between managers and artists over the years. Some end up in court, many more settle before they get that far – even at the doors of the court. Most people don't want to air their dirty linen in public. It's not a pretty sight when you're sitting in court and the reporters are all lined up on the benches behind you ready to take down every sordid detail. One time I was in court and found myself sitting next to a journalist from one of the tabloid newspapers. He was obviously bored with the lack of juicy scandal and kept popping in and out of court. In one of the gaps in the proceedings, I asked him if he'd been going out for a cigarette. 'Nah, love,' came the reply, 'I'm checking with my bookie who won the last two races at Sandown Park.' He then asked me if I fancied a bet on the outcome of the trial and could I tell him what he'd missed while he was outside on the phone. Journalism at its finest.

The judgements in certain cases which did get to court helped to establish what lies behind the management relationship in legal terms, what duties the manager has towards an artist, and what is acceptable in a management contract. One of these cases involved Joan Armatrading.

Armatrading v. Stone and Another ([1985] unreported)

Joan Armatrading is a singer-songwriter who is still recording and performing. The case was about an agreement that Armatrading signed when she was young and relatively inexperienced and before she became famous. This is a theme that comes up regularly in these cases.

Stone was a partner in the Copeland Sherry Agency, which had signed a management agreement with Armatrading in March 1973. This was shortly after she released her debut album *Whatever's For Us*, which was produced by Gus Dudgeon, who also worked with Elton John. Copeland is Miles Copeland, who managed The Police and Sting for some time. Stone advised Armatrading on business matters. Armatrading took charge of most creative issues herself. It seems she was confident enough to select the studios and producers she wanted to work with without needing advice from her managers, but didn't have a clue when it came to the business end of things.

In 1975, Armatrading released her second album *Back To The Night*. It didn't reach the charts. She then began work on an album that turned out to be the first to bring her properly to the public's attention.

In February 1976, as the term of the original management contract was about to run out, she signed a new contract under which Stone was to manage her on his own. He may have been worried she would go off to another manager when the original contract ran out and just as her career was starting to take off, although he denied that in his evidence. The album that she released in 1976, *Joan Armatrading*, went into the Top 20 in the UK and one of the singles released off it became her most famous and successful song. It was called 'Love And Affection' and it reached the Top 10.

Things continued to go well for her at first and in 1980 she released her most successful album to date, *Me, Myself, I*, which also contained the hit single 'All The Way From America'. Shortly after that, she seems to have become disillusioned with Stone and commenced proceedings for the management contract to be declared void on the grounds that Stone had used undue influence to get her to sign the contract and that the terms were unreasonable and a restraint of her trade.

It became clear from the evidence given in the case that the lawyer who drew up the contract had been introduced to Armatrading by Stone and had done some work for him. Coincidentally, I worked with that same firm of lawyers for a couple of years. The contract was done before my time there, but the court case was going on when I was there and I know it caused a lot of strain on everyone concerned. When preparing the management contract, it seems the lawyer acted on the instructions of Stone and not Armatrading. In particular, Stone asked for two specific things to be added to the draft contract. The lawyer billed Stone for the work and it's clear from the description on the bill that he thought he was acting as Stone's lawyer.

At a meeting on 4 February 1976 at the lawyers' offices, Armatrading received a copy of the draft contract to take away with her. She returned the next day to sign it. She didn't ask for any changes to be made to it.

Stone claimed that the lawyer acted as lawyer for both of them. When he gave evidence, the lawyer said that he thought he was just acting as lawyer to Stone. A very confusing state of affairs. Stone and Armatrading were both present at the meeting with the lawyer on 4 February when the contract was discussed. That must have been very awkward. If a manager turns up at a meeting I'm due to have with an artist to discuss a management contract, I insist on him staying outside while I take the meeting. I can't be open with the artist about what I think about the contract or the manager if the manager is in the same room. The same would apply the other way around.

The contract was drafted in Stone's favour. It was for five years and during that time Armatrading was exclusively tied to Stone as her manager. The contract didn't say that Stone had to do very much at all for her. He could manage other artists. He was to be paid a management commission of 20% (which, as we will see, is quite common) but 25% on any new recording or publishing deals she signed (which is not common). He got 20% commission on touring whether or not the tour made a profit. The court thought this was particularly harsh, as was the fact that Stone's right to commission was open-ended. For example, if Armatrading signed a new record deal in year three of the five-year management term, Stone would be entitled to 25% commission. He might stop being her manager two years later, but he'd still go on earning at 25%. If Armatrading got herself a new manager and he negotiated some improvements to the recording contract in return for, say, a two-year extension on the record deal, then Stone and not the new manager would get commission at 25% on the extended term. Not much of an incentive for the new manager (or expensive for Armatrading if she had to pay out two lots of commission to the original and the new manager).

When he gave evidence, Stone agreed that he knew that he had a duty to act in Armatrading's best interests and that she had trust and confidence in him. This fiduciary duty already existed when the 1976 management contract was being discussed. Stone knew that his interests under this contract were not the same as Armatrading's and yet he still seemed to think that the same lawyer could act for both of them.

Stone admitted that it was very likely that Armatrading didn't realise she should have separate legal advice. Even though he accepted his fiduciary duties existed, he didn't seem to accept the idea of a conflict of interest and couldn't seem to see that if something in the management contract was in his interests it would not necessarily be in Armatrading's best interests. This doesn't mean that a manager can't look out for his own interests just that it's up to him to make sure that the artist has separate advice and is able to come to an informed decision.

The court found Stone's evidence very contradictory. It decided that Armatrading relied heavily on Stone in business matters. She trusted him and he'd told her that he would look after her. The court thought it was clear that he had influence over her. She didn't look at the detail of the contract. She relied on Stone, who told her that it was a standard and fair contract, even though he had asked for two specific changes to be made to the draft.

The court decided that the contract should be set aside by reason of undue influence by Stone. The terms of the contract were said to be unreasonable ('unduly onerous and unconscionable' in the words of the judgement). The contract was voidable and not void from the outset.

The fact that Armatrading didn't have separate legal advice was seen as very important. On its own this wouldn't have been enough to set aside the contract. For example, if the contract had been a perfectly reasonable one, so that any lawyer who advised on it would say it was all right to sign it, then the absence of that advice would not have been fatal. The absence of separate legal advice coupled with the particularly harsh terms of the contract was enough to convince the court to set it aside. The court found that, although she had some experience of the music business, because she concentrated on the creative side it was important that she be given a proper understanding of the business side of the contract. She hadn't understood the implications of the open-ended commission clause and hadn't been able to form an independent view after full, free and informed thought. She had signed the contract relying on her manager's claim that it was fine. He had failed in his fiduciary duty to her. She was freed from the contract and went on to record several more successful albums.

Although this case wasn't reported in the Law Reports, it had a very significant and practical effect on management contracts. We lawyers still use it as a yardstick to measure the reasonableness of management contract terms. It's also quoted as an authority for saying that artist and manager should have separate lawyers when discussing the management contract and whenever their interests are not the same.

After this case, it became usual to add a clause to management contracts saying that the artist has been advised to take independent legal advice. I don't think this goes far enough. Just advising someone they should get advice and then not making sure that they do is not good enough. I think that the manager should insist on the artist having separate legal advice from a lawyer who understands the music business, and should make sure he understands what he's being asked to sign, but sometimes they just refuse so you have to take them at their word.

The Armatrading case also cast doubt on whether a five-year contract term was reasonable. After the case, some managers decided to go for a shorter term or otherwise tried to make their contracts more reasonable. No manager wants to risk having an artist walk away from a management contract at the height of his success. However, as we shall see below, the trend these days is back to longer minimum management terms, because it is taking longer to break an act.

The Judge was also quite critical of the 25% commission rate on new record and publishing deals. A 25% rate is now rare, but is staging a bit of a comeback as I write this, with one or two lawyers advocating that higher rates might be acceptable if the manager is providing exceptional services or financial support. The Judge in the Armatrading case was even more concerned about the fact that Stone took commission on touring money even if the tour made a loss. Music business lawyers reacted to these criticisms by introducing new protections for artists in these areas.

Elton John (John v. James [1991] FSR 387)
Another case on management contracts that was reported in the tabloids as well as the Law Reports involved Elton John.

Elton John signed a series of publishing, management and recording contracts starting in 1967, when he was still under age and unknown. Although these themes come up quite often in these cases, each case has played its own part in developing how the business operates and how contracts have to be adapted to deal with criticisms made by the Judges.

Elton John and his lyricist, Bernie Taupin, were originally taken on as in-house writers for James's new publishing company, DJM. It's said they were on wages of £10 per week. It took quite a while for them to be commercially successful. The first successful album was produced by Gus Dudgeon and was called *Elton John*. The 1972 album contained the now classic work 'Your Song'. Seven consecutive number one albums followed in the next seven years.

Although Elton was making a lot of very successful records, he didn't seem to be seeing much of the proceeds. For example, the publishing set-up consisted of a number of inter-related companies, each taking its own slice of the income, so that a very small amount was left for Elton. What he did get he had to pay management commission on.

He sued to try to recover his copyrights and damages for back royalties. He relied on the same argument as in the Armatrading case that he had signed the contracts under undue influence and that they were an unreasonable restraint of his trade.

He hadn't taken separate legal advice before signing any of the contracts. He'd placed trust and confidence in James. The contracts weren't as beneficial for him as they could have been had they been with independent companies. The publishers could take rights in his songs and not have to do anything with them. They could be shut away in a drawer and never seen again and Elton couldn't do anything about it. He was also signed up exclusively, so he couldn't take his songs to another music publisher.

The court decided that in these circumstances it was to be assumed that there was undue influence at work and that it was up to the manager to show that he didn't use his influence in the wrong way. The court found that James had failed in his fiduciary duties to Elton. It felt that James couldn't be acting in the best interest of Elton if James's publishing and recording companies were also entering into contracts with him. How could James be advising Elton as his manager while he also had an interest in making as much money as possible for his record and publishing companies out of those contracts?

Once again, the decision in this case had a knock-on effect on the music business. It was fully reported in the Law Reports, so had authority and it confirmed the existence of the fiduciary duty owed not only by the manager, but also by any companies under his control. It also brought home the importance of separate legal advice.

The other important thing it changed was what happens where your manager also has a record or publishing contract that he wants you to sign up to. If your manager also has an interest in a record or publishing company, the management contract will now probably ask the artist to confirm that he won't consider it a failure of the manager's fiduciary duty to him if he signs up to the record or publishing company on the manager's advice. I don't think this would be enough to get the manager off the hook if he did, in fact, break his duty to the artist especially if the artist hadn't had separate legal advice. There's also usually a clause that says the manager can't take a double hit on the income from the record or publishing deals. For example, if the artist releases a record on the manager's record label, the manager should get his money from the record label's profits on the record sales. He shouldn't also take a management commission on the artist's record royalties. As we shall see below, this blurring of the edges between the roles of managers is becoming a key issue and a potential future problem area.

In 2010 the footballer Wayne Rooney was sued by his former managers for breach of contract.

The Wayne Rooney Case (Proactive Sports Management Ltd v. Wayne Rooney [2010] EWHC 1807 (QB))

This case was reported in July 2010. Although it involves a sports personality, the principles contained within it are relevant for entertainers. It is a useful case in that it considered many of the elements that govern or underpin music management agreements.

The brief facts are that in 2003 the company that Wayne Rooney had assigned his image rights to (Stoneygate 48 Ltd) ('Stoneygate') entered into an exclusive worldwide image rights representation agreement with Proactive Sports Management Limited ('Proactive'). Rooney was under age (17) at the time the contract was entered into and had not had the benefit of legal advice; there was little negotiation of the terms. The agreement ran for eight years and Rooney was to pay Proactive commission at the rate of 20% for all services, such as negotiating and concluding sponsorship agreements, provided by Proactive to Stoneygate. In December 2009, Stoneygate purported to terminate the agreement and Proactive took this as a repudiation of the contract, which it accepted and then sued for unpaid commission due up to the date of termination as well as for commission it said it was due after termination and damages for breach of contract.

Stoneygate defended the claims and contended that the contract was unenforceable as it was in restraint of trade and unreasonably so. Proactive claimed as an alternative that if that were correct and the contract was found to be unenforceable it was still entitled to recover payment for the work it had done on a *quantum meruit* basis, i.e. a fair price for work done.

The Judge found that the contract was a restraint of trade saying in his judgement that *'the Agreement imposed very substantial restraints upon Wayne Rooney's freedom to exploit his earning ability over a very long period of time on terms which were not commonplace in the market and which were not the outcome of a process of commercial negotiation between equals'.* He found the restrictions to be unreasonable and that Proactive was not entitled to its unpaid commission either before or after the contract had terminated. As it was an unenforceable agreement, he also declared that Proactive could not claim damages for its breach but did find that Stoneygate and Rooney had freely accepted services provided by Proactive and Proactive was, therefore, entitled to payment for that work. The Judge did not set a value on that at this hearing because there was insufficient evidence before the court but he did say that it would not be a simple matter of a 20% commission as that would just be an indirect means of getting

---

around the unenforceable nature of the contract. Instead, he would want to hear evidence and take into account other factors such as what Proactive would save in not having to provide the services.

The Judge made several interesting comments in his judgement which are relevant for music management agreements. In considering whether this was a contract in restraint of trade, the Judge said that, whilst not all contracts which impose restrictions on a person's freedom to trade are subject to this doctrine, he was entitled to look at whether there was some kind of *'exorbitance or special feature'* in the contract which would bring it within the ambit of the doctrine. He considered that one special feature might be the inequality of bargaining power. He found that there was *'a very substantial imbalance in bargaining power between the parties'*. Rooney was 17 at the time, had no commercial experience (similar point to the Armatrading case above) and had not had independent legal advice. On that last point, Proactive's lawyers argued that this should not be held against them because there was a clause in the contract which said that both parties confirmed they had had independent legal advice and agreed that all terms were reasonable. In a restatement of what artist lawyers have long believed to be the case, the Judge confirmed that in cases of restraint of trade it was a matter of public policy and therefore the parties could not contract out of it by agreeing not to take legal action.

When looking at individual aspects of the contract, the Judge considered the fact that it was exclusive and was for an eight-year term which Rooney could not get out of unless Proactive breached its terms or became insolvent. Because of the relatively short time span of the working life of a sportsman (an argument that might also apply to some performers), the Judge considered that an eight-year term might amount to half Rooney's playing career. In criticising the length of term, he compared it with the two-year FIFA players' contracts saying that a two-year contract with Proactive for the image representation rights would be *'entirely reasonable'* and that even a four- or five-year term *'might'* be reasonable. The argument that an eight-year term gave more time for an overall strategic approach to the exploitation of the image rights did not, in the Judge's view, provide any justification for an eight-year term. This ties in with my view that a management contract of up to four or five years might be reasonable but that anything longer than that is potentially an unreasonable restraint of trade.

The fact that Rooney could not easily get out of it earlier other than by reason of Proactive's breach or insolvency was also a factor and this is reflected in the already common practice in music management cases of there being a 'get-out' after a period of time if certain aims haven't been achieved. In the Judge's view, had Rooney had independent advice and if there had perhaps been a little competition from other agents, the eight-year term might well have been negotiated down.

In the face of this inequality of bargaining power restrictions have to be seen to operate fairly.

WHAT TO LOOK FOR IN A MANAGER

This all depends on what you expect your manager to do for you. You may only need a manager to advise you on business matters. You may also be looking for creative advice, comment and guidance. Some artists already have a clear idea of what they are doing creatively and have a good business sense and grasp of contracts. They don't want an all-round manager and may only be looking for a good organiser. We saw in the Armatrading case (above) that in effect Stone only looked after Armatrading's business interests. She looked after the creative side herself. This tends to only apply to more established artists. Those who are new to the business tend to look for all the help they can get from a manager.

You may be looking for a Svengali, someone who will come up with the cast-iron plan for world domination in three years. Such managers do exist, for example, people like Tom Watkins, Jonathan Shalit, an early manager of Charlotte Church, and now behind several successful acts, and of course media moguls like Simon Cowell and Richard Griffiths of Modest Management. Another, Simon Fuller, used his marketing background to exploit the worldwide branding possibilities of an act like The Spice Girls as well as steering the careers of artists like Will Young, and sportsmen like Andy Murray and David Beckham.

When you expect a manager to devise an all-encompassing game plan and then to implement it, you can't expect to get away with no effort on your part. You and your manager will have to put enormous amounts of time and energy into making the plan work and both of you must completely buy into the whole idea behind it. There is, of course, also the type of artist who's come together for a particular purpose, such as those who have won reality-TV competitions such as *Britain's Got Talent* or *The Voice*. Provided the artist fits in with this game plan, then all is well. It's only when the artist, or one or more members of the group, starts to rebel or baulk at the situation that problems occur. Acts that win a TV talent show often struggle when it comes to the cut and thrust of the music industry and many fail to have a long-term career beyond the album that comes out quickly when they win the competition. For every Leona Lewis or Susan Boyle, there are many artists who don't make it.

Is it Essential to Have an Experienced Manager?

Someone who hasn't managed anyone before can make a good manager if they have the flair for it. They may have been a musician themselves, a tour manager, a producer or may have worked in-house at a record or publishing company. Those with a marketing background can be very useful in developing a strategy to get you noticed. These people will have seen how the music business works and can bring valuable experience to the job of manager, as well as some contacts. However, their skills are not necessarily those that make a good manager, so be careful. On the other hand, a manager may be experienced and still not be right for you because his experience is in a different arena (for instance, as a tour manager) rather than skilled in managing an artist's career. So take your time before making up your mind and ask for a trial period if you are unsure.

Qualities to Look For in a Manager

The manager has to be a diplomat, motivator, salesman and strategic planner – and has to have the patience of a saint.

Record and publishing companies like to have managers around to act as middlemen so they don't have to have unpleasant conversations with the artist direct. They'd like the artist to choose someone who's already successfully steered an artist through getting a deal, getting a record made and who's already done the whole touring and promotion side of things. This doesn't mean to say that they won't work with an inexperienced manager, just that they would prefer one who was not. They would also like you to be managed by someone they already know, someone they know they can work with. This doesn't necessarily mean that that manager will be in their pocket. It could mean that they have a healthy respect for him for being tough but fair, someone that gets the job done, but, if you are being pushed by your record company towards a particular manager, take the time to stop and ask why and to do some research of your own before meekly accepting their choice. Labels may seek to reduce their risks by only working with artists who have a manager on board that they like or with whom they have an existing relationship. This can work well but you need to be sure the manager has the necessary degree of independence.

WHAT DOES A MANAGER DO FOR YOU?

Personal Managers

A personal manager looks after your day-to-day needs. This usually includes some advice on the creative side of things. The personal manager also acts as go-between with the record and publishing companies and the outside world. This might involve working with you on creative issues such as the choice of songs. A personal manager is also usually someone who organises your life and tries to make everything run smoothly. They put into action plans others have come up with. They don't necessarily get involved in day-to-day business decisions or strategic plans.

BUSINESS MANAGERS

A business manager doesn't usually involve himself in the day-to-day business of running your life. It's the job of the business manager to work out where you should be in terms of business planning and to help you put the plan into action. He will liaise with the record and publishing company, but usually more at the level of negotiating deals, changes to the contracts, setting video and recording budgets, and getting tour support when it's needed.

It's much more common in the US to have a separate business and personal manager. There the business manager is often an accountant or financial adviser. The idea of these roles being filled by different people hasn't yet become popular in the UK. What tends to happen here is that one person will do both jobs, sometimes with the assistance of a personal assistant (see below) or you have co-managers with complementary skills.

If you do have separate business and personal managers or co-managers, you need to be sure that you're not paying too much by having two people on board instead of one.

Don't assume that because you have a business manager you can do away with the need for an accountant. You will need one to oversee your tax and possibly VAT returns and someone to prepare company or partnership accounts. Bear this in mind when you agree what to pay your business manager. If you're paying your business manager 20% of your income, your personal manager another 10% and then paying an accountant, that's not a great bargain.

The manager is there to advise you, to guide you through your career in the music business. A successful career as a performer or songwriter can lead into other areas such as films, television, writing or modelling. One of the many things you have to consider in choosing your manager is whether the manager can also look after these other areas of your life.

The manager should spend a reasonable amount of time on your affairs and your career. He should help you to get a record and/or publishing deal, live appearances, sponsorship and merchandising deals or to develop a strategy for releasing records independently.

The manager should advise you whether or not you should take up a particular offer. It may not fit in with the game plan that you and the manager have worked out. Putting together that game plan is a very important job for your manager. You and he need to be on the same wavelength on it.

PERSONAL ASSISTANTS

As you become more successful so the manager may employ someone to act as your personal assistant (PA). If the PA is working full-time for you, the manager will probably expect you to pay their wages. If they work some of the time for you and the rest on general work for the manager or for other acts that he manages, then the cost is likely to be shared between you. If the PA works most of the time for the manager and only occasionally runs errands for you, then you would expect the manager to bear all the cost.

FIDUCIARY DUTIES AND PROBLEMS WITH BANDS

As we saw in the section on the cases (above), the manager has to always act in the artist's best interests. He has a fiduciary duty to the artist, which means that he has to always act with the utmost good faith towards that artist.

This duty can cause problems when dealing with a band. Something that may be good for the band as a whole may not be good for one of the band members. There's a very narrow line that the manager has to tread. Sometimes you may feel that the manager has stepped the wrong side of that line. This also has to be carefully considered if your manager is also your publisher. Bucks Music Group is the latest to launch a management arm in June 2016.

This issue was one of several behind a dispute between Nigel Martin-Smith and Robbie Williams.

The Robbie Williams management case (Martin-Smith v. Williams [1997] unreported)
I have to declare an interest here, as this was a case I inherited when I became Robbie's lawyer a few years ago. Martin-Smith was the manager of Take That from the early days to the height of their success. Take That was made up of five members, including Robbie. He became fed up at the direction his life was taking and was thinking about leaving the

band. His version of events is that he was prepared to see his commitments to a major tour through to the end before leaving the band. He says that, on advice from Martin-Smith, the band sacked him. The other members and Martin-Smith say he walked out.

When Martin-Smith later sued Robbie for unpaid commission (Robbie had refused to pay him), one of the arguments that Robbie used was that Martin-Smith had failed in his fiduciary duty to Robbie and was not acting in his best interests in advising the band to sack him.

Martin-Smith acknowledged that it was very difficult in such circumstances to advise a band when he also had a duty to each of them as individuals. He admitted that he had had discussions with the other band members about Robbie and how disillusioned he was, but he said he also tried to advise Robbie on what was best for him. He said that he had acted in the best interests of the band as a whole, while trying to balance this against the interests of the individual members. He denied that he'd advised the band to sack Robbie.

The Judge accepted his evidence that he had acted in good faith and was not in breach of his fiduciary duty to Robbie. The Judge acknowledged the difficulties that a manager faces in such circumstances, but decided that in this case Martin-Smith had stayed the right side of the line.

If you're in any doubts as to the good faith of your manager, you should seek independent advice, if only to be aware of your legal position.

ALTERNATIVE BUSINESS MODELS

There is a growing trend for managers to also take a financial interest and possibly ownership of rights in some other capacity. For example, a manager may say that he also wishes to act as your record label or your publisher. These are big issues and are driven by the fact that as manager he doesn't have any ownership of rights and can only take a financial cut on catalogue sales of records or songs for so long as his management contract allows. Some managers now feel that is not enough. They say it is taking longer to get an artist a deal; that each album is taking longer to make and that the promotion associated with it is even longer. On a basic three- or even five-year management term, the manager may, at best, only get paid on songs and recordings on a couple of albums. Some managers want more. They are also aware of the personal nature of management contracts and that their artist may leave, so they seek to gain some future security through ownership of recordings or of rights in songs. While the commercial reasoning behind these actions is easy to see, it doesn't necessarily mean it's a good thing. The skills that a manager brings to bear may not be the same ones that are needed to successfully release and sell records or promote uses of songs. This needs to be carefully investigated.

There is also the problem of potential conflict of interest. As your manager, he has to put your interests ahead of his own. What would happen if he felt, as your publisher, that it would be best for you to put one of your songs in an advert for a particular brand of lager as it would earn a lot of money but you feel that this would jeopardise your image as an artist popular with the 12–15-year age group. Who would fight your corner? Finally, there is also the issue of the manager having more than one source of income, i.e. he has his management commission on your earnings but also his profits as your record label or publisher. It is very important that the management contract doesn't allow the manager to take commission on any source of income that he has other interests in, e.g. record sales or income from songs. We saw the importance of this in the Elton John case above. If he does 'double-dip', is there very good justification?

Seal v. Wardlow (John Wardlow v. Haney Olusegun Adeola Samuel [2006] EWHC 1492 (QB) June 2006)

A more recent case on this point involves the artist Seal. John Wardlow began working with Seal who was then an unknown artist in 1987. Mr Wardlow provided studio time, instruments and musicians free of charge. Over the next two years, he helped Seal to record some demos and in time his role grew into that of a manager. He had very little experience of management but that in itself is no bar to being a good manager in this industry. The efforts of Mr Wardlow did not at this time result in any deal from a record label or publisher, and in 1988 Mr Wardlow went into business as a music publisher himself as part owner of the company, Beethoven Street Music. That company entered into a publishing agreement with Seal to publish his songs. Seal had legal advice before signing that deal.

The following year, Seal collaborated with Adamski and they had a number one hit single with 'Killer'. In 1990, Seal signed a record deal with ZTT Records and a couple of months later finally signed a written management agreement with Mr Wardlow. That deal allowed for Mr Wardlow to receive commission at 20% on Seal's income, including publishing monies. As we have already noted, as Mr Wardlow also benefited as publisher, it is usually unacceptable for him to also then take commission on the publishing money paid to the writer. In this case, this so-called 'double-dipping' went on for some time. By 1995, Seal felt he had outgrown Wardlow's capabilities as a manager and ended the management agreement. Seal continued with more experienced US management and a settlement agreement was entered into between him and Wardlow in 1995. He continued to pay Mr Wardlow in accordance with that settlement through to 2000 when he stopped. Mr Wardlow sued for what he said was properly due to him. Seal was trying to get out of his agreement to pay on the basis amongst other things that Mr Wardlow had used undue influence when in 1988 he had gone behind Seal's lawyer's back direct to Seal to persuade him to enter into the publishing agreement and accept the double-dipping. The Judge said that Wardlow had not convinced him that he had not used undue influence in relation to that agreement. But the Judge thought it was academic as the settlement that they had entered into in 1995 put in place new arrangements, was not a variation of the original agreement and superseded it. The settlement had not been entered into using undue influence; Seal had independent advice and the help of his more experienced new manager. It was a settlement by which Mr Wardlow gave up rights to income from future albums and the settlement was meant to draw a line under these issues.

Seal did not accept the decision and appealed to the Court of Appeal. In February 2007, the Court of Appeal upheld the earlier decision and went slightly further to say that it did not matter if the settlement was a variation of the original agreement or a new set of arrangements; it was intended to replace the earlier agreement and was not entered into through undue influence. The Court of Appeal Judges felt that by 1995 Mr Wardlow could not have been in a position of trust and confidence with Seal to exercise undue influence; by that time he was no longer the manager.

Some commentators have suggested that this case now takes over from the *Armatrading v. Stone* case (above) as the definitive view on undue influence in management cases. In fact, the two continue to exist side by side as the Judge in this later case found that there was a clear distinction between the two cases on their facts and on what was in the two management contracts so a direct comparison could not be made.

It is a fact of the current music business that such arrangements exist and you may well be offered such a deal and may have no alternative than to accept it if you want to work with a particular manager. Many of these arrangements work very well, but before you go into them take legal advice and be aware of potential pitfalls.

WHAT IS IN A MANAGEMENT CONTRACT?

Once you've found yourself a manager you think you can trust and who will do a good job for you, you need to think about putting a contract together between you.

What you want out of this contract will be different depending on whether you are an artist or a manager. In what follows I'm going to look at things from the artist's viewpoint, but in my time as a music lawyer I've acted for both artists and managers and so I'll try to present both sides of the argument.

Independent legal advice

As we've already seen, when negotiating a management contract the artist must have separate legal advice. The manager may decide not to take legal advice at all but this is rare. He may be experienced enough to feel comfortable with the deal he's prepared to do and doesn't need advice. If he's experienced with management contracts this isn't really a problem. If the artist decides that he doesn't want legal advice, then this is a problem for the manager. The manager should insist on the artist getting separate advice from someone who is familiar with the music business and with management contracts.

What if you haven't got the money to pay for a lawyer? The Musicians' Union (MU) has a limited free legal advice service for its members, but you can't expect it to be as detailed as if you were paying proper rates for it and it may take some time for you to get the advice. Some managers will lend you the money to take independent legal advice because it's in the manager's interests to make sure you're properly advised. If the manager does lend you money to get a lawyer, he will usually put a limit on how much he'll contribute. You'll either have to get the lawyer to agree to do the work for that amount or you'll have to chip in as well. The manager will get his contribution back out of your first earnings. Your lawyer may agree to accept payment by instalments if you ask and if he thinks he'll get more work from you in the future.

Territory

The first thing you have to decide is what countries the contract will cover. We call this the territory of the deal.

The manager will probably want to manage you for the world. This isn't just so that he can get as much commission as possible, although that is a factor. He may want to keep overall control of the game plan, which he won't be able to do very easily if he only manages you for part of the world.

You may be fine about this because you're confident that he can look after your interests around the world. But you must bear in mind that the way the music business operates elsewhere, in the US in particular, is very different from the UK. Does the manager have an office in the States? Does he have an associate there? Or will he be spending half his time on planes crossing the Atlantic? If he is, who's going to end up paying for that? Sometimes it'll be the record company, sometimes it'll be part of a tour budget, but sometimes it'll be you.

If you don't think that the manager can successfully look after your interests worldwide, you could insist that he only manage you for part of the world, for example, the world outside North America.

Even if you aren't sure he's up to being a worldwide manager, you could initially give him the benefit of the doubt. You could make it a worldwide deal to start with and, if he's not up to it, you could insist that he appoint a co-manager, probably for the US but possibly for other parts of the world, like Japan, to look after your interests there. This is a very personal thing and both you and your manager should agree the identity of this co-manager.

The co-manager is usually paid out of the commission you pay to the manager. Apart from the co-manager's expenses, you shouldn't end up paying out more in total commission just because there's a co-manager on board.

There are several ways that the manager and co-manager can split the commission between them. They could just take the total worldwide commission and split it down the middle. They could each just take commission on the income earned by you in their particular areas of the world. For example, the co-manager could take commission on the income you earn in North America and your original manager on the rest of the world income. The manager could decide not to share his commission but to put the co-manager on a retainer or pay him a fee. It's a complex subject and the manager should take legal advice on it.

Activities covered

The next thing to think about is whether the contract will cover everything you do in the entertainment business or just your activities in the music business. You might start out as a songwriter or performer and later move into acting or writing books. The manager may be perfectly capable of managing you for all those activities, or he may be an expert at the music business and know nothing about the business of writing books or acting. If you're not convinced he can look after your interests across the whole of the entertainment industry you should limit it to the music business only. The manager may be unhappy about this. He may think that it will be his management skills that will help turn you into a success in the music business which will in turn open doors to acting or writing books. He may feel that he should share in your income from those other activities. On the other hand, you may be concerned that he's not up to representing your interests and may want a specialised acting or literary agent involved.

Many managers will agree to compromise and say they have no objection to you bringing in specialised acting or literary agents if you are in acting roles or writing books that have nothing to do with you being a successful musician or songwriter. If the acting role or book is directly connected to the fact that you are an artist, they will want to share that income and manage those projects. For example, if you are asked to write a behind-the-scenes look at your time out on the road with the band, the manager will expect to take commission on your income from that book. If, however, you are asked to write a book on climbing in the Himalayas that clearly has nothing to do with your fame as a successful musician or songwriter, the manager may agree not to take commission on that income.

By the time you get a manager, you may already have established yourself in another part of the entertainment business. For example, you may already be a successful TV actor or model. The manager may agree not to manage those areas of activity. He may also agree not to manage or take commission on work that comes from a particular contact or source of work, such as a recording studio, which was in place before he came along. If, however, you ask him to manage projects that come from that source, perhaps by setting up the deal or chasing them for payment for you, then it's only fair that the manager should be allowed to take commission on that project or work.

In an economic climate where making enough money as a manager is challenging, to say the least, you can expect the manager to push to manage the widest possible range of activities.

Exclusivity

Once you've decided what activities he's going to manage and in what parts of the world, the manager will expect to be your exclusive manager for those activities and those areas. You will not be able to manage yourself or to ask someone else to manage a particular project unless he agrees. This is not only reasonable, it's also practical. You can't go around accepting work without referring it to your manager as it might clash with something he is putting together for you.

Key-man provisions

What happens if your manager manages other acts or is part of a management company that manages a number of people? How can you make sure he'll be there for you when you need advice? How do you make sure you aren't fobbed off on to someone else because your manager is busy with the other acts he manages? Well, first of all you make sure that your management contract says that he has to spend a reasonable amount of time on a regular basis on managing you.

You could possibly go further and insist on what we call a 'key-man' clause being put into the contract. This term comes from insurance policies that are taken out on the life of key individuals in an organisation, which pay out if the key-man dies or is unable to work. You name the manager as a key-man and say that if he's not available to you as and when you need him, you can bring the contract to an end.

Your manager may be very flattered at being named as a key-man, but he or his bosses may feel that it's a bit harsh to allow you to end the contract so abruptly. He may want to say that you can only terminate the contract if he has regularly not been available to you or has been unavailable to you for over, say, six weeks at a time. You have to be sensible about this. If you're buried in a residential studio in the depths of the country, writing or rehearsing material for your next album, it may not be reasonable to expect your manager to be there all the time. If you're in the middle of a major renegotiation of your record contract, however, you can reasonably expect him to be around.

These key-man clauses are also sometimes put into record or publishing contracts, but companies hate them because they give the artist and the key-man a huge amount of power. If they sack the key-man, you can end the contract. It is becoming increasingly difficult to get such provisions into contracts as the industry becomes more uncertain as to its future profitability.

How long should the contract run?

The contract could be open-ended and carry on until one side or the other decides it's over. This is a very confident position for the manager to take as in theory the artist could dump him just as things are starting to come good and few are this brave.

It could be for a fixed period of, say, one or two years and then, if everything is going well, could continue until one party wanted to end the relationship.

More usually it's for a fixed period of three to five years and at the end of that time the contract is renegotiated or it just ends.

Until the early 1980s, you often saw terms of five years or longer, but the Armatrading case cast some doubt on that and this has been reinforced by the Wayne Rooney case (see above). In the US, terms of five years or longer are common and, given that artists seem to take longer to record and promote each album, terms of five years are becoming more common in the UK too. However, as was clear in the Rooney case, exclusive deals that run for more than a couple of years are potentially seen as being in restraint of trade and care needs to be taken by managers that the deal they do is reasonable overall.

I can usually be persuaded to advise a client to agree to a five-year term with the artist having an option to end it after, say, two years, exercisable only if the manager has failed to achieve something for the artist – what I call hurdles.

Hurdles

A hurdle could be that the artist has to have a record or publishing deal or have earned a minimum amount of money within the first two years, although it's difficult to say what the right minimum level of income is and I generally resist such clauses as they are difficult to draft with sufficient clarity.

A get-out based on the manager not getting you a decent record or publishing deal in the first two years is a much more common hurdle. Or perhaps if he got you a deal in that time and it's come to an end and he hasn't got you another one within, say, six to nine months.

Album cycles

This is originally a US concept, but has gained ground in the UK. The length of the contract is linked to an album cycle. An album cycle starts with the writing of the songs to be recorded on an album, and runs through the recording of the album and all the promotion that then goes on after its release. The cycle ends with the last piece of promotional work for that album.

My problem with it is that it's very difficult to say how long it will last. You don't know at the beginning how long it will take to write, record and promote an album. I'm uncomfortable with agreeing to two- or three-album-cycle deals, which could easily run for six years or longer. If you're offered this type of deal, I advise you to put a time backstop on it, for example, two album cycles or five years, whichever comes first. It can, however, be a neat way of an artist bringing a manager on board for one album only.

Ending the term early

Sometimes an artist or a manager wish to part company while the term of the contract still has some time to run. If it's all amicable, then that's one thing and an agreement on the manager's share, if any, of future income earned by the artist can be reached and put in writing as you would in, say, an amicable divorce.

If, however, one party wants to go and the other doesn't agree or thinks there are any grounds for an early termination, then the matter is more complicated. In such cases, if a settlement can't be reached by negotiation the matter ends up in court. Sometimes you get a settlement which one party then becomes discontented with, as in the Seal case above. That old adage of 'where there's a hit there's a writ' certainly seems to hold true.

THE MANAGER'S ROLE

I've already explained a little of what you can expect the manager to do for you. What you can't do, though, is list every single thing that you expect a manager to do. It will be the very thing that isn't listed that causes the problem. There are still some contracts around that try to list things the manager is expected to do: for example, the manager will advise on clothes, image, voice training etc. I think these have an old-fashioned feel about them. My management contracts just say that the manager will do all he reasonably can to further the artist's career and to do all the things expected of a manager in the entertainment or music business.

What is the manager paid?

Some would say too much, but if you ever saw a manager working round the clock, seven days a week to make an artist successful, with not even a thank you from him, you'd say it wasn't enough. It is a measure of the fact that many managers are branching into publishing or setting up as production companies that they are unable to make a good living from an averagely successful artist once they've paid their staff, overheads and taxes.

The average rate of commission for a manager is 20%. If you're very successful the 20% could be negotiated down to 10–15%. Some record-producer managers only charge 15% because, arguably, there is less management of projects or a career than there is with performing artists. Very few managers try for a 25% rate, though there are some circumstances in which it could be justified. The manager may have invested a lot of his own money in making an artist successful and may want to get that back in commission as soon as possible. He may agree to reduce his commission down to 20% when the artist becomes successful and he's got his investment back.

Percentage of what?

A percentage of your gross income but net of some expenses is the simple answer. For example, if you were paid a £100,000 personal advance on signing a record deal, the manager on a commission of 20% would take £20,000.

What if you have to use some of that money to record your album or pay a producer? What happens if you are advanced money by your record company (which they get back or 'recoup' from your royalties) to make a video or to underwrite losses on a tour? Is it fair that the manager takes 20% off the top? The answer is no, it's not. There are a number of exceptions. It's not usual for the manager to take commission on monies advanced to you as recording costs, video costs and payments to record producers or mixers, sums used to underwrite tour losses and sometimes monies advanced to you to buy equipment.

Example: The record company sets a budget of £200,000 for you to make an album, £50,000 to make a video and £100,000 for you to live on for the next year. The manager usually won't take commission on the £200,000 or the £50,000, but will take commission on the £100,000, i.e. £20,000.

Depending on the manager and the contract, the manager may say that if you decide to use £20,000 of your £100,000 to buy some equipment, then that's your choice and he's still going to take commission on the full £100,000. Or he might treat the £20,000 spent on equipment as an exception and take his commission on the balance of £80,000.

Commission on earnings from live work can be a problem. The manager usually has to work very hard putting together and running a successful tour. He may feel that he should take his 20% off the top from the income that comes in from that tour. What if the expenses of putting on the tour are so high that the tour makes little or no profit? For example, you take £50,000 in ticket sales and the expenses are £40,000. If the manager took his 20% off the £50,000 (i.e. £10,000), there'd be £40,000 left, which would be wiped out by the expenses. As an artist performing every night of the tour, you may start to resent the manager making £10,000 when you are getting nothing. As we saw in the Armatrading case, the Judge was very critical that Stone took 20% of gross income on touring regardless of whether the tour made a profit.

What tends to happen is that the manager takes his commission on net income on live work after some or all of the expenses are taken off. There are various formulas to arrive at a fair compromise; your lawyer will advise.

Trent Reznor Management Dispute

In June 2007, a US court awarded Trent Reznor of Nine Inch Nails approx. $2.9 million in his claim against his former manager John Malm. He brought the case back in 2004 alleging that Malm had mismanaged his finances and in effect defrauded the band out of money by tricking them into signing a contract that gave Malm the rights to 20% of the band's gross income as opposed to the net income. The manager claimed to have not taken advantage of this and that he had not actually collected the additional money. He also pointed out (presumably as evidence of his good character) that he had worked for no money for many years. The court nevertheless found that he had taken funds that he was not entitled to and awarded damages to Mr Reznor.

This case shows the difficulties managers can get into when they step outside the established norms.

Post-term commission

This means how long after the end of the management contract the manager continues to get paid commission. It's sometimes referred to as the 'sunset clause'. It has two sides to it. Firstly, should the manager take commission on albums made or songs written after the end of the management term? Secondly, for how long should he earn commission on albums made or songs written while he was the manager?

What is commissionable?

Until the early 1980s, it was quite usual to see management contracts that allowed a manager to go on earning on things the artist did long after he'd stopped being the manager. If he negotiated a five-album record deal while he was the manager and he stopped being the manager after two albums, he'd still take commission on the remaining three albums because that contract was done while he was the manager. Some contracts also allowed him to continue to take commission after he stopped being manager if someone else negotiated an extension of or substitution for that original contract. Again, because he had done the original work. This led to some very unfair situations. The new manager had no incentive to improve upon deals because it was the former manager who got the commission. Artists found it difficult to get new managers and were forced to stay with the original manager or the artist ended up paying out two lots of commission. This situation was strongly criticised in the Armatrading case and led directly to a change in the way UK managers operated and it is this aspect that the Judge distinguished in the Seal case in saying that the facts of the two cases were not the same. UK managers usually now accept that they only get commission on work done, recordings made and songs written while they are the manager, or which are completed within, say, three months thereafter.

How long should the manager continue to receive commission?

After it was established that managers should only take commission on what was recorded or written while they were the manager, the question then came up of how long they should go on earning commission on those recordings and songs.

Some managers, although now not many, still take the view that they should go on earning commission as long as the artist goes on earning income from a particular song or recording. I can see the logic in this but again it can lead to some unfairness. A manager might have only been around for one album's worth of recordings. It may be a second manager that makes the artist successful. Fans of successful artists want to own all the artists' back catalogue of records and so buy the first album, or a track from the first album may go on a Greatest Hits album. The first manager has done nothing to help ongoing sales of that first album. Should he get full commission on it? Most managers accept that after a period of time their influence cannot be affecting continuing sales of early records, so they agree to a reduction in their commission rate. Most also agree that it should stop altogether after a given period. For example, the first manager could agree that his commission on the first album drops to 10% after ten years after the end of the management term and stops altogether after twenty years. This means the artist can give the second manager an incentive by giving him 10% of the income on the first album after ten years and 20% after twenty years. Or the artist could keep the saving himself and give nothing to the second manager.

These periods of time are negotiable. Some music lawyers insist that the commission stop after two or three years. This may be too short for a manager to be properly compensated for the work he has done. It may, however, be acceptable if the artist is established and successful and has greater bargaining power than the manager.

What happens if there's no written contract?

A few managers prefer to work without any written contract. They say they'd rather work on a good-faith basis, trusting you to do the right thing by them. This is a comparatively rare situation but it is also possible for a manager to work for a trial period and then not carry on. Sometimes the manager just can't get the artist to commit to a contract and carries on reluctantly without one. Even where there is no written deal, you still have to deal with what the manager gets paid for the work he did. It is, of course, perfectly possible for there to be a verbal contract in place. The difficulty with verbal contracts is that it's very hard to prove what exactly was agreed.

If it's not possible to show that there was any sort of agreement, the manager has to rely on what would be a fair price for the work he has done (a *quantum meruit* claim). If you and the manager can't agree this and there is a court case, the Judge will take expert evidence of what's usual in the music business and will make an order of what he thinks the manager should be paid. The court will order payment for the work already done, but it's rare for them to order payments going forward. For example, if the manager got a record deal for you, then the court might order that he's paid a percentage of the money payable on signing that deal; but rarely does it order that the manager is paid a share of ongoing royalties. So the manager wouldn't usually get post-term commission and is therefore at risk of not benefiting from his work in the future. For these reasons it's usually more important for the manager to have a written contract to protect his commission on future royalty income than it is for the artist. However, both sides may want the certainty of knowing where they stand and want to reach some form of agreement.

Who collects the money?

It's very important to know who's looking after the money. The manager may be unhappy at the thought of you looking after the money just because you're an artist. Artists are notoriously bad at hanging on to money (they say). 'They can't even keep the money back to pay the VAT or the taxman; how can I trust them to keep enough back to pay me?'

On the other hand, you may be very responsible with your money. You may not want your manager controlling your money, but also may not want to have the bother of looking after it yourself.

A compromise would be for you to appoint an accountant. The money is paid into a bank account in your name looked after by the accountant. The manager sends in an invoice for his commission and expenses. The accountant checks the sums are right and either makes the payment or advises you of what is to be paid. The accountant may also deal with the VAT and he'll almost certainly advise keeping some money back for tax. What happens with the rest of the money depends on what you've told him to do. He could pay it into another account for you or leave some in the bank account to meet expenses.

Expenses

On top of his commission, the manager is entitled to be repaid his expenses. That doesn't mean everything he spends. The costs of running his business, his office, staff, computers, etc., are all paid for by him. These are called office overheads. If he pays for a taxi to pick you up from the recording studio or for a courier to deliver your demo recording to an interested A&R man, then he will probably reclaim that money from you.

He should keep receipts and bills and have them available for you or your accountant to check. He should also agree that he won't run up expensive items in expenses without checking with you first. I wouldn't expect him to buy a plane ticket to New York without checking that you're all right with him spending your money in that way. On the other hand, it may not be practical for him to have to come running to you for every small item of expenses, in which case you might agree a float account. This is a special account with a fixed sum of money, say £500, in it. The manager is authorised to draw money out of that account for expenses and the account is then topped back up to £500 on a regular basis, like a float in the till of a pub or shop.

Tax

You are responsible for your own tax and National Insurance and for paying your VAT. Don't expect the manager to do it for you. As we saw in Chapter 1, your accountant is a very important part of your team. Your accountant may keep the books, do the VAT returns and prepare the tax return for you. This doesn't mean you can sit back and do nothing. You have to tell your accountant what has come in and give him receipts for anything he might be able to reclaim or recharge.

Your accountant will also advise what you can expect to have to pay in tax and ways in which you can, legitimately, pay as little tax as possible. But remember, there are, they say, only two certainties in this world – death and taxes.

Signing agreements

It's practical to allow the manager to sign one-off short-term contracts in the artist's name. For example, when an artist does an appearance on *Later with Jools Holland* or *The Graham Norton Show*, the television company needs him to sign a short release or consent form before he can appear and get paid. If you are busy rehearsing, it's all right for the manager to sign that form for you.

What isn't acceptable is for the manager to sign a long-term contract, or indeed anything more than a one-off. It's dangerous for the artist – who won't know what's in it or what's been agreed. It's also dangerous for the manager. You may not object at the time, but when you find something in the contract that's not to your liking you can be sure you'll blame the manager for not telling you.

CONCLUSIONS

- Separate lawyers must advise the artist and the manager on the management contract.
- Treat with caution any management contract capable of running for longer than five years.
- 20% is the average management commission for artist managers. Commission is on gross income net only of certain exceptions which should be set out in the contract.
- Commission on 'live' work should be after deduction of some or all of the expenses.
- The management deal doesn't need to be for the whole world.
- Make sure it is clear who is handling the money.
- Only the artist should be able to sign potentially long-term contracts.

Chapter 3

What Is A Good Record Deal?

INTRODUCTION

Everyone's idea of what's a good deal is different. For some it's a question of how much money is on offer. For others it's how much commitment there is from the record company. Some artists are more interested in how much control they have over what sort of record they make. We call this creative control.

I'm going to look at these different ideas of what's a good deal. I will do so from the artists' point of view because that's what I know best. But, because I've negotiated so many record deals over the years, I've heard all the arguments from the record companies, so I'll try to put their side too.

There's more than one type of record deal. I'm going to look at four basic types of deal – the licence, the exclusive recording contract and a sub-category called a development deal, the 360-degree model and the production deal. A new addition, the label services arrangement, will be referred to but is dealt with in more detail in Chapter 5. The production deal and 360-degree model are currently the most popular.

You won't be surprised to learn that there have been some celebrated cases over the years to do with recording contracts. I'm going to look at four in this chapter to see what the problem was, what the court decided and what the music business learned from them.

THE STATE OF THE INDUSTRY

The mergers which have dominated developments in the major labels over the last five years or more has now settled down. We have three major label groups, Sony, Warner and Universal with BMG coming up fast on the inside. As a direct consequence of concerns over monopolies or dominant positions, the majors have had to divest themselves of some labels. EMI Records was sold off to Universal, who had to sell off some labels including Parlophone, which ended up at Warners. Warners is in the process of selling off several dance labels, some of which have been bought by independent companies. In a quirky twist of history, Chrysalis Records was bought in a deal led by Blue Raincoat Music's Jeremy Lascelles and Robin Millar CBE. This saw the original owner of Chrysalis, Chris Wright CBE, reunited with the label, returning as non-executive chairman some 27 years after he sold the company to EMI.

Within the majors there has been a continuation of their cautious approach to signings. They are fewer in number, the money is generally tighter and the reliance on tried and tested production companies and producers as sources of new talent continues. However there are signs at Universal, in particular Island Records, of a return to favour of a development-style deal, which may be an indication of majors returning to their traditional role of developing artists.

In the absence of much signing activity at the majors, and indeed in some cases as a positive rejection of major label conservatism, the independent sector has taken up the slack as well as significant numbers of artists self-releasing their first recordings online. Both the IFPA and BPI released very upbeat reports on the state of the digital market and the music industry in 2016 – with a distinct feeling that the music industry has turned a corner in its battle to get proper remuneration for online use of music content and reporting a period of strong growth of over 5%.

Independents cannot compete with major label budgets or international distribution networks so may have to accept a deal for a limited territory such as the UK or Europe as opposed to a world deal. They may offer digital release only worldwide with physical releases following only if the sales warrant it. They can take more chances in what type of artist they choose to record or release, but that makes it commercially risky for them so they cannot afford to absorb too many failures.

At the other end, the growth and greater stability of the online market makes it easier for artists to record and promote their own releases bypassing labels altogether or perhaps relying on local licence deals for international releases. At this lower end, access to mainstream radio is hard to achieve and so marketing needs to be ever more innovative. However, the growth of streaming (which is covered in depth in Chapter 7) has seen the development of playlists, and in some senses led to stagnation in the charts. Changes in how the charts are compiled which came into effect in January 2017 are intended to address this.

Artists who are unable or unwilling to sign to major label deals find it hard to survive on income from record sales and publishing revenue alone. The 'live' scene remains a vital source of income. It is also increasingly important that artists are clued up about, and plugged into, all online services in order to access the revenue that is being generated by them.

Production companies continue to act as feeders or nurseries for the major labels, and some have also branched out into releasing records by artists they are developing, where they have not been able to attract the interest of more established labels. The Internet makes the release of single tracks or EPs easier to achieve and these can act as a 'calling card' or taster for more tracks to come.

In an attempt to fully utilise their manufacturing and distribution networks and marketing departments in the face of fewer releases of their own, the major labels have begun offering paid-for label services to independent labels and artists. See more in Chapter 6 on Distribution deals.

THE HYPE OF THE MILLION-POUND RECORD SIGNING

We have all read in the press about new, unknown acts being signed supposedly to million-pound deals. Can you believe what you read? Well, I guess in one or two cases it could be true, but it's pretty unlikely if it's a completely unknown artist. Also have you noticed how it's always a million-pound deal not 1.2 million or 1.5 million?

What is much more likely is that the deal has been hyped up in the press to make it seem bigger than it is. If you add up all the money that the record company could spend on making an album you could get to a million pounds. That would include the recording costs, the cost of making one or two videos, marketing and touring costs. In 2010, the International Federation of the Phonographic Industry (IFPI) issued a report called 'Investing in Music' stressing the investment made by record labels in artists and seeking to debunk suggestions that an artist can develop careers in the business without needing a label.

The report claims that it can take up to $1 million to break a new act in major markets. Typical record label investment in developing a new pop artist in major markets was put at $200,000 for the advance, $200,000 in recording costs, $200,000 in making three promotional videos (one per single), $100,000 in underwriting shortfall on live shows and a whopping $300,000 in marketing and promotion.

So, when the press or record companies talk about the £1 million deal, all these factors and elements are taken into account. The artist might only see a fraction of that money in his bank account.

HOW DO RECORD COMPANIES KNOW WHAT TO OFFER?

When record company executives are making up their minds about what to offer you in terms of a deal, they will look at a number of things. First, and most importantly, how much they want to sign you to the company. If they desperately want you, they may pay over the odds to get the deal done. If you've got more than one company fighting over you, then you've much greater bargaining power. Your manager and lawyer can play one company off against the other and get you a better deal. There is less of that going on at the moment, but you do still occasionally get major companies trying to outbid each other.

If the record company is doing it scientifically, they'll use various formulas to work out what's a reasonable deal to offer. There are computer models that they can use. They look at the type of act, at how much they think it's going to cost to record the album and to make videos and to promote. They also look at other commitments, possibly to touring. They put these estimates into the model and it tells them how many records would have to be sold, or paid for streams or downloads before they break even. If they think that's an unrealistic number they may scale down the offer. This is the theory anyway. I suspect that they do this number crunching then go with their hunches to some extent anyway as to how well they think you're going to do. There are also other factors at play, such as whether it is a good deal to sign in order to get a good slice of the market (so-called 'market share') so as to look good for the shareholders. Sometimes a deal is done for strategic reasons in order for a particular label or label head to set out their stall as being an important player or wanting to attract a particular type of artist.

We saw in Chapter 1 some of the ways in which you can increase interest in you as an artist. The 'hotter' you are, the more the record company is likely to pay or the better overall deal you'll be offered. The better your lawyer is, the less likely it is that the record company will get away with paying below the odds – a very good reason to get a good lawyer on your side.

Your manager should sit down with you and discuss what's important to you. Are you only interested in big-money advances, or would you prefer to go for a smaller advance in return for creative control or more commitment from the record company? Once he knows what you want, your manager can make his 'pitch' to the record company along those lines.

It should be a balanced contract, where the record company can reasonably protect its investment, but also one where you get some commitment from the record company and the chance to earn a decent living from the deal.

THE LEGAL PRINCIPLES

Before I look in more detail at these questions of money, commitment and creative control, I need to run through the guiding legal principles in deciding what is a good record deal.

Restraint of trade

We have already seen in the cases of *Armatrading v. Stone* and *John v. James* (Chapter 2) that the courts can be highly critical of clauses in contracts that are unfair on the artist.

In deciding whether a contract is fair, the court looks at a number of things. It looks at the bargaining power of the artist and the company. It will also look at whether the artist had independent specialist advice before he signed the contract, and at how experienced the artist was in the music business at the time the contract was signed. It does this against the background of what was the norm for these contracts at the time.

Another guiding principle behind the court's decisions is that of restraint of trade. The basic principle behind the doctrine is that, where someone has to provide services or be exclusively employed and the contract contains restrictions on what someone can and cannot do, that contract is automatically a restriction on the ability to earn a living, or trade. Because it's an exclusive arrangement, the person concerned cannot earn money in any other way than through that contract. In the UK it was decided long ago that these contracts were contrary to public policy. A person should be free to earn his living wherever he can. That said, the courts recognised that there would be circumstances where it was commercially necessary to have restrictions in contracts. They decided that such restrictions would be allowed if they were reasonably necessary to protect the legitimate business interests of the person imposing the restrictions. If the restrictions were unreasonable, the contract would be unenforceable.

Because it was so important to the music business, the case of *Macaulay v. Schroeder* went all the way to the House of Lords before it was finally clear that the doctrine did apply to recording and publishing agreements.

Macaulay v. Schroeder (Macaulay v. Schroeder Music Publishing Co. Limited [1974] 1WLR 1308, HL)

Macaulay was a young and unknown songwriter who entered into a music publishing agreement with Schroeder Music Publishing Ltd. It was an exclusive agreement for his services for five years. The contract was in a standard form used by the music publisher. Macaulay's copyrights in the songs he wrote were assigned for the life of copyright throughout the world. The contract specifically prevented him from working as a songwriter for any other music publishers during the five-year period. There is nothing wrong in signing someone up to an exclusive deal, but, because it restricts that person's ability to go and work for anyone else, we have to look at whether as a whole such a contract is fair, and whether the restrictions still allow him to earn a reasonable living. The House of Lords looked at the specific terms of the agreement to see if, taken as a whole, they were reasonable. It found, in fact, that they were unduly restrictive and an unreasonable restraint of trade. Macaulay didn't have a reasonable chance to earn a decent living from his trade of songwriting. The contract was therefore said to be unenforceable.

In contrast, the *George Michael* case described later in this chapter is an example of an exclusive contract that was found to contain reasonable restrictions.

CREATIVE CONTROL VERSUS LARGE ADVANCES

Earlier in this chapter I spoke of getting the right balance in the contract terms. Behind that statement lies the principle that any restrictions in an exclusive services contract should be fair and only go so far as to protect the record company's interest. They should not unreasonably restrict an artist's ability to earn a living. So let's look at some of these terms.

WHAT IS A GOOD RECORD DEAL?

Do you go for the money or try to protect the integrity of your art?
Of course it's important for you to be able to eat, to have somewhere to live, and transport to get you to and from gigs, rehearsals and the recording studio, but it may not just be a question of money. For many artists, creative control of their work is at least as important. Being able to make a record with minimal interference from the record company is crucial to some artists.

If creative control is the most important thing for you, then getting that control would mean you had a 'good' deal, even if there was less money on the table as a result. Some record companies are more flexible than others on questions of creative control. If this is an important issue for you, you need to look at this before you get into a deal. You should ask the record label people what their attitude is to this issue. What is their track record? If you can, you should talk to other artists signed to the record company to find out their experiences. Some may well have been quite vocal online. You should also ask if the record company is prepared to guarantee creative control in the record contract. Sometimes they'll say it but won't put it in the contract so you can't rely on it.

Your wish to have creative control must be balanced against putting so many restrictions on what the record company can do that they can't sell your records properly. They may in such circumstances choose to use another artist's recordings – one who isn't so particular about creative control. For example, a proposal comes in from an advertising company to put one of two tracks into a major new car campaign. Artist A has full creative control in his contract and is known to be completely against the idea of his work being used in ads. Artist B, on the other hand, has an eye to the integrity of his work but realises that a campaign like this, if done properly, can really help him break into the big time. Artist B says yes and the record company puts his track forward not Artist A's.

You may be very interested in getting as much commitment as possible from a record company. If so, then you'll concentrate on getting them to confirm a specific figure in marketing 'spend' or to underwrite tour losses up to a fixed amount. The record company may be reluctant to go this far. They'd be in difficulties under the contract if, for example, there weren't enough suitable tour dates or they were unable to find the money to pay for the full marketing spend. It used to be the case that artists were concerned that there'd be a commitment to make at least one promotional video per single release, or to get a commitment to the release of a minimum number of singles. Now with the increase in popularity of single track downloads release of singles is rarely the issue. Physical single sales are almost unheard of. The problem now is how to make sure that you make money from all places where your work is used, whether that's actual record sales, downloads and streams or as a taster to drive the fans to buy the album, a ticket to your live show and a T-shirt at the show.

Despite the rapid growth of online streaming activity, traditional radio play continues to be important in promoting a new release; A&R people are very interested to hear tracks that they know will get radio play to promote the artist. There is a strong belief amongst labels that in order to get commercial success in terms of number of sales you need to get radio exposure, preferably 'A' or 'B' list at Radio 1 or 2. To some extent, therefore, marketing is driving creativity, and artists who are not necessarily radio-friendly have to look for other ways to attract the attention of the public. So make sure you are signing to a label who understands where you are coming from on these issues. Chapter 7 deals with the importance of playlists in more detail.

There are few music programmes on terrestrial television which are likely to show a promotional video. This has led to a down-sizing in the spend on promotional videos. On the other hand, music is now often consumed in conjunction with visual images on websites like YouTube or on satellite TV shows featuring music videos where the visual material is made quite cheaply. So the quality and cost of video has declined overall, but the number of videos being made has increased.

Whatever the issue may be and no matter what big statements and promises the record label makes when they want you, if it's not specifically in the contract you will have little chance of making them keep their promises if they go back on what they said or if the person who said it is no longer with the company.

Whatever your particular needs (and it may be a mixture of all of these things), if you get a reasonable number of them in your record contract, you'll have what is a good deal for you.

This whole issue of creative control versus money has caused a lot of problems over the years. It's one of the reasons why Prince became 'Symbol', became The Artist Formerly Known As Prince, then The Artist, before finally reverting to Prince. He may have believed that by changing his name he could use a loophole to get out of his record contract. The rumour I heard is that his contract gave his label exclusivity over him under any name under which he recorded, so by recording as a symbol rather than a name he may have hoped to get around the exclusivity of his contract. He was probably also hoping that it would show his record company, Warner Bros., the strength of his feeling over the type of records he wanted to make. Since his untimely death in 2016, there have been a number of legal disputes, including a well-publicised one with streaming service, Tidal. His home is to be opened to the public and his estate has done a major music publishing deal for his catalogue. It remains to be seen how closely control over how his music is used is continued after his death.

Disputes take place on a daily basis between record company and artist or manager as to how an artist is presented creatively, as well of course as to whether the artist is getting paid a fair price. It is part of the normal cut and thrust between them. I regularly have to arbitrate or advise on issues like who has final say on choice of single, or the look of the artwork for the new album because artist and label have different views. Another area of common dispute is what happens when a label decides after hearing the finished album that they don't want to release it. Most of these disputes don't get to court. One that did was the acrimonious case between George Michael and his record company, Sony Records.

The George Michael Case (Panayiotou v. Sony Music Entertainment (UK) Limited [1994] EMLR 220)

To understand the case and the decision, you need to know a bit about the background.

As we all know, George Michael was part of the very successful pop duo Wham! along with Andrew Ridgeley. The first exclusive record deal that George and Andrew signed in 1982 was with the record company Innervision, owned by Mark Dean. As is often the case, they were young, unknown and inexperienced. The record deal was for up to ten albums, which was a lot even in those days. They were exclusively tied to the company until they'd delivered all the albums that Innervision wanted from them. Applying the doctrine of restraint of trade, the restrictions in the contract were immediately contrary to public policy and were unenforceable unless they were reasonable.

Innervision was a small record company. It had a deal with Sony whereby Sony provided funding and facilities for the manufacture, sale and marketing of Innervision's records. The Innervision contract with George and Andrew, therefore, also included Sony's standard business terms. If the Innervision contract was criticised as being unenforceable and an unreasonable restraint of trade, this could also have been an indirect criticism of Sony's terms of business.

At first things went well, and their second release, 'Young Guns', was a UK Top 10 hit in 1982. This was followed by 'Bad Boys', 'Club Tropicana' and the chart-topping album *Fantastic*. By 1983, however, the relationship between Wham! and Innervision had broken down. Andrew and George sued the company to get out of the contract, arguing that it was an unreasonable restraint of trade. The case was settled before it got to court. It was part of the settlement that George and Andrew signed an exclusive recording contract direct with Sony label Epic Records. Again, that contract contained Sony's business terms, but an experienced music business lawyer negotiated it on George and Andrew's behalf.

Once again, things went well at first. Their first single on Epic – 'Wake Me Up Before You Go Go' – went to number one in the UK and was followed by four further number ones in quick succession.

In 1986, George and Andrew parted company. George embarked on a solo career with Sony. It was a very successful one, beginning in 1988 with the release of 'I Want Your Sex', which was a deliberate move to break with the playboy Wham! image. George's first solo album, *Faith*, was a huge success, selling over 10 million copies. On the back of that success, George renegotiated his contract with Sony, again with the help of an experienced music business lawyer.

In return for a substantial sum of money, George agreed to record three solo albums in the first contract period and gave Sony options for up to five more albums. *Faith* counted as the first of the three albums and he went on to record and release a second hugely successful album, *Listen Without Prejudice* (Vol. 2), which also sold millions. His star was also rising in the US, where he had a number one with 'Praying For Time', a single taken off that album.

Not surprisingly, Sony wanted George to continue in the same style with his third solo album. By this time, George wanted to move away from the out-and-out commercial pop style of records. He wanted to be regarded as a serious artist.

Because the contract ran until he had delivered up to six more albums, or for a maximum period of fifteen years, George couldn't record for anyone else. Sony also had the final say on whether an album by him met the necessary artistic and commercial criteria. They could go on rejecting more serious material from him, so a deadlock existed.

George sued, arguing that the record contract was an unreasonable restriction on his ability to earn a living, and as such was an unenforceable contract.

He refused to record for Sony and instead did a number of projects with other artists that were within the terms of his contract, just. For example, he did guest spots on other people's albums. He also concentrated on live work.

The case finally came to court in 1994. The decision to throw out George's case was made on somewhat surprising grounds. The Judge ruled that, in order to decide if the 1988 renegotiation of the contract was an unreasonable restraint of trade, he would also have to consider the earlier 1984 contract. He decided that he could not reopen a review of the 1984 contract because it had been entered into as a result of a settlement of a dispute. It's contrary to public policy to reopen something that was agreed by the parties as being a final settlement of a dispute.

It wasn't difficult to imagine that George would appeal. Perhaps the Judge realised this because, even though he had decided that he could not look at the 1988 contract, he went on to say what his conclusions would have been if he had done so.

The contract was an exclusive worldwide deal. It was for potentially a very long time and Sony had the absolute right to reject recordings and a limited obligation in the contract to do much with any recordings that it did accept. Obviously, Sony argued that the contract represented only the contractual obligations that it had and that, in fact, it would have done far more to help sell as many records as possible. In deciding whether the contract was unfair and unenforceable as being an unreasonable restraint of trade, the Judge looked at the relative bargaining power of the two sides. By 1988, George Michael was a very successful and powerful artist and well able to stand up to Sony. He had had the benefit of advice from his longstanding lawyer, who was very experienced in music business contracts. Finally, the Judge looked at what George would get out of the contract. Financially, he stood to get a great deal.

Balancing out all these factors, the Judge decided that the benefits George got out of the contract meant that the restrictions in it were reasonable to protect Sony's investment and its legitimate business interests.

While the case was going on, it was much easier to get improvements in record contracts, particularly those parts of the contracts that George was specifically attacking. For example, on CD sales, Sony was only paying 75–80% of the royalty at the time. While the case was going on, Sony was much more inclined to agree a 100% royalty rate. George, as expected, appealed. The thought of prolonged, expensive litigation with an artist who clearly wasn't going to record for Sony, and who could see his own recording career stalling with all the delays, led to a settlement before the appeal was heard. George was released from the contract and signed to Virgin/Dreamworks in return for a payment back to Sony. As part of the settlement, he later recorded some new tracks or new versions of old tracks for a greatest hits album that was released on Sony.

Aston Barrett v. Universal Island Records and others

In a dispute over monies due to the bass player for Bob Marley and the Wailers, Aston Barrett sued Island Records and the Marley family on behalf of himself and his brother, Carlton (who was the drummer with the band and was murdered in 1985). Aston argued that he had not received the money they were due after Marley's death in 1981. Aston and Carlton had played on a number of Marley albums. They had had their own successful act The Upsetters and joined Marley after Peter Tosh and Bunny Livingstone left. Their claim for royalties arose out of a contract made in 1974. Aston was also suing separately for his proper share of songwriting royalties on songs he co-wrote with Marley. Originally, Marley and the two Barrett brothers had shared royalties equally. It was alleged that under a new agreement made in 1976 Marley took 50% and the Barrett brothers shared the remaining 50% between them. In 1994, Aston took part in a settlement where it was said he agreed to forgo any right to future royalties in return for a share of a $500,000 settlement paid by Island Records. At the trial, Marley's widow and the founder of Island Records both played down the role played by the Barrett brothers and said that the 1994 settlement represented a fair share to them for what they had done. The Judge accepted that and refused Aston's claim. He also did not accept his claim that he had co-written several of the songs. Aston was something of a serial litigator having sued three or four times before. The Judge ruled that he would not be allowed to start any more litigation unless allowed to do so by a court.

TYPES OF DEAL

What types of deal may be on offer, what basic rights does a performing artist have, what is copyright and what rights does the record company need in order to release records?

Although there are many variations, some of which will be looked at below, there are two basic types of record deal – the licence and the exclusive long-term recording contract. Variations include the production deal, which contains elements of the latter two types, the development deal and the so-called 360-degree model, which embraces not only recordings but also other areas such as publishing, live and endorsements under the one umbrella deal. A new development is the offer by the majors of label services to support independent releases by artists not exclusively signed to them. See Chapter 5 for more detail on this.

Licence Deals

Legal principles and definitions
Licensor is the technical term for a person or company who owns rights, which it is licensing to someone else.

Licensee is the person or company to whom the rights are licensed.

A *licence* is an agreement to allow the licensee to do certain things with the rights that the licensor has to a particular product – a recording, a song and so on. A licence can be for as long as the life of copyright (see below) but is usually for a shorter period. The licensor continues to own the rights but gives someone else permission to use some or all of those rights.

In contrast, an *assignment* is an outright transfer of ownership of rights by an owner to someone else. It's usually for the life of copyright, although sometimes the rights are returned (reassigned) to the owner sooner than that. The assignment can be of some or all rights and can have conditions attached.

The *assignor* is the owner of the rights being assigned. The assignor no longer owns the rights once they have been assigned.

The *assignee* is the person or company to whom the rights are assigned.

You will often see in agreements a reference to rights being granted for the *life of copyright*. This is now the same period throughout the EU. For literary and musical works (e.g. songs) it's seventy years from the end of the year in which the author dies. For sound recordings and performer's rights it's now seventy years from the date on which the recording was released or the performance was made.

This change came about in 2011 when the European Parliament passed a variation to the 2006 Copyright Extension Directive (2011/77/EU) which extended copyright in sound recordings and performances from fifty years to seventy years following first publication (i.e. release) of the recording. The UK Government finally brought this into law in the UK on 1 November 2013 by means of The Copyright and Duration of Rights in Performances Regulations 2013.

The extension did not have retrospective effect beyond two years before 1 November 2013. So if the sound recording went out of copyright in, say, 2009 it will not revive. There are also innovative new arrangements for this extended period, including 'use it or lose it' notice provisions, a clean slate for recoupment purposes and the record labels have to set up a fund to support session musicians with a share of revenues from sales in this extended period. After the fiftieth year following the publication of a recording, a non-featured performer (i.e. one who signed over their rights to the owner of the sound recording copyright in return for a single payment) will receive, annually, an equal share of a sum equivalent to 20% of revenues from the physical and online sales of their recordings. These funds will be administered by the collecting societies that represent the interests of labels and performers, namely PPL in the UK. Under the 'use it or lose it' provisions if, five years after its release, the sound recording copyright owner is not commercially exploiting a sound recording the performers on the sound recording can reclaim their performers' rights if they serve a notice on the owner of the sound recording and within a reasonable period that owner fails to make the sound recording available for sale (both physically and online). The sound recording copyright will go into the public domain but the performer's rights in their performances will continue for the extension period allowing them to regain control of their performances and to release them themselves. The third innovation, the 'clean slate', means that revenue from sales in the extended period cannot be used to recoup any unrecouped amounts on the artist's account. Royalties must be paid through to the artist. These rights apply in the EU only.

To continue with our definitions, the *author* is the first owner of the copyright (*ss.17-27 CDPA*). In the case of sound recordings, the Copyright Designs and Patents Act 1988 (CDPA) declares this to be the 'producer'. This could be confusing, and for a time record producers were claiming they were the copyright owners. The position is, in fact, the same as before the 1988 Act. The copyright owner of a sound recording is the person 'who made the arrangements for the recording to be made'. This is generally taken to mean the person who paid for the recording to be made. With the changing role of managers and producers in making independent recordings, there will be issues about whether the artist, the manager, the producer or even the studio owns the copyright. I regularly have to deal with situations of multiple ownership of copyright with the attendant problems of trying to decide mechanisms for what is to happen to the copyrights when it comes to commercial exploitation. The artist may need to rely more than ever on his performance rights to ensure a measure of control and also through songwriting where he is the writer of the songs being recorded. There is more of this in Chapter 4 on publishing deals.

Copyright is the right that an author has to prevent anyone else doing certain things with his work without his permission. It underlines all creative aspects of the music industry so it is important to get to grips with it. The basic rights of copyright are the right to copy the work; the right to issue copies of the work to the public; the right to rent or lend out copies of the work to the public; the right to perform, show, play the work in public or communicate the work to the public; the right to make an adaptation of the work and the right to do any of these acts in relation to that adaptation. Before anyone can do any of these things with a copyright work, they have to get the permission of the owner of the copyright. This may be the author as first owner or he may have assigned his rights to someone else or given someone else an exclusive licence to deal with the copyright instead of him. The definition of what constituted communicating and making available a copyright work to the public was clarified as including Internet, cable and satellite broadcasts and also includes on-demand services. The law applies to authors, record labels, film producers, broadcasters and performers.

There is much debate about the exemptions to the basic rule requiring the copyright owners' permission to reproduce the whole or part of a copyright work. Indeed in the US this 'fair use' (as they refer to it there) has been a key tenet in the arguments of various ISPs that the content they use does not require permission and therefore there is no need to pay a fee. In the UK we refer to these as 'fair-dealing'. There are some genuine exemptions where, for example, an excerpt from a recording or part of a video is reproduced for purposes of a critical review or commentary. There is greater scope for abuse of this exemption in the fast-moving online world. Further extensions have been introduced such as an exception for parody or pastiche. These are dealt with in more detail in Chapter 13.

Performing rights are the rights performers have to prevent someone else from doing certain things with their performances, or with recordings of their performances, without their permission. The basic performing rights are in some respects similar to the rights associated with copyright. They are the right to prevent someone making a recording of a live performance; the right to prevent the communication of it to the public. It is also a performer's right to prevent someone from making a recording of his performance directly from a broadcast or cable programme. The performer's permission has to be obtained to do any of the above. Recordings of performances for personal use are allowed. The performer also has the right to refuse to let someone make a copy of a recording; issue a copy of a recording to the public; rent or lend copies of the recording to the public; play a recorded performance in public; or include it in a broadcast or cable programme service. The performer's rights also extend to online methods of making his work available to the public. The performer should make sure he only grants his performing rights when he is reasonably sure that the agreement under which he does so gives him either contractual control over how his work is used or sufficient financial reward for losing that control. As we saw earlier the performer's rights are also now extended from fifty to seventy years after the date of the performance being recorded, or if it is made available to the public the date on which that occurred. The 2013 case of *Jodie Henderson v All Around The World Recordings Limited* confirms that performer's consents to the use of their performances do not need to be in writing or in any particular form but can be implied by conduct. For example, if a performer goes into a commercial studio to make a recording of his performance knowing that it was intended that that performance is commercially released he would probably, by implication, have consented to the reproduction and distribution of that performance. Of course the scope of that consent might be a matter of fact in each case. For example you might consent to that recording being released but not to a remix of it being done and released without your knowledge or agreement. This stresses the importance of getting a clear written consent and setting out clearly the terms on which that consent is given. In recent years we have seen a growth in interest in the rights of performers and indeed a new collective licensing for performers. These rights are sometimes referred to as 'neighbouring rights' i.e. rights akin to copyright owned by performers. Under the UK system there are sub-classes of performers which break down into featured performers, non-featured performers and the performing producer's share. Between them they share fifty percent of the total performing rights fees and the record label retains the remaining fifty percent. It is important that your performance is logged, as is the nature of the performance i.e. in which of the three categories it falls. The performing producer should get the agreement of the featured artist to share in the performer's fifty percent as not all performers would agree that the producer has performed on the recordings concerned. The collection society operating in the UK for administration of these rights is Public Performance Limited (PPL), but there are also now several commercial organisations who will administer this for you. In 2016 Kobalt acquired one of the leading neighbouring rights companies, Fintage, as part of its plan to offer a full neighbouring right collection service. Even before this acquisition of its major rival, Kobalt reported that its neighbouring rights gross revenues grew to $20.9m, up 127% on 2015. (Source: MBW).

Licence versus assignment

There is an important distinction between a licence and an assignment. When an owner grants a licence, he keeps the underlying copyright. He only gives the licensee permission to do certain things with the copyright for a period of time (the licence term). In contrast, when rights are assigned then ownership and control of the copyright has passed from the owner to the assignee.

Courts are reluctant to order the return of copyrights or other rights that have been assigned, mostly it seems because to do so would upset business arrangements that have been already entered into. If it's a licence then the underlying copyright has not been assigned; there is no copyright to be returned to the original owner because it never left him. So, from the point of view of an artist, a licence should always be preferable to an assignment, all other things being equal.

There are two problems with this. The first is that the record company will in many cases be the one who made the arrangements for the recording to be made (i.e. paid for it) and so will be the first owner of copyright. The artist may have his performing rights, but will probably not own the copyright in the sound recording. The second is that record companies don't want to do licence deals if they can take an assignment of rights instead. They have investments to protect and want to own the copyright outright. They don't want to lose their rights when a licence ends, because these rights represent assets of the company and have monetary value to the company. The longer they have them and the more secure the ownership is the more value they have.

The more successful an artist is the more chance he has of being the owner of the copyright in the sound recording and in a position to license it to the record company. In production deals or joint ventures, it is more likely that the artist and label will jointly own the copyright and may well be in a position to keep that copyright and license it on rather than assigning these rights away. The argument would be that the bigger label has not taken the commercial risk in investing in the making of the recordings so should not take ownership either at all or unless the money paid is significant. If the artist has paid for the recording he'll be in a good position to argue for a licence rather than an assignment. In recent years, however, record labels have begun to do licence deals rather than assignments but with a long licence period, in excess of fifteen years in many cases and with the option to extend on payment of further advances or to assignments but with reversion of rights after an extended period of time.

Exclusive and non-exclusive deals

You might license rights in a recording that you own to a record company for inclusion on a particular compilation only and in that case probably on a non-exclusive basis. You might want to put the recording out yourself or license it to another company for a different compilation. You couldn't do that if you'd given the first record company an exclusive licence. The same principle applies to the grant of the right to put a recording in a film or advert.

On the other hand, you may be an artist or a small label that has recorded a track or an album yourself and own the copyright in it. You may not have the financial resources to do anything with that recording. Perhaps you can't afford to press up copies of it to sell or you can't promote it properly. You might go to another record company for those resources. In such cases, the licence is likely to be an exclusive one to protect their investment.

The licence term

How long should the licence last? If it's non-exclusive it doesn't matter as much. An exclusive licence could be as long as the life of copyright or as short as a year. Five- to ten-year licence terms are common. The licensee wants to have long enough to get a reasonable return on his investment, but if it's a short licence term the licensor will get the rights back sooner and may be able to re-license them to someone else (perhaps with a new mix) or release them himself. Most licence deals I'm doing at the moment are for five years or longer, with European and US companies often wanting seven to ten years. As usual, it's down to knowing and using your bargaining power.

Territory

It could be a worldwide licence or it could be limited to particular countries. If, for example, you've already licensed the rights exclusively to a company in the US, you can only then grant other licences in the same recordings for the rest of the world outside the US.

A distinction used to be made between the UK and other European countries, but one of the consequences of closer European integration has meant that Europe-wide deals, including the UK, are now as common as UK-only deals.

The disadvantage of individual-country deals is keeping on top of a number of different licensees. Record releases and marketing campaigns have to be co-ordinated and there isn't just one company to chase for payment of royalties. The main advantage is that there is the chance to license the recording to the company that most wants it in each country. You may also be in the fortunate position of ending up with more in total advances from individual-country deals than you'd get from one multi-territory deal, and may also receive more than you need in contributions to make videos or do remixes or in contributions to touring.

Deals involving online releases are almost invariably worldwide deals, but geo-blocking means that it is possible to limit it to, say, the US only.

Options

When you're doing a non-exclusive licence of a single track for a compilation, you don't usually give the licensee any options to any further recordings you may make. It's usually a one-off.

If it's an exclusive licence for something other than just a compilation, the licensee may be keen to get rights to release follow-up recordings. The licensee may be encouraged to invest more in promoting the first track or album if he knows he's going to get the follow-up.

When doing your exclusive licence deal, you can agree up-front the basis on which you are going to give them any follow-up product or you can leave it to be agreed at the time they exercise the option. This latter approach can be to the owner's advantage if the first track has been successful, as his bargaining power will be higher. It's not a very certain state of affairs though and often leads to problems, so I generally recommend that the terms are fixed at the outset.

Another possibility would be to give the licensee the opportunity to be the first to try to do a deal with you for the follow-up. For example, you might deliver a demo of the follow-up and give the licensee the exclusive right for a month to try to negotiate a deal with you. If no deal is done in that time, you can take it into the marketplace. This is called a first negotiating right.

You could give the licensee a matching right. This is the right to match any offer for the follow-up that you get from someone else. You have to tell the licensee the details of the offer, and if the licensee matches or betters it within a given period of time then you must do the deal with him.

Sometimes you do a combination of the two known as a 'first and last matching right', i.e. they get the first option to negotiate; if that fails you can go into the marketplace to seek a deal; if you get one you must give the first company a chance to match it; if they do they get to do the deal. This can be difficult to handle but you will at least know you tested the market for the best deal available and you know the label really wants it.

EXCLUSIVE RECORDING CONTRACT

This type of deal may give you the greatest potential investment and commitment from a record company but in return, of course, the record company will expect to be able to protect its investment and is likely to seek greater financial and creative controls.

A fair deal

It will be up to your advisers to make sure that whatever contract you are offered is a fair one. It should also be in the record company's interest. If the contract is so unfair that it's an unreasonable restraint of trade, it will be unenforceable. Most major record companies have now moderated their contracts to deal with this issue and, while individual cases of unenforceable contracts will, I am sure, still arise, you should never enter into a contract thinking you can tear it up if it no longer suits you. Quite apart from this being a very negative approach, it is likely that you will not just be allowed to walk away and may get embroiled in a lengthy dispute or court case. While this is going on it will be difficult for you to carry on with your career and could stall it permanently.

It's likely under an exclusive recording contract that the sound recording copyright will be owned by the record company either outright or for an extended period in excess of fifteen years. The contract will also make sure that the record company will be able to exploit the performances by getting all necessary performers' consents. So it is important that the contract is also balanced by suitable controls over what the record company can do with the recordings and performances.

One thing you might not want them to do is to put your recording with an advert for a product that you don't approve of. I was once involved in a case where Sting was upset that a recording of his track 'Don't Stand So Close To Me' was used in an advert for deodorant. Tom Waits also took exception to a use of one of his songs in a Levi ad. Not everyone wants, or perhaps needs, to make money at any cost. In fact, Tom Waits is something of a serial defender of his image and creative output. You would have thought by now that advertising companies thinking of using his work or that of a sound-alike would have learned that he does not take kindly to this, as on more than one occasion he has taken a company to court to protect his position.

Term of the contract

The contract will usually run for an initial period, normally of one year, but possibly shorter if it's a development deal. The record company will usually have a number of options to extend the contract term. In each contract period they'll expect the artist to record a minimum number of tracks. It could be single tracks or enough tracks to make up an album. The commitment is generally for an album unless it's a development deal when they might call for five or six tracks to start with and then decide whether to go for the balance of an album. Despite the fact that there has been a significant growth in downloads and streaming of single tracks, the emphasis in contracts is still very much on the delivery of enough tracks to make an album. There are, however, some signs that record labels are looking at different models and the arguments continue to rage as to whether or not the album format is dead. Artists like DJ Calvin Harris have declared it to be over but there are others such as Glenn Peoples writing in *Billboard* in the 15 November 2013 issue who argued that the album remains a viable format, particularly for the consumer wishing to become fully engaged with an artist. He also argued that some of these reasons are cultural – album charts, award ceremonies for album of the year adding to the culture of society. Interestingly, it is in the area of publishing agreements, which we will look at in the next chapter, that the shift away from an album commitment is becoming more widespread.

Each contract period is usually extended by up to six months after the artist delivers the last of the recordings the record company wants. The more slowly these are recorded and delivered, or the longer it takes to release them, the longer each contract period will be. It is, however, generally accepted that there should be a maximum backstop for how long each contract period can be extended. Otherwise, the fear is that the contracts will be unenforceable as they are too open-ended and potentially a restraint of trade. Two- to three-year backstop dates are common.

Why is it only the record company that has options?

The record company will have invested a lot of money in making the records. It may also have made videos and probably have supported the artist while he's been out touring. These costs are recoupable (i.e. the record company gets some or all of them back from royalties from sales or exploitation of records) but, if the artist doesn't sell or stream enough records, or the artist leaves before the record company has had the chance to recoup its investment, then all these unrecouped costs would be down to the record company. Very rarely can the record company get them back from the artist.

Then there are the promotional and marketing costs, which for a major release can run into hundreds of thousands of pounds, as well as the manufacturing and distribution costs. In many record deals these costs are non-recoupable from the artist's royalties. If the artist could just up and walk away from the contract whenever he felt like it, the record company wouldn't be able to protect its investment, its business interests. This is why the options are in the record company's favour not the artist's.

Why can't you get your copyright back once you are recouped?

It is easy to understand why a record company justifies its ownership of copyright in the recording for as long as possible by the fact that it's invested a lot of money. What is less easy to understand is why the company won't transfer ownership to the artist once they've recouped that investment.

Record companies claim that the vast majority of artists don't recoup their investment, possibly as high as 95% of all artists. So, for the foreseeable future record companies are going to insist that the record companies continue to own the copyrights of the small minority of artists who are successful, as without these assets their companies become a lot less valuable. However, as already mentioned, there is a distinct trend to either allow an automatic reversion after, say, twelve to fifteen years, or to have an option to extend the ownership period for further periods on payment of a further advance, often linked to the last two or three years' royalty earnings. Record companies also say that they have to spend a lot of money in researching and developing new talent. If they had to return the copyrights of successful artists, they say they wouldn't be able to invest as much in new artists in the future and that the culture of the nation would suffer as a result. Whilst some labels are coming back to the idea of doing development deals in order to find and break new artists, many record companies are not developing artists but are waiting until they are presented to them almost fully formed with a body of songs, many of which will have been recorded and produced to a high standard and with an artist with professional managers or production companies in place. However, the reality is that most artists just aren't going to get those copyrights back automatically on recoupment.

How many options should the record company have for future albums?
Most major record companies in the UK want options on three or four further albums. In the US, options for six or seven further albums can still be found. Independent record companies may accept less. That said, every now and again one or two unusual deals occur where record companies are so keen to sign up particular artists that they do non-exclusive, one-album deals, with no options. In some cases, the deals are seen as purely short-term ones to improve the record company's share of record sales in a particular quarter or before a company's financial year end. A good or improved slice of market share can significantly improve the company's share price and possibly the A&R or label head's end-of-year bonus, but in other cases it's because the artist may not be perceived as having a five-album career ahead of them. If this turns out to be wrong and they wish to renegotiate, then the artist will have the upper hand.

The number of options, and therefore the overall length of the contract, is a key issue when considering if a contract is an unreasonable restraint of trade. This issue came up in the *George Michael* case against Sony (see above) and was at the heart of a major court case between Holly Johnson of Frankie Goes To Hollywood and his record company ZTT. (He also had a similar dispute with the sister publishing company, Perfect Songs, which I will deal with in Chapter 4 on publishing deals.)

ZTT v. Holly Johnson (Zang Tumb Tum Recordings Limited and Perfect Songs Limited v Holly Johnson [1983] EMLR 6)

Holly Johnson and the other members of Frankie Goes To Hollywood were unknown when they attracted the interest of the directors of ZTT, Jill Sinclair and her husband, the highly successful record producer Trevor Horn. The band was broke and very keen to work with Mr Horn. They were told that ZTT would only do the record deal if they also signed an exclusive publishing deal with Perfect Songs. Now you might detect a whiff of undue influence here but, in fact, this point was not seriously argued in this case. The band signed up to both deals. Although they were inexperienced and had very little bargaining power, they were represented by a lawyer who was experienced in music business contracts.

Frankie Goes To Hollywood had two very successful singles with 'Relax' and 'Two Tribes', both of which attracted a great deal of controversy because of the subject matter in the case of the first and the video for the second. At one stage the tracks were Nos. 1 and 2 in the UK singles charts. The band's first album *Welcome To The Pleasuredome* sold well and produced two more hit singles. They failed to make it a success in the US and by 1986 the pressure was on them for the second album to be a success.

The band had a lot of trouble with the recording of this album, to be called *Liverpool*. Trevor Horn controlled the recording costs, he was the record producer and the recordings were being made in his studios. The costs were escalating alarmingly and the band was, it was said, horrified by how much they would have to recoup. After a lot of problems, the band split up but ZTT (and Perfect Songs) wanted to hold on to Holly Johnson. Johnson didn't want to continue with them and sued on the grounds that both the recording and publishing contracts were an unreasonable restraint of trade.

The term of the record contract was for an initial period of six months and was extendable by two option periods and up to five contract periods, all in favour of the record company. Each contract period was to be for a minimum of one year and extendable until 120 days after they fulfilled their minimum obligations to the record company (known as the Minimum Commitment). There was also no maximum extension of each contract period. It was open-ended and depended entirely on when the band fulfilled its Minimum Commitment.

The Minimum Commitment was one single in each of the initial period, first and second option periods and one album in each of the third through to seventh option contract periods. This is an unusual way of structuring a contract, but basically it meant that if the record company exercised every option the band had to record three singles and five albums.

The record company was free to bring the contract to an end at any time. The record company also had the right to reject recordings delivered to it by the band. As the term continued until after delivery of recordings that were satisfactory to the record company, this meant that the record company controlled how long the contract lasted. There are echoes of this in the *George Michael* case.

The court decided that the contract was one-sided and unfair and was an unreasonable restraint of trade and unenforceable. It thought that the potential term of the contract was far too long, as it could easily last eight or nine years. In that time, the court felt that the band wouldn't have had the opportunity to earn a decent living from their work. The record company wasn't obliged to do very much with the recordings. There was no commitment to release them. The court freed Mr Johnson from the contracts and awarded him compensation.

Probably as a result of this case, UK record contracts now almost without exception contain a clause committing the record company to releasing records in at least the home country. If records are not released the contract usually gives the artist the right to end the contract and sometimes to get the recordings back, possibly in return for a royalty (called an override royalty) payable back to the record company.

Two-album firm deals

If you've enough bargaining power, it is possible to get a record company to commit in advance to a second album. These types of deal are called 'two-album firm' deals. They are not currently common. Record companies are more likely to agree to these when they're in competition with another record company or perhaps where they are licensing in a finished album (so know what they are getting) and are then more inclined to take the risk on committing to a second one. Most record companies don't want to give this commitment. They want to see how the first album does before committing to a second. Some artists and managers favour them because they believe they provide commitment and certainty, which allows them to do some forward planning. Others feel they only work if things are going well. If things aren't going well, the record company will probably try to get out of their commitment after the first album. If your only alternative is to sue the company for failing to honour their side of the bargain, you'll probably agree to accept the offer they make to end the contract, so the commitment may not mean much in the end. Sometimes the record label will give the commitment but will insert what is sometimes called a 'disaster clause', where if the first album does not sell over a given number of units the record company does not have to make the second album. To my mind, this type of clause negates the whole point of seeking the certainty of a 'two-album firm' deal.

Territory and split-territory deals
Long-term exclusive record deals will usually be offered on a worldwide basis. This may be perfectly acceptable, particularly if the record company has a strong presence in most major markets of the world. However, because the US is a very different marketplace from that of the UK, an artist sometimes asks for what is known as a 'split-territory deal'.

This means that you do one deal with a record company for the world excluding the US and another deal with a different record company for the US. To make these types of deal work, the artist and his manager have to juggle the demands of two record companies. Record companies don't like doing these kinds of deals, because they say they need a worldwide market in which to recover their investment. They also say that their own companies are strong worldwide and should be given the chance.

Split-territory deals are therefore usually offered to artists with considerable bargaining power. Sometimes these deals are done because the record company has a strong reputation in one part of the world but not in another. A US branch of a UK record company may not have a track record in 'breaking' non-US artists in the US. With the growth of worldwide online marketing and distribution these arrangements are becoming less common in exclusive artist contracts although they do frequently exist in global licensing arrangements.

Smaller record companies may not have their own offices in all parts of the world. They may have a network of licensees in different countries. Those licensees might take all the records they produce. These are called catalogue licence deals. Alternatively, the UK company may look for different licensees for each artist. For example, the UK record company could do a deal with Atlantic Records in the US for all its acts or it could do a deal with Atlantic for its mainstream acts and with a smaller US label for its indie acts. Whatever the situation, you need to know who the licensees are going to be. They need to be well-established, trustworthy companies that will do a reasonable job of selling your records in the country concerned. Be a little cautious if an overseas licensing network is not in place when you do your record deal. Can you get a right of approval when the label negotiates its international licensing set-up, so that you know who will be releasing the album overseas?

Smaller companies use overseas licence deals to help to fund their operation in the UK. For example, a company in Germany could pay an advance against the royalty it expects to pay on sales of records in Germany. It may also pay a contribution to the cost of doing a remix in return for the right to use the remix in Germany. If the artist does a promotional or concert tour in Germany, the German licensee may provide some financial back-up. If you have a small low-key deal in the UK with a label that can't afford to pay you very much up-front, you could ask that some of the advances paid by overseas licensees of your recordings should be paid through to you. For example, if the German licensee paid an advance against royalties of €100,000 you might get 25% (i.e. €25,000). This will help to make up for the low advances in the UK. This is something that should be negotiated at the time the original UK record deal is done.

OTHER FORMS OF RECORD DEAL

Development deal

A variation on the exclusive recording deal is a development deal where the record label signs an artist up exclusively for a period of time during which it may record some demos or enough tracks for one or more EPs. The artist is given a recording budget and the means to pay for a producer but not usually much by way of money to live on. It is not yet time to give up the day job. If things go well with the development stage, then the record label usually has the option to decide to go on to make the rest of the album and probably then have options to more albums as in a normal exclusive record deal. If you get offered a development deal, you may initially be disappointed that it isn't a commitment to the full exclusive album-based record deal with all the financial commitment it promises. But it is a foot in the door and if you make the most of it you can use it as a stepping stone to your end goal. If they don't proceed with the deal, you can ask for the initial recordings back so you have at least got some well-recorded material with which to continue your search for fame and fortune.

360-degree deals

These have become the default business model adopted by most UK record labels for exclusive record deals. They are not new – variations on them have been around for years and the Robbie Williams deal done in 2002 was a particularly striking example.

They are now mainstream and represent a source of additional revenue for the record labels, which in some cases can be at least as financially beneficial as income from declining record sales, with merchandising and the live sector being particularly lucrative. UK Music's report *Measuring Music 2016* reported a steady growth in the whole sector, with the UK music industry contributing £4.1 billion to GVA in 2015, with the recorded music sector contributing £610 million and the live sector £904 million (a slight decline on 2014 live sector figures, put down to a dropping away in grass roots live events). However, these deals have not turned out to be the answer to all the problems and the label services deals and the drive to monetise streaming is a reflection of how record companies are still seeking other ways of broadening the income they can generate from their existing infrastructure. In many cases the difficulties of administering all bar the highest earning artists with these kinds of deals has made them less attractive.

So, what are these deals? They have acquired the name 360 degree because they involve all important aspects of an artist's career. A record label may say to an artist – in effect – 'We cannot make enough money just from selling your records to justify the level of advances, royalties and recording costs you want us to pay. We cannot invest the kind of marketing budget this record needs because we can't make enough money from record sales alone. So if we are going to sign/extend your record deal we can only do so on the basis that we also get a share of the money you make from other activities.' These activities might be songwriting but more commonly it means they want a share of the money the artist makes from selling tickets to their live concerts, from selling merchandise and from any sponsorship deals the artist does. The reason the record labels originally latched on to this is because for the last six or seven years the live industry has been doing well in relative terms. Prices of tickets to live events have risen and, as fans have been known to spend another £20 to £30 or more a head on merchandise once they get to the concert, this can prove a very lucrative business for the artists. The record companies have convinced themselves of the rightness of their stance by the fact that they feel it is their work in promoting the album and the artist that is at least in part responsible for the artist being able to sell so many concert tickets and therefore they should share in that money.

All the major record labels and many of the smaller ones are now doing some form of 360-degree deal. In the case of the majors these may be the only deals on offer.

These 360-degree deals can take a number of forms, but in essence the negotiation centres on what do they get a share of, for how long, and at what rate? The record company is usually looking for a share of income from things like the artist's website, merchandising, sponsorship and ticket sales and publishing income if it can get it. The artist may agree to pay over a percentage of this income together with supporting statements which the label can check or the record label may require that they are accounted to direct. The percentages are variable with figures around 10–20% being common but 50% not being unheard of. In these types of deals, the record label may not interfere, but just collect a share of the money. In other cases, the record label may insist that it controls things like the merchandising and sponsorship deals that the artist does. It is here that many artist advisers start to get more nervous as this gives the record company a great deal of control over the artist's wider career.

One deal that I did was an innovative variation on this 360-degree model which involved the artist and the label setting up a partnership which would hold assets like recordings, trade marks, videos, artwork etc., but which the artist ultimately owned. These assets were licensed to the partnership for a period of time before reverting to the artist. The partnership embraced recording and all other activities that the artist undertook in the entertainment industry other than songwriting as that deal had already been done. There was, however, no other reason why songwriting could not form part of such an arrangement if all agreed. The partnership was initially funded by the record label 'partners' and it was based on the parties sharing net profits. So far, it was reasonably similar to other joint ventures but with added income-producing areas. Where it was innovative was in what happened after the contract term ended. The artist was then free to go off and sign to another company if he wished, but for a period of time after the end of the contract term the artist would continue to pay a percentage of his profits from live work and other non-songwriting activities back to the record label 'partners' but these types of deals have not gained much traction.

Many managers were initially up in arms at the 360-degree model because they saw it as the record label taking slices of income that traditionally they were not entitled to and arguably therefore reducing the monies that the artist receives and which are then commissionable by the managers. However, managers are nothing if not pragmatic and in the majority of cases, as these are often the only deals on the table, they have learned to accept them while seeking ways to reduce their impact. These deals are now very common and most new start-up independent labels are at least advised to consider whether they should spread their risk by taking a share of other income. They are often the default offer from the majors. But there are also positive signs of how an artist signed to a 360 deal can benefit from the fact that their label has a vested interest in the live income, such as Universal Music UK launching a live tour initiative for selected numbers of its newly signed artists to tour towns and cities not on the usual touring schedules on one big sleeper bus. We are also seeing moves by labels into a form of legitimate ticketing business, such as demanding a guaranteed ticket allocation and record labels requiring artists to perform for a separate fee at events organised by the label. What these all have in common is a wish to monetise as much of the artist's potential as possible. Nevertheless, the argument that they cannot make enough money off record sales is looking less sustainable with every report which suggests that the industry has turned a corner and is now making good money (at least for the record labels) off streaming.

Production deals

The production deal has grown significantly in importance over the last ten years. It is usually a form of an exclusive recording agreement for the world, but one where the record label is an offshoot business of a record producer, or recording studio owner, or a manager who has access to cheap recording facilities, or a fan, or a songwriter who has decided to set up his own 'label' to record an artist he has found who he thinks is talented. These production companies may be partially funded by a bigger company and act as a talent outsource, e.g. their studio rent and other office overheads may be wholly or partially met by a major record label, or they may be self-financed. For a while the funding for some of these deals came from venture capitalists who set up schemes to invest in artists and labels and in so doing exploit legitimate tax arrangements to maximise the investors' tax breaks. But the squeeze on tax revenues saw greater scrutiny of these types of deals and effectively a closing down of this type of tax scheme. Many production deals are self-financed, or use what we call 'friends and family' funding – which as its name suggests means funding provided not by official financial institutions but by people known to the label owner, or are crowd-funded by fans.

These production companies aim to exclusively sign up artists at an early stage in their careers before there is too much interest leading to a possible bidding war. So the advances and recording budgets are likely to be low. The production company will expect to own the copyright for life of copyright and to have at least a couple of options to extend the contract beyond an initial period, although you can usually negotiate a shorter rights period. The aim of these production companies is either to record up to, say, five tracks to good demo or master quality and use these to tempt a bigger company to come on board, or the production company records and releases some recordings themselves in order to hopefully create interest and have the bigger company come along and either buy the contract off them or license the rights off them exclusively in return for an investment into marketing and promotion and reimbursement of recording costs. The production company will obviously also hope to make a profit on the deal.

There is some debate as to whether these production deals are a good thing. I tend to take the pragmatic view that these structures are here to stay and, if this is the only type of deal on offer, you should think carefully before turning one down. There may seem to be a distinct advantage in signing direct to a bigger label, not through a small production label. On the other hand, at least you are very important for the small production company who is likely to give you more attention and perhaps more creative control than you might expect from a bigger label with other artists to also deal with. The big potential downside is that many of these deals are on the basis that the artist shares net profits (sometimes called 'net receipts') with the production company, usually an equal split. Sometimes it is a little more in the artist's favour, but in the early stages most are 50:50.

Why is this a potential downside? Well, in an ordinary royalties deal only the recording, video costs, personal advances and possibly a percentage of independent promotion and tour support is recoupable from royalty earnings. With a net profits or net receipts deal all costs are recoupable.

With an ordinary royalties deal the record company recoups the recoupable sums just from sums earned in royalties. With a net profits or net receipts deal, all costs are recouped from all income attributable to the recording, i.e. including advances/fees paid by licensees, the record company's share of earnings etc.

So all the income generated by the recordings goes to recoup all the expenses and any profits or receipts left at the end are divided between the record company and artist in the agreed proportions.

At the outset, net profits or net receipts deals work quite well for the record company, as that is when costs are high. The record company still bears the risk on costs initially, but it doesn't pay out anything to the artist until the deal goes into profit. Also, the record company gets to recoup costs it wouldn't be entitled to under a regular exclusive recording contract, such as manufacturing and promotional costs. The artist can still receive an advance to live on. Where these deals start to become less attractive to a record company and much more attractive to the artist is when the initial costs have been recouped and ongoing costs are going down. If the record continues to sell well and the artist is on 50% or more of net profits, he will be doing considerably better per record sold than he would be if he were on a straight royalty basis.

To explain further, such deals almost inevitably benefit the label in the early days because they do not have to pay the artist anything until the deal goes into profit. This means they have all their costs of recording, manufacturing and distributing the records repaid first as well as things like press and promotion costs. Only once all those costs have been recovered and the project goes into profit do proceeds start to get shared. If the artist has had an advance against his share of profits, he will have to also repay that before he sees anything more. Once the costs have been recouped and start to tail off, then if the records continue to sell the label in theory should be making larger profits. These profits are then shared with the artist who stands to do much better out of it than he would if he were on a royalty from a bigger label. So if costs are kept under control and the record sells both sides stand to do very well.

Where the scales tend to tip away from the artist is if the production company sells on the contract to a bigger label. The production company may then recover some or all of the costs it has paid out for recording and so is doing quite well, but may not yet be in profit, so perhaps the artist may not have seen any more money at this point. The bigger label is not likely to do a net profits deal. They are much more likely to pay a royalty to the production company – let's say 22% of the dealer price of the records. That then is the 'net income' that comes into the production company for sales of these records. That 22% is then what the production company shares with the artist. If it splits it 50:50 the artist is, if you like, on the equivalent of an 11% royalty deal. Now that doesn't sound so good, does it? So it is often the case that the lawyer for the artist will ask for an increase in the share payable to the artist to, say, 70% if a deal like this is put in place to give the artist a better 'royalty equivalent' deal. Even though it may seem that the artist has not done as well here as he would have with the bigger label, that bigger label was not showing any interest at the time the artist signed. The production company was prepared to invest in the future of the artist, and maybe helped nurture his creativity – so is it wrong to say it shouldn't get a fair reward for that investment? You decide.

Alternative sources of funding/crowd-funding

If you are looking to source funding yourself, there are a number of funds available such as those run by companies like Pledge Music and Kickstarter. They are web-based services which use investment from fans to part fund recording or promotional activities. Investors get access to things like specially packaged limited edition copies of an album or privileged/early access to the album or tickets for live shows. The artists retain copyright in their recordings.

These are, of course, only a small sample of the types of funding arrangements out there and, as with any commercial transaction, I would advise you to check out the companies involved and make sure that you have the structure fully explained to you before you sign up to them.

OTHER ASPECTS OF RECORDING CONTRACTS

Now that I've looked at the main types of deal and some of the things that distinguish them, I want to look at some aspects of contracts that are common to all types.

DELIVERY REQUIREMENTS – MINIMUM COMMITMENT

Each type of record contract has a minimum that is required from the artist. Licence deals can be for single tracks or albums. Development deals may start out as being for four or five tracks and then develop into a commitment to record albums in exclusive record deals. With the 360-degree variant the commitment will be an album initially, usually with options to acquire further product in the form of further albums. Production deals will be either for four or five tracks with options on further recordings or an album commitment with options. One of the artist's obligations is to deliver the required minimum number of recordings.

This obligation may be simply to deliver the masters of these recordings to the record company. More often, however, the commitment is not fulfilled until the record company has agreed that the recordings meet the required standards. As we saw in the *George Michael* and *Holly Johnson* cases, if these standards are not met, the company can reject the recordings and make the artist re-record them until they are satisfied. It's important that these standards are realistic and that they are set out in the contract. They could be technical requirements, commercial ones or a combination of both. What you should try

WHAT IS A GOOD RECORD DEAL?

to avoid is a subjective standard. This is someone else's view of whether the recordings meet the required standard or whether the recording is commercially satisfactory. What a record company executive thinks is commercially acceptable may not be anything like your own views on the subject. It's best if you can try to set an objective standard, a standard against which the quality of your recording can be measured. For example, measuring it against a recording of yours that the record company has previously accepted as being satisfactory.

It is also usual to try to put a time limit on when the record company has to give an answer as to whether a recording is satisfactory. It must be a realistic time period, as the company may have to go through various stages and processes before it can give an answer. The A&R man will have to listen to it and probably play it to his colleagues at the weekly A&R meeting. He may talk to record producers to get their views of the recording. He'll probably talk to the artist's manager for his views. He may have a hunch that the record could be improved if one or more tracks are remixed by someone other than the record producer or original mixer. Depending on the contract, he may have to get the artist's permission before he does that. The contract with the record producer may mean that he has to give him the first chance to remix the track in question. Now obviously it's unlikely that the A&R man will be hearing the recordings for the very first time. He is likely to have been involved in the process to a greater or lesser extent at an earlier stage, but nevertheless this approvals process takes time.

Once the record company is happy with the standard of the recordings, it may say that the recordings have been accepted and that the Minimum Commitment has been fulfilled, but most companies want more information from you before they do that.

Acceptance or fulfilment of Minimum Commitment usually means that the record company has to start planning the release and maybe has to pay a further instalment of the artist advance. The record contract may set a last date by which the record must be released. The record company won't want that time to start running until it is in a position to start the processes for a release. This means that they usually require you to hand over a number of other things before delivery is said to have taken place and before the label accepts the recordings. This could be artwork for the packaging of the records, details of who performed on the masters, and confirmation that those performers have given their performer's consents. If there are samples of anyone else's recordings or songs in the masters, the record company will want to know that you have permission from the copyright owners of those recordings or songs to use the samples (see Chapter 13). If permission to use the samples hasn't been agreed, then the record company can't put the recordings out without being in breach of copyright. With a production deal, it is likely that the delivery of the five or more tracks will start the time running for when the production company has to get a bigger company on board, release the records themselves, or release you from the contract. So they are going to be pretty sure they have all they need before they officially accept the recordings.

Because it's important to know when a recording has been accepted, I often ask the record company to agree that the recordings are said to be accepted if the record company has not said that they aren't within four to six weeks of delivery of the masters, artwork, etc., to them. Depending on how long they think it will take for them to go through the acceptance process, they may agree to this or they may not.

With a production deal, you are more likely to be closely involved in the whole process with the label and you may be choosing songs, producer, remixer, etc., together. There is less likely to be a very formal procedure for notification of delivery and acceptance in such cases, but they will still want to know they have all the parts they require to get a release and the artist will still want to know that he has done all that is required of him for the moment.

ADVANCES

For many artists, this is one of the most important issues. Remember that these monies will have to be recouped out of the royalties earned from sales or other uses of the recordings. Unlike a loan, however, advances aren't usually repayable if the record company doesn't sell enough of the records. That's the record company's risk. If, however, the artist takes his money and then doesn't deliver any recordings, the record company may try to come after him to get the advance back. If it's all gone, they may not bother to sue because it would cost them more in legal fees than they would get back. I wouldn't like to rely on this though.

What's a good advance on an exclusive recording agreement?
A good advance is one that meets your needs. You may only care about getting as much money as possible and aren't concerned if you never sell enough records to recoup. There are a lot of cynical managers with that view in the business

– take the money and run. In that case, you'll just be looking for the most money you can get up-front. It's a short-term view because the greater the record company's investment in advances, the more pressure there is going to be on you to perform and the more likely it is that the record company will want to dictate to you. If you go for a more reasonable advance payable in reasonable instalments, the record company may put you under less pressure to deliver. You should also recoup the advances sooner out of your royalties. Because so few artists recoup advances and costs, this will put you in a strong bargaining position with the record company. I have, however, heard a very successful and influential music manager take completely the opposite position. His view is that an artist who has proved that he can sell records if the record company does its job properly can get more commitment out of a record company by being unrecouped, as this will encourage the company to work harder. This could well be the case with certain labels or individuals, but I'm not convinced that this applies to everyone; particularly in the current climate when so few artists are getting beyond their first album. One of the reasons the contract does not go further is because overall it is just too expensive. A prudent manager would consider renegotiating if the label was otherwise a good bet to stay with. If, however, the A&R or MD who signed the act is no longer there, then you may be better off cutting your losses, walking away from the debt and trying to start again.

Whatever the position on recoupment, a good advance is going to be one that allows the artist to live and have a roof over his head for at least a year (preferably eighteen months) while the recordings are being made and then promoted. It's a good idea for the artist or his manager to do an outline budget of what he may need.

If a manager is only interested in getting as much of the advance as possible as early as possible, as an artist I would be suspicious. Is he only concerned about his commission? Is he only in it for the short term? Doesn't he expect to be around when the record is finished or when it's time for the option to be exercised? Whose interests is he looking after – the artist's or his own? It may be the correct approach, but perhaps the artist should not accept it without question. If the manager is pushing for a very short deal with most of the money up-front, is it an agreed approach of 'take the money and run' or doesn't he have faith that the artist can cut it beyond one album?

The artist may accept a lower advance in return for other things such as greater creative control. It's possible to get both, but usually only when you have a lot of bargaining power. If you go for a lower advance, you should also be able to argue for a higher royalty and this argument also holds good in production deals, but do not expect the production company to necessarily move beyond a 50:50 deal in the early stages when their risk is at its highest. Advances on production deals are, in any event, usually significantly lower than from a major or larger independent. They are mostly self-funded and would prefer to spend their money on recording costs and promotion.

Min-max formula

The level of advances payable could be calculated according to a formula (called a 'min-max formula'). Under this formula a minimum advance is payable to the artist and a limit is also set on the maximum the company will pay. The actual amount is calculated as a percentage of the royalties the artist earns. The formula usually applies from the second contract period or album onwards. This method of calculating option period advances is often favoured by production companies as it allows them to reward sales success.

At the beginning of the second contract period, the record company looks at how much the artist has earned from sales of the recordings he made in the first contract period. It then takes a percentage of that and, if the amount then arrived at is more than the minimum and less than the maximum, then that is the advance payable for that period. For example, in the twelve months following the release of the first album, the artist may have earned £100,000 in royalties. The formula for calculating the advance for the second contract period is linked to 66% of those earnings; 66% of £100,000 is £66,666. The minimum advance payable in the next contract period is, say, £50,000. This is above that. The maximum advance payable is, say, £100,000, but it's not got to that point so the advance payable is £66,666.

This formula can work and many record companies favour this system because it gives them a degree of certainty for budgeting purposes and a payment linked to success. The artist needs to make sure that the minimums are enough to meet his minimum living requirements. In the example I gave above, could he live on £50,000 for a year or longer in the second contract period?

The maximums are usually double the minimums, but may be higher in later contract periods. Is the maximum a reasonable advance if the artist is doing very well? To be honest, I don't worry about the maximums as much as the minimums. If the artist is hitting the maximums, it's because he is doing well and the record company is more likely to want to keep him happy by renegotiating these figures upwards.

Payment terms

Advances are normally paid in instalments, usually one on signing the deal, another when the artist starts recording the Minimum Commitment for that contract period, and the final instalment either on delivery of the completed recordings to the record company or on commercial release of the recordings. With a production deal, the later instalments may be linked to the production company getting a bigger company on board. As the release could be some months after delivery, the artist will want the final instalment to be paid on delivery. The record company may want to protect itself by only paying the last instalment when the record is released, when there is a reasonable prospect of record sales reducing its financial exposure. However, a lot can happen between delivery of the finished masters and their release. A client of mine once delivered finished masters to the record company and they were accepted. A few months later, and before the last date on which the record company had to release the recordings, the company closed down and the copyright in the client's recordings was transferred to another record company. That record company then hesitated for a few months more about whether or not they were going to release the album. In the end the artist's manager asked me to send the record company a formal notice under the terms of the record contract requiring the record company to release the album and pay the final instalment due under the deal. When the record company got the notice, it rang me up and said that it had decided that it didn't want to release the album. It offered to give my client the copyright in the album back in return for an override royalty until such time as it had recovered the recording costs that had been spent on the album. The client and his manager decided to take this offer, but more than seven months had passed since the recordings were delivered and the artist didn't get the advance due on release of the album. From the artist's perspective, therefore, it would have been better to have had payment linked to delivery of recordings not their release.

Costs-inclusive advances

The advances I have been describing so far are personal advances. They go towards the artist's personal needs. The costs of making the recording are separate recoupable amounts (see Chapter 5). The record company may offer an advance which includes the costs of making the recordings. These costs-inclusive deals are often called 'recording-fund deals'. Both artist and the record company have to be quite careful that the amounts advanced under a recording-fund deal are at the right level. The artist has to be sure that he can make the album he wants to make with the available funds and still have something over to live on. Often costs-inclusive deals work out at less money than one for a personal advance plus recording costs, unless the artist can record very cheaply. The record company has to know it's not being too generous, but also that the artist won't run out of money before the recording is finished. If he does, the record company inevitably ends up paying out more money if it wants to get the recording finished. Recording-fund deals can work for established artists, for those with their own recording facilities, or for more mature artists who can be relied on to make the recording without spending all the money on themselves.

RECORD BUDGETS

If a record company is not offering a recording-fund deal, you'll need to have some idea of how much it's going to cost to make the recordings. You need to know that the record company is committed to spending that amount of money. If you're doing a licence deal, you'll usually have already finished making recordings, and so the issue is whether they will compensate you for the costs you've incurred. So you need to know what you've spent.

The budget must take into account how much it will cost to rehearse the material, to do any necessary pre-production (preparation for recording and programming), to record the material in the studio, to have it produced, mixed and edited. Some record companies include the cost of cutting or digitally mastering the recording in the budget. This can add thousands to the deal, so, if the budget is tight, try to get them to pay for that separately. You also have to bear in mind the cost of hiring in specialist equipment and engaging the services of additional musicians and vocalists. The budget also usually includes what are called per diems, an expression meaning a daily expenses payment to cover food and drink and sometimes also transport to and from the studio.

The record company may commit to a guaranteed minimum spend on recording costs in the contract, but most are reluctant to do that. This is either because they're afraid they may get it wrong, or because setting a minimum figure means you tend to spend that amount of money whether it's necessary or not. On the other hand, the artist will want to know the record company is committed to a particular level of spend so that he knows that he can make the kind of record he wants. Both sides must be realistic. It's no good a record company thinking you can make an album for five pence, but neither is it any good you thinking the record company will let you have a blank cheque. This is where a decent recording budget is invaluable.

Recording costs are usually fully recoupable. There are, however, some elements of the recording cost budget that may fall outside the regular costs. A classic example is the costs of remixing. Mixing costs can be very expensive. If you're on a tight budget, these costs can take a lot out of the total. The record company may want to commission a remix that you don't think is necessary. Who is to pay for this and are the costs to be recoupable? Some record companies will agree that the first mix comes out of the recording budget as does any remix that you want to do, but if the record company wants to do additional remixes they pay that on top of the recording budget but of course still recoup the cost from royalties. So, you know what to do – make sure it's the record company that asks for the remix, not you.

ROYALTIES

This could be the subject of a whole book in itself. No two companies calculate royalties in exactly the same way. This is an area where there is really no escaping the need for experience and legal advice.

Record company executives usually have guidelines as to what is or is not allowed. Certain top artists may have been given 'favoured nations' terms. This means that they have the best deal that the record company can offer on that particular point. If any other artist is offered better terms by that record company, the artist with the 'favoured nations' provision must also be given these better terms. As this has potentially huge financial implications for the record company, an executive crosses these boundaries at his peril. It may be impossible to do so and will definitely require agreement from someone high up the corporate ladder.

Retail versus dealer price

Until about ten years ago, the majority of UK record companies calculated their royalties as a percentage of the retail price of the record in question. However, the retail price is not within the record company's control and varies considerably. All UK companies have, therefore, moved over to using the dealer price of the record as the basis of calculation. For online sales it's usually the price at which, after tax, the track is made available to the end purchaser.

What percentage of sales?

Is the royalty calculated on all records sold or on a lesser percentage? Some record companies, particularly in the US, build in a 'free goods' allowance of up to 15% of total sales on which they do not pay a royalty. In the UK it is almost always on 100% of net sales.

Packaging and other deductions

Until about seven years ago, the most common deductions were packaging deductions, sometimes also referred to as container charges. This is a charge supposedly to cover the cost of making the cases or other packaging in which the record is sold. In reality, the actual cost is usually far less than the average packaging deduction and is, in fact, a way by which the record company artificially reduces the royalty paid to the artist. Now most record labels have dispensed with packaging deductions altogether as part of a drive for simpler contracts and greater transparency.

There should certainly be no packaging deduction on downloads, but some record companies still sneak it in under another name such as fulfilment or credit card charges.

Other traps for the unwary are the reductions that some record companies apply to certain types of records. For instance, sales by mail order, through record clubs or at budget prices will be at a lower royalty rate. The principle behind all these deductions is that, where the record company gets less than the full price for a sale, it will reduce the amount payable to the artist on that sale. A record sold as a budget record will usually attract a 50% reduction in the royalty rate. A 50% reduction also applies to records advertised on television, sold by mail order or through record clubs.

A detailed exploration of all the royalty reductions is beyond the scope of this book. Your lawyer and accountant will be familiar with these. Most UK record companies usually apply the principles behind the reductions in a similar way, but the details will differ a great deal.

What's a good royalty?

As a very general guideline, an acceptable basic royalty on CD sales of albums would be at least 18% of the dealer price (PPD) calculated on 100% of records sold with no packaging deduction. It's unusual to see royalty rates of more than 24% of the dealer price for new signings to exclusive record deals. These are reserved for the megastars or very hot acts. However, royalties on licence deals could exceed 24%, because the record company is getting a finished recording and can assess the commercial potential up-front. The record company also hasn't taken any risk on the recording costs. On non-exclusive licence deals between record companies, for example for a compilation, the royalty may well be more than 24% of the dealer price with no packaging deductions. The royalty rate for downloads may be a fixed percentage similar to the CD royalty rate or it may be a percentage of receipts from such sales. There have been a succession of legal disputes (including class actions) in the US by various artists (mostly those under older-style contracts) where the artist claims that their record company should be paying them on a different basis on digital sales. For example, if a digital download is treated as a sale then it is arguable that the royalty should be based on a percentage of that sale at the album or single royalty rate, let's say 20%. If, however, you can successfully argue that the digital sale was in fact by a third party, such as iTunes under a licence deal from the record label, then you could argue that the licence rate should apply – generally closer to 50% of what the record label receives. This could, of course, make a major difference to the artist. Cases which have come to court so far seem to turn on their individual facts without, as yet, an overall clean line emerging on the central issue. Significant settlements have been reached in class actions brought against major labels but those who could benefit from the settlement pot tended to be the more successful artists who could meet the specific criteria set out in the settlement.

Release commitments

Obviously, once the album has been delivered and accepted, it would be good to have some kind of assurance that it's going to see the light of day and not just sit on the shelf. You need a commitment from the record company to release the record in at least the home market and preferably also the main overseas markets. The release should usually take place within four to six months of delivery of the recordings. If it doesn't, the usual remedy is to serve a notice telling the record company that if it doesn't release the record within another two to three months then the artist has the right to end the contract and not have to deliver any more recordings. Even better would be a commitment from them to return the unreleased recordings to the artist (perhaps in return for an override royalty until the recording costs have been recouped). Some record companies don't want to do this, because they would rather negotiate such things at the time. They may also want to hold on to the recordings in case another company has better luck in making you successful. They then have back catalogue material which they might try to release to cash in on this success. I think this is pretty daft because, while the tried and true fans will buy all records, there's no artist to promote the record so it's unlikely to go very far. Sometimes, though, they hold on to the unreleased recordings to try to sell it to the artist's new record company later, and this strategy is often successful.

Overseas, if the record isn't released within four to six months of the UK release (depending on the contract – it might be longer if it's a small label), you can serve another notice of sixty to ninety days; if there hasn't been a release, the artist may have the chance to find a licensee and make the record label then license it to that licensee to release. The label is unlikely to automatically give the recordings back, as they know it's difficult to make their overseas companies or licensees release recordings. It's mad though if you think about it – why bother to do a worldwide deal if you can't even guarantee that your sister companies overseas will even release the records in their territory? It's all part of that argument, 'We have to do this because for the few that are international artists we would look stupid and get fired if we didn't have world rights.'

If it is important to you that both physical copies, in the form of CDs, and digital downloads of your album are made available you must spell this out in the contract. Digital-only releases are becoming very common and as it is relatively cheap to do this with little or no marketing it may not represent a decent commitment to a proper commercial release. So you may wish to specify a minimum promotional or marketing budget.

Accounting

The artist should get paid at least twice a year, possibly four times if it's a smaller company doing its own distribution. The accounts statements will be sent out sixty to ninety days after the accounting date. If all advances are recouped (oh happy day!), the statement will have a payment remittance with it. If you aren't certain what the statement says, check it with your accountant. If he doesn't think it's right, you should challenge it, but don't leave it too long as you probably can't object after a period of time, say one to three years. You have the right to audit (inspect) the books at least once a year. Send accountants in to audit if you've had a successful period or at the end of a deal that has gone well but it's an expensive process so don't do it unless you are advised it is worthwhile.

CONCLUSIONS

- There are four main types of record deal – licences, production deals and exclusive recording agreements with a sub-category of development deal and 360-degree deal. Label services are a new variant of distribution with additional functions.
- With each type of contract, you need to work out how much exclusivity you're going to give and what territory the contract is to cover.
- Advances against royalties can include recording costs or these can be dealt with separately. Recording and personal advance budgets are useful in setting the level of the deal.
- Check the price basis on which the royalty is calculated.
- Record contracts often contain reductions in royalties on certain types of sale or method of distribution. Check if these are reasonable.
- Net profits deals work for the record company at the beginning but the scales can tip in favour of the artist after the initial costs have been recouped.
- 360-degree deals may be all that is on offer, in which case be pragmatic about sharing other income sources.

Chapter 4

What Is A Good Publishing Deal?

INTRODUCTION

In this chapter I'm going to look at what rights a songwriter has and what he can expect from the various types of publishing deals. I'm going to ask whether you need to do a publishing deal at all. If so, whether, ideally, it should be before or after you've done your record deal. Just as we have seen with recording deals, there have also been changes in how publishing is viewed by the smaller operators. There has been a move amongst managers and smaller record labels to also take an interest in publishing rights. I will explore how they do this and whether or not I think this is a good idea.

Before I go into any detail about the contract, I need to look at how you find a music publisher, what a music publisher actually does and what rights a songwriter has. You will not be surprised by now to learn that the doctrine of restraint of trade comes up here too.

STATE OF THE BUSINESS

Publishing is also changing rapidly to face the challenges of the market. The publishers have grown more vocal and adept at political lobbying. They have also started to step out from behind the scenes and to take a more proactive role in marketing their catalogues to third parties. Publishing companies have got involved in raising the profile of songwriters by funding recordings and releasing them on their own label, but it has not proved to be easy to move these acts onto bigger labels for the next phase of the profile/income-raising activities. Publishers are also reaching out more directly to the consumers of music such as advertising agencies, television and film companies, mobile phone companies, computer games developers, online company websites and more recently have become involved in the collection of so-called neighbouring rights income, for songwriters who also own their own recordings.

One publisher, Kobalt, has bought into a collection society and Bucks Music Group now has a management arm. Several publishers are also setting themselves up as administrators of neighbouring rights i.e. moving into the area of performer rights and away from traditional songwriting. Sony/ATV has diversified into this area adding Sting and Lady Gaga to its roster in 2016.

HOW TO FIND A MUSIC PUBLISHER

Music publishers employ A&R people and scouts in the same way as record companies do. They're on the lookout for talented songwriters who either perform in a band or as a solo artist, or who mostly write songs for or with other people. Hopeful songwriters send demos to publishing companies in the same way as artists do to record companies, usually in the form of an MP3 or web link.

You can find lists of UK music publishers in the *Music Week Directory*. All the major record companies also have well-established music publishing companies within their group of companies. For example, there is a Universal record label and a Universal publishing company.

Following the breakup of EMI in 2012, an investor consortium led by Sony/ATV Music Publishing acquired the bulk of the publishing interest, with the combined company operating as Sony ATV Music Publishing. Some catalogues had to be sold off as part of the anti-competition rulings and BMG Chrysalis/BMG Rights acquired many of these, including Virgin Music. In 2016 Sony acquired the remaining share of the ATV Music catalogue from the Michael Jackson estate, which includes a large part of the Beatles catalogue. This was the subject of a monopolies enquiry by the European Commission but was unconditionally cleared. Although Sony had administered the ATV catalogue for some time, and therefore, the number of copyrights under its control did not increase (around 4.2 million songs) the difference is that now the ATV catalogue is no longer subject to consents and approvals from the Jackson Estate. As I write, Sir Paul McCartney has begun what some see as a pre-emptive strike to obtain a US court ruling that he is entitled to the return of some of his earliest rights under the 1976 US Copyright Act, which created a reversionary right in the US to copyrights after 56 years, provided notice is served in the correct form and in time. Apparently McCartney has been serving notices for some time, but says that Sony has refused to tell him if they would object to the rights reverting. This would seem to be a reaction to a recent court ruling in the UK in the Duran Duran case (more on which below). It is possible that Sony was waiting for the outcome of this case before responding to Sir Paul and that Sir Paul has in his turn decided to take the issue to the US courts instead.

There are, of course, also independent music publishers that aren't associated with record companies, for example Peermusic or Bucks Music Group, as well as administrators such as Kobalt. Some of these independents, notably Kobalt, have also expanded into related activities such as direct licensing of certain digital rights, label services (with Kobalt's acquisition of AWAL [Artist Without A Label] and developing its neighbouring rights collection service). Your lawyer, accountant and manager can all refer you to publishers they think will be suitable for your style of songwriting. Organisations like the Music Publishers Association (MPA) and BASCA can also provide information.

WHAT DOES A PUBLISHER DO?

Have you ever wondered why we call them publishers? As far as I can work out, it comes from the early days of the music business when music was published in the form of sheet music in the same way as a book is published. Nowadays, of course, sheet music forms only a small part of the income that a songwriter and a publisher can make. These days the largest share of income comes from the use of songs on sound recordings (mechanicals) or with TV, film or other moving images (synchronisation). As digital distribution of music develops, the rights in a song may well prove to be far more valuable than a physical sound recording.

Publishers have traditionally had three main roles. Firstly, they issue licences to people who want to use music. Secondly, they actively look for ways to use music – for example, putting it in an advert or on a film soundtrack. Thirdly, they collect the income from those licences and uses. The first and last of these roles are often done in conjunction with the collection societies locally and through their links with international societies and in the developing area of cross territory licensing and direct digital licensing.

Some publishers are better than others in finding uses for music and collecting the money earned. Obviously, a songwriter must be satisfied that they can do a reasonable job of collecting in the money. Whether he also needs them to be good at finding uses for his songs will depend on the type of songwriter he is. If he's part of a band he may be self-sufficient, if not he might need more help in talking him up with co-writers or artists. Most can help in finding co-writers and collaborators and synch users.

So that people know who to approach when they want to ask to use a song, and in order to track the money and collect it properly, the publisher registers the songs with all the main collection societies around the world. Sometimes this just requires that the songwriter fills in a form and files it with the society concerned. Sometimes they also have to send in a recording and a written copy of the words and music, called a lead sheet.

If the music publisher is one of the bigger publishers, it will have its own companies in each of the major countries in the world. One or two of the independent publishers also have their own companies worldwide too. Most of the independent and smaller publishers don't have the resources to set up overseas companies. They appoint local publishers in the country concerned to look after their interests there. This is called sub-publishing.

The traditional roles of the publisher are, however, changing as they too look for different ways of making money in a difficult marketplace. One of their traditional main sources of income has been mechanical royalties on record sales, and as CD sales are declining so their income is also dropping. They are looking to streaming services to pick up some of the shortfall, but this area is fraught with difficulties. Unfortunately music publishers are not doing as well as record labels from streaming income, receiving a small fraction of what the record labels get in royalties for the master rights. Publishers have to supplement their income in other ways, as well as becoming better at collecting it and more efficient in running their companies. They will also now do some of the things that were originally only done by record companies. They will provide studio time for an artist or songwriter to record demos. In order to get interest from record companies to sign singer–songwriters, some publishers act almost like record companies, putting records out in limited editions, usually online, as a way to attract record company interest. There are even some that will provide financial support for a songwriter when he is out on the road promoting his records, or extra funds for promotion or press coverage. These costs and payments are usually recoupable from the songwriter's publishing income. The main reason they do these things is in order to give the writer a bit of a boost, a head start, or to top up funding that may or may not be provided by the record company.

They have become more innovative in finding new ways to use the copyrights, including licensing song lyrics for inclusion on merchandise like mugs and T-shirts. Licensing songs for use in ads and films has become more important and most publishers have strengthened their synchronisation departments. Neighbouring rights have become another possible source of revenue. The UK Music 2016 report shows music publishers generating £412 million in 2015. The rather odd sounding term, 'neighbouring rights', covers the rights, akin to copyright, that performers have in the use of 'fixations' of their performances, e.g. a recorded broadcast on radio or television, a CD, a digital download of a recording of their performances, the playing of recordings of their performances in pubs, clubs, shops, restaurants and places of work. In some countries neighbouring rights also include the so-called 'blank tape levy' paid as compensation to rights owners when blank tapes (or CDs) are used to copy music. In Europe these rights – and the rights of the performers (and performing producers in the UK) – are treated as analogous to copyright, i.e. its neighbour. Collection societies like Public Performance Limited (PPL) have collected these rights both on behalf of the sound recording copyright owners but also the performers. Now other companies, many of whom are publishers, are getting in on the act, collecting the revenue paid by broadcasters and websites to play the recordings and after deducting a commission paying the balance to the performers. In the UK PPL makes a distinction between featured, non-featured and performing producer performances with each group commanding a share of the 50% of the revenue allocated to performers. This is not a universally accepted method of distributing revenue and in fact each country that recognises neighbouring rights has different criteria and distribution methods. In the US the organisation SoundExchange collects fees and pays royalties to the featured artist and the owner of the copyright in the sound recordings from non-interactive digital sources, namely digital radio. It is crucial that you register with PPL or another performers' collection society and that you ensure that your database of information with that society is accurate and up to date.

106

WHAT ARE MUSIC PUBLISHING RIGHTS?

Before you can have any rights in a literary or musical work (*s.3(1) CDPA*) (i.e. in lyrics or music), you have to establish that the words and music are original and that they have been recorded in some way. This could be sheet music, with the words and music written down, or a demo of someone singing the words and music (*s.3(2) CDPA*).

HOW DO YOU PROVE THAT YOU HAVE COPYRIGHT IN A WORK?

In the UK we do not have a formal copyright registration scheme but certain methods have developed as ways to prove that a song was written at a particular point in time. You could put the sheet music or demo recording in a safe deposit box marked with your name and the date on which you wrote it and get a receipt. You could send it to your lawyer and ask him to write back to confirm when he received it from you. Not all lawyers will do this as it's quite a responsibility. They don't have any direct knowledge of who wrote the song or when. They can only say that you sent a CD to them on a particular day. The most popular way is to put the lyric sheet and recording in an envelope addressed to yourself that you then post to yourself by recorded mail (so you have a receipt). When it arrives, you keep it unopened in a safe place. The postmark and the fact that it's still sealed means that you have proof that that recording/lyric sheet must have existed some time before the postmark date. So, if someone later copies the song illegally, there is evidence that your version was written before theirs. Or you could ask the studio engineer or producer to swear a statement that they witnessed the recording being made or the song being written in the studio in their presence. If you are first publishing in the US or there is to be a release there you should consider registering with the US Library of Congress.

WHO OWNS THESE RIGHTS?

The first owner of the copyright in a musical or literary work is the person who is the 'author' or creator of an original work and records it in a tangible form (*s.9(1) CDPA*).

There can be more than one writer or composer (*s.10(1) CDPA*). These are called co-writers. One person might write the words and the other the music, or the co-writers might all work on both elements.

Famous examples of successful co-writing partnerships are Elton John and Bernie Taupin, Andrew Lloyd Webber and Tim Rice and, more recently, Robbie Williams and Guy Chambers. It's perfectly possible for two separate publishers to control parts of the same song. Where there are co-writers, the song is jointly owned, and it's very important to record who owns what part of the music or lyrics. When you finish a new song and give it to your publisher, they fill in a form on your behalf called a Joint Registration Form. This is the form needed to record the details about the song, which is then sent to the collecting society, the Mechanical Copyright Protection Society Limited (MCPS) and the Performing Right Society Limited (PRS). The form contains the title of the song, who wrote it, what shares of it they wrote and if there are any restrictions on what can be done with it. If you don't have a publisher and you're a member of PRS, you should complete and file that form yourself. This can be done online, as can your application for membership. At the moment, one form filed with PRS acts as a joint registration because PRS provides back end administrative support for MCPS. However, in a bid to test if this was a good value deal the MCPS has put that contract out to tender and is in the process of evaluating offers so this may change.

Most publishing agreements will say that all songs are assumed to be written in equal shares by all co-writers unless the publisher is told something different when the work is completed and details given to them for registration. The whole question of who wrote what can be the cause of major arguments between co-writers, who are often members of the same band or the producer of the album. This can be the case even where not all members of a band contribute to the writing. Those members that do write resent those that don't. These issues ought to be sorted out at an early stage before they become a real issue.

You won't be surprised to learn that disputes over ownership are commonplace. A well-publicised 1999 case over songwriting shares involved members of Spandau Ballet.

Spandau Ballet Case (Hadley and Others v. Kemp and Another [1999] Chancery Division)
Spandau Ballet was formed in 1979 and made up of the two Kemp brothers, Martin and Gary, together with Tony Hadley, John Keeble and Steve Norman. They were part of the New

Romantic movement and, after turning down a record deal with Island Records, they set up their own label that they eventually licensed to Chrysalis Records. Their first single, 'To Cut A Long Story Short', went Top 5 in the UK. They released a couple more singles before having a Top 3 hit with 'Chant Number 1'. They released six albums plus a Greatest Hits compilation. The last of these, called *Heart Like A Sky*, was released in 1989. Ten years later they were in court arguing over song royalties. Martin Kemp was not involved in this case.

Everyone agreed that Gary Kemp had written the lyrics to all the songs. The dispute was over who composed the music. Gary Kemp's company received all the publishing income from the songs. He volunteered to give half of this money to the other band members, but stopped this arrangement in 1987. The other band members sued, saying that there was a legally binding agreement to continue to pay this money. They also argued that, if there was not a binding agreement, they were entitled to the money anyway because they were co-writers of the songs and therefore co-owners of the copyright. They said they'd contributed enough to the music to make them co-writers. The Judge decided that there was no binding legal agreement. He ruled that Gary Kemp was sole writer of all the music save for a song called 'Glow'. The Judge also confirmed that to be a co-writer you have to have contributed to the song's creation, not just to its interpretation.

So, if a drummer just adds a short drum loop which doesn't make any material difference to the song, that won't qualify for a claim that he has co-written that song. A bassist who takes the melody line and just converts it into a part that is suitable for his instrument will also probably not have claim to being a co-writer.

Mark Taylor v. Rive Droit Music Limited (Nov. 2005 (unreported))
Another case that made it to court was a claim by Mark Taylor, who was co-writer of Cher's hit record 'Believe'. He brought a claim against music publishers Rive Droit Music Limited (RDM). Many of the problems that surround this case turn on bad drafting of a publishing agreement and a dispute as to who owned two songs that Mark Taylor co-wrote and which were recorded by the artist Enrique Iglesias.

In 1995, Mark Taylor entered into two agreements with RDM, the second of which was a written publishing agreement which was renewed twice, the second time in 1998. At the end of November 2000 Mr Taylor stopped working for RDM and joined a rival set-up, Brian Rawling Productions Limited (BRP). Brian Rawling had originally been recruited by RDM to bring together a stable of songwriters. Songs written by these songwriters would be pitched to other record labels and artists. The idea was that RDM would produce the subsequent recordings of those songs and receive both a production fee and royalties from sales of the records and a share of the songwriting royalties.

Mr Taylor collaborated with Paul Barry (another songwriter signed to RDM) and together they wrote a number of songs including 'Believe' which made their name. Mr Taylor entered into the third publishing agreement with RDM in about December 1998.

Two years later in early December 2000, Mr Taylor and Mr Barry went to America and worked on songs which were to be recorded by Enrique Iglesias. On 6 December, Mr Taylor decided to end the production arrangements with RDM with effect from 1 December 2000 and sent the owner of the company a fax to that effect.

In April 2001, Mr Taylor sought a declaration from the court that his 1998 publishing agreement had expired on 30 November 2000 and that he was due royalties. RDM disputed this interpretation of the contract and said that the term of it was three years not two. Presumably on the basis that they may have been found to be wrong on this, they also tried to argue that they had the rights in the two Iglesias songs which Mr Taylor was arguing were written after the end of the 1998 publishing agreement, because he had in fact not created new works but adapted parts of songs written by Mr Barry (who was presumably still under contract). RDM alleged this amounted to an infringement of their copyrights and asked the court to award them damages.

At the first hearing, the Judge found that it had been a two-year contract and that Mr Taylor was under no obligation to deliver to RDM any song written in whole or in part after 1 December 2000. However, Mr Taylor did not have it all his own way because the Judge also found that some of the two Iglesias songs had in fact been in existence on 1 December 2000 and the copyright in those parts belonged to RDM. Taylor felt that RDM didn't acquire the copyright until he had delivered a completed song. So both parties appealed to the Court of Appeal which finally gave judgement on the case in November 2005.

There were considerable difficulties in deciding what the publishing contract entered into in 1998 actually meant. The term appeared to be for two years, but then in another clause this was contradicted by a reference to three twelve-month periods not two. Eventually, the Appeal Court Judges agreed that it was two years not three and that the earlier clause which defined the term was stronger than the later, contradictory one. The court also decided that the relevant point for determining the ownership of the copyright was when copyright subsisted and when it was intended that that copyright could transfer to another. The Judges accepted this was not always easy to determine, but in this case decided that copyright vested in RDM at the moment there was a complete work. Now this could have implications for drafting of publishing agreements in future, as many publishers take the view that even if a song is a work in progress they still own rights in it. There were also echoes of our old friend the doctrine of restraint of trade in that if they were to decide that this meaning of composition included the entire writer's output then that could be seen as a restraint of his trade. As a post script to this case, in late 2007 Rive Droit Music Limited went into administration. In 2009 a company which had taken an assignment of rights from Rive Droit Music Limited, Crosstown Music Company LLC, brought a case against Mark Taylor and Paul Barry seeking, amongst other things, a declaration that the publishing rights in the songs had not reverted to the writers under the terms of the original publishing agreement. The claim was rejected.

While the arguments surrounding these cases may suggest they turn on their own facts, there are clearly lessons to be learned: be clear in your drafting, and make sure all rights of session musicians and band members are clearly set out. This point will emerge again in a later chapter when we look at the rights of session musicians, but before we leave this area let's look at a case (which went on appeal all the way to the House of Lords (now the Supreme Court)) which seems to throw some doubt on what rights the original composer of a song has when part of that song is then replayed by a member of the band.

The 'Whiter Shade of Pale' Case (Matthew Fisher v. Gary Brooker [2006] EWHC 3239 (Ch) 20 December 2006; [2009] UKHL 41 (30 July 2009)

This was a case decided some forty years after the song was originally written and recorded and became a massive hit for the band Procol Harum. Mr Fisher was the band's ex-organist and he argued that he was entitled to a share in the musical copyright (not the lyrics). The song was originally released as a single on 12 May 1967 and was a huge hit, going on to sell over 6 million copies worldwide. Around the time of the release, the two authors Mr Brooker and a Mr Reid assigned their copyright in the words and music to Essex Music Limited; those rights are now owned by the successor to Essex Music Limited, Onward Music Limited. When the song was being written, the two were forming a band which Mr Fisher joined as Hammond organist. In rehearsals Mr Brooker and Mr Fisher improvised their respective piano and organ parts over the original chord sequence that Mr Brooker had composed. It is this improvised organ accompaniment that formed the basis of Mr Fisher's claim for a declaration that he owned 50% of the copyright in the music. Mr Brooker argued that Mr Fisher's organ solo was essentially the same as the original piano composition. The Judge preferred Mr Fisher's version of events and ordered that Mr Fisher was entitled to claim a share in the music. Having decided that Mr Fisher had made a significant contribution to the original musical work so as to make him a co-author with Mr Brooker, he decided that that contribution was not as 'substantial' as Mr Brooker's contribution so awarded him a 40% not 50% share. The Judge also ordered that Mr Fisher was not entitled to any royalties for the time before he brought the case on the basis that ignorance of his rights to claim was no defence to the fact that Mr Fisher had sat back for over forty years and allowed the collection societies and publishers to collect the money and distribute it on the basis of a 50:50 split between Mr Brooker and Mr Reid. The Judge said that if Mr Fisher allowed the collection societies to collect and pay out despite his view that he was entitled to a share then he must have in effect granted a free licence for all this time to use his share of the song. As it was a licence, he was entitled to end it and is deemed to have done so by bringing this claim.

The publishers who stood to lose their publisher's share of the 40% interest in the music now attributed to Mr Fisher appealed the decision alongside Mr Brooker to the Court of Appeal who agreed that Mr Fisher was a co-author and joint owner of the musical copyright, but held that he was not entitled to revoke the implied licence to Brooker and Onward because of the delay in enforcing his rights.

Mr Fisher appealed to the House of Lords. The House of Lords handed down judgement in favour of Mr Fisher and restored the declarations made by the original Judge that had been set aside by the Court of Appeal. The House of Lords Judges identified three key issues in the case: did Mr Fisher impliedly assign his interest in the song to Essex? Did the recording agreement entered into between the members of the band and Essex include an assignment of Mr Fisher's interest in the musical composition? Had Mr Fisher lost his interest in the copyright as a result of the equitable doctrines of estoppel, laches or acquiescence?

On the first point, Mr Brooker and Onward had argued that, as Essex had taken an absolute assignment in the music and lyrics of the song in its original form, and all parties intended Essex to exploit the song as developed for the first recording released by Decca, it must have been intended (including by Mr Fisher) that Essex would be the sole owner of the copyright in the song. The Law Lords held that, for this to be the case, there would have to have been an implied assignment of Mr Fisher's share in the copyright in the song to Essex. To show this, Mr Brooker and Onward would have to show that it would have been obvious to Mr Fisher that such an assignment was taking place and that the commercial relationship between the parties could not have functioned without such an assignment. The Law Lords found that Mr Brooker and Onward had not established these requirements at trial (and decided it was not the House of Lords' place to revisit the factual findings of the Judge on these issues), and that, even if they had, an assignment of Fisher's share in the copyright (particularly a gratuitous one) would have been more than was necessary to give business efficacy.

Then they considered the terms of the recording contract. Although they agreed with the original Judge that the contract did not operate as an assignment of the copyright in the song (dealing as it did with the sound recording copyright), they also said it might be possible to argue that the wording did give rise to a licence to use the song in the original recording. They made no definitive ruling on the point but merely by raising it they may have started another line of argument. If the Law Lords' suggestion that the recording contract granted a royalty-free licence to Essex to exploit the song in the medium of the original recording then this would take a lot of the sheen off Fisher's victory. Mr Fisher would still be entitled to royalty income from cover recordings and live performances, but, if the court is right, he would not be entitled to royalties from the song as it appears on the first recording.

On the last point, perhaps surprisingly given the length of time that had passed, the Law Lords were not persuaded that this claim should fail on these grounds – the length of time (and indeed the motive for bringing the case) were not, they decided, relevant for this point. The mere passage of time did not of itself undermine Mr Fisher's proprietary claim in copyright.

Source: *Jon Baker of Michael Simkins LLP as published in The Reporter issue 45*

One lesson to be learned from this case is to make it quite clear at the time what claims any interested parties may have in the work. If at the time it was first written Mr Fisher had signed an acknowledgement that he had no rights in the composition, then this claim would never have arisen. It also militates in favour of co-writers always agreeing at the time of creation of a song their relative shares in that song.

Orphan works

These include compositions but also photographs and other copyright works. The Enterprise and Regulatory Reform Act 2013 permits the Government to bring in regulations to enable licensing of copyright works in the UK where the rights holder cannot be located. Prior to the existence of this scheme, where the rights holder could not be found, the work could not be legitimately used. As part of its overall wish to make licensing and use of copyright material easier the Government launched a scheme in October 2014 whereby, subject to certain safeguards, orphan works can be licensed for use following a diligent search for the owner and payment of a licence fee to be set aside for the rights holder should they reappear. The licence is non-exclusive and applies to uses in the UK only. The term of the licence is up to seven years but it can be renewed. Uses can be both commercial and non-commercial. To get an orphan works licence you have to apply to the IPO online at the IPO.gov.uk website and after following the guidelines (including a diligent search to find the owner of the work(s) in question), and completing a short questionnaire, if the work and the usage is eligible (and not falling within one of the exceptions to uses requiring a licence) an orphan works licence will be issued. This will be on standard terms and conditions, and requires payment of the appropriate fee which is on a sliding scale, currently from £20 to £80 for commercial uses (depending on the number of such works you want to licence) and £0.10 per work for non-commercial uses. Orphan works are listed on a searchable register. If you are a rights owner and you think you have a legitimate claim to a work classed as an orphan work you can also complete a form to register your interest. If ownership is established no more orphan work licences will be issued for that work. There is ultimate appeal to an Ombudsman. In its first full year of use the scheme attracted 48 applications for over 300 works, 79% of which were for still images.

Alongside the UK orphan works scheme the Government also implemented the EU's Orphan Works Directive (2012/28/EU) which is more aimed at allowing publicly accessible archives of cultural and heritage-type organisations (but including public-service broadcasters) to make certain of their works available in digital form on their websites for access across the EU. Here again a diligent search for the owner of the copyright is required and the IPO acts as the UK's central reference point for these enquiries in the UK. It is not known if this will continue post-Brexit.

DURATION OF COPYRIGHT

The copyright in a musical or literary work lasts for seventy years from the end of the calendar year in which the author dies (s.12(2) CDPA). If a song has been co-written, the rights last until seventy years from the end of the calendar year in which the last surviving co-writer dies (s.12(8) CDPA). If the lyrics are written by one party and the music by another and their interests are not specifically merged then a situation could arise where the copyright in the lyrics and music end at different times depending on when they die. However, the Regulations which brought into the UK the extension of the term of sound recording copyright to seventy years (The Copyright and Duration of Rights in Performances Regulations 2013) also provide that where the music and lyrics in a musical composition are written specifically for each other, the term of copyright in each shall last until seventy years following the death of the last surviving of both (or all) of them. The new rules will only apply to co-written works where the music and words were originally written to be used together and where the collaboration is indistinguishable. The new law applies to co-written works made on or after 1 November 2013 and well as to any previous co-written works where the musical work and/or words are still in copyright in the UK on 31 October 2013 or where music or the words are protected in at least one member state of the EEA on 1 November 2013. As you can see therefore there is the possibility that works that had previously gone out of copyright will be revived but if you exploited these works or made arrangements to exploit these works, e.g. by a licence deal, then these actions will not be an infringement of the revived copyright. When dealing with older compositions it is essential to also look at the laws which pertained at the time and what effect subsequent laws have had on the position. The co-owners are deemed to be held in equal shares, but you can specify otherwise, and the consent of all co-owners will be required to licensing. If that is going to be difficult in practice then consider a written agreement between the co-owners as to what can be done with the joint work.

Gloucester Place Music Ltd v. Simon le Bon [2016] EWHC 3091 (Ch)

Gloucester Place Music Ltd (GPM) (now owned by Sony Music) entered into various music publishing agreements in 1980 with the members of Duran Duran. These assigned the copyright in works written by the group members worldwide and for the life of copyright. These agreements ran until 1983 when they were terminated and new agreements were entered into on 1 June 1983 by the service companies of the group members, with an inducement letter from each group member. The group's major hits, including songs such as 'Girls On Film' and 'Hungry Like The Wolf' were written during the term of the original 1980 agreements, which covered some 37 songs in total.

Under s203 of the US Copyright Act 1976 and in respect of agreements entered into on or after 1 January 1978, composers have the right to acquire a reversion of the copyright in their works after a period of 35 years. There are complicated rules for the timing of notices and effective date of the reversion. The purpose of this section of the Act is to protect authors from the consequences of agreements assigning rights for life of copyright, something which is considered undesirable in the US, but which was perfectly common practice in the UK at the time these agreements were entered into. The members of Duran Duran and their various service companies served notice for reversion of the copyright in the 37 songs.

GPM sought a declaration from the court that the members of Duran Duran and their service companies were in breach of their publishing agreements by serving the notices, or would be in breach of contract if they did not withdraw them. In other words, if the US notices were valid and the copyrights reverted this would be contrary to the worldwide assignment that the group members and their service companies had entered into. This might also be referred to as being in 'derogation of the grant of rights'. If they were or would be in breach of contract then they would be liable to pay damages in compensation to GPM. GPM argued that the worldwide life of copyright assignment was all-encompassing and did not reserve to the members of Duran Duran the right to terminate under s203. Duran Duran in contrast argued that the assignment did not address the matter and did not expressly prohibit them exercising their rights under s203.

The Judge hearing the case, Arnold, noted that the agreements were subject to English law and conferred exclusive jurisdiction on the English courts and that any interpretation of the agreements would be under English legal principles. He rejected arguments that the US legal position should be taken into account. He ruled that the meaning of the assignment clause in the agreements was to assign the 'entire copyrights' for the 'full term' of the copyrights and that this implicitly precluded the group members from exercising

---

any rights under US law, which would result in GMP's ownership of the copyrights coming to an end before their expiry. This interpretation was, he said, supported by the doctrine of non-derogation of rights. So he found that the members of the group were in breach of the agreement by serving the notices, or, where the notices had not yet taken effect would be in breach if they were not withdrawn.

Now, you might think that this case is limited to its particular facts and does not have any wider import. However, as you can imagine there are a number of songwriters from this period who are now either about to or who may also have served similar notices. The wording of the clause is a fairly standard one for the time and if their agreements are also under UK law they would also find that they were facing a similar dilemma. There is also speculation in the business that the reason Paul McCartney has commenced proceedings for a declaration in the US is in order to try and bypass this case and bring the matter before the US courts. We do not know if the Duran Duran case will be appealed.
(Source: The Reporter issue 119).

WHAT RIGHTS COME WITH OWNERSHIP OF COPYRIGHT?

The copyright owner of a literary or musical work (i.e. a song) has rights very similar to the recording copyright rights we looked at in the last chapter (*ss. 16–21 CDPA*). The main ones are the right to authorise the reproduction of a musical or literary work with or without visual images (mechanical and synchro-nisation rights); the right to authorise distribution of the work; the right to rent or lend the work to members of the public; the right to authorise public perfor-mance of the work, or its making available to the public, and the right to make an adaptation of the work, or to do any of the above in relation to an adapta-tion. As the copyright owner, you can allow or prevent someone from doing all or any of these things either throughout the world or in a particular country. When you do a publishing deal, you are giving someone else the right to deal with some or all of these matters on your behalf. The publisher might do this itself throughout the world or may sub-contract the rights to a sub-publisher.

WHERE DOES THE MONEY COME FROM?

Mechanical licences and royalties
Originally, when a recording was reproduced it was literally done mechanically, using mechanical piano-rolls. So the licence to reproduce the song on a sound recording is called a mechanical licence. It remains a major source of income

for most songwriters. If a record company wants to record a performance of a song, it has to ask permission from the author or the publisher or the person who administers the song. This may seem a bit strange where you've written a song that your band wants to record. It seems odd to have to ask permission from someone else to record your band performing it. But remember that different people may control the rights in the sound recording and the rights in the song. They are separate copyrights and the same people will probably not control both. The record company has to pay a licence fee to the owner of the rights in the song. The fee for this, the mechanical royalty, is either fixed by negotiation between representatives of the record and publishing companies in the country concerned or set by law or legal tribunal.

The present licensing system in the UK was the result of a referral to the Copyright Tribunal in 1992. The record and publishing companies couldn't agree on what was a proper licence fee. The scheme approved by the Copyright Tribunal is operated by the MCPS on behalf of most of the music publishers in the UK. The current licence fee on physical CDs is 8.5% of the dealer price of the CD. The MCPS can only license the mechanical reproduction of a song if it's a straight 'cover', i.e. a faithful reproduction of the original by someone other than the original performers. If it's not a faithful reproduction, then the MCPS does not have the authority to issue a licence and permission has to be asked from the writers or their publishers.

Until recently, mechanical reproduction took the form of a physical product such as a vinyl record, or a CD. With the coming of the digital era and music being delivered online, the law had to adapt to deal with this new means of distribution. The download of a computer file containing music is treated as a reproduction akin to a physical reproduction such as a CD. This was confirmed in UK legislation by the 2003 amendment to the 1988 Copyright Act, introduced by the Copyright and Related Rights Regulations, 2003.

The mechanical royalty rate for digital downloads is 8.5% of the published dealer price (PPD) or 8% gross revenue for downloads and there are also licences available now for many types of music online, such as podcasts and streaming.

Controlled compositions
Although in this book I'm mostly dealing with UK copyright and licensing schemes, the situation in North America is important as it can have a huge impact on publishing income coming from the United States (and to a lesser extent, Canada, a much smaller marketplace).

In the UK, we have a licensing scheme and a fixed rate that has to be paid for a licence. In the US, the law also sets a fixed rate (currently 9.1 cents for recordings of a song five minutes or less, and 1.75 cents per minute or fraction thereof for those over five minutes) for the right to reproduce a song on a record, but in the US the record industry has more bargaining power than the music publishers. It lobbied the legislators and got a clause included in the law that allows a different rate to be set by agreement. Well, surprise, surprise, the record companies have insisted on a different rate. And is it higher? What do you think? The position in the US is that many record companies will only pay 75% of the fixed rate on physical product at least. This is referred to as a 'controlled composition' or 'reduced mechanical royalty' clause. They are called 'controlled compositions' because the compositions and what happens to them are under the control of the writer or his publishers. Obviously, you can only agree to a reduced rate if you're the owner or controller of the song. Many US record deals start from the standpoint that you will agree to this 75% rate for physical records. This means that you're losing a quarter of your US publishing income from the reproduction of your songs on records sold in the US. The pressure will be on you to accept this and if you really want to do the US deal then there may be little you or your advisers can do about it. However, if you already have a publishing deal you probably won't be allowed to accept this reduction without your publisher's agreement. You can use this to get your publisher to fight on your and its behalf to get improvements on this rate. If you've a lot of bargaining power, you can get a 100% rate. If you've medium bargaining power, you can get them to agree to increase the 75% rate to 85% and then to 100% based on sales of a given number of records. Sometimes they will not budge at all and in most cases you have to give in or not do the deal. A 100% rate however is the norm on digital downloads and indeed I understand that save for some heritage releases all new digital releases in the US should be at full statutory rate under the Millennium Copyright Act. The digital rate is to be revisited in the US at a hearing scheduled for Spring 2017. Already there is heavy political lobbying on both sides, but with a slight preference perhaps on the publishers' side, to a per use fixed fee as opposed to a percentage-based scheme.

Most US record companies try to further reduce their liability to pay full mechanical royalties by limiting the number of songs on a record that they will pay royalties on. This is usually no more than ten or eleven. If you have twelve different songs on your album, you may not get a mechanical royalty in the US on at least one or two of those tracks with such a limitation in place. Perhaps a reason for aiming to keep the number of tracks on your record within the ten- or eleven-track limit.

Synchronisation licences and royalties

If you're a songwriter who writes mostly music for films, adverts or computer games, then your main source of income may not be mechanical royalties but fees from the issue of licences to use your music with visual images. This licence is called a synchronisation licence, because it gives the right to synchronise music with visual images. The publisher also licenses and collects income from these licences. The fee for this use is called the synchronisation fee. Synchronisation income has become much more important as a source of revenue with the decline in mechanical royalties on declining record sales and the rise in advertising agencies using music creatively to build brand loyalties.

In recent years the battle has been to get your song or your artist's performance on the Christmas ads for the major campaigns such as Marks & Spencer or John Lewis. The high profile and frequent rotation of these ads can 'break' a new artist or revive the fortunes of another. The John Lewis Christmas ad has established a practice of using a new artist to record a cover of an old song. In 2016 the ad was set to a cover of the Randy Crawford classic 'One Day I'll Fly Away', recorded by the British band Vaults. The publishers of the song will have done well out of this but often the performers are expected to do it at a low rate because, arguably, of the 'free' publicity they are getting. Sync fees are a growth area and for the right music an advertising company will pay a lot of money – £50–70,000 or more as a synchronisation fee for the right work isn't unheard of. I should just say, though, before you all rush to get your music into adverts or films, that many advertising companies pay a lot less than this. Many also commission writers to write songs that sound like, but aren't, famous songs or which are in the then current music style. Some songwriters make a career of writing music for adverts or in composing sound-alike songs. For some this is their main source of income. Others do it as a way to fund the writing of that film soundtrack or concerto they otherwise wouldn't have the money to do.

In some countries, there's a fixed rate for synchronisation licences. In most cases, though, it has to be fixed on a case-by-case basis. So this again is an area where your publisher, or lawyer, or manager (if you don't have a publisher) will negotiate a good deal for you.

If you want to put one of your songs in a promotional video for one of your singles, your publisher will probably give you a free synchronisation licence. They will want a separate fee for any commercial use such as inclusion in a DVD or for some online/website uses or permanent digital downloads.

If there is a synchronisation fee payable it is usual for the songwriter's share of the income to go towards recouping any advances which have already been paid to the songwriter. The publishers will keep their publisher's share of the income. For example, if the songwriter is on a 75:25 split of royalties in his favour the publisher would keep 25% of the fee for itself and use the remaining 75% to help recoup the advances.

A situation may arise where a songwriter is commissioned to write some music or a song for a specific project like a film soundtrack. Publishing contracts will often say that even though the publisher may have an exclusive arrangement with the songwriter, the songwriter can do these deals and keep any commission fee, that is a fee for the writing services, provided the synchronisation fee for the right to synchronise it with visual images, is paid through to the publisher. Now, it doesn't take much intelligence to work out that, as a songwriter, you may want to increase the commission fee and decrease the synchronisation fee. Publishers are obviously wise to this and may also try to apply some of the commission fee to recoupment. It's a matter of negotiation.

It's interesting to see the positive effect a successful music-based television show can have on publishing income. The *X Factor* and *Britain's Got Talent* and *The Voice* contestants regularly top the singles charts and in 2010 it was the television programme *Glee* which did the trick, building on successes for UK writers in US TV shows like *The OC*.

Music featured prominently in the opening and closing ceremonies for the 2012 Olympics and the artists performing, particularly Emeli Sandé, saw significant increases in record sales, with her album jumping five places in the week following her performance. There was, of course, also the worldwide exposure to an audience of billions. Not a bad night's work, even if they did all apparently perform for only a nominal £1 fee.

Performing rights

We have looked so far at two main sources of publishing income: the mechanical licence and the synchronisation licence. The third significant source of income is the right to publicly perform a song. Public performance doesn't just mean live concerts – it includes the playing of music in shops, restaurants and clubs; in fact, anywhere that music is played in public.

Most songwriters who have had some success become members of the PRS or one of its overseas affiliates. The PRS is the only UK performing right society for the administration of the right to perform a work in public and it is responsible for the collection of income generated by the public performance of the music. The income comes largely from licences taken out by broadcasters, shops, pubs and so on. When you become a member of the PRS the rules say that you have to assign your performing rights in your songs to the PRS. If you end your membership the performing rights are returned to you. The performing rights controlled by the PRS are the right to publicly perform a work, the right to broadcast it and to make it available to the public, and the right to authorise others to do any or all of the above.

The PRS monitors use of music on TV and radio programmes by means of cue sheets. These are lists of music played on each programme, which the station producers complete after each show. The PRS has a random sampling policy for live shows. They couldn't possibly cover all live gigs, but do monitor the main venues and a selection of the smaller ones and they keep the type of venues monitored under review.

In order that there doesn't have to be a separate licence every time a song is played in public the PRS has entered into licences with most of the broadcasters and with major places of entertainment like clubs and restaurant chains. These are called 'blanket licences' because they cover all songs controlled by the PRS. If you've a blanket licence you don't have to worry about whether you can play a particular song, provided you've paid the annual licence fee negotiated with the PRS. So every time your song is played on television, radio, cable or satellite you'll receive some income from that use of your song. Blanket licences are also available for a variety of uses of music on websites where the PRS now licenses use of music for TV, radio, mobile and other online uses. In fact, it is probable that you will now be able to find a licence for most of what you want to do. The PRS website is a useful source of information on the right licence for what you want to do and, in many cases, the application form can be downloaded. If you plan to use music in a way which is not covered by one of the current licences you can apply to their commercial committee with details of your proposal and ask them to propose an appropriate rate, which in many cases is open to some negotiation, particularly while you are establishing the commercial viability of your scheme.

There is, however, pressure from Government to make the licensing system even more streamlined, in particular for pan-European uses of music, and as we will see in Chapter 15 on collection societies steps are being taken to achieve this as well as direct licensing by publishers of digital rights they have withdrawn from the societies (e.g. ICE).

Through the cue sheets, samplings and the data they collect from online uses, the PRS gets a good idea of what music has been performed and calculates the amount due under the various blanket licences. The share due to the songwriter members of PRS is paid out at regular intervals (four times a year) after the PRS has deducted its fee for doing the administration.

The PRS rules require that at least six-twelfths (i.e. 50%) of the performing income is paid to the songwriter direct. This money does not, therefore, go through the publisher's hands to be used to recoup any advances, but goes direct to the songwriter. This can be a valuable source of income for an impoverished songwriter who is unrecouped and can't expect any royalties or further advances from his publisher for some time. It doesn't have to be 50:50 but in the majority of cases that is how it is divided. The other 50% can be paid to a publisher nominated by the songwriter as having the right to publish his songs. This 'publisher's share' can also be divided between the songwriter and the publisher. If the publisher does share any of it with the songwriter that share usually goes first towards recouping any outstanding advances. If there isn't a publisher the songwriter can collect 100% of the performing right income himself, but may have difficulties in collecting or administering it and may need to get an administrator on board to help. The PRS's role is not a proactive one. It does not actively seek ways in which to exploit the performing rights in the songs, but is there to make sure that public places playing records do so under a proper licence scheme, so that there is a chance of earning some money from this use of music. The PRS acts as a sort of clearing house, collecting in this money and paying it out to its members, both songwriters and publishers. The publishers are happy to allow the PRS to do this job for them, provided, that is, that it doesn't charge too much – there are periodical renegotiations of the collection fee.

Print

Although not as relevant these days, the publisher also has the right to issue licences for a song to be reproduced in printed form as sheet music. It is comparatively rare that the publishers do this themselves now; usually it's third-party specialist print companies who do it under a licence arrangement with the publishers. The exceptions tend to be classical music publishers. While print income from sales of sheet music isn't a large source of income for a popular-music songwriter, for classical composers it can be a good source of income because included in this print category is the hire-out charge the publisher makes to orchestras wishing to have access to the 'parts' of the work, i.e. the sections written for the different instruments in the orchestra.

As publishers look for new ways to make money from the songs they control, we may find that the print music royalty or other miscellaneous royalties payable to songwriters increases in importance. I am thinking here of licensing lyrics for merchandise. The publisher would charge the merchandiser either a flat fee or a royalty per unit sold and the songwriter would to be entitled to a share of such income.

Grand rights

There is one final source of revenue and that is from exercise of the somewhat archaically named Grand Rights. These are the rights to use your songs in theatrical stage productions and musicals. Obviously, it is a somewhat special-ised area as not every song is going to be suitable. There is a fashion for creating stage shows around the story of an artist's life, however loosely. For example, *We Will Rock You* (Queen), *Mamma Mia* (Abba) and *Thriller* (Michael Jackson). Deals may be based on a flat fee and/or a share of box office. And then there's the income from spin-offs like cast albums. There are also several examples of what are called Jukebox Musicals with little or no dialogue, minimal sets, just back-to-back music, like *Let It Be,* the Beatles story.

The songwriter will usually try to have contractual approval in his publishing contract over the exercise of his grand rights.

RECORD DEAL BEFORE PUBLISHING?

It used to be invariably the case that you did your record deal first and got a publishing deal later. Nowadays, the publisher fills many of the same roles as a record company, finding the right co-writers and producers, and even in some cases recording and releasing limited edition single records. The decision there-fore becomes much more of a personal one. For some, it's important that they have got a deal, *any* deal. So, if the publishers come courting first, they will do the publishing deal first. Others stick to the tried and true method of getting a record deal first and then hoping that that deal and the success of their first release will push the bidding up for their publishing rights. This can be a dangerous game as, if the first release doesn't prove to be a success, the publishing offers may dry up. You may be a songwriter who wants to hang on to your publishing rights for as long as you can, in which case you're going to be concerned to get a record deal that will give you enough by way of personal advances to live on for a reasonable period of time without having to go looking for money from a publisher.

If a songwriter doesn't need to do a publishing deal in order to get some money or other form of 'leg-up', he can become self-published. This way he fully controls the copyright in his songs and how they are used. How do you do this? You would start by becoming a member of the various collecting societies like PRS. The collection societies fulfil a lot of the administrative functions of a publisher, but a self-published songwriter still has to do a lot of work himself. The collection societies don't always notify all foreign societies of their interest in a particular song or chase up individual payments. Disputes over ownership can also clog up the works. The songwriter will have to track down where the music is being used and check if the song is registered locally and if the right amount of money has been paid.

Most songwriters will seek some form of assistance, either signing up to a full-blown exclusive publishing deal or by appointing a publisher or other third party to administer the rights for them.

TYPES OF PUBLISHING DEAL

There are three basic types of music publishing agreement: the administration deal, the sub-publishing deal and the fully exclusive songwriting deal. Within the category of exclusive songwriting deals, there is a sub-category where rights are just assigned in a single song. This is called, unsurprisingly, the single-song assignment.

THE ADMINISTRATION DEAL

Administration deals are popular with songwriters who have a small but potentially lucrative catalogue or collection of songs. It may not be worthwhile for them to join the collection societies and be self-published. They may not have the necessary time, energy or organisational abilities to go tracking down the income. They may prefer to employ someone to do it for them.

124

These types of deal also appeal to established songwriters. They may not need a publisher to try to exploit their songs. They may be disillusioned with exclusive publishing deals or want to own their copyrights. They may not need up-front advances against income and may relish the increased control that they would have if there were no publisher in the picture.

The administrator doesn't usually take an assignment of any interest in the copyright, but is granted a licence for a period of time. If an administrator asks to take an assignment of rights outright, I would need to be convinced that there was a very good business reason to do it. If you assign your rights, you aren't in a position of control and there isn't very much of a difference between this and exclusive publishing deals, except you're likely to see only small or no up-front advances. At least if it's for a licence term then you retain control of the underlying copyright. A licence term can vary greatly from one year upwards, but with a three- to five-year licence term common. If it is a licence and things go wrong the songwriter wouldn't have to worry about getting his copyrights back, as he would have held on to ownership and merely licensed the rights.

As the name suggests, the administrator administers the songs for the owner of the copyright. The administrator registers the songs with the various collection societies and licenses others to use the songs, collects the income from these licences and prepares accounts showing how much has been earned. The terms of the contract dictate whether the administrator has complete freedom to issue whatever licences he thinks right for the songs, or whether he must first consult with the songwriter. It may say that commonplace licences, such as the right for the writer to record his own songs, can be issued without asking him first, but if someone wants to use a song in an advert or a film the songwriter has to first give permission. I would advise against putting too many restrictions on what licences the administrator can grant if you want to maximise what can be earned from the songs. By all means put a stop to something that is a real issue, for example if you are a vegan you may not want your songs used in adverts for beef burgers, but think carefully before you block all uses of the songs in adverts, because you are cutting off a potentially very valuable source of income.

The administrator could be a company that specialises just in administration, however, most music publishers who sign up songwriters to exclusive deals will also do administration deals in the right circumstances.

The administrator will usually charge around 10–15% of the gross income in fees, although some with high volumes of turnover can charge less than 10%.

You wouldn't usually expect an administrator to pay any advances. Payment will only be made when the administrator has collected in some money. It's therefore very important to know how often the administrator will account. They should pay at least every six months and preferably every three months. It's also important to check out their reputation for efficient collection of money, particularly outside the UK. The administrator may be very good in the UK, but overseas he may not have the necessary resources or contacts. In which case, it's likely that all he will do is collect what comes through collection societies overseas that are affiliated to PRS and MCPS. If this is the case, then you have to ask yourself whether it's worth it, because you can get this income yourself through direct membership of PRS and MCPS. You ought to be getting some kind of added value by having the administrator on board. It may be as little as taking the load off you, but it wouldn't be unreasonable to ask the administrator to try to track down unpaid licence fees or royalties on your behalf, and if he has a worldwide deal with you he shouldn't just limit his activities to the UK.

A songwriter will often do an administration deal when he isn't too concerned about getting other uses for his songs. If you know people will either not want to put your songs in a film or advert, or if they do your songs are so well known you don't have to sell yourself and they will come to you, then you needn't worry about someone going out and actively looking for these extra uses. Administrators will look after the administration side but may not be out there pitching your songs to advertising agencies or film companies. However, even those who have old catalogues of songs which are more or less dormant can still be tempted by promises of a bit of an extra push on their songs and a bit of extra cash, in which case perhaps a more proactive arrangement would suit them better than a pure administration deal.

The Sub-publishing Deal

The sub-publishing deal is a mixture of an administration deal and an exclusive publishing agreement, but it is more commonly applied where a smaller publisher engages the services of a larger one for some or all of the territory that it has rights for. The owner of the copyrights sub-licenses some or all of these rights to a publisher. The original owner usually keeps the copyright, so it's normally a licence rather than an assignment of rights. These types of deal come up in two very different circumstances.

Established songwriters or songwriters who want to own or control their copyrights and have their own small publishing company, may want something more than a pure administration deal. If so, a sub-publishing deal may suit. They may not need an advance or may be prepared to do without an advance in return for keeping control of the copyrights. That isn't to say that a sub-publisher won't pay any advance at all. They may pay modest sums in advances, but they may not be as big as you'd get under an exclusive publishing deal. Why? Because the sub-publisher doesn't get as much ownership or control from a sub-publishing deal as he would from an exclusive songwriting deal.

If a songwriter needs someone to go and search out deals for him, then he may not get that from an administrator, so a sub-publishing deal may work for him. Under a sub-publishing deal, the songwriter gets someone actively looking for other ways of earning money from his songs.

In some cases, the publisher will want an assignment of the copyright. As you know, my advice is to avoid this if you can but if you don't have much choice then try to get them to agree that this is only for a limited period of time. This period is called 'the Rights Period' or 'the Retention Period'. The shorter you can make it as a songwriter, the better in terms of your control of the copyrights. Bear in mind, though, that the shorter the period of time that the sub-publisher controls the copyrights, the fewer opportunities he has to make money from the songs and this may be reflected in the level of deal he offers. If you do get a publisher to agree a licence term, then currently in most cases this is likely to be for at least three years, which may be extendable by the publisher if, for example, you haven't recouped an advance in the first three years.

The sub-publishing deal also appeals to smaller publishers, ones that don't have their own established systems overseas. Instead of the cost of setting up their own companies in each of the main overseas countries, such publishers do sub-publishing deals in those countries. They keep the rights they have, but grant the overseas publisher the right to use some or all of those rights in their country for a period of time.

Whichever type of deal we are talking about, the sub-publisher needs to have the right to register the songs, to license some or all of the main publishing rights such as mechanical and synchronisation rights, and to collect in the income.

The sub-publishing contract will set out the extent to which the songwriter or original publisher has the right to approve the grant of licences to exploit the publishing rights. Don't be surprised if the sub-publisher presses for overall control and only wants to have to get approval on certain very specific matters, for example, approval over alterations to the songs or over the grant of licences to include them in adverts for certain products that you may disapprove of, e.g. alcohol or personal hygiene items. If you tie the sub-publisher's hands too much, then they can't easily get further uses for the songs. You're employing a sub-publisher and paying them a large fee to be proactive on your behalf, so you need to balance the need for creative control against commercial realities.

How much you have to pay a sub-publisher will depend on a number of factors such as your bargaining power, how much the sub-publisher wants to control your catalogue of songs (whether for market share or income or to have the kudos of having you on their books), and how much you are expecting them to do. I recently had a bidding war going on for an old catalogue of songs because they were very iconic and 'of their period', and it happened that this was a period that is popular at the moment for films and ads and so the publishers involved in the bidding war could easily see how there was a lot of money to be earned from licensing these songs.

The fee is likely to be more than you would pay under an administration deal but probably a little less than under a fully exclusive songwriting agreement. A sub-publishing fee of 15% of the gross income received is common. If you expect an advance, then that may increase to 20% to compensate for the additional risk the sub-publisher is taking. The sub-publisher has paid out some money to you on the strength of what it knows about you and your potential. If you don't live up to that then that's the sub-publisher's risk. The contract very rarely allows the sub-publisher to demand that money back, but they may extend the licence Rights Period until your account is recouped.

What does a sub-publisher do?
A sub-publisher should provide the same basic services as under an administration deal, including registering the songs, granting licences, collecting income and accounting on a regular basis.

Some larger publishers can account and pay you what you're due in the same accounting period that they receive the monies from overseas. For example, the sub-publisher grants a mechanical licence to reproduce your song on a record in the US. The record sales take place in the period between March and June 2017. Say the US record company pays the mechanical royalty in the next three months, so it will be in the sub-publisher's account by the end of September 2017.

The contract with the sub-publisher says that it accounts in September for income received in the period up to the end of June. In the scenario I have given, the income won't have come in until after the end of June. If the deal were that you got paid in the same accounting period, you would get it in September. If it's not then you'll get it at the next accounting date, which would normally be March 2018. This is a six-month delay which, when you're waiting for your money from overseas, can seem a very long time. If prompt payment and cash flow are important to you, and let's face it, they are to most of us, then you need to check this out carefully.

In addition to the basic administration services, the sub-publisher should give you more for the extra fee it's getting. This could just be payment of an advance, but the sub-publisher should also be more proactive, going out and looking for other uses for the songs, suggesting co-writers, finding film projects or adverts and so on.

A smaller publishing company appointing a sub-publisher overseas would expect them to act as if they were a branch of their company overseas.

If you are a songwriter with your own publishing company you may not notice any difference between what a sub-publisher does and what you'd expect from an exclusive publishing agreement. The sub-publisher will usually expect exclusive rights to sub-publish your songs and will charge a similar fee to an exclusive publisher. The crucial difference is that you retain the copyright in your songs and have more control.

THE SINGLE-SONG ASSIGNMENT

The single-song assignment is a bit of a halfway house. It's not an exclusive publishing agreement. The songwriter is free to publish individual songs himself or through a variety of different publishers. Unlike under a sub-publishing agreement, he usually assigns the rights in a song to a publisher; he doesn't license them. The assignment could be for the life of copyright or it could be for a shorter Rights or Retention Period. There may be an advance, but it's likely to be small. The publisher is likely to get a fee of about 20–25% of the gross income received.

Deals such as these would be attractive to a songwriter who only writes a small number of songs on an irregular basis, or who wants to keep his options open. The publisher still gets the rights it needs in the particular song and market share in that song. Because the publisher controls the copyright in the song, it's in its interests to get as many other uses for the work as possible. The publisher will also carry out all the usual administrative functions and should account regularly. The same comments that I made above about accounting delays apply here. The song assignment will decide how much control the songwriter has over how the song is used. Because it's a one-off, he may not have as much control as with an exclusive deal for all his songs, but if he has enough bargaining power he should certainly be able to prevent major changes to the words or music and some control over the use of the song in films or adverts.

A client of mine had a song on a number one album but was undecided about whether to sign up exclusively to one publisher. An offer was made by a major publisher to just publish this song under an exclusive single-song assignment. This proved just the ticket.

EXCLUSIVE PUBLISHING AGREEMENT

If none of the above options appeals or is on offer, then there is the exclusive publishing agreement. For most songwriters this is important at some stage in their careers. Getting an established publisher behind them means that they've arrived, that someone else has faith in their work and is prepared to put money and commitment behind that conviction. In many cases, a publisher is instrumental in getting record company interest. There are stories of music publishers of songwriters who are now household names who spent months knocking on record company doors trying to convince them of the strength of the songs. Sometimes it's just a case of waiting until your time has come while honing your craft in the meantime. It can be good to have a music publisher supporting you during this development phase.

RESTRAINT OF TRADE

As we saw in Chapter 3 on record deals, whenever there is an exclusive arrangement containing restrictions on what you can and can't do, there is an assumption that it is in restraint of trade. We also saw that the leading case in this area, *Macaulay v. Schroeder*, had decided that this doctrine also applied to exclusive record and publishing contracts. We know that the contract was found to be an unreasonable restraint of trade and, as such, unenforceable, but so far I have not gone into any details as to why the contract was found to be unreasonable so let's do so now.

> *Macaulay v. A. Schroeder Music Publishing Co. Limited ([1974] 1WLR 1308)*
> The particular parts of the contract that led the court to decide that it was unenforceable
> were that it was an exclusive arrangement, it required absolute commitment from Macaulay,
> but there was no corresponding commitment on the part of the publishers to do anything
> with the songs. They could accept them and tuck the copies away in a drawer, or put them
> on a shelf and forget about them. The term was for five years, but Schroeder could extend
> it for a further five years if more than £5,000 worth of royalties had been earned in the
> first five years. This was not a lot of money even then. Macaulay had had to assign the
> copyright for the life of copyright. Even though in those days this was fifty years after the
> end of the year in which he died not seventy years, it was still a long period of time to
> have a publisher controlling the copyright in his songs exclusively without having any obliga-
> tion to do anything with them. The advance that he received was very low. It was £50 with
> further payments of £50 as each earlier advance was recouped. This was almost like putting
> him on a wage, but with no guarantee of when he would receive his next pay cheque. The
> court felt that, taken as a whole, the contract was an unreasonable restraint of trade.

As a result of this and later cases, there was a change in UK music publishing
contracts. The length of the term is generally now limited with a maximum
backstop, usually no more than three years per contract period, although some
publishers do hold out for longer periods. There is also usually a requirement
that the publisher has to do something with the songs. For example, the contract
will often say that if the publisher has not granted a mechanical or synchronisation licence for a song, or no sheet music has been printed of it or it has not
been performed in public within, say, a year or two of the song being delivered
or after the end of the contract term, then the songwriter has the right to ask
the publisher to do something with it. If nothing happens within another three
to six months, the songwriter can usually get the copyright in the song back.

WHAT IS IN A TYPICAL PUBLISHING CONTRACT?

Exclusivity

If you sign an exclusive publishing deal you are usually agreeing that the
publisher will own and control all your output as a songwriter during the term
of that contract. In return for that exclusivity you can expect a commitment
from the publishing company to do something with your songs. You can also
usually expect that your publisher will be reasonably proactive on your behalf.

Even though it's an exclusive deal, there can sometimes be exceptions. As I
explained earlier, the exclusivity may not apply where you're commissioned to

write a song or some music specifically for a film. The film company will usually want to own the copyright in that piece of music or song. Your exclusive publisher may agree that these commissioned works are excluded from your publishing deal. This could be agreed at the time the contract is done as a blanket exception or your publisher could agree to consider specific requests on a case-by-case basis. If you are regularly commissioned to write music for films, your publisher isn't going to want to automatically exclude all these from your agreement. By not automatically agreeing that the film company can own the copyright, your publisher may gain some bargaining power with the film company to get a better deal.

Occasionally, a publisher will agree that the songs you write for a particular project are excluded from the deal. For example, you might write some songs for a largely uncommercial project that the publisher isn't interested in. In a deal I did, the songwriter did a bit of 'bread and butter' work writing for a library music company and it was agreed that these songs, which earned very little money, could be excluded. If you've a lot of bargaining power, you could insist that songs you write for a particular commercial project are excluded from the deal but this is rare. Just bear in mind that the more songs you keep back from your publisher, the more likely it is to reduce the size of the deal on offer.

Rights granted
The publisher will expect to take an assignment of the copyright in all your songs already in existence and not already published by anyone else. The assignment is usually of all rights in those works, subject to the performing rights that you may have already assigned to the PRS.

If you have done a publishing deal before, then another company may still have the right to act as publisher of those songs. If the Rights or Retention Period of that earlier deal runs out while your new publishing deal is still running, the new publisher will expect to get the right to publish those songs too. If you don't think they should, then you need to argue for this at the time the new publishing deal is done.

It's possible, if uncommon, to grant a publisher some but not all of the rights of a copyright owner. In deals I've done, I've given a publisher the right to issue mechanical licences but not synchronisation licences. Obviously you can do this if you've the necessary bargaining power, but there's no point in doing it unless you can do something with the rights you've kept back. Remember also that the more rights you hold back the more likely it is that you'll get a less attractive deal from the publishing company.

Territory

The rights that you assign could be for a particular country or worldwide. We saw in Chapter 3 that it was reasonably common to have split-territory deals with one deal for the US and another deal for the rest of the world. These deals aren't at all common in exclusive publishing contracts. Depending on who the publisher is and what its overseas set-up is like, it may have sub-publishing deals for some overseas countries. As a songwriter you should find out what the situation is overseas. You need to know that the sub-publishers are good, efficient companies and that there won't be any accounting delays.

Rights period

You could assign rights for the life of copyright or for a shorter Rights or Retention Period, which runs from the end of the term of the publishing contract. This period can vary considerably from anything as short as two to three years to more than twenty years. For the last three or four years, the average deal on offer from the major publishers has been twelve to fifteen years.

The Rights Period often gets shorter when there is a more positive economic climate and if there is a lot of competition to sign good songwriters. Ten years ago, I could get Retention Periods from some of the major music publishers as short as five years. This was when there were lots of good songwriters and a lot of money around. Publishers were going for short-term market share and weren't as concerned about hanging on to copyrights for any length of time. Many of the copyrights were for dance music songs and I guess they gambled that most of these would have a short lifespan. Now there's less money around and songwriters are expected to prove their worth over a longer period of time. It's difficult to get Rights Periods of less than fifteen years now unless you've got a lot of bargaining power. There are, however, always the one-off deals for one album or song which are ludicrously short, say two or three years, often for short-term market share to boost a publisher's standing in a particular quarter, possibly to impress their shareholders or other investors but again all down to bargaining power and the marketplace.

Term

The term of a UK music publishing contract is usually shorter than that of a record contract. It's quite common to find a publishing contract with an initial period of one year and then options in the publisher's favour for a further two or three option periods. Each contract period is usually for a minimum of twelve months, but can be longer depending on how long it takes to fulfil the minimum requirements that a publisher has for each contract period. For similar reasons to those given for record contracts, the options are in the publisher's favour not the songwriter. The publisher has too much invested to allow the songwriter to just walk out the door when he wants to.

Fixed terms and rolling advances

Some publishers use a different basis for the term of the publishing contract. Instead of a term made up of a number of optional contract periods, the publisher fixes the term up-front and says it will run for, say, three or five years with no options. That fixed period may be extended until the songwriter has fulfilled a minimum requirement, but often there is no minimum requirement; the publisher just publishes anything written during the fixed term. This is a risk for the publisher to take. The songwriter could take the advance payable on signing the deal and then not write another thing. To offer this kind of deal, the publisher has to know the songwriter well and be convinced that he is going to continue to write good songs. For such a songwriter this show of faith from the publisher can also be a relief. He won't have to worry about fulfilling a minimum requirement or delivering songs to order.

With a fixed term the songwriter often gets an advance when he signs the deal recoupable from his earnings in the usual way. When the initial advance has been wholly or partly recouped, he may be paid a further advance. This is called a rolling advance.

The publisher won't usually pay you an advance in the last twelve to eighteen months of the fixed term because it won't have enough time to recoup it before the deal runs out. When working out how recouped you are, to see if you are eligible for a further advance, you should try to get the publisher to take into account income that's been earned from your songs but hasn't yet come through to its or your account in the UK. This is called 'pipeline income'.

Minimum commitment

There are a number of different types of Minimum Commitment, i.e. the minimum that the publisher requires the songwriter to deliver in each contract period. The simplest is where the requirement is just to write a minimum number of songs. If you co-write, your share of all the co-written works must add up to an equivalent number of whole songs. For example, if the Minimum Commitment is to write five new songs and you always only write the lyrics, therefore only control at best

50% of each song, then you'll have to write ten half-songs to add up to the five whole ones. This type of commitment may work best for a pure songwriter who writes for others and doesn't perform and record his own material.

There may be an additional requirement that, in order to count towards the Minimum Commitment, the song must be exploited in some way, for instance commercially released as an A-side of a single or as an album track. This puts a greater burden on you if you're a pure songwriter who can't easily control whether anyone else will want to record your songs. The publisher usually insists on this when it wants to be certain there will be some form of exploitation (and hopefully some income) before it commits to any more advances or decides whether to exercise an option to extend the term.

There may be a requirement that you have to write a minimum percentage of the songs on an album. That percentage varies depending on the songwriter and the style of music. The requirement is usually that you have to write at least 80% of the songs on your own album but this can be less if there are many co-authors. There is also usually a requirement that that album has to be commercially released. This sort of arrangement works better for a songwriter who also performs and records his own material. In the past two years I have seen a move away from an album commitment to a number of songs or 'cuts' either on the songwriter's own album or on other people's recordings.

Advances

It's usual under an exclusive publishing agreement for the publisher to pay advances. As we saw with record contracts, this is a pre-payment of the songwriter's share of the gross income from the use of the songs. It's not a loan and isn't repayable to the publishing company – if you never earn enough from the songs to cover the amount of the advance, then you usually don't have to pay it back. But if you take the money and run, never delivering a single song, your publisher may get a bit upset and may sue for return of its money on the basis that you've failed to fulfil your side of the bargain.

What size of advance can you expect? Your bargaining power, the number of co-writers there are, how much is your own material and how much is sampled from others will all help to determine the figure. It will also depend on how much the publisher thinks it's likely to earn on average from your songs. If the record deal has already been done, the publisher may take its lead from what it knows of the level of that deal. If that was a particularly 'hot' deal, the publisher will know that it probably has to increase the overall terms of its offer. There are also financial models that help a publisher to decide how much it can realistically risk. Some publishers rely solely on these models, most work on a combination of gut instinct and financial modelling. You also have to factor in market forces. If the publisher really wants to sign you up, whether to increase the profile of the company, for market share or just because the A&R man wants it, then that publisher will pay whatever it takes.

The higher the advance, the more the publisher will expect from you in return and the larger percentage of the income that the publisher may keep as its fee. The publisher will be more reluctant to pay a higher than average royalty if it's had to pay out a high advance – £75,000 for a writer for 80% or more of the songs on an album isn't unreasonable from a major publisher. Much higher figures can be expected if there is 'hype' or if the songwriter has a proven track record. If the publisher knows that there is already some income out there from your catalogue waiting to be collected, or that you have a song on the next album to be released by a chart-topping act, it's more likely to risk paying higher advances. A recent deal doubled in value when in the course of the negotiation it was confirmed that one of the songs was to be covered by a top artist and included on his next album which was expected to sell in the millions. A smaller publishing company cannot usually hope to compete just on money and if you are considering a deal with a smaller publisher you have to weigh up things like the greater degree of control versus level of advances.

The publishing deal is likely to recoup a lot faster than a record deal because with a publishing deal you only have to recoup the advances and maybe some money in demo costs, or a little tour support or marketing spend. There aren't generally the additional recoupable expenses like recording costs and video costs and the greater part of tour support. Also, the publisher pays through to you a much larger percentage of the income earned for the use of your songs than most record companies do with the income from sales of your records.

Royalties
The publishing advance is recouped from your royalty earnings after first deducting the publisher's fee. For an exclusive publishing deal this fee will usually be about 20–25% of the gross income.

Royalties can be calculated in one of two ways, either 'at source' or on 'receipts'. 'At source' means that (after the collection societies, the VAT man and payments to any arranger or translator) there have been no other deductions made by anyone from the gross income earned from your songs. In a 'receipts' deal in addition to these basic deductions, the publisher's sub-publishers overseas have to be paid and these fees are deducted from the gross before the income is paid through to you.

Let me give you an example. Ten thousand Euros are earned in France in mechanical income from use of songs on a record after paying the collection society and the tax. If it is a 'source' deal, then, as far as you're concerned, nothing else gets deducted from that €10,000 by the sub-publisher in France before it's paid through to your publisher in the UK. The UK publisher would deduct its fee of, say, €2,500 from the €10,000 and pay through €7,500 (or the sterling equivalent) to the songwriter. With a 'receipts' deal the sub-publisher in France would first take its 'cut' of, say, 15% (€1,500) leaving €8,500 to be sent through to the publisher in the UK. The UK publisher takes its 25% of that €8,500, leaving the songwriter with just €6,300.

As a songwriter you should try to get an 'at source' deal, but your publisher may not have any choice. The deals done with its sub-publishers may mean it has to do deals on a 'receipts' basis in order to make any money out of use of your songs overseas. If you're offered a 'receipts' deal, the very least you should do is to try to limit the amount the sub-publishers can take off the 'gross' income. For example, you might want to say in the contract that the sub-publishers can't deduct any more than 15–20% of the gross. We saw in the *Elton John v. Dick James* case that the sub-publishers were spread all over the world and many were associated with Dick James and his UK companies. There was no limit on what these sub-publishers could take off the top as their cut. As Elton was on a 'receipts' deal he could, and did in some cases, find himself in a situation where the sub-publisher took 50% or more, leaving small amounts to come into the UK, where a further percentage fee was deducted by Dick James – leaving very little over for Elton. Putting a 'cap' on the deductions would have gone some way to reduce these problems.

Synchronisation and cover royalties
Sometimes the publisher justifies taking a larger slice of the royalties by saying that, in order to do certain work for you, it needs the incentive of getting more of a fee. Part of me says that getting 20–25% of your income should be enough for most purposes. The reality is that it is accepted that publishers get a larger fee for these types of work and it's hard to buck the trend unless you have a

great deal of bargaining power. The two areas where the publisher usually takes a larger fee are synchronisation licences and covers.

Publishers usually expect to get about another 5–10% for obtaining synchronisation licences for your songs, so, if you were paying your publisher a fee on synchronisation royalties of 25%, you would see that increase to 30–35% for synchronisation royalties on projects actively procured by the publishers.

A cover is a recording of a song by someone other than the songwriter. So, for example, if a song written and first recorded by U2 is later recorded by Sinead O'Connor, Sinead's version would be the cover. Once again, the publisher will probably want an increased fee for finding other artists keen to cover your works. Try to make sure that a use doesn't count as a cover unless the publisher has actually done something positive to get it. For example, if you bumped into an artist at an awards show and he was raving about what he thought he could do with one of your songs, and then goes on to cover that song, it hasn't happened because of anything the publisher has done. The publisher should not get an increased fee for that cover.

You have to be particularly careful where you're a songwriter who doesn't perform his own songs. Otherwise, you'll find that you're paying the higher fee for most of what you're doing, because the recording will always be by someone other than the person who wrote it, i.e. you, and everything will be a cover. In these cases, I always push for all recordings to be treated in the same way and not as covers. The publishers are sometimes reluctant to do this, saying that getting anyone to record a song requires effort and that it's harder if the songwriter isn't the performing artist. You have to stand your ground on this. If you're a songwriter you'll be paying a publisher to find ways to use your songs. You shouldn't expect it to increase its fee just because you aren't going to record your own songs.

Performing income

The PRS rules require that at least six-twelfths (50%) of the performing income has to go to the writer/composer. This is called 'the writer's share'. The other six-twelfths is called 'the publisher's share'. Depending on the deal you have, the publisher will either say that it intends to keep the whole of the publisher's share or it will agree to share some of it with you, the writer. You get to keep the writer's share and don't have to put it towards recoupment of your advances. Your share of the publisher's share will first go towards recoupment of any unrecouped advance.

138

When you're dealing with contracts for the use of music in a film or TV programme, it's still common for the publisher to insist on keeping the entire publisher's share and not putting any of it towards recoupment. TV and film publishing deals have lagged behind popular-music deals, where it's usual for the publisher to share the publisher's share with the songwriter. But in film and TV deals it is possible for the songwriter to own more than a minimum 50% writer's share. Writers for film and TV programmes can, if they have the necessary clout, argue that the writer's share should be 60–70% or even higher with the publisher only keeping the remainder.

Accounting

The publishing company will usually account to you every six months. You'll be sent a statement of what use has been made of your songs in the previous six months and how much income has been received. It should show the percentage that your publisher has kept as its fee and the amount that has been credited to your account. Your share of income will go first to recoup advances. After that, your publisher should send a cheque or remittance advice with the statement for the royalties due to you. Even if the account isn't recouped, you or your representatives should check these accounting statements to see if they seem right and that the correct fee has been deducted. If, for example, you know that your music was used in an advert in the last six months but there is no mention of income from this in the statement, you should ask your publisher to explain. It also pays for you to audit the books of the publishing company from time to time. You don't want to be doing this every five minutes, but you may want to run a check after you've had a particularly successful period. You'll probably also want to think about doing an audit when the deal comes to an end, as that is going to be your last practical chance to check up on your publisher. Because it can be very expensive to carry out an audit (£10,000 plus isn't unusual), you only want to do it when you think there is a reasonable chance of getting something back from it. If the audit shows up serious errors in your favour, you should expect them to reimburse you the main costs of doing the audit as well as paying you whatever sums the audit has shown are due to you.

You shouldn't delay in raising any concerns you might have about an accounting statement, as the publishing contract will probably put a time limit on your doing so. Usually, if a statement hasn't been challenged for three years, sometimes less, then it's said to have been accepted and no objection can be raised to it after that time.

139

WHAT CAN YOU EXPECT FROM A PUBLISHER UNDER AN EXCLUSIVE PUBLISHING AGREEMENT?

We've already seen that there is a presumption that an exclusive songwriting agreement is in restraint of trade and it's up to the publisher to show that the contract, taken as a whole, is reasonable to protect its interests and fair to the songwriter. As we saw in the *Macaulay v. Schroeder* case, a publishing contract should require the publisher to do something with the songs that it controls, and if your publisher doesn't manage to do so within a reasonable period of time you should be able to get those songs back (see the cases below). The publisher has to ensure that it does what it can to get the songs used, to maximise the income from all uses, to make sure the songs are properly registered, and income properly collected and accounted through to the writer.

Your publisher should also take steps to protect your songs from unauthorised uses, e.g. sampling of part of your songs. It's up to the publisher either to prevent such uses by court action or, if you and your publisher are prepared to allow the sample use, to ensure a proper amount is paid in compensation (see Chapter 13). Open-ended contracts are likely to be seen as unfairly restrictive, as we see in the case of Holly Johnson and Perfect Songs.

Frankie Goes To Hollywood (Perfect Songs Limited v. Johnson and Others [1993] EMLR 61)
This case came to court at the same time as the related case involving Johnson's record contract. Both the record and publishing companies were trying to get an injunction to bind Holly Johnson to the contracts, even though the band he was a member of, Frankie Goes To Hollywood, had disbanded. Holly Johnson argued that both agreements were unenforceable as being an unreasonable restraint of his trade.

When the court looked at the publishing contract, it found that it was potentially a very long contract; that it was exclusive, but there had not been equal bargaining power when it was entered into. It found that the restrictions in the contract were not reasonable and declared that the publishing agreement was unenforceable. The Judge was concerned that Holly Johnson and his fellow band members had not had any choice in whether they did the publishing deal. It was offered as a package with the record deal. There was also no obligation on the publisher to do anything with the songs. There was no reassignment of the rights in the songs if the publisher failed to exploit them in any way. The Judge also thought that it was unfair that Perfect Songs had full control over what happened to the songs once they were delivered. The songwriters had little or no creative control. The Judge considered what financial benefits the songwriters got out of the deal and found that the 35% fee retained by the publisher was too much.

Stone Roses Publishing Dispute (Zomba v. Mountfield and Others [1993] EMLR 152)
Another case that has had an effect on the form of publishing contracts is the Stone Roses publishing dispute.

The Stone Roses were a Manchester band that had a hit with an album called *The Stone Roses*, released in 1989. They were signed to the Silvertone label, part of the Zomba Group. The members of the Stone Roses were also offered a package deal. They couldn't do the record deal without also signing the publishing deal. As we saw in the case of *Armatrading v. Stone*, it's very important that the songwriter gets independent advice from his own lawyer, someone who is familiar with the music business and its contracts. In this case, the songwriters had their own lawyer but he was not experienced in music contracts and made hardly any changes to the terms of the contract from the initial draft that the publishing company's lawyer gave to him. There was no equality of bargaining power. The agreement was an exclusive one and the rights were assigned for the life of copyright. There was a limited obligation on the publisher to do something with the songs under its control. After five years, the Stone Roses could ask for the rights back in any of their songs that hadn't been exploited. The first contract period was linked to that of the record deal. The court found that the first contract period of the record deal was capable of being extended indefinitely. As the two were linked, this meant that the publishing agreement was similarly open-ended and, as such, unreasonable. The court also found that the advances were not reasonable and objected to the lack of artistic or creative control by the songwriters. Because Zomba had obtained an injunction preventing the band from recording for anyone else, they couldn't bring out any more records until this case had been decided. When it was, they signed a big deal with US label Geffen. The band went on to release another album called, appropriately enough, *The Second Coming*, but split up shortly afterwards.

As a result of this and similar cases, it's now common to have clauses in UK publishing agreements making it clear that the publisher has to do something with the rights it has. Also that the songwriter should have some say on what happens to the songs once they're delivered. It's usual to say that no major changes to the music or any change to the lyrics can be made without the songwriter's approval. The criticism of the 65:35 split has led to the average publishing royalty in the UK rising to at least 70% in the songwriter's favour and in many cases to 75% or 80% with the publisher keeping the remainder but this is by no means universal and 65:35 deals are still being done. In the TV and film industry and in library music deals 50:50 deals are still common.

MORAL RIGHTS AND CREATIVE CONTROL

A songwriter may have strong views on what he wants or doesn't want to happen to his songs. For example, a songwriter may believe passionately that no one should be allowed to alter the words or music without his approval. This doesn't usually extend to straight translations. Those are taken to be a logical part of the exploitation process. But if, in the translation, the translator wanted to give the lyrics a different meaning and the songwriter objected to this, his contract with his publisher will say whether he is entitled to prevent this happening. Obviously, I'm not talking about minor changes, but major ones that change the meaning significantly. This contractual control overlaps with a songwriter's moral rights. Moral rights are described in more detail in Chapter 12. Where you're able to retain your moral rights, then you should do so. The reality is that, because our copyright laws acknowledge these rights but allow you to waive them, all publishers have put clauses in their contracts requiring you to waive these rights. What lawyers now do is put contract clauses in to give you the same or similar rights to what you would have got from using your moral rights. So you might ask why we bother with this farce. Why don't we acknowledge that the songwriter has certain rights to object to what is morally being done to his songs? Well, the essential differences are that the moral rights are wider than what you might get under your contract and a moral right is capable of being enforced by you even if your publishing company doesn't want to take any action.

Other creative controls may involve the songwriter reserving a song for himself or his band to record and stopping another artist applying for and getting a mechanical licence to record that song first. The publisher will usually agree not to issue a first mechanical licence to another artist where the songwriter wants to reserve it, but will often require that there is a time limit of, say, six months on this. If it hasn't been recorded in that time, then the restriction can be lifted. If you want to have this right when you register a song with PRS for Music you now have to write to them to say so. Previously you could just tick a box on the registration form.

Finally, of course, the songwriter will want to ensure he is properly credited.

WHAT TYPE OF DEAL SHOULD YOU DO?

How do you decide which deal is best for you? To some extent, this may be out of your control. You may not be offered anything other than an exclusive publishing agreement. You may not be able to afford to keep control of your copyrights. You may be able to afford to do so but haven't got the organisational talents necessary to make sure that your works are properly protected and the income collected. In these cases, the exclusive songwriter agreement is for you. But if you aren't bothered about getting an advance and you do want to control your copyrights, you may want to go for either a sub-publishing or an administration deal, depending on how much activity you require from your publisher.

NEW BUSINESS MODELS

As we saw in relation to management deals in Chapter 2, some managers now insist on taking an interest in your publishing as well. You also have to consider the issue of a potential conflict of interest between the manager's role as your manager and as your publisher. There are also many more package deals involving a production company acquiring rights in your recordings as well as your songs. Try to make sure that the set-up is a proper, arm's length one; that the manager/publisher/production company has thought about how he is going to administer the rights he is getting, and make sure that the manager does not take management commission on your publishing royalties for so long as he is also acting as your publisher of those songs. And, of course, there are the 360-degree deals where not only publishing and record rights are involved but also live and merchandising rights. Look back at the last chapter for the reservations I have expressed about these deals. I would always try to keep the publishing rights out of the 360-degree type deal if I could.

CONCLUSIONS

- Decide what type of publishing deal would ideally suit you: administration, sub-publishing or exclusive songwriting agreement.
- Decide if you need an advance and this will help you decide the type of deal to go for.
- You should try to do deals where your share of the income is calculated 'at source' – but if you have to have a 'receipts' deal then make sure you put a limit on what the overseas sub-publishers can deduct in their fees.
- If you're receiving 75% or more of the gross fees, you're doing well.
- Look at the Minimum Commitment. Is it realistic? Can you achieve it within a reasonable period of time?

- If you're a songwriter who doesn't also record your own works, try not to agree to a contractual commitment that means your songs have to be exploited in some way, as this will be outside your control.
- If you're a songwriter who doesn't record your own songs, hold out for no reduction in the amount of royalty you receive on 'covers'.
- Make sure there's as little delay as possible in you receiving your money from overseas.

Chapter 5

Getting a Record Made

INTRODUCTION

Just to make things a little clearer, in this chapter I'm going to assume that you've signed a record deal and that the money for making your record will come from the record company, either as a separate recording budget fund or as an all-inclusive advance. At the end of the chapter I'm going to look at other ways of making a record, for example, where you're funding the making of the record yourself, including the crowd-funding phenomenon.

PRODUCTION DEALS VERSUS DIRECT SIGNINGS

Before I go into the process of getting a record made, I need to look at two different ways of structuring a record deal. This has an impact on how the recording process is organised. We covered both types of signings in Chapter 3 – the direct signing and the production deal. Now we're going to take a closer look at the production deal and compare the pros and cons of both.

PRODUCTION DEALS

As we've seen, a production deal is one where someone (whether it's an individual, a partnership or a company) acts as a middleman between the record company and the artist. This middleman is the production company. Don't confuse this meaning of 'production' with the process of producing a record by a record producer which I'll deal with below.

Sometimes a smaller label, a record producer, or manager finds a talented artist. They may not have the necessary funds to make the record or, even if they can afford to make it, may not have the necessary wherewithal to set up decent manufacturing, distribution, marketing or promotion. They often sign up the artist and then look for a company with more resources to fund the recording and all aspects of putting out the record. In effect, they sell on the rights they have to the artist's services, either by a licence or an assignment of rights.

The contract between the production company and the artist is called a production deal. More established production companies may already have a link with one of the major labels and act as a kind of out-of-house developer.

What is a production deal?
The contract may look very similar to a record deal, more details of which are in Chapter 3. The production company could sign the artist up to record an album with options to make further albums. There may be fewer options, perhaps two or three instead of four or five. The money available will often be significantly less than in an exclusive record deal with an established, larger record company and, in some ways, may resemble a development deal. In all likelihood, the deal will be a 'net receipts' deal as opposed to one where the artist is paid a royalty as a percentage of the record sales price.

It's a little difficult to agree up-front what sort of deal might be done with the larger company. If I'm acting for the artist I usually try to ensure he gets the chance to be involved in the negotiations with that larger company whenever that happens. The larger company needs to know the artist is on side, so should want to co-operate. If the larger record company is going to pay advances to the production company, the artist will want to know that he'll get a decent share of them. Also, if the artist is on a 'net receipts' deal, he will need to know that the royalty being paid is high enough when it's split between him and the production company. For example, if the artist is on a 50:50 net receipts deal and the royalty is 18%, then he'll be on a 9% royalty, as will the production company. Maybe the artist's share should be higher – 65% or 75% instead of 50%. If you're the production company, you should work out what's a good deal for you and should be looking at getting a clear profit. A share of at least 25% is probably appropriate, but possibly higher for the first couple of albums. Obviously each negotiation is different so these percentages are guidelines only.

What's in it for the larger record company?

The larger company has the advantage of having someone else find and develop a new artist. By the time the project is brought to them they can hear what it's going to sound like. Some of the risk has been taken away. If they're licensing a finished record from a production company, they know exactly what they are getting. There's also a middleman to deal with the artist – who becomes someone else's problem. One downside for the larger company is lack of control. They need to be confident that the production company can deliver the goods, so they are more likely to trust someone who already has a track record.

What's in it for the production company?

The production company has a much closer involvement with the artist. It has the thrill of discovering an artist early and of developing him. It gets another company to take the risk on manufacture, distribution and marketing costs, but at that stage it loses overall control. If the larger company then fails in what it has to do, all the production company's work will have been wasted. For the production company it's essential they choose a larger company with a good marketing department and that they try to get a clause in the contract which allows them to insist on outside press and marketing people being brought in if necessary. If it all works out all right, the production company get their costs and expenses repaid, the financial risk on the manufacture, distribution and marketing taken off their hands, and a decent royalty into the bargain.

What's in it for the artist?

If a production company is interested in an artist, then it's a step up the ladder. If it knows what it's doing, there will be a second chance later of getting a larger company involved, one with greater resources. There should also be greater artistic and creative freedom, unless the production team are control freaks. The downside for the artist is that, if he doesn't get the deal right, he could end up sharing a larger than necessary piece of the pie with the production company. He is also a further stage removed from the larger record company that's promoting the record, so it's that much harder to get his views

147

heard, and therefore it's important that there are plenty of creative controls in the contract.

FINDING A STUDIO

Whether you are signed direct, or via a production company, or financing it yourself, one thing you'll have to do is to find a suitable recording studio. It could be as simple as the studio in your back bedroom or a full-blown commercial studio like Abbey Road or RAK and all stages in between. Before you decide on a studio, you should look at several, checking out the ambience as well as whether it has the necessary equipment. If equipment has to be hired in, it will add to the recording costs. You should listen to material produced in the studios and, if you can, talk to other artists who have used them. You should also talk to any in-house engineer or producer. How enthusiastic are they about the place and how it's run? If you have a record producer in mind or a favourite engineer, ask them what they think of the various studios on your shortlist. They will have their own favourites and some producers may have their own studios and be able to do some pre-production work there, in theory saving you some money.

You also need to think about where it is. Is it easy to get equipment in or out? Is it secure? You'll have seen stories in the press of recordings being 'leaked' from the studio on the Internet. Record companies are doing what they can to tighten security but do check if the studio keeps recordings safe and secure, and who is responsible for this. Can leaks be traced? Also, provided you can keep it safe yourself, consider making a backup copy of the final versions of the recordings and keeping it somewhere outside the studio. This might prove invaluable if there are problems of security or if the studio proves difficult in releasing the final recordings. I have known studios hold artists to ransom asking for a bigger fee in return for release of the master recordings. Most studio owners do not descend to this level, but disputes can arise over what is properly due, and the studio may legitimately have a hold over the recordings until this is resolved.

A studio can either be one that you go to day to day or a residential one where you stay in accommodation at or near the studio. Your own personal arrangements and budget might decide which is better for you. Some bands respond best when they're immersed in the project in a residential studio. For others, the idea of spending 24 hours a day, seven days a week with the other band members is their idea of hell.

STUDIO PACKAGE DEALS

The recording studio may block out a period of time and the studio is yours for the whole of that time. These arrangements are sometimes called 'lockout' deals. Other deals are for a fixed eight- or ten-hour day. If you overrun, you may either find that the studio has been hired out to someone else or that there are financial penalties. Some studios will give you discounts on their usual rate if you record at times when the studio wouldn't normally be in use, for example, in the early hours of the morning. This is called 'down time'. It's fine if you're on a very tight budget, or if you just want to record some demo tracks. But if you're planning to use down time to record your whole album, you're putting very great limitations on yourself. It's mentally and physically tough recording an album without adding to this by having to record it all at two in the morning. These deals are much less common than lockout deals.

Some studios will offer a package deal that includes mixing and mastering of the finished recordings. There are two things to bear in mind here. First, the studio must have the technical capabilities to do a good job and, secondly, the price offered should represent good value.

Your A&R man or production company representative is going to be an important source of information on where you choose to record. These people also have a vital role to play in giving you feedback on how the recording is going. It's far too easy to lock yourself away in a studio and become isolated from reality. You'll need feedback and constructive criticism. The A&R man won't be sitting at your shoulder all the way through the recordings, but he will want to visit the studio regularly during the recording process. Don't surround yourself with yes men – you'll need people who can be objective and whose opinion and judgement you respect.

Once you've chosen your studio, you need to haggle on a price – or your manager, production company or A&R man will do it for you. Before you book the time, make sure that any people are available who you want to help with the recording, such as a producer, engineer or session musicians. If you really want to work with a particular person then you may have to adjust your recording schedule to work around their availability. If they live outside the UK they may need a permit to work in this country. This can take time and has to be factored into the recording timetable. If you want to record overseas you may need visas or work permits so allow time for those to be put in place too.

Another key factor in the choice of the studio is whether you can afford it. Studio costs and fees to a producer usually make up most of the recording costs. You'll have to recoup these, so it's important that you keep an eye on them.

It is becoming quite common for a record producer to offer an all-in rate for his services which includes studio costs. This of course assumes the producer either has his own studio or open access to one. With these deals in particular you need to be sure that the studio is up to the job in hand.

THE RECORDING BUDGET

When you or your manager were pitching for your record deal you may well have done a 'back of an envelope' calculation of how much it would cost you to record the album. Now you're going to have to do a much more detailed budget. You and your manager are going to have to work out how long you think you're going to take to record the album, how many days of studio time, and what that will cost at the studio of your choice. You need to know how much your producer of choice will charge, how long a mixer will take to mix it, and what he's likely to charge. If there are session vocalists or musicians you need to know how much they will charge per day or session. There are minimum rates set by bodies like the Musicians' Union and Equity, but good people will want more than the minimum rate. By the same token some non-union musicians may offer you 'mate's rates'. If special equipment is required you need to work out how much this will cost to hire, and whether it's more cost-effective to buy it. It may be a piece of equipment that you'll need to have later when you're out on the road promoting the album. You may have an equipment budget as part of your deal, or the cost may be built into the recording budget. Another possibility is that you'll have to buy the equipment out of your personal advance.

Don't forget rehearsal time. You don't want to spend expensive studio time rehearsing the songs until you're ready to record them. Do this before you set foot in the studio. Whether you do this in a professional rehearsal room or in a room over the local chip shop will depend on your budget. Managers sometimes help out with the cost of hiring rehearsal rooms, but this will probably be on the basis that the cost must be recouped.

Once you've thought of everything, you should add at least 10% to it. This is called a contingency. It's to cover extra costs when you spend another day in the studio, or on mixing, or when you have to hire in equipment because yours or the studio's isn't up to the job.

If you have a recording fund deal, your budget should not exceed about 60% of the total advance in order to leave you with enough to live on. If you have a deal where you have an advance plus a recording budget, you'll have to keep within the maximum set by the record company, and you'll have to take your finished outline budget to them for approval. Very often the product manager at the record label will assist you in this whole process but you should, nevertheless, have an idea of whether the figures you are being told seem realistic. Bear in mind that most record contracts say that if you overrun the agreed budget without first getting clearance from the record company, you'll be liable for the extra expense. It will be deducted from your royalties and possibly also from any further advances due to you under the deal.

MASTERING AND DIGITISATION COSTS

These are a grey area. Mastering costs are the costs that are involved in getting the final mixed recordings into a state ready to be made into records. Where those records are to be made available as digital downloads then the masters have to be digitised. I'll deal with the process in a little more detail below. The record contract will say whether these costs are to be included in the recording budget or not. Mastering can cost several thousand pounds, so it's important to know this when setting your financial budget. The situation with recharge of digitisation costs is in a state of flux. Some companies treat these as part of the costs of online distribution akin to the transport costs they incur for physical distribution. Others pass on the costs as a recoupable amount. I have noticed, and there's no surprise here, that most labels are now seeking to recoup digitisation costs.

THE PRODUCER

The role of the producer has been described as getting the dynamics and emotion of the music to come out in the recording. The producer makes your material come alive. It's possible for you to produce yourself and many successful artists do. By the same token, most artists, particularly when they are starting out, might find it difficult to have the necessary distance in order to hear how the music will sound to an outsider. The producer can be your external critic. You're going to be working closely together, so it's helpful if you have similar musical tastes and influences. You have to like working with them, respect them and have a common vision of how the music should sound.

Your A&R man can be very helpful in pointing you in the direction of possible producers. They can do a lot of the filtering process. They may play your demo to a series of different producers to see who's interested. They may invite producers to come to your gigs to get a feel for how you sound. Some vocalists need a little help in the studio to keep in tune. A good producer will realise that when he hears you play live. Increasingly, the producer is, through necessity, taking on the role of a finder and developer of talent, sometimes as a formal production company but sometimes just by default as part of his role as record producer. It is this more proactive role that is leading some producers to believe they deserve a bigger piece of the pie than the fee or advance referred to below. Some set up production companies as we saw in Chapter 3. Others look for higher royalties or a share of another revenue source such as publishing income or a performer royalty. This is a thorny subject: when does a producer add sufficient to a song being recorded that he becomes entitled to say he is a co-writer and when does a producer's normal role spill over into him being a performer? The PPL already recognises a category of 'producing performer' to cover such instances. Anyone who is eligible would take a piece of the overall 50% of performing income collected by societies like PPL. The performing producer has to get the featured artist's permission before he can be registered for this share but most producers and their agents or managers do ask for this as part of the deal negotiation. Songwriting is a potential minefield, particularly with producers who also have a career as songwriters. It's a fine line and varies from project to project. If the producer makes an actual contribution to a song, e.g. changing a lyric, strengthening a melody line, then it is perhaps reasonable to acknowledge that that contribution gives him an entitlement to be credited as co-writer and to a share of publishing royalties. As with all things communication and clarification is everything. You need to establish at the outset what the expectations of both sides are and ensure that both sides can emerge from the process feeling their contribution has been properly rewarded. If, for example, a producer is producing a recording speculatively for little or no money and is having a significant say in the shaping of the material being recorded he may well expect some of the publishing income as a way of 'topping up' the low or non-existent fees he gets for his production work.

Fee or advance

A producer will usually expect to be paid a sum of money per track that they produce. This could be a pure fee, which isn't recouped; it could be an advance against the producer's royalty; or it could be part non-recoupable fee and part advance. Good producers can charge £5,000 plus per track and many of those will expect some of it to be a non-recoupable fee. Whether they get that will depend on the negotiation. If it's being recorded in the producer's studio they may include recording costs in the fee so the total may be nearer £10,000 than £5,000. That said, these rates are always negotiable and with fewer signings to major labels there are more producers chasing the work and a good project may well cause them to lower their rates. But note what I said on this above.

Royalty

The producers may just work for a fee, but they will often expect to receive a royalty calculated in the same way as the artist's record royalty is calculated. A good producer may insist on a royalty of up to 5% of the dealer price; 4% is commonplace. They may ask for increases in the royalty if sales exceed a given amount. Producers who work with very commercial acts see themselves very much as key parts of the team and charge royalties accordingly. The rates will definitely be higher if the advance is low in order to compensate for the lower up-front monies and greater risk that the record will not generate enough sales to make it commercially worthwhile.

Recoupment of costs

Another big bone of contention is whether the producer receives the royalty as soon as he has recouped any advance he has received, or if he has to also wait until his royalty, together with the artist's royalty, has also recouped the recording costs on the tracks he has produced. If he agrees to the latter, the producer may say that, once that's achieved, his royalty is calculated as if he had been paid from record one after recouping his advance. Let me give you an example:

A producer is to be paid a 3% royalty and has received a £30,000 advance. The recording costs on the tracks he worked on came to £200,000. The artist's royalty together with the producer's 3% is 12%. Say each record sold makes the artist £1.25. He'd have to sell £230,000 ÷ £1.25 = 184,000 copies of the record in order to recoup the recording costs and his own advance. Say the producer's 3% royalty earns him 31p. To recoup his £30,000 advance he'd have to sell £30,000 ÷ £0.31 = 96,774 copies. If he's on a deal where he's paid retrospectively, he would then get paid on the number of copies sold between 184,000 and 96,774 copies, i.e. 87,226 x £0.31 = another £27,040. If the artist sells 96,775 copies, the producer recoups his advance and receives the extra £27,040, but if the artist doesn't sell more than 184,000 copies, he doesn't recoup the recording costs and the producer gets no more royalties. So the producer is taking a risk, but if it pays off he gets a windfall.

The producer of an entire album is expected to wait until all recording costs have been recouped. Often it's only with great reluctance that record companies accept that the royalty should then be paid retroactive. Where the producer doesn't have to wait until any recording costs have been recouped and is paid his royalty as soon as he has recouped his advance this can be a problem for the artist. He can probably only do it if his record company agrees to advance him the money to pay the producer. The artist is unlikely to be recouped as he will have all the recording costs, video costs and so on to recoup first. This pushes the artist further into debt, but he will often agree to this if it's the only way he's going to be able to do the deal and get that particular producer but he will have to have his record label on board and the earlier the better.

Who does the contract?

In the UK it's usually the record or production company that will do the deal with the producer, issue the contract and negotiate its terms, although sometimes the artist's manager will have issued a deal memo, outlining the deal beforehand. At the very least, the artist should have approval of the royalty payable to the producer, because it will usually come out of the artist's royalty, and also approval of the advance, which will usually be a recoupable recording cost.

In the US the artist issues the contract and negotiates the deal with the producer – or his lawyer does. The contract isn't with the record company, but is between artist and producer. If the artist doesn't pay, the producer can only sue the artist, who may not have the money. In the UK the contract is between the record company and the producer, so if anything goes wrong the producer can sue the record company not the artist. This puts the producer in a more secure position. The US record company will usually do the royalty calculation and, if asked, will pay royalties direct to the producer as a favour, not as a legal obligation.

Remix royalty reduction

The royalty to the producer almost invariably comes out of the artist's royalty, so it's in the artist's interests to keep the royalty at a reasonable level. If the record is to be mixed or remixed by someone else, then a good record mixer will also want to be paid a royalty. You could try to get the record producer to agree that if the mixer is paid a royalty the producer's royalty is reduced by the same amount. Some producers will agree to this. Others are adamant that if they've done a good job of production there shouldn't be any reduction in their royalty just because the record company or artist decides to bring in another person to mix the records. If this becomes a real sticking point, it's sometimes possible to get the record company to contribute to the royalty for the mixer, perhaps by paying another 0.5%.

Credits
The producer will usually want to receive a credit on the packaging of the record, in metadata for digital releases and sometimes also in marketing material.

Sometimes a 'name' producer will insist on having the right to remove his name from the packaging if his work is remixed and he doesn't like the end result or doesn't wish to be associated with it.

Standard of work
Whether it's the artist or his record company that's doing the contract, they'll want to know that the producer's work will be of a high standard. There will probably be instalment payments to the producer so that he isn't paid in full until recordings of the required standard have been delivered. So what is that standard? Well, just as we saw with record contracts, it's usually a question of whether the producer has to deliver technically satisfactory recordings, or whether they have to be commercially acceptable. The latter is, of course, a very subjective test and the producer may well argue that he has no say in what the artist chooses to record, so it's not his fault if the finished recording isn't commercial. A common compromise is to say that it must be a first-class technical production and of at least the same high standards as the producer's previous production work on other projects.

Rights
The producer usually assigns any and all copyright he has in the sound recordings he produces to the artist (US deals) or to the record or production company (UK deals). The recordings may have been made in a studio owned by the producer. In that case there is a possibility that the producer made the arrangements for the recording to be made. If so, the producer could claim to be the

first owner of copyright. The record company will therefore want to make sure that it takes an assignment of any copyright the producer may have.

In the US they deal with it slightly differently. There the contracts will say that, for the purposes of copyright, the producer is employed by the artist. Under US copyright laws the artist owns the copyright in anything a producer creates where he is employed by the artist. This is called a 'work for hire'. If you are, in fact, doing a licence not an assignment of copyright you will want to get rid of these 'for hire' clauses in a licence deal.

The producer may perform on the recordings. He may play an instrument or programme a keyboard. He may therefore have the same rights as any other performer. The record company will therefore want to know that he has given all the necessary consents to his performances being used. The fee or advance that the producer is paid will usually include any fees for his performances.

If the producer has made any original creative contribution to the writing or composing of the music or the words then he may have rights as a co-author of that song. If the artist and producer agree on what each has contributed this isn't usually a problem. The artist will want to know that a mechanical licence will be available on standard industry terms so that the producer's share of that song can be included on the recording. If the artist has agreed to reduced mechanical royalties in the US and Canada (the so-called Controlled Compositions clauses as explained in Chapter 4), then the artist should make sure the producer accepts the same reductions. The producer may, however, refuse to do this and there is no requirement that he must agree. If the producer co-writes a number of the songs on the album this could affect the artist's ability to fulfil the Minimum Commitment requirements that he may have in his publishing deal. This must also be taken into account when agreeing what share is allocated to the producer. If a producer co-writes the songs, he will have moral rights in his work. He may also have moral rights as a performer. The contract will usually require him to waive those moral rights (for more on moral rights, see Chapter 12). If he hasn't co-written any of the songs or isn't claiming any publishing rights, the contract will require him to confirm this by giving a warranty.

Producer's duties
In addition to making sure that the production is of the required standard, it's also the job of the producer to try to keep the recording costs within the budget and to let the artist/record company know if it's likely to run over budget. The

contract will make the producer responsible for any overrun on the budget which is his fault.

The producer is responsible for getting all session musicians to complete the necessary forms, buying out their rights and getting all the necessary performers' consents. He has to deliver these signed forms to the record company with details of who did what on each recording.

He also has to keep all recordings safe and deliver them up to the record company when asked to do so. It is usual to make one or more backups. The delivery requirement includes all outtakes, i.e. recordings that didn't end up in the final mix on the record.

One case in which these 'outtakes' then found their way onto a commercially released record involved Bruce Springsteen.

The Springsteen Case (Springsteen v. Flute International Limited & Others [1998] Ch Div.)
Bruce Springsteen had had agreements early in his career with a record company called Flute. Those agreements had been declared to be void from the outset in a previous court case. Springsteen therefore argued that he was the owner of the copyright in all previous recordings, including any outtakes or other unreleased material. He couldn't produce any evidence in court to back up his claim that all copyrights had been reassigned to him, but the court accepted that he was the owner of the sound recording copyright and therefore could control what happened with them. The court decided he was within his rights to claim that CDs containing outtakes of his recordings released by Flute were an infringement of his rights.

While a record company is unlikely to risk upsetting an artist by releasing records containing outtakes whilst the artist is still under contract, it may not have any such qualms after the end of that contract. The producer will have handed those outtakes over to the record company, so the artist's agreement with the record company should cover what can or can't be done with those outtakes, e.g. giving the artist a right of approval over their use at any time.

MIXING

This is the stage between production (i.e. the recording and capturing of the essence of the song) and mastering (when the recording is made ready for duplication) or digitisation.

The mixer selects from all the various recordings he has of a song those that will be mixed together to make up the final version. He also chooses which aspects to emphasise, for example a guitar part or a vocal might be brought into more prominence.

The producer might do the mix and, as he's been close to the recording process throughout, you'd think he would be best placed for the job. He may be, but very particular talents are required for mixing and sometimes a fresh 'ear' can hear things that the producer and the artist can't.

There are also mixers who take the finished, fully mixed recording and play around with it – maybe changing the rhythm or bringing in elements either sampled from the recordings themselves or from elsewhere. These are called remixers and the resulting recordings are called remixes. When samples are being introduced from other recordings as part of this process, the artist has to make sure that all necessary rights have been cleared and that the mixer has permission to include them (see Chapter 13). Remixes are often done to create a different sound for radio or to play in clubs or to refresh an old record on re-release.

MIX CONTRACTS

The contracts for mixers and remixers are very similar to and follow the same format as producer contracts.

Fees and advances

A mixer or remixer may only receive a non-recoupable, one-off fee for his work. This can be as much as £10,000-plus for one track to be remixed by a big name (if it includes recording costs).

Increasingly mixers demand an advance, which as with producer deals is sometimes partly non-recoupable, and partly on account of royalties. The same comments apply here as with producer deals above.

Royalties

If a mixer has enough bargaining power, he can ask for and get a royalty of up to 1.5–2% and 1% royalty rates are now commonplace. The royalty is usually calculated in the same way as the artist's royalty. As we saw with producer deals, the artist has to work out if there is enough left for him after producers and mixers have received royalties, whether the producer will take a reduced royalty, and whether a royalty has to be paid to a mixer, or if he will take a fee instead.

These same issues apply to mixer deals as to producer deals: who does the contract, whether the mixer gets his royalty only after all mix costs have been recouped, and what standard of work is expected of him.

Rights

As with producer deals, the record company will usually require the mixer to assign any sound recording copyright to the record company. Remixers sometimes argue for the right to retain a separate sound recording copyright in their mix. It's possible, if they have added enough original elements or have re-recorded the track as part of the remix process, to create a separate sound recording copyright. I think if I was the artist I would be nervous about some mixers owning a version of my track, and I'd want to have restrictions on what they could do with it. If they just wanted to put it on one of their own record compilations that might be all right. If I were the record company who had paid for the remixes, I'd want to own them, and perhaps license rights back to the mixers for that compilation.

Mixers don't usually contribute to the creative writing of the song. Some remixers may claim that they have added enough original elements to create a new work. This may be true, depending on what they have done, but more likely they will be said to have made a new arrangement of it and, if agreed, can receive performance income on that version. This eats into the writer's performing income and most publishers will expect it to come out of the writer's share. This must be agreed with the publisher. The remix contract could ask the mixer to confirm he has no interest in the underlying song at all which is preferable. As we saw with producer contracts, if he is a co-author the contract will say that licences to use the remixer's part of the song will be granted without difficulties on usual industry terms.

MASTERING

This is part of the post-production process when the recordings have been produced and mixed to everyone's satisfaction.

The final stage before the recording goes to be manufactured into records is mastering. It covers aspects of both recording and manufacturing. It's not just a mechanical process of ensuring all the right digital notes are in the right places.

It's the means to give it a final 'tweaking' before the record is released. A person skilled in mastering can make the sound punchier, warmer, deeper or louder. He can bring out details not already obvious. Mastering is a separate process from the mix and needs a different set of 'ears'. Some bands swear by a particular person mastering their records in much the same way as film directors have their favourite editors.

The mastering process helps the recording sound great no matter what medium it's manufactured in and whatever hardware it's played on. I'm sure you can think of albums that sound fantastic played over headphones on your iPod but awful on the car CD player. This could be a problem of the mix, but it's just as likely that someone didn't get the mastering process right.

When mastering a recording, equalising and compression of the sounds gives a consistency from track to track. Have you ever found yourself constantly having to adjust the volume between tracks on a compilation? It's either earth-shatteringly loud or so quiet you're straining to hear the words. That's an example of bad mastering. Radio really brings out the difference, as the radio process itself compresses the material. If a recording hasn't been properly mastered it can sound thin and weak.

Purists also believe that the compression involved in creating an MP3 loses a great deal of the original, in particular the top and/or bottom registers. The average listener will not know what he is missing, and most now consume their music on a less-than-studio-quality phone, tablet or through tinny headphones, so no one is any the wiser. But some wonder if we aren't cheapening the listening experience.

When you've spent a small fortune on making a recording, you shouldn't spoil it for a few thousand pounds in mastering costs.

The person doing the mastering is engaged to do the job by the record or production company. He either provides the mastering suite and equipment or the company hires or pays for one. He is paid a fee for his work. The record company usually pays it and, depending on the contract, will either treat it as a recoupable recording cost or as a non-recoupable manufacturing cost.

DELIVERY REQUIREMENTS

There are a number of things that have to be delivered to the record company before the artist can be said to have completed his side of the recording process.

As well as the finished, fully mixed and edited recordings, he will also have to deliver up all outtakes and all copies of the recordings. He may also have to deliver finished recordings of additional tracks to act as B-sides or bonus tracks, and will definitely have to deliver up all signed session forms and clearances for any samples that have been used in the recording.

The artist will have to deliver a list of all the tracks on the record in the order in which they appear (called a track-listing). He'll also have to provide 'label copy'; that is, all the information that has to appear on the label and packaging of the record. This includes things like who performed on each track, who wrote each track and who publishes those songwriters. If there is an agreement to give credits to producers and mixers or a name check to the studio, then those details will have to be given to the record company. This is also when the artist gets to say thanks to particular people who have been helpful or supportive.

The contract will be very specific about what has to be delivered and to whom. It will also be quite technical about the form in which the recordings are to be delivered. It's very important that the artist delivers all that is required of him. If he doesn't, then he'll find that all sorts of things don't happen. He won't get the instalment of advances due on delivery; the manufacturing process won't start, time will not start running for when the record company has to release the record.

The artist should try to get written confirmation from the record company confirming that everything has been delivered from the person identified in the contract as the person to whom delivery has to be made, for instance, the head of A&R or label head.

ARTWORK

One key item that usually has to be delivered is the artwork for the cover of the album. Without the artwork the record can't be released in its physical form and rather naff generic 'covers' have to be used for digital downloads, so it may be reasonable to assume (depending on the contract and individual circumstances) that delivery has not taken place until the record company has the finished artwork.

Some talented bands do the artwork themselves. Some leave it to the record company's art department. Many hire someone else to do a design to their brief or specification.

If the record company is doing it the artist should try to make sure he has final approval. If someone else is being brought in make sure they have a good, professional reputation for their work. The artist should look at covers he admires and who designed them. It's wise to interview a few designers and ask to see examples of their work. Remember that if a potential customer doesn't know who you are, they may be attracted to pick up your CD or vinyl record by the striking artwork on the cover or by an image used online. You could use art students or friends to do it on the cheap, but then you could end up spending a lot of time supervising the work, might end up with a sub-standard product, and would have been better off using a professional in the first place.

The artist's logo should be on the artwork as well as the label or production company logo and name. This is all part of making the package look inviting and identifiably part of your image. Striking artwork and logos repeated on the website and in any other marketing and promotional material not only make the association easier but also help to brand the artist, and to make his work stand out from the crowd. Sometimes artwork is used as a marketing tool in itself, either by design or by accident. Take the artwork for a Beck album. It was released with a variety of different stickers that the buyer could use to customise his own copy. The company in charge of the Charts decided that there were too many versions to count for the album charts and debarred the release. This potential disaster was turned into a classic example of 'marketing' spin to raise awareness of the album in the press and amongst the public.

Once the artist has decided on a designer who he thinks can do a good job in the required time, terms need to be agreed. You need a contract setting out what they are going to do, by when and for how much. You may want to make payment in two instalments, one when they start work and the other when they deliver satisfactory finished work.

If photographs are to be used, the artist needs to agree who is going to be responsible for supplying those and at whose expense. The record company will usually organise and pay for a photo-shoot, but it may not necessarily be with the top-name photographer the artist would like to use if the budget won't stretch to it.

Whether or not there are to be photographs, there needs to be an agreement with the designer or photographer that confirms that the person commissioning the work is the owner of the copyright in the photographs and the copyright as well as any design rights in the artwork and graphics. There should be an assignment of any copyright or design rights they might have acquired. Ideally, there should be no restrictions on what can be done with those designs and photographs. However, designers and photographers are now wise to the fact that they can earn more money if you have to go back to them for permission to re-use their work. For example, they may now agree to license the artwork or photo for the album cover only. If the artist wants to use it on a poster, T-shirt or other merchandise, or as a backdrop on live stage shows, then he'll have to come back to the photographer or designer for further permission. If they give it – and they don't have to – then they will probably want another fee for it.

The cost of commissioning someone to create original artwork depends on who you use, but record companies don't usually want to pay more than about £2–3,000 for the basic design. They will go higher if it's a top designer or 'name'. The record company doesn't usually have any rights to use the artwork in any form of merchandise other than sales of the album, so it will only be interested in getting album cover rights. If the artist thinks he'll want it for other purposes, he'll probably have to pay for those himself. The cost of originating the artwork is usually non-recoupable and the record company will usually give the artist the right to use the artwork for other purposes, for example, for merchandising, if he pays 50% of the origination costs.

The value that attaches to a distinctive artwork design was highlighted by the application for an injunction made by Creation Records (Oasis' record label at the time) against the publishers of various newspapers, including the *Sun*.

The Oasis Case (Creation Records Limited v. News Group Limited EMLR 444 1997 16)
Oasis was going to release an album in the autumn of 1997 and decided that the photograph for it should be taken at a country hotel. Noel Gallagher, the lead guitarist and deviser of the band's artwork, had a particular idea in mind, a kind of homage to The Beatles and their cover of the *Sergeant Pepper* album. The hotel swimming pool was drained and a number of different objects were delivered to the hotel, including a white Rolls-Royce. This was lowered into the pool at an angle and Noel Gallagher supervised how the other objects were to be placed. A professional photographer took a number of photos from various angles so that the band had a choice of different images in different lights. Oasis thought it was essential that the plans for the photography were kept secret, and only a few people were allowed in on it.

Inevitably, perhaps, word leaked out and a couple of newspaper photographers turned up including one freelancer attached to the *Sun*. One of the photos he took was published a few days later in the *Sun*. It was very similar to the one chosen for the album cover, but had been shot from a different angle. The *Sun* offered copies of the photo for sale to readers in a poster form. Although other newspapers also published photos, it seems none was very clear and none was offering posters of them for sale.

Creation got an immediate injunction restraining the *Sun* from publishing any more photos or from offering copies for sale. The Judge then had to decide if that injunction should continue.

Creation Records were arguing that the freelance photographer had infringed their copyright or had breached confidence.

The Judge rejected the argument that the way the scene was put together attracted a copyright as a dramatic work. He also rejected the argument that the scene was a work of artistic craftsmanship, a sculpture or a collage (those lawyers were trying hard, weren't they!). A film set can sometimes be said to be a work of artistic craftsmanship, but the Judge decided that this was just an assembly of disparate objects without the necessary element of craftsmanship.

Creation Records and Oasis might have been thought to be on stronger ground in arguing that there was copyright in it as an artistic work of collage – being a collection of unrelated items. Their barrister argued that it should be put in the same category as the infamous Carl André bricks displayed at the Tate Gallery or Gilbert and George's living sculptures. The Judge declined to agree with that line of argument, as the assembly of objects didn't have the same degree of permanence – it was going to be dismantled after a few hours. This is a very restricted view of what would be entitled to copyright protection.

The Judge did, however, find that there was copyright in the photograph, but the *Sun* didn't copy that original – the freelancer took his own photograph of the same scene. This was why Creation Records was trying to establish some kind of copyright in the scene.

So, having failed on all their ingenious copyright arguments, the lawyers then argued that the freelance photographer had breached confidentiality. Here they had more luck. The Judge decided that any reasonable person would have assumed that, in viewing the scene, they were getting confidential information and so the freelance photographer was obliged not to photograph the scene. The *Sun* had admitted their photographer had to get around a security cordon to get the film out, so they must have known it was intended to be confidential.

On balance, the Judge decided Oasis/Creation Records had more to lose if the *Sun* were to continue to be allowed to sell posters and continued the injunction on the basis of breach of confidence. If he had not, then potentially huge sales of posters and other merchandise by the band and their record label would have been lost.

Once the artwork is delivered, the artist should then be in a position to press for a release date for the album. This will depend on a huge number of factors, some of which I'll deal with in the next chapter, but once a provisional date has been set, then the manufacturing process can begin for the physical release, and the online set-up, marketing and promotion should start to swing into action.

If the artist or production company intends to release a record themselves then they will also attend to all the other formalities such as sample and session work clearances, obtaining barcodes, getting a mechanical licence and paying the licence fees. These are dealt with in more detail in Chapter 6. The other thing they have to worry about of course is getting the necessary funding. In this area there have been a number of initiatives. In 2013 the PRS for Music Foundation in conjunction with the Arts Council, England set up the Momentum Music Fund providing a pot of over £500,000 of funding for grant applications from artists seeking sums of between £5,000 and £15,000 to further their careers. Bands and artists from many parts of the country have benefited including Laura Mvula, Let's Eat Grandma and Ghostpoet, and decisions on who to give grants to is made by a panel of industry representatives. For more details check out www.prsformusicfoundation.com. The BBC Music Horizons project, which helps new Welsh bands reach a wider audience, will be extended by an extra year into 2018.

Then there is the crowd-funding craze which began in the US and is not unique to the music business. All sorts of businesses use it to raise funding. It even has its own association, The UK Crowdfunding Association, which claimed at its 2016 general meeting that its members had facilitated fundraising of in excess of £5 billion. There is usually a platform, a website where investors can check out offerings that they might want to get involved in. Examples of platforms aimed at the music business are Pledge or Kickstarter. The idea is that in return for certain benefits you invite people to invest varying sums of money into your business. For example, you want to raise the funding to record an album. You may offer potential investors, many of whom may be actual or potential fans, to pay say £2 to get a copy of the album when it's finished and before general release. But the offerings get ever more inventive. On one recent crowd-funding I was involved in the band got most money, £800 a time, from those who wanted to have the opportunity to sing as backing singers on the album. The next favourite was to receive copies of the CD signed by the band – a snip at £20. For one thousand dollars fans of a Californian band, Ozma, received a signed copy of the album and a hand-written lyric sheet. American Idol contestant, Scott Macintyre, offered, amongst other things, for his Kickstarter campaign a personal phone call and email and a 'follow' on Twitter from his official account. Others have offered tickets to secret gigs. Crowdsourcing service Indiegogo announced it had teamed up with Island Records in February 2014 to launch a new music-based fan-funding operation called Fan Republic. The site is also intended to act as a talent-scouting resource for Island's A&R team. According to its website it has facilitated 11 campaigns so far, raising $78,041. Increasingly crowdfunding through services like Pledge are used to raise funds for marketing campaigns and direct to fan engagement.

CONCLUSIONS

- Choose your studios well. Decide if they'll be residential or not.
- Set a reasonable recording budget and stick to it.
- Get the best producer and mixer you can afford and be clear on their terms.
- Don't skimp on mastering costs, but keep an eye on remix costs, as these can get very high.
- Check you've complied with the delivery requirements in your contract.
- Try to get copyright ownership of the artwork.

Chapter 6

Manufacture and Distribution

INTRODUCTION

Until about ten years ago there was no serious viable alternative to the tried and tested method of distribution, whereby you finished your record, it was mastered and 'cut' – literally cut into the vinyl or digitally mastered (i.e. put in digital form in a computer program from which digital records such as CDs and DATS could be made). The physical CD, tape, or vinyl record was then packaged up and distributed out to the record stores in the back of a van.

This all changed with the shift to online, digital releases. As we will see in the next chapter, at first this took the form of digital downloads and it was therefore possible to replicate the physical distribution with distribution deals for online sales. This has changed again with the shift to streaming, where the distributors are, if you like, the ISPs like Apple Music and Google. Although illegal downloads remain a major problem and challenge, the industry began to turn a corner commercially with the arrival of services such as iTunes and there was a rapid increase in the number of companies providing online distribution services – some alongside physical distribution and some as digital download distributors only. Such was the growth in the digital side of the business that there grew up a class of middlemen 'aggregators' who sign up labels and artists and then offer the catalogue to a bigger online distributor. There is no longer a commercial physical singles market and all single tracks are now being offered as permanent digital downloads alone or bundled, or by means of streaming, many on sites like iTunes or on individual artists' web pages or online stores. Many album or EP releases are now digital only. Artists or small labels don't want to go to the expense of pressing up physical copies of a record; they wait first to see how well the online release goes in publicity terms. Major record companies have either pulled out of physical distribution themselves or are combining their manufacturing and distribution operations either in one place in Europe or through deals with other companies. By pulling out of these two traditional means of earning profits, the record companies may be saving millions of pounds in overheads but they are also focusing their money-making activities on the more risky aspects of the business, the marketing and promotion of artists and their records. So the stakes are now higher and the pressure on to get these aspects right more often than they do at the moment. This of course feeds into the more cautious outlook referred to in Chapter 3 on record contracts and on the greater use of middleman production companies to filter out some of the artists less likely to succeed commercially. It is also reflected in the growing requirement of the major labels that they participate in income from other areas of an artist's working life such as live gigs through the 360-degree rights deals we saw in Chapter 3.

In an effort to target the numbers of artists and small labels releasing records themselves the major labels (and some of the independents) have started to offer label services, a kind of pick and mix of services you can buy in from them as needed. These are looked at in more detail below. And finally, of course, there is the commercial revenue to be earned off streaming and the unique challenges involved in shifting consumer habits to subscription models, the problems of obtaining fair value for such uses and transparent accounting. More of this in Chapter 7.

MANUFACTURING

The compact disc remains a significant carrier of albums, even though year-on-year sales have declined. In 2015 it formed less than 50% of the market for the first time. The prediction of the death of vinyl was premature. It survives and thrives in a startling way, beloved by DJs and specialist collectors and in fact at one point in November 2016 the number of vinyl records sold exceeded downloads. Now who would have predicted that? Sales of vinyl albums were up to 3.2 million in 2016 representing a 53% increase on 2015's total.

Most mainstream albums and certainly those released on major labels are still made available in physical format and many artists are insisting on a vinyl pressing. This is putting pressure on the few remaining digital pressing plants – largely in continental Europe – so new ones are having to hurriedly be brought back on stream. Long lead times are reported for a vinyl release so plan ahead. Independent releases and self-releases now tend to be digital only. If you have a publishing deal then you have to be careful to make sure that a digital-only release will fulfil your Minimum Commitment. That will often specify a physical release in reasonable commercial numbers. If you've paid for the recording yourself or via a production company, then you won't have a record company to organise the manufacturing for you. You're going to have to seek out specialist CD manufacturers and shop around for a deal. You need to make your arrangements with manufacturers at least four months before you intend to release physical copies of your record, and even longer at popular times such as Christmas. This is to try to ensure that the manufacturing/pressing plant has capacity and won't squeeze your record out because a release by a big star is slotted in, but it is also in order to give you enough time to set up the promotional and marketing aspects of your release. Until a couple of years ago it was usual to release records to radio stations (via pluggers if necessary – see below) at least a month before they were available in the shops. There was considerable pressure to reduce this time lag by retailers and etailers as the long time gap between a fan being able to hear a new track by their favourite artist on the radio and being able to buy it legally was driving a significant proportion of these fans to get the tracks in the form of illegal downloads. In July 2016 the general release date for new records in the UK was moved from Monday to Friday, ostensibly to be more in tune with international release dates and with a view to thereby reduce the chances of piracy and increase legitimate sales.

When picking your manufacturer, you also need to ask what services each company provides. Is it a full-service company that will produce a production master from which to reproduce the CDs, or will you have to find a company to make a production master for you and deliver that together with the artwork to the manufacturer? If so, would it be cheaper, easier and quicker if you looked for a full-service company? You'll need to check the small print very carefully. What hidden costs are there? Do they charge you to deliver the finished records to you? Can they offer a distribution service or any marketing services such as sales teams? If they do, is it better to use them for these services or to look for separate companies to do them? Look at the quality of their work. Ask to see samples. Do they do everything in-house or is it farmed out? Who else do they work for? Can you get recommendations?

Once you've narrowed down your choice, you have to look at how quickly they can turn things around. They may have a minimum production run (say 5,000 copies). Is that all right for you or were you looking for a more modest 500 copies? To be honest, if you're going for a very short production run, possibly for promotional purposes, you might be better off burning the CDs and putting the finished product together yourself.

Once you've decided on your manufacturer, you'll need to agree a price, the number of units to be produced and a time for delivery. You ought to try to keep some of their fee back until you see things are running according to plan, but if you're a small unknown company they're likely to want cash up-front. Even so, keep an eye on things. Check the quality of the sound and of the artwork. Is the running order correct without any gaps in the songs? Have all the names been spelled correctly and correct credits given? If anything is wrong, pull them up on it immediately. Always check a sample of the finished product.

You also have to be sure that they can continue to manufacture repeat orders as your first batch, hopefully, sells out. You need to keep close contact between your distributor and your manufacturer so that you can put your repeat order in as soon as your distributor sees stocks are dwindling. This need for close co-operation is one of the reasons why some people prefer to keep production and distribution with the same company.

P&D DEALS

As you can probably guess, 'P' stands for production (i.e. manufacture) and 'D' for distribution. A P&D deal is one that combines both of these services in one contract with one company. Companies that offer P&D deals can often also offer marketing services like a telephone sales team (telesales), a strike force (a specialised team targeting record stores to take your records) or pluggers, who try to persuade radio stations to play your record. Whether you want these additional services will depend on your overall marketing plan and on the price and reliability of the service.

You should ask the same questions of P&D companies as you would of a manufacturer, but you'll also have to ask another set of questions about their distribution operation. Who do they supply records to? Is it just the small specialist stores or can they get into the few remaining retail chains and do they supply major supermarkets?

MAJORS VERSUS INDIES

Until recently all the major record companies had their own distribution facilities. Mergers in recent years have resulted in some of those facilities being combined to save costs by pooling operations. The recession of 2008/2009 had a major impact on the physical distribution network in the UK as well as on the high street retail stores. We lost Woolworths, Zavvi (aka Virgin Megastores) and more recently many of the HMV stores, leaving many towns without any high-street record store. HMV has since staged somewhat of a comeback in the UK at least, and in the twelve weeks to 25 September 2016 it overtook Amazon to become the UK's largest physical music retailer. It did not do so well in Canada where it went into liquidation in January 2017 and it was announced that over 100 stores would close. Other retailers like Fopp and a plethora of small town independent stores are also trading on the upsurge in vinyl sales.

As a direct consequence of the decline in high-street competition the big supermarket chains now dominate the retail market, driving down the cover price of CDs and ultimately therefore the dealer price and price on which the artists receive a royalty. A side effect of their dominance has been greater emphasis on mainstream releases as opposed to the more risky offerings of the indie labels. This has all helped reinforce the growing conservatism about what to release. Supermarkets like Sainsbury's have dipped in and out of CD sales and Sainsbury's also started to stock vinyl records in certain stores in 2016. There are some chinks of light – a growth in independent retailers and a number of 'pop-up' temporary stores in shopping malls and more unlikely places as busy Christmas periods as well as the success of Record Store Days has helped to promote the independent stores.

Of course, one direct effect of the decline in the numbers of retail outlets has been a greater focus on online, digital distribution and, of course, mail order sales via online retailers like Amazon.

Digital distribution deals have tended to follow the principles laid down in physical product distribution contracts, although without issues such as warehousing costs, stock losses etc., which means they are somewhat simpler than their physical equivalent.

The independent sector has companies like PIAS, Proper, Believe and Absolute but also check out other niche distributors online.

Without an efficient distribution system, all your talents and efforts in making the record and the marketing people's work in getting you noticed will mean nothing if the distribution company doesn't have the records in the stores or available for download for the public to buy or stream.

All distributors have to balance efficiency with a speedy response. If they can't meet demand quickly, your records won't be available, the customers won't be able to buy them and you won't get your chart position. I had an horrendous situation where someone within the distributor label failed to upload a single for a download in the week of release. The physical sales alone meant that it charted outside the Top 10. The label pulled all further spend on promotion, failed to push the album and ultimately the artist was dropped.

As well as dealing with their own artists' records, some of the majors act as separate distribution companies for other companies' records as well as now all offering some form of label service to small, independent labels or artists.

If you aren't signed to a major or can't get a deal with a major distribution company, you may not have any alternative but to go to an independent distributor.

You also need to be aware that some smaller distributors are a bit like production companies and pass on the job of actual distribution to another company. If that's what your chosen distributor does, you should try to find out how reliable and financially stable that other company is, particularly in the light of the events of the last couple of years. As we'll see below, there are some things you can do to protect yourself by retaining ownership of the records until you've been paid.

LABEL SERVICES

Whilst not entirely new, in the sense that some distributers would say they have been offering these kinds of services for years, what is new is the extent to which they are being offered by the major labels and are being targeted at independent labels and artists.

These deals allow the artist or indie label to pick and choose the elements they require. For example, you may have marketing covered in the UK but need some marketing help overseas. Artists who have benefited successfully from these deals include Nick Cave, Travis and Noel Gallagher's 'High Flying Birds'.

And it is not just the majors who are offering these deals. Some companies better known perhaps as traditional distributors like PIAS or the label services division of Kobalt, better known for its publishing and more recently neighbouring rights collection services and BMG Rights Management offering a one-stop rights clearance service for songs and recordings.

Advantages of these deals are that the artist or indie label is not locked exclusively into the deal. The artist retains ownership of the copyright and can control how he is presented. The artist/label is also in control of the services it needs and has much greater transparency on the finances.

The downsides are that there may no advance and so investment either has to come from the artist or a third party. This may mean that these deals are better suited to more established artists but, in theory at least, the same services could be used to launch a new act, as indeed was shown by Warner's ADA division with Macklemore & Ryan Lewis. In 2016 Sony announced a commercial tie-in for label services with long-standing independent label, Cooking Vinyl.

When an artist chooses the non-traditional route to release his records there is undoubtedly a greater workload on him and on his manager. Indeed, the manager may be the one that fronts up the investment to get the project off the ground. This might prompt a re-think as to whether it is appropriate in these circumstances for the manager to continue to just earn his 20% management commission. Then again, the potential profit margin is also much higher and the accounting probably more frequent so it is not a foregone conclusion that the manager should be remunerated in some other way.

What do these deals cost? Well, as usual it's negotiable and down to your bargaining power and things like your likely turnover. Distribution rates as low as 5% of net receipts are possible but perhaps 15–20% is more usual. Similarly for the other services in some cases a flat fee might be appropriate, in others a percentage of net receipts. Sometimes the label will advance a marketing fund but if they do then it will be recoupable.

Label services are either coordinated centrally, as you would find with a worldwide exclusive recording contract, or they are on a territory by territory basis as you might find with a series of separate licence deals. But remember, the service company does not own your rights and you can be very flexible as to how you use the services.

CATALOGUE OR SINGLE RELEASE DISTRIBUTION DEAL

Most of what follows in this section is geared towards physical distribution as well as online downloads. Distributors will often offer both physical and online distribution, although some specialise in only online distribution. Streaming services are dealt with separately in Chapter 7.

So are you doing a deal for all the records you're likely to produce in the next year or so? These are called 'catalogue deals' and would be suitable for a small record label or production company. They would also work for a company that was going to license in rights to records by other artists, and also for an artist who has decided that he doesn't want or need the facilities of a record company and wants to distribute his own recordings. In recent years some very successful artists have bypassed record labels. Radiohead looked like they were going down that road when they announced online sales of their album at prices to be set by the customer. However, they used a traditional record label for first international and then physical distribution of this new album. In a variation on this Beyoncé released an album just before Christmas 2013 in both audio and visual versions providing full length videos for each track. It was exclusively available on iTunes, thereby upsetting the usual retail outlets and other etailers. There had been no prior warning and no marketing build-up. The first fans and the industry knew of it was on Twitter. Following perhaps in the steps of David Bowie who released an album earlier in 2013 with no prior build-up or anyone even knowing he was recording it, and again shortly before his death in 2016. Once again this shows that a new angle can often drive significant sales, but would this campaign have worked for an artist with a much lower profile?

If you aren't doing a catalogue deal, you could just give distribution rights for a single release to a distribution company. You might choose this route if you were just seeing this release as a stepping stone to getting a record company interested in you. Just bear in mind, though, that, if the distributor is only dealing with one release for you, you'll not have much bargaining power and will have to push hard to ensure that you get any kind of priority. These days you'd probably elect to raise profile by doing an online release of a single track yourself with some marketing.

EXCLUSIVE VERSUS NON-EXCLUSIVE

Catalogue distribution deals are likely to be exclusive, but there may be one or two exceptions to the exclusivity. For example, you could have the right to put tracks on compilations or to distribute small quantities of the records yourself to one or two specialist outlets, or to sell at your gigs.

Term

This is really only relevant for exclusive catalogue deals.

The distributor deals with your entire product over a period of time. This could be open-ended, continuing until one of you gives notice, usually three months' notice at least. Other possibilities are a firm period of one year with the distributor having the option to extend the term for another year. Or the term could be for one year with further one-year extensions unless you give notice before the end of that time that you don't want it to carry on. You have to be careful with this one because, unless you're good at remembering when to give notice, or have an efficient reminder system, you might miss the relevant 'window' and find yourself locked in for another twelve months. Some distributors are now insisting on three years initially, but that is usually negotiable.

If you think you might want to move your label and catalogue at some point to a bigger distributor or major, the more flexible the term is and the easier it is for you to get out of it will be important. It could also be very important if you aren't sure how good the distributor is. On the other hand, the distributor might have greater commitment to you and be more inclined to give you priority if they know you're going to be with them for a pre-determined minimum period of time.

Territory

The distribution deal for online sales will usually be a worldwide one, but a physical distribution deal may be for a limited number of countries, for example just for the UK or the UK and rest of Europe. If you're a UK artist or label looking to distribute your records beyond Europe (for example to the US), then you're much more likely to do it through licensing the rights to another record company with its own distribution set-up (see Chapter 3). It is possible to have deals where you ship finished records to a licensee and they distribute them. They are sometimes referred to as 'consignment' or 'sale and return' deals and

Japanese labels are quite keen on them, as are some Canadian and US labels where it isn't worth them manufacturing copies locally, and it is cheaper for them to do it on a sale or return basis.

There is a problem, though, with physical distribution deals for just one country, for example the UK, and that is imports or, more particularly, what is often referred to as 'parallel imports'. For example, you have the rights to distribute a particular track in the UK. Another record company has the rights to distribute the same record in France. If the record is released in France first, the French record company could export the records into the UK, where they might take some of your market from under you. You may think that wouldn't be allowed as they only have French distribution rights, but there is the principle of a common marketplace throughout the European Union (EU), which is meant to encourage the free movement of goods. So, within the EU, it's illegal for you to outlaw these imports. You can tell the French distributor that he isn't to actively try to get orders from outside France, but it's very difficult to police it. How do you know who approached who?

It's easier, in theory, to prevent parallel imports coming in from outside the EU. For example, if you were giving one UK distributor European distribution rights and licensed the rights to a record company in the US for North America, your contract with the US record company could specify that they aren't allowed to ship records outside the US. The problem is that there are specialised exporting companies who also act as genuine domestic distributors. The US record label could legitimately sell records to such a company and then deny any knowledge or responsibility if that company then exports the records to the UK.

This is why you might try to ensure that a record is released simultaneously in as many countries as possible, or to ensure that there is something special about the release. For example, Japan, which has suffered badly from cheap imports, often insists that releases in Japan have extra 'bonus' tracks to make the records more attractive to the domestic market than the imports.

There is also pressure on price levels within the EU. The idea is that, if the dealer prices are the same throughout the EU, there is less demand for imports which are cheaper than the domestic product.

Rights granted
If you're doing a P&D deal you'll be required to give the distributor the right to reproduce the sound recording and the right to distribute and sell those copies whether that is as physical copies or in the form of digital downloads.

Price

The distributor will take a fee off the top of the price they get paid. So, for example, if the distributor gets paid £6 for each record sold, they take a percentage of that as their fee.

The percentage can vary a great deal depending on how many additional services they provide, for example, a telesales service or a strike force dedicated to pushing your records. It can be as high as 28–30% of the dealer price if you're unknown or only have one track to distribute. Deals of 15–18% or less are available to successful independent companies with a high turnover of successful product or to well-known artists or those with a guaranteed fan base. Major record companies can pay distribution fees in single figures but that will often be based on volume sales. Sometimes the percentage the distributor gets as a fee goes down as the turnover increases. A good average amount for a distributor to charge in respect of physical product would be 20% to independent record labels or artist production companies. And as we saw in Chapter 3 disputes rumble on about the correct basis of paying royalties on digital sales.

The distributor will also usually have a discount policy. This is a sliding scale of discounts on the dealer price that have to be given to the various retail outlets. For example, major national supermarket chains would be able to command a discount on the price because they order in bulk and are such important outlets for the music. You'll have little or no say on these discount rates, nor have a chance to change them. However, you should know what they are in order to check you're being paid properly. Discounts haven't yet fully established themselves in the online world but as volume increases then they may well follow.

Payment terms

The distributor will often pay half of what is due within 30–45 days of receiving the payment from the retailers and the balance within 60–80 days. So if they get paid for a record sold on 28 February, the label might get half of their money by the end of March and the rest by the middle of April. Make sure that for online sales all the necessary technical requirements of the online distributor are in place to ensure that you can track the number of sales and check whether you are getting paid correctly, not just for online sales, but also the payment of mechanical royalties for reproduction of your songs. As we will see in the chapter on collection societies, there are now licensing systems and rates set for most uses. The challenge now is to ensure that these rates are paid.

So check who is responsible for ensuring mechanicals are paid – you, the distributor or the retailer. Many small labels fall down on this assuming the distributor is deducting and paying it; some do but not all.

The distributor will probably keep back some of the money due to you as a reserve against records which are returned. This, of course, only applies to physical sales as, in theory at least, the customer should not pay for a download which fails. Distributors usually have a fixed policy on this, but will sometimes negotiate the level of reserves. The reserve on albums is higher if the album has been advertised on television. Retail stores may take copies of your record on a sale-or-return basis. So, although the distributors have sent out, say, 1,000 copies, they don't know how many have actually been sold and won't include these copies as sales until they've been paid. They keep back a reserve against these returns and any other returns that appear to be sales (i.e. they've been shipped out but may be returned to the distributor for some legitimate reason such as being damaged or faulty). The distributor has to hold back money against the possibility of them being returned.

The distributor won't usually take responsibility for bad debts. It also won't usually pay out before it gets paid, because that can lead to big problems. For example, you do a P&D deal with a local distributor who agrees to pay out on the number of records it actually sends out, less a reserve against returns. It ships out 1,000 copies of a record to the retail stores and pays you on 750 copies, keeping back a 25% reserve, until it has received payment of the 1,000 sales. Months later, the stores return not 250 but 500 copies; the distributor is then out of pocket by 250 copies and will look to you to pay it back. Even worse for you is the case where you do a deal with a local distributor who pays you on what it gets paid. It does a deal with a bigger distribution company and ships records to that bigger company. The bigger company sells those records but, for whatever reason, fails to pay the smaller distributor, who can't then pay you (even though records have been sold) because they haven't been paid for them. This problem should not arise to the same extent with online sales because once the customer has paid and received his download there is a limited possibility of returns.

Retention of title
A way of protecting yourself when you're in a chain of deals like the one described above is to retain your title (your ownership) of the records until you've been paid. These sections of the contract have to be very carefully drafted

in order to have a chance of working. Assuming the bigger distribution company has gone bust, the liquidator of that company will want to hold on to whatever stocks, i.e. records, that he can. He'll want to sell them to raise money for the creditors of the company, so he'll want to get around the retention of title if he can legitimately do so. Specialised legal advice is needed on this and again it should not be necessary with online sales. There the issue should be making sure that once the deal has ended they take down the copies off the Internet and do not continue to sell them. Most will offer to use reasonable efforts to do this, but will not guarantee it as the online world gets 'populated' with the tracks very quickly.

Most will agree to take down copies once they are brought to their attention, but none of them will take responsibility for illegal copies offered for free download.

Advances

Will a distributor give you an advance? Well they might if you've got a good track record for finding hit records or have a catalogue that has a regular turnover, but it is less likely in the current economic climate. No advances are likely to be offered for small independent labels or individual artists. As with most advances, these sums aren't usually returnable if you don't sell enough records, but they are recoupable from monies you would otherwise receive from sales.

CONCLUSIONS

- Decide on whether you need separate manufacturing and distribution deals.
- Check the returns and discounts policy of your distributor and for any hidden costs.
- Try to retain ownership of the records until you've been paid.

Chapter 7

Digital Downloads, Streaming and Marketing

INTRODUCTION

I suppose the biggest story for this edition has been the rapid speed of change in how we consume music. When I was writing the 6th edition in late 2014 it was all about downloads: pricing, payment and how quickly they would overtake physical sales. A side story was the surprising revival of sales of vinyl albums. Of course, there was streaming and discussion around new models such as subscription and/or ad-funded services. The main players were still the major labels, either directly in the form of their dominance in the download market, or through share investment in companies like Spotify, and Amazon music services were just a gleam in some developer's eye.

A mere two years later and we have seen the download market peak and collapse in favour of streaming. For the first quarter of 2016, digital albums dropped 30.5% year-on-year. It is, however, possible that fans of certain genres will continue to buy downloads, particularly if the audio quality is higher. Dance music DJs may also still want downloads for where internet connectivity is poor or inconsistent. Major labels are still players, but now alongside them there are the communications companies and internet service providers.

The physical market is holding up well, standing at around 46% of the total UK market for paid music in the first half of 2016. Vinyl goes from strength to strength, prompting concerns that the remaining production hardware is too fragile and the number of pressing plants too few to keep up with demand. In one week at the end of November 2016, the value of sales of vinyl records exceeded those of digital downloads. This may have been a headline-grabbing blip but is indicative of how rapidly the download market is declining. 'Now' compilation sales were down nearly 21% year-on-year by mid-2016.

OVERVIEW

The traditional record labels are doing very nicely with the major record labels having a global turnover of $5.18 billion in the first six months of 2016. Universal is the biggest recorded music company, although Sony announced in late 2016 that it had a war chest and was looking for companies to buy. The rights management company BMG is coming up fast on the inside. Their reported revenues topped $200 million by the end of the first half of 2016 and were expected to be close to $500 million by year end.

However, the major label dominance of the recorded music marketplace is under serious threat from the new players led by Google (owners of YouTube), Spotify, Apple Music, Tidal, Pandora and Amazon, with a host of others crowding the stage. The remaining download market is dominated by iTunes owned by Apple, but that too is being reconfigured in favour of their streaming service. Paid subscriptions have become the business model of choice (with or without a premium service, or at the other end of the spectrum, an introductory or basic 'Freemium' service). Spotify is expected to have more than 50 million subscribers by March 2017, while still showing a net loss for 2015 of $119.4 million on revenue in excess of $112 billion. Spotify claims to have paid out $1.83 billion in 2015 in 'royalties, distribution and other costs'. Its per stream rate gross of distribution fees in 2016 was .00437 cents down 16% on 2014 rates. In an interesting development, in August 2016 it was reported that Spotify was making its own records and putting them on its own playlists. This has echoes of what happened at Ministry of Sound whose owners decided to make their own records to include on their compilation records as more economical than licensing the masters in from the majors. In a move which took things full circle, Ministry of Sound was bought by Sony in 2016 and cited as amongst its reasons for sale were the difficulties of breaking artists internationally in what is rapidly becoming a global market place, and the struggles it was having as an independent label in getting on the all-important streaming playlists.

Apple Music had around 20 million subscribers by December 2016 and the second largest amount of streaming revenue. Apple's gross per stream rate in 2016 was .00735 cents, twice that of Spotify. However, Spotify continues to dominate the streaming market with 69% of all streaming revenue.

Tidal, part-owned by Jay Z's company Project Panther, posted a net loss of $28 million in 2015. There were questions around how sustainable this was as it was posting losses of $2 million a month and was reported in September 2016 to be seeking additional finance. It had about two to three million subscribers by December 2016. What sometimes gets lost in the financial headlines and talk of exclusives is the fact that it is the only one of the streaming services which makes a virtue of the higher sound quality offered by its service. In January 2017 Tidal announced that it had sold 33% of the company for approximately $200 million to US telecoms company, Sprint – which has around 45 million retail customers. As part of the deal, Tidal will make exclusive content available to Sprint customers, thereby greatly expanding its reach.

Pandora is best known as an internet radio service and has been the subject of some disquiet amongst rights owners and performers for allegedly not paying fairly for the use of the music. However, in 2016 it announced it was moving away from this model to offer on-demand streaming, putting it into competition with Spotify and Apple Music. Pandora said it was close to striking deals with major label rights holders for the right to use the music (at least in the US). Its free service is also said to be going to continue and possibly expand globally and it is apparently looking to improve its marketing reach by analysis of the data it collects.

Amazon announced the launch of Amazon Music Unlimited in October 2016 and an exclusive with mega-star Garth Brooks, available as a stream only on Amazon Music.

YouTube leads the streaming world and concerns continue to be raised about how much it pays per stream compared to, say, Spotify or Apple Music. Google is seen by many as the bad guy, in that its dominance of the market for consumption of music and visual images through its YouTube service means it is difficult to negotiate terms with it for a fair rate for use of the music. As one commentator involved in these negotiations said: 'How do you say no to YouTube?' In the US they are relying on their government to come to the rescue. US labels are trying to get this issue on to the political agenda of the new President Trump.

In Europe, the new digital copyright proposals may see the issue being addressed in legislation, but the extent to which the UK will even be at that negotiating table is currently unknown. YouTube of course works on the 'click-through' ad-funded model as opposed to a subscription model. The conversion rate of the big data behind the consumers' viewing habits enables very targeted marketing and potential for cross-over sales.

I Heart Music has announced a Napster tie-up for its fully on-demand service, providing an enhanced service for a monthly subscription. The aim is to integrate its traditional radio stations and programmes into the on-demand streaming experience. Napster also offers the opportunity to take the service beyond the US using Napster's global reach. I Heart Media, Shazam and MTV (in partnership with Pepsi) unveiled a new music platform called The Sound Drop to offer emerging artists a stage to promote themselves; they are looking to launch 10 artists a year.

ISSUES

There is intense competition between the various streaming services and one of the ways in which they have sought to gain an edge is through *exclusives*. This is where an artist or rights owner agrees to release a new record through one service for a limited period of time – perhaps a week following release – before making it available on other streaming services. If you are a subscriber to the service which has the exclusive all well and good. If you aren't you either have to wait until it is more generally available or you also subscribe to the exclusive service. Although these exclusives apparently only affect less than 1% of available music, they have a disproportionate effect as some of the major players are involved. Amongst those offering exclusives were Frank Ocean, Drake, The 1975 and Taylor Swift. A variation on this is 'windowing', when a release is only available for a limited period of time on a premium service. In 2016 Apple Music was involved in a series of exclusives where it invested money (in payments to the artist/master rights owner and in marketing) to steal a march on its competitors. With subscriptions running at around £10 a month is this too much to ask for the earliest possible access to your favorite artist? This goes to a much wider issue of what a consumer will pay for music. Spotify in particular was reported to be unhappy with these exclusives. Bear in mind here that the major labels have a share stake in Spotify so potentially a conflict of interest. There were reports of Spotify black-balling or not supporting or promoting artists who had given an exclusive to Apple Music. Katy Perry's new single's disappointing performance was said to be down in good part to its lack of support and non-listing on Spotify playlists. In contrast, however, Drake was the most streamed artist of 2016 on Spotify despite having given an initial two week exclusive to Apple Music. He racked up over 4.7 billion streams. The single 'One Dance' was streamed 960 million times and generated an estimated £3.9 million in royalties [Source: Mark Savage: BBC Music 1/12/2016]. In the summer of 2016 Universal announced a ban on artists' exclusives. Spotify also announced that it was considering 'windowing' certain releases on its premium service for a time.

Artist Stagnation was another perceived problem when the method by which the Official Chart Company counted streams led to very little movement in chart positions from one week to the next, with artists like Drake spending 15 weeks at the top of the UK singles charts in 2016. Streaming now accounts for more than 80% of all single sales. This stagnation led to a feeling that in 2016 there were few new acts breaking through. In December 2016 the Official Chart Company announced it was revising its criteria for its singles chart to try and address the issue. As of January 2017 the total number of streams required to equal one download increased by 50%.

Chart Dominance by the Majors

Connected with the perceived stagnation of the charts was an alleged dominance of the playlists by releases from the major labels. Major label singles are auto-matically placed on the new music playlists on release. There is a lively debate as to whether independent releases are underrepresented in the charts and there is some statistical evidence that they **are** under-represented in the upper reaches of the charts, but of course the same could be said of the difficulties independent releases have always had in competing for market share up against major label marketing budgets. One of the difficulties with the main playlists is that they are the source of most subsequent user-generated playlists leading to more streams and therefore higher chart positions and a further perpetuation of the situation. If you don't get your release on the main playlists you stand to lose out on the user-generated plays too. It is said that 60–90% of the total plays come from these user-generated playlists.

The Challenge of Discovering New Music

This all feeds into an issue around how you discover new music. Is it enough to rely on computer algorithms? These are mystical formulae by which a service can suggest: 'If you like X you might like Y'. Initially this was the method by which people were referred to other music, but it quickly came to be seen as a bit crude. Just because I have one blues record does not mean I *only* like blues music. Most people have more eclectic tastes. The analysis of big data means that the algorithms and the suggestions have become more sophisticated. Both Spotify and Apple Music have also hired people known to be good at discovering new talent to add a human dimension. Apple Music were first to raid BBC Radio 1 to hire lead tastemaker Zane Lowe, followed a few months later by Spotify's hiring of BBC Radio 1's George Ergatoudis. Alongside human intervention artificial intelligence is also being brought into play to add your locality and mood into the equation.

What of the Publishers and the song?
The focus is often on the master rights owners as opposed to the composers and publishers. A large part of this is due to the profit margin being much higher for record labels than for music publishers. So where a group company has both master and publishing interests – as in the case with all the majors and several mini-majors like BMG and Kobalt – then they have been happy to direct the revenue to the master uses. The US Copyright Royalty Board is to hear evidence for the setting of a new streaming royalty rate in Spring 2017. The major labels are lobbying for a low rate. Some independent publishers are arguing that the best way forward would be to set a per stream payment as opposed to a percentage of revenue. It is rumoured that Apple supports such a system.

REPRODUCTION AND DISTRIBUTION

As we saw in more detail in the last chapter, distribution contracts for online distribution take the same form as for traditional physical distribution, with the distributor putting the record out through aggregators or direct to retailers online, collecting the income generated, and paying the rights owner after deducting its cut. The percentage the distributor keeps is open to negotiation and will often start at around 15–20%. Just as you'd check or expect your label to check quality of CD pressings and availability of stock, so you need to make sure the tracks are correctly digitised and that the correct metadata is included with the online file to enable the downloads to be tracked and payment made. Make sure it's uploaded in good time. If at all possible, do a trial run or a 'soft' release, where you let the track out a few days before the official release date or just through one or two key outlets to test all is well. I had one client who was releasing his latest track online. He had all his promotion lined up: a live date; some radio; and some press ads and articles all directing the fans to buy the release through certain websites and services. The release date came and with it a host of complaints from the fans that they could not get the record or that the download had failed but the company had still taken their money. The release was a disaster and the artist had to make up a great deal of lost goodwill with his fans. The response of the distributor was a very nonchalant: 'Oh yes, we sometimes get teething problems but they sort themselves out in time. Complaints from fans help us find what's wrong.' Well, needless to say we were not impressed with this line and the client will not be using that distributor again.

RECORD COMPANIES AND OTHER PLAYERS

How else have the companies sought to improve their position on this new playing field?

Innovations in marketing
Record labels and artists are also looking at innovative marketing ideas to drive customers to their product. As already indicated, one of the main issues is how to discover new music and the use of algorithms and analysis of big data to tailor suggestions. There remains a challenge over how to access independent music and in effect we need to see the online equivalent of a BBC 6 Music station. Changes to the Official Chart Company rules on counting streams for the charts may help a little, but as ever it is innovative marketing ideas which are going to grab the headlines.

In 2016 one company stood out as coming up with those new ideas. Kobalt announced a number of initiatives, such as the same 'pre-order' function on Spotify as would be available for a CD/download. They call this Pre-Save. The first artist to benefit from this was Laura Marling whose new album *Semper Femina* was offered via this service in March 2017. Kobalt sees this as an extension of the label services function it offers. Similarly, it announced another 'first' with its marketing of David Gray's *Best of* album release in 2016. Alongside the standard CD and vinyl release it was also released as a dynamic playlist on Spotify. The playlist changed every Monday to allow newer tracks to be listened to alongside older tracks. The more fans that streamed a track in a week, the higher up the playlist that track featured the following week.

Artificial intelligence (AI) is also being brought into play on marketing, with artists like Olly Murs and Robbie Williams using 'chat bots' to interact with fans. These bots answer fans' questions and drive them to online e-tailers. The same AI will be used to further personalise the recommendations the user will receive e.g. using bots to track where you've been, the day of the week, your likely mood and then offer suitable listening. It can identify, for example, that you like a particular musician and offer you more tracks on which that musician features. This might help the jobbing session musician as well as the featured artist. Analysis of users uploading their own music to services like YouTube is used to track those who start to get some following or traction. One such service is backed by a major label which has gone on to sign some of the artists discovered by this means to development deals. Redundancy of the human A&R? Probably not but an interesting development.

PIRACY

Piracy and illegal downloading remains an area of concern and this subject is covered more fully in Chapter 14. The music industry is probably fighting a lost cause in trying to prevent illegal downloading, which, after all, is just a particularly invidious form of piracy. Individuals are now pirates as well as the large-scale commercial operations. The genie is already out of the bottle and isn't going to go back in. We now have a generation who is used to free or cheap availability and exchange of music. Even those who will pay for it are unwilling to pay at the levels they were in the days of physical-only carriers. They may only be interested in paying for single tracks rather than 'bundled' albums. Making legal downloads easy to get and of a superior quality to the illegal versions may go some way to help but not for those who do not care overmuch about quality and who just want the latest stuff for free. Educating these people may help a bit, but probably not a great deal, so one way to get them may be to get them to pay for something else that they do value, such as a mobile phone service or artist exclusives or the inside track with an artist, and include in the price they pay an element for the music content of that service. However, the problem is becoming a little less of a commercial concern with the growth of online, on demand streaming services. To access the full benefits provided by many of these services you need to either pay a monthly subscription or (if you choose the 'freemium' services) to endure some form of ad-supported listening/viewing. But there is still concern over the number of 'ripped' streams there are out there.

The problem of leaking of albums via the Internet ahead of their commercial release is a serious one. It is extremely difficult to track how or where the leak occurs: it's not as if someone were smuggling a large tape reel out of the studio. There are examples of almost 'Mission Impossible'-style scenes where reviewers are searched before entering dedicated rooms where they listen on a special machine to one numbered copy of the album. The intention being that if the reviewer makes an illegal copy it will be tracked back to him. But even such measures don't stop the determined pirate. The long-awaited Coldplay album was available in full on the Internet days before the official launch. This was despite strenuous efforts by their record company, EMI, to prevent this. EMI made the best of a bad job by bringing forward release plans. Record companies also try to get the websites offering the albums shut down but they do not always get the co-operation of the ISPs and where they do it may already be too late. All this of course makes Bowie's announcement that he had recorded an album and was releasing it with no previous inkling that he was even in a studio all the more remarkable. You have to have loyal friends in order to achieve that level of secrecy. I remember one artist who had all the musicians sign confidentiality agreements not to divulge what they were working on or with whom. It was all for nothing as one of the musicians, apparently without thought, Tweeted his day's activities to all his followers. It was then too late to stop the word getting out and we had to make the best of a bad job.

Alongside legislative initiatives such as the Digital Economy Act and pressure from the European Commission for a co-ordinated cross-European approach to piracy and licensing, there have been cases which have shown the way to how courts may be prepared to make ISPs responsible for what they carry.

SABAM v. Scarlet

Extended SA

The first landmark case to take this line was brought by Belgian collection society SABAM against Scarlet, formerly a branch of the Italian ISP Tiscali in 2007. A court in Belgium confirmed that an ISP must take responsibility for stopping illegal file-sharing on its network by using file-filtering systems. The ruling was the first of its kind in Europe and, as you might imagine, was welcomed by the international record industry, which has been pressing for action by ISPs to curb piracy on their networks. The case seems to have turned on a determination of which of two pieces of European legislation should have precedence. The first to be implemented was the E-Commerce Directive (2000/31/EU) which declared that ISPs as intermediaries were not liable for the content on the websites that they host. However, the later Copyright Directive amending the copyright laws to cover online uses said that in some circumstances copyright owners could get court orders against ISPs if websites using their services were being used for piracy or infringed the rights of copyright owners. This was the first case to decide that the Copyright Directive had precedence. Not surprisingly Scarlet appealed to the Belgian Court of Appeal saying that it was impossible for them to comply with the injunction on practical grounds but also that it was contrary to Article 15 of the E-Commerce Directive because in order to comply Scarlet would have to generally monitor communications over its service and that was contrary to this Article. Finally Scarlet argued that it would infringe the laws on protection of personal data and secrecy of communications. The Belgian Court of Appeal referred a point of law to the Court of Justice of the European Union. That court decided that imposing an injunction on an ISP requiring it to install a filtering system to prevent illegal downloading is unlawful under European Law; that the European Charter of Fundamental Rights from 2007, whilst giving protection to intellectual property, had to be balanced fairly against the rights of individuals to be free to conduct a business. It also found that it would infringe the right of individuals to protection of their personal data and the freedom to receive or impart information. The UK secured an opt out from the provisions of the Charter of Fundamental Rights but this latter point could potentially prove a problem in the European Courts if the provisions of the Digital Economy Act are fully implemented as that Act provides for ISPs to notify their subscribers of copyright infringement and provide copyright owners with subscriber data. Is this striking the right balance, i.e. not requiring active monitoring of all communications but still requiring the ISPs to cooperate in the protection of copyright holders from infringement of their rights?

HARGREAVES REVIEW AND RECOMMENDATIONS

In May 2011 the review by Professor Ian Hargreaves of intellectual property was published under the title: 'Digital Opportunity: A Review of Intellectual Property and Growth'. This was a wide-ranging review which took into account a large body of evidence and submissions from interested parties. The guiding principle behind the review was to consider economic impacts. Was the current intellectual property framework sufficient to promote innovation and growth and were any elements acting as a hindrance to this?

Hargreaves concluded that the current system was a hindrance to economic growth and that the copyright law in particular was blunting Britain's competitiveness. Copyright was biased towards the needs of the creator and, as far as the music industry was concerned, was preventing research and development in the Internet-based economy.

One recommendation was to permit format shifting for personal use by means of a specific fair dealing exemption to copyright. Format shifting is where you wish to make a copy of, say, a piece of music you own on your iPad for use on your mobile phone or by burning a CD copy of it. The Government was minded to introduce such an exception but without any form of compensation for this in the form of a levy, similar to the blank tape levy already in place in parts of Europe. However, this fell away when the Musician's Union and other interested parties could not agree on the details, and there are no plans at present to resurrect it.

Alongside his various recommendations, Hargreaves sought better enforcement procedures alongside better education about copyright and creative rights. In the spirit of education ISPs began to send out information notices to infringers at the end of February 2017 advising those apparently using music illegally that they were breaching copyright laws. However, this falls considerably short of the three strikes and you are banned from the net which some have been militating for.

In terms of what is available by way of additional enforcement procedures there is, of course, the Digital Economy Act 2010. The Act envisaged a Code of Conduct and regulations for the sending of warning notices to those identified as downloading pirate material. Three such notices could result in the ISP being required to bar that user from its service. Initially the ISP is required to notify its subscribers if the IP addresses associated with them are reported by copyright owners as being used to infringe copyright; secondly the ISPs must then keep track of the number of reports about each subscriber and compile, on an anonymous basis, a 'Copyright Infringement List' of those subscribers who are reported on above a certain threshold. This allows the most persistent alleged infringers to be targeted. The copyright owners can then apply to the court for an order to obtain the personal details of those included in that list and take legal action against them. However, as always the devil is in the detail. The Act provided that the implementation and regulation of these steps must be set out in a Code approved by Ofcom. Draft Codes have been circulated but the whole process was initially slowed by litigation from companies like TalkTalk and BT and then from debates around who is to pay for these measures. The Government has announced a review of the implementation of the Act and so it is at present in a limbo state. Organisations like UK Music continue to argue for an amendment to enable a code of conduct between the search engines and rights holders governing online infringement.

NEW BUSINESS MODELS

Of the various methods which have been tried, the following have gained a hold.

Track downloads

The simple model of a single track or bundled download, sometimes with a refinement that in some cases the customer can buy the right to listen to a piece of music for a limited period of time before he has to buy it in order to keep it permanently. With these systems, the customer 'owns' the tracks downloaded and pays about 59–79p per track or more for the premium version. The tracks paid for are then transferable to portable devices and can be burned to disk. As already mentioned, these are more popular with certain genres of music (like classic rock), amongst those who like a higher audio quality and seek big resolution downloads, and with DJs.

Subscription services

Subscription models have gained greatest traction. They allow subscribers access to all the music they want for a monthly fee, sometimes with an option to purchase selected tracks or to access more or exclusive services on a premium subscription. Sometimes the service is offered free for a limited, introductory period. Once the subscription ends, the music is no longer available. This was seen initially as a disadvantage but many users have become used to the idea of impermanence. One of the chief business challenges to companies reliant on a subscription-based system was how to move their users across from the minimum 'free' element to the full fee-paying service. It is here that exclusives originally came into their own, albeit as we have seen there are many who object to them.

Ad-funded streaming services

As we have already read, certain streaming services allow the consumer purchasing the basic service to pay less or get some services for free but in return has to listen to or watch ads alongside the music. This is the model currently adopted by Google for its YouTube service. The debate continues to rage over whether Google pays a fair price for the use of music content and attempts are being made to move this on to the political agenda of US President

Trump. In Europe the proposed EU Directive modernising EU copyright for the digital world has focused on services like YouTube, which rely on user-uploaded copyright to get around paying more for content, proposing that they should pay for a licence if they provide a search facility or other functionality.

Paying the artist

On the other side of the coin, the debate continues as to how the copyright owner – usually the record company – will account to the artist for the income from streaming and subscription or ad-funded services.

When online revenue first became a reality, the royalties were generally treated as similar to a flat fee per use charge that the artist might get from licensing a piece of music for a one-off use, e.g. on a compilation. The share of receipts from online was also generally the same as for flat fee uses at around 50%. This way of calculating shares of income still tends to apply with income that is linked to subscriptions or where the service is provided by a third-party unrelated company.

Later, the record labels began to realise that they should think again about how they account to their artists if they weren't going to end up paying out more to them than they wanted to. In other words, greed kicked in and the model shifted to a royalty basis. The royalty rate used is now about the same as applies to a physical CD sale and the price is that which the record label receives from the online etailers or aggregators or from the mobile phone companies. This method of calculating shares of income works well for downloads or per use payments but is not so effective for subscription revenue. What is of course important is to have as transparent a deal as possible on online income.

In the past the existence of non-disclosure agreements meant that the labels were able to claim that they were unable to disclose the details of deals struck. A couple of high-profile leaks, plus statistics emerging from the services themselves, as well as amounts being paid to independent master rights owning artists has enabled us to see behind the curtain. There is a feeling that the labels are not paying through a fair share of the revenue. A high-pressure campaign by artists and their representatives resulted in some of the major record labels agreeing to share out a proportion of the monies it receives when/if it sells shares it holds in these streaming services. There is also focus in commercial contract negotiations on getting a share of so-called 'black box', the hole into which allegedly non-attributable income is being placed. On the political stage the proposals to modernise EU copyright rules have focused on Article 14 of the E-Commerce Directive arguing for greater transparency.

MOVE AWAY FROM ALBUMS?

The debate has continued for some time now as to whether we will see a switch away from the traditional album format. Now that consumers on streaming and download services can pick and choose the tracks they want to make up their downloads or playlists, to some extent the focus has switched to the single track. There is, of course, still a market for the album in the CD and vinyl market so we are not going to see it disappear anytime soon. However, Calvin Harris announced in 2016 that he was no longer going to make albums and instead was going to focus on singles. I haven't seen much evidence yet of that filtering in to contracts, but there is some movement detectable in terms of the minimum contract commitment in publishing deals changing to a number of tracks as opposed to a percentage of an album. Labels like Island and Warner are also returning to the development model of a couple of four or five track EPs per contract period as opposed to album commitments.

SOCIAL NETWORKING SITES AND RECOMMENDATIONS

As we saw at the beginning of this chapter, one of the interesting effects of the growing influence on the music industry of the Internet is the extent to which the consumer is starting to drive the sort of music he wishes to listen to and purchase. Recommendations from online 'friends' are as influential as hearing a track on the radio. Consumer-generated playlists have allowed the individual to tailor his listening and one of the side effects of this is that many of the single tracks downloaded off the Internet are back catalogue both recent and decades old. Interest in old tracks can be boosted by an appearance in a Hollywood film or on an influential television show like *Grey's Anatomy*. The US series *Glee* gave rise to a revival in the back catalogues of many 'heritage' artists. *Glee* is no longer on UK television, probably as a result of the judgement in a long-running case brought by Comedy Enterprises, the owners of comedy venue 'The Glee Club' which resulted in them successfully winning their case that the use of the title 'Glee' for the television show was an infringement of their trademark.

> *(Comic Enterprises Ltd v. Twentieth Century Fox Film Corporation [2016] EWCA Civ 41).*
> This case is also important because it confirmed that in considering allegations of trademark infringement, it was possible to use reverse evidence i.e. that someone wrongly believed

193

that the party using the infringing name was connected with the party who had the legitimate right to use it. In this case there was some evidence that potential visitors to UK comedy venue 'The Glee Club' thought the club was connected with the US TV show.

Slightly more controversially, there are privacy issues over the use of the information provided on these websites and around the collection and analysis of so-called big data.

MARKETING ONLINE

Official websites

The Internet has proved to be an excellent means of marketing the 'brand'. Artists now link their online marketing efforts with those of their record company and their own efforts in terms of live work as a matter of course. Artists can successfully sell out a concert in minutes when tickets are advertised for sale on their website and now many artists make a proportion of the tickets available for sale solely on their official website thereby cutting out the fees to the middleman and providing the opportunity for an exclusive offering to fans. By selling tickets online, the artist or his advisers also have the opportunity, with the right permissions, to create a database of committed fans keen to learn more about what the artist has planned. This gives the artist a ready-made mailing list. Many artists now use websites to communicate directly with their fans in the form of online diaries or 'blogs' and as we have seen the use of Artificial Intelligence has resulted in some artists using 'chat bots' to engage with their fans. Of course you must always ensure that the website is regularly updated. Most exclusive artist contracts with the majors now insist that the artist commits to writing a blog or giving 'copy' regularly to a staff writer at the record company to write one up for them. Others require the artists to record snippets for sale as mobile phone ringtones and to take part in online chats with fans or agree to Tweet regularly on Twitter.

A couple of years ago, we were very concerned to ensure that artists retained ownership of their domain names and official websites. Most record companies now don't insist on ownership of all variations of the artist's domain name and, even where they do, they provide links to the artist's or fan-club sites. Most will now agree that their ownership and control only lasts during the term of the record deal and will make arrangements for transfer of names at the end of the deal. In some cases, they only require ownership of one domain name with the artist's name in it, for example a .net or .org domain name, and are happy for the artist to retain all the other names. There is then usually a require-ment for the artist to provide links from his website to the domain name which is used for the 'official' record company website page for that artist. There are, however, still some record labels who would like to control all aspects of the artist's online presence. I have some clients who really aren't bothered about this and who are unlikely to ever do a good website themselves, so in these cases I usually do not resist the record company having these rights exclusively during the term of the contract. But at the end of the contract the rights should transfer to the artist.

The increasing use of Apps has meant that the ownership of the domain name is becoming less important than having an App with an instantly recognisable icon. All the more reason to check out your trade and service marks.

Record companies have in some, but not all, cases shown that they have the resources and skills to create interesting, even dynamic websites. Most of the major record labels now focus heavily on the artist's website as a means of cross-selling their product – CDs, downloads, merchandise – with whatever other activities that the artist may be doing – such as gigs or personal appear-ances. Record companies who are insisting on 360-degree models are keen to ensure they control the websites so that any revenues generated online, e.g. from ticket sales or sales of T-shirts, also come to them. As with all things that make up an artist's brand, the artist should have creative control of the 'look and feel' of any website dedicated to them and maybe also of the designers/ artwork providers or other creative elements.

A well-thought-out campaign can be very effective. If all promotional material contains a website address or link to an App and Facebook page – all of which are vibrant and informative – you create a receptive audience for the marketing material you want to target at potential consumers and buyers of the various products you have on offer.

WEBSITE AND APP DESIGN RIGHTS AND COPYRIGHT

If you do create your own website or App, you may decide to employ someone to design it. The website or App is likely to be made up of many different elements, all of which could be the subject of copyright or other legal protection.

The website or App will no doubt contain visual images or graphics. These could be still photographs, moving images or film. Each of these could have its own copyright. The website or App will be made up of a number of computer programs which are also protected by copyright. The designer will have copyright in the original design drawings; he may also have a design right.

When commissioning someone else to design a website or App, you have to make sure that all rights have been cleared for use in the website or App design, so that you have all the rights you need to do what you want with the website. You also need to find out whether these rights have been 'bought-out' for a one-off payment or if there is an ongoing obligation to pay for the use. It's possible that in order to use the music or a sound recording you'll have to pay a royalty or further fee.

If the person commissioned to design the website or App is your employee, then you'll own the copyright in their original work, but the other rights may still have to be cleared.

If you ask someone who isn't employed by you to design the website or App, you must make sure that you take an assignment from them of all rights in the work they have done. You could make this a condition of the commission fee, or it could be the subject of a separate fee, or occasionally a royalty. The designer may grant the right to use the work only on the website or App and not, for example, to print design elements from the website or App and sell them separately as posters or otherwise as part of a merchandising campaign (see Chapter 8). These additional uses could be the subject of a separate fee.

Assignments of copyright should be confirmed in writing. A written agreement also establishes what rights you have and on what terms. It should contain a confirmation from the designer that he has all the necessary rights from third parties for the use of any or all elements of the design.

Both the website and the App may rely on certain elements which are generic or not specifically created for you. In that case you must make sure the designer can and does grant you a licence to use those elements.

DATA PROTECTION

If you're putting together data on people electronically, you have to register with the Information Commissioner. You can't do what you want with the data you collect. You have to get permission to use it for a purpose other than that for which it was collected. You'll have seen this on websites for a particular product. If you send off for that product or for details about it, you'll invariably be asked to register and to fill in a form with your details. The product owner may want to try to sell you other products that he has in his range, or to sell his list of customers and their product preferences to another company. He can't do this without your permission. There is often a box on the form that you have to tick if you don't want your information to be used in this way. This 'negative' consent technique is lawful, although the Information Commissioner is in favour of you having to tick a box if you *do* want more information rather than the other way around. You'll often find a box that has to be checked or unchecked to block your information being used in other ways. If you're compiling a database and you don't comply with the rules on passing on information, you can be fined.

If, however, these data protection hurdles are overcome, a database of consumer profiles and information is a valuable asset. If you own your domain name, then, you'll usually also own the data collected in relation to that website.

BIG DATA

I take this to mean the collection and analysis of information on an individual's preferences culled or 'scraped' from information available on Internet websites, often by combining information from a variety of different sources with real-time analysis.

The gathering and analysis of this information and the uses to which it can be put are governed by rules and regulations on the protection of personal and business data (such as the 1998 Data Protection Act) and by rules and regulations intended to encourage commerce and economic activity (such as the Data Protection Directive). The two are not always aligned and clashes frequently occur.

Collection and analysis of huge quantities of data is now big business. The data is used for many purposes, including tracking your whereabouts, your purchases, the websites you visit, the preferences you state when selecting music or films etc. Advertisers use the data to target users with other products and services. The analysis could, in theory, be done manually by human agency, but is much more likely to be done with the aid of computer algorithms. Up-to-date analysis of huge quantities of data is vital to business, and to research and development arms of companies considering future products and services and strategic decision-making. But what of the rights of privacy? Individuals have the right to know and have a measure of control over how personal data is used, and businesses have a right to protect sensitive information. Every website must have a privacy policy setting out details of the data it collects and the uses it puts that to. App settings on your phone allow some flexibility on the information you give out, and the use of cookies on websites must now be declared and you opt in to their collection (EU Privacy Directive 2010). But, of course, if you want to use the website or App then you are going to have to accept some invasion of your privacy. In the EU the focus has been on measures to protect the dissemination of personal data and to prevent such data being sent to countries where the protection levels were not at the necessary level. In practice, the sending of information outside the EU to the US has been governed by a regime known as 'Safe Harbor' where US companies could self-certify they provided 'adequate' protection for data. However, high-profile cases like that involving Edward Snowden and a 2015 case brought by Max Schrems against Facebook led the European Court of Justice to rule that the existing Safe Harbor regime did not adequately protect data of EU citizens and so it was no longer an acceptable way of transferring data. The alternative that was put in its place is known as the Privacy Shield, a system which does meet EU standards placing strong obligations and monitoring of US organisations. (Source: Richard Kerr, Practical Law 2016).

DESIGN

One of the big challenges of marketing online is to make sure that fans come to a particular website and, once they have found it, come back to it over and over again. The design of the website is, of course, crucial. It should be eye-catching and user-friendly and scaled to work on laptops, tablets and mobiles. The text used in it should be designed so that it features prominently in the first twenty websites that come up when key phrases are used to search for information using one of the search engines like Google. Website optimisation is an art form in itself and is becoming more difficult to achieve but specialist web designers could be used, or consider paying to be a sponsored site.

The website should be regularly updated. And updating should be a simple process. Sites like Wordpress specialise in user-friendly website design, hosting and updating.

The website should be different – it should have something that will raise it above the general 'noise' online.

CONCLUSIONS

- Artists can use the Internet and crowd-funding to partner up with investors from outside the music industry, or to distribute their own records.
- Marketing is vitally important in raising your music above the noise.
- Artists should try to own their own domain name and database.
- If you commission someone to design your website, make sure they give you ownership of all the various elements of it and make good hosting and maintenance arrangements.

Chapter 8

Branding, Marketing, Merchandising

INTRODUCTION

In this and the following chapter I'm going to look at the whole area of branding and marketing: first by looking at marketing and then at merchandising deals, at how you get a trade mark and at the benefits of building up a reputation in your name and how to protect it; and then, in the next chapter, I'll be looking at sponsorship deals.

MARKETING

Once you've got the recording, mastering, digitisation and distribution sorted you need to turn your mind to how you are going to market it, to let the public know about you and your record. The marketing process has many elements to it and it's an ongoing process. You've got something to sell – a record, live performance, merchandise – and you need to tell people about it. In the 'noise' of the online world and with the globalisation of the marketplace, marketing is of vital importance. Having a good record in the first place is a given, but that often isn't enough. You need to draw it to the attention of your likely market. Do you know that market? Do you know who you are targeting? If you don't, then its time you learnt, fast.

It is essential that your marketing is part of an overall plan linked to release dates and touring plans. If you are not already an established name (and sometimes even when you are if you've been away for a while), it is important that your marketing is innovative but true to your brand (more on which below).

Indeed some self-sufficient artists engaged in self-release of their recordings are bypassing the traditional record label route altogether and relying instead on the links and exposure (as well as funding) provided by brand partnerships.

Iron Maiden promoted their album *The Final Frontier* via a new online game that they created with game developers Matmi. In the game, Iron Maiden travel deep into space to play their first intergalactic gig but they are attacked by space pirates who scatter their instruments around the galaxy. They have to be collected up again before they can play the gig.

ARTWORK

Getting the right artwork for the record is important and it should form a key part of the whole campaign. It could be used as the backdrop to a stage show and on a poster campaign. It could appear on T-shirts and other merchandise. Make sure you own the copyright in the artwork and that there are no restrictions on what can be done with it. The challenge for artists and graphic designers is a design that works well online and uses the interactive technology and the global possibilities of the Internet to the fullest extent. Simple versions of the artwork can be made available as a download when you buy the record online. Packaging must contain the correct copyright notices and the all-important barcode and the correct tracking information must be embedded in the metadata for online releases. For online sales, make sure that all necessary technical requirements of the online distributor are in place to ensure sales are correctly tracked and fed back to you.

PHOTOGRAPHS AND BIOGRAPHIES

You're going to need to have some decent photographs. They'll be needed for information packs, for the press, for letting overseas licensees or associated companies abroad know what you look like. You'll also need to post photos or graphics up on your website or page on Facebook. The costs the record company pays for are not usually recoupable or repayable by you unless you want to use the photographs for merchandising, for example on a T-shirt or poster, when you may be expected to repay at least half the costs.

If there's an exclusive record contract in place, it will usually, but not always, give the artist approval over which photographs are used. It will also usually give the artist approval of the official biography. It also ensures that a consistent message or image is presented of the artist, which forms part of the brand. Many record contracts now also require the artist to contribute to online blogs or to Tweet regularly. Instagram and Snapchat are more recent ways to connect with the fans – to make them feel part of your life.

IN-HOUSE OR EXTERNAL MARKETING

Most big record companies will have in-house marketing and press departments. These are staffed by dedicated people, one or more of whom will be allocated to marketing your product. You need to be sure that these people understand the game plan and, preferably, that they love your music. At the very least they should like it, because otherwise they won't sound convincing when they try to sell you to the press, radio, TV and so on.

If the marketing is to be done in-house it will normally be paid for by the record company on a non-recoupable basis. The position changes if it's a smaller company without its own in-house marketing departments or where outside specialists have been brought in for particular aspects. The costs are then usually partly or wholly recoupable from the record income.

Whether it's being done in-house or with a number of outside specialists, the whole campaign has to be co-ordinated. The sales force and any special strike force have to be primed with artwork, photographs, biographies and campaign details. Promotion packs have to be sent out to any exporters, to clubs, DJs and to some retail outlets. Much of this is now done by email especially EPQs (see below). For bigger releases the record company may arrange for a private 'play through' of the new album to selected key retailers, reviewers and tastemakers.

The fact that the record is being released has to be notified to the music press, to the chart compilers and to MCPS and PPL to get the relevant mechanical licence and details registered for when the record is performed publicly. Each release has to have its own catalogue number. It is usual to prepare a summary of all the information, known as 'presenters' or 'sales sheets', of about a page long, consisting of the name of the artist, the title of the record and a picture of it, its catalogue number, barcode, dealer price and release date. You should then add details of how to order it and contact details plus some brief points on what the marketing campaign is.

The adverts for a co-ordinated advertising campaign will have to be designed and approved well in advance so that they're ready for distribution at the same time as the promotional packs, posters, promotional items and so on.

The strike or sales force goes into action several weeks before the release date, trying to get orders from the retail shops and retailers with online pre-sales charts now providing valuable pre-release indicators of how well a particular record is being received. It will help determine the chart position, it tells the marketing people how much more work they have to do, and pre-sales figures can give you some information to pass on to your physical manufacturer and distributor to help them assess how many copies of the record will be needed. The figures may also tell you in what areas of the country the record is selling best, so the distributor can know to make more copies available in those areas. Pre-sales for online sales help to determine a chart position in digital charts and greater exposure for the artist. Most of the major labels consider the statistics from these online sources a vital part of their market research and mainstream radio will often not playlist a record for its primetime shows. So a large part of the marketing is now to ensure that there is the right level of activity on the social networking sites as well as in pre-sales and digital sales.

Since the last edition we've seen the *NME* go free following the business model of advertising-driven income generation adopted by other publications like *Time Out,* or driving traffic instead to online sites, but nevertheless, print media is still an important driver of news in the UK. If a daily newspaper prints an exclusive it will be immediately picked up by the online sites like Google News, and most of the print/broadcast media corporations now have online versions of their papers, with tablet editions too. Don't forget the local newspapers; regional press can be very useful in targeting your audience and some have large circulations. But alongside the established print media it is now essential for any marketing campaign to build up the statistics of hits, viewings, as well as reactions from influential bloggers to show the requisite levels of take up and buzz around an artist. There is also the international aspect of these Internet blogs which can help to spread the word worldwide. Artist Imogen Heap tells of how she saw that a significant number of comments were coming from people based in Indonesia, not an area she would normally have targeted.

She asked her live booking agent to look into doing a gig there. A 4,000-capacity gig in the capital, Jakarta, then followed and was a sell-out which helped to fund her Australian tour.

Sending out press releases is also now a much easier task if it can be sent in an email as opposed to the laborious process of printing and posting thousands of copies out. But now of course the trick is to make sure that your press release doesn't just go into Junk Mail or the recycle bin. What is clearly true now is that, if an artist's online presence is not up-to-the-second, active and relevant, this will have a negative impact on that artist's chance of success.

Let's say you have come up with a marketing plan which raises your music above the 'noise' of all the other competing releases that week. Why should a potential customer listen to and possibly buy your record over anyone else's? How do they even know you have a record released? You need to come up with a marketing plan or idea that makes your release stand out. This takes talent and you may need to bring in specialist marketing people. As with all experts that you engage, make sure it is clear in writing what you want them to do, how they will be paid and what constitutes a successful outcome.

If you are targeting online streaming services how are you going to ensure you are recommended or playlisted? Is the service based on human curation or algorithms? Have you got access to the streaming data? Do you know what to do with that data when you see it? Is a data marketing specialist required as part of the marketing budget?

TV ADVERTISING

If you are on a major record label (or perhaps an independent one owned by a millionaire!), then part of the marketing campaign might be to advertise the records on television. This is an expensive business. A basic television campaign in four ITV regions can easily cost £75,000. The record company is only going to want to spend this money if it thinks it will earn it back in extra record sales or online revenue. To keep its risk to a minimum, the record company will try to recoup some or all of these costs, either as a further advance or by reducing the royalty payable to you. The record company may reduce by 50% the royalty it would otherwise have had to pay on sales of the records until it has recouped (from that reduced royalty) 50% or more of the costs of the TV ad campaign or the whole cost may be treated as a further recoupable advance. It will say which in the contract.

We lawyers try to get artists the right of approval over whether an advert is made but have to fight for this. Otherwise, we try to limit the ways in which the artist's income is affected, either by restricting the reduction to sales in the country where the campaign is run, or limiting the time over which they can recoup the costs from reduced royalties, or both.

Be aware of the cynical attempt to reduce royalties to you when your record has been particularly successful. The record company may rush out a cheap TV campaign in the same accounting period as your album is released and achieved most of its sales. By doing this, the record company can add a further advance to the bottom line or halve royalties on all sales in that accounting period even if those sales happened before the ad campaign. Don't think this is fanciful. One of my colleagues found that a major record company was trying to do this with an artist who had had a very successful debut album. A TV campaign wasn't needed and the lawyer and manager had to fight hard to get a deal whereby the royalties were not artificially reduced. It is also true that record company executives might panic you into doing a TV campaign when they fear that the sales are not at the level they expect. It is the job of a good manager to try to decide whether the fear is real and would be helped by a campaign. I know of one very experienced manager who had to persuade their artist's record label not to rush out a TV advert for an album at Christmas. The label was afraid that they had over-supplied the stores and would get masses of returns in the New Year. The managers had to fight long and hard to stop this happening but they did have an ace up their sleeve – they **knew** that the next single was a winner, stood their ground, were proved right and the artist went on to have a very successful album. Of course, nowadays with the value of actual physical sales declining, the focus of TV adverts may be in driving customers to particular online services, but nevertheless this point about the potential for reducing royalties holds good then too.

TV AND RADIO PLUGGERS

Even though everyone can stream their own records and videos online now it's still very important and, in the case of pop records, I would say essential to the success of a record that it gets exposure on radio. Unless the record gets a decent number of radio plays, it's unlikely to enter the charts. The world of radio is a very fickle place. An artist who is adored by radio for his first album may be ignored by radio on the follow-up even though the songs are just as commercial. The reasons are often unfathomable and depend on factors such as personal taste, political issues and just the way the wind is blowing, but there is also a greater reliance than ever on the statistics from online activity on Facebook, YouTube, as well as the pre-sales online when deciding whether or not to playlist a particular record.

The people who decide what is played on Radio 1 or 2, 6 Music, or Radio X and other pivotal regional radio stations are therefore very powerful. It is generally the producers of the shows rather than the DJs who decide what should be added to the playlist of tracks which must be played on the mainstream programmes. There are three levels of listing: A (the holy grail), B or C with each dictating the number of 'plays' per week. A listing may well encourage the record label to release more funds for additional marketing. The TV and radio pluggers have the tough job of trying to get records playlisted. They are either employed in-house by the record company or are from outside agencies that specialise in this work. Their costs are dealt with in similar ways to press agents (see below).

WHAT DO YOU PAY EXTERNAL PLUGGERS AND PRESS PEOPLE?

There are several different ways of paying for external marketing and press work.

Retainers
Press and pluggers could be on retainers. These are regular, monthly payments that are made to keep them on board as the press agent, constantly having an eye on press opportunities. When an artist isn't actively doing any promotion, for instance when he is in the studio recording the next album, the level of retainer could be quite small. It would then increase when press/promotion activities rise around the time of the release of the record. However, in the current economic climate most are now only paid when they do some work, with retainers being a distant fond memory for many. Those who do commercial press for companies as opposed to individual artists may do better on the retainer front as they need to hold a working brief.

Fixed fees
They could be on a fixed monthly fee, possibly with bonuses linked to success.

Bonuses

If someone is on a retainer or a fixed fee, they may be paid a bonus for achieving certain targets. For example, a press officer could get paid a bonus for every front page/cover he gets that features a particular artist.

A plugger might get a bonus if a record goes into the Top 10 or is playlisted on a streaming service or mentioned by an influential blogger.

Royalties

Good pluggers and those in great demand (usually the same ones) can insist on 'points', i.e. a royalty (usually 0.5–1%) on each record sold. If you want the best you may have to pay this. It will either come out of the artist royalty or be paid by the record company, or a combination of the two.

Where do you find them?

The usual ways – word of mouth, those companies already on a retainer arrangement with your record company, those companies known to your manager as doing a good job in this area of music. The *Music Week Directory* carries a list of press and promotions companies, but it would be a good idea to get a recommendation from someone in the business before you choose one.

Do they want a contract?

If they're on a fixed fee, they will probably just invoice you for the fee when the work is done. If you've agreed they'll undertake something out of the ordinary, or you're putting them on a retainer, you'll probably want a simple contract. If they're being paid a royalty, you'll definitely need a contract setting out how that royalty will be calculated and when it will be paid. The simplest way to do this is on the same basis as you get paid your royalties under your record deal.

EPQs

This abbreviation means electronic press packages. That is pre-recorded interviews, photos and biographies, together with promotional clips of your latest release, which are put together by your in-house or external press officer. These usually take the form of a DVD or an email attachment with links to external sites and they're sent out to reviewers, press reporters, DJs, radio station controllers and so on as an additional means of promotion.

VIDEOGRAMS

Promotional videos are a key part of the marketing process for most artists who are aiming for a commercial chart position and they are essential for social networking sites like YouTube. In October 2016 it was announced that YouTube had finally reached a deal with the German collection society, GEMA, to make music videos available in Germany. This settlement brought to an end a dispute dating back to March 2009. The details of the settlement have not been released.

A pilot scheme that required music videos to be classified by the British Board of Film Classification (BBFC) will be continued on a permanent basis. All videos that might be considered to be inappropriate for viewers under the age of twelve must now pass on the BBFC guidance to the hosting site, such as Vevo or YouTube.

Kobalt struck a new partnership with multi-platform media company AwesomenessTV (co-owned by Comcast, Hearst and Verizon). It has a multi-channel network of over 90,000 YouTube channels. Ad agency Omnicon will have the first look at opportunities to use the music by Kobalt's roster of clients in ads, and artists coming through AwesomenessTV will be able to have their songs administered through Kobalt. (Source: *Music Week*.)

However, videos can be very expensive to make and there's no point in making an expensive one if your record doesn't get radio plays or TV airtime. It will be a waste of money and you'll end up paying for it in one way or another. It has to fit in with the overall marketing plan so don't overspend. If you can pull in some favours and get your mates who've studied film-making to make a cheap video for you – good enough for YouTube and maybe as a video mobile phone clip – then that may be worth doing but again only if it is part of a well thought-out campaign.

The creative elements such as what the story is going to be (the storyboard), who's going to produce and direct it, and when and where it is to be shot will probably be agreed between the artist and record company. Depending on the contract, the artist may have a final say on some of these things and the record company on others.

LONG-FORM DVDS

Unlike promo videos which are generally there to accompany a single release or as a trailer for an album campaign, a long-form DVD may well be a full-length 60-minute production, using the medium as a marketing tool for the artist, but also as a commercial product in its own right. DVD releases can also help to keep the artist in the public eye in between album releases. For example, if no new album is expected for a year, then it might be worth putting out a DVD of the last tour to keep fans interested.

Cinemas have been used innovatively to relay live broadcasts of sporting events, concerts and live theatrical performances and are a potential revenue stream but perhaps more in the live sector than DVDs. However, it can also be a good marketing tool, for example, the film of the story of The Rolling Stones entitled *Ladies and Gentlemen....The Rolling Stones* went out to 800 cinema screens worldwide.

It is also important to see a DVD, commercial video or film as part of a cross-media marketing push that can include the showings live in cinemas or live venues, online and as a sales promotion, as well as making available the physical copies. There is a growth in deluxe packages which combine the DVD with the CD as part of a special package at premium prices to target events like the gift market for Mother's Day or Christmas. The Blu-Ray format allows additional functionality so that consumers with Internet connectivity can download additional features off the Internet, which in turn also allows for the possibility of the gathering of yet more data on the consumers of these products.

But it does seem at the moment to be the more successful or established artists who are able to benefit from the long-form DVD as a source of additional revenue. The opportunity to get record company funding for a full-length DVD only comes well on in an artist's career.

Rights

The record company will usually expect to own all rights in any audio-visual recordings of the artist's performances it has paid for.

Some artists or DJs have people who film them going about their professional business, doing public appearances, backstage at gigs etc. and use some of that footage in a DVD or an online TV channel, YouTube, or their own webpage. The important thing here is to ensure you have the right to use the footage of other people who may get on the film, such as backstage crew or audience members, but lawyers can advise how to do that.

The record company may have the exclusive right to make long-form DVDs, or it may have the first option to bid for the right to make one, or the right to match an offer to make one that someone else may have made.

The cost of making a long-form DVD is usually mutually agreed between the artist and the record company and a separate account is set up. The artist usually gets to dictate, or at least approve, all the creative aspects of the long-form DVD.

Royalty

The royalty rate will be the same or slightly lower than that for records: around 80–90% of the record rate at the moment. There may be an advance payable for the long-form DVD or the record company may have had to match any offer made by a third party. The advance and the costs should only be recoupable from the royalties on this long-form DVD. Income from records or any commercial use of promotional videos should not be used to recoup these costs.

BRANDING

Branding is the way in which you use your name, logo and reputation to build up a particular image in the public mind and is intrinsically linked with the marketing of you and your product whether that is on record, or live, or in the products you want to sell off the back of your name. You may think that image and brand aren't relevant for an artist just starting out in the business. It's true that new artists are going to be more concerned at getting that first record deal than in worrying about their 'brand'. However, you only have to look at many of the boy and girl bands, and at the image-making that surrounds TV artists such as Taylor Swift or Little Mix, to be able to see that putting a bit of thought into branding even at its simplest level can pay big dividends. Not everyone can be or wants to be an *X Factor* or *Britain's Got Talent* winner, but all artists should think about getting some of the basics of branding right from the beginning. It can be as simple as getting a good, memorable name and registering it as a domain name. With those two small and cheap steps, you've already started to establish a brand. Add a visual and you've the makings of a brand to use in-App icons or to create a distinct online presence. At a conference I attended in Palo Alto in 2016, the App designers were commenting that your domain name was becoming of less relevance because of the rapid growth of access to websites via App icons on your phone.

Late in 2016 Guess joined forces with Republic Records to launch Guess Music. At its launch it featured an exclusive 24-hour window for the video of the new single 'Side to Side' by Republic Records artist, Ariana Grande (featuring

Nicki Minaj). In the video Grande is seen wearing Guess clothing and introducing a new Guess athletics line and giving viewers the opportunity to shop for outfits worn by her in the video.

Branding is big business and the growth of online activities on the Internet has added to the commercial outlets for the brand. At its most straightforward it's the building up of an artist's name and reputation in order to help to sell more records and concert tickets. At its more sophisticated, a name, reputation and public image can help to sell other things, not necessarily ones that involve music. Artists like The Spice Girls used their names, likenesses and the 'girl power' image originally to sell everything from crisps to soft drinks and sweets and revived that with their 2007/08 reunion tour when once again they used their brand image to sell products and supermarkets in TV advertising. Also bear in mind many successful 'live' artists make as much money from sales of merchandise at the venues or online off artist websites as they do from the ticket sales.

This idea of branding isn't anything new. All successful companies have invested a lot of money in the company name and logo and in establishing name recognition for their products. Think of Heinz, Sainsbury's, Coca-Cola or McDonald's. Companies such as Virgin turned branding into an art form. Sir Richard Branson realised the value in the Virgin name, in the fact that the consumer immediately recognises it and the familiar red and white colours. By putting that recognition together with a reputation for being slightly anti-establishment, he gets consumers to buy into almost everything that the name is linked with. A healthy dose of self-publicity from Sir Richard himself kept the name and the brand in the public eye.

A new trend in the area of artists and branding is the appointment of a (usually) high-profile artist as a brand ambassador for a company promoting the company's products more widely and in many instances supposedly involved in the development of the new products to be offered by that company. In January 2014 Will.i.am was appointed Chief Creative Officer for 3D Systems. They are a 3D printing firm and his role apparently includes shaping and driving the company's initiatives to make the use of 3D printing mainstream.

In the last ten years there has been an explosion in the number of acts that seek fame and fortune not through the traditional route of hard slog on the gig circuit, but on a fast track through appearances on reality television shows. These are, if you like, the 21st-century equivalent of the talent show. This started with *Popstars*, which spawned Hear'Say. The runners-up on that programme were Liberty, who, as a result of an unsuccessful court case, had to change their name to Liberty X, but nevertheless went on to international success. Then there was the *Pop Idol* phenomenon, where telephone voting by members of the public spawned a lucrative new source of revenue for the TV broadcaster and maker of the programmes. This has since been taken to new heights with the *X Factor, Britain's Got Talent*, as well as by the BBC on *Strictly Come Dancing* and more recent arrival, *The Voice*. The final of an *X Factor* series attracts many millions of viewers with the attendant increase in advertising revenue as well as the revenue from telephone votes.

In most cases the contestants, or at least the finalists, are required as a condition of their participation to sign up to recording contracts and also to sponsorship and merchandising contracts. The TV production company and the broadcaster take a piece of all this income. In some cases, the TV production company making the programme is in business with a manager who has an option to manage some or all of the successful artists. The artist is offered these contracts at a time when they have relatively little bargaining power and, although there can be some tinkering around the edges, the basic deal is usually already set and non-negotiable. Of course, once the artist is successful, renegotiation becomes a possibility but not a guarantee.

There are some signs in the ratings listings that indicate that the British public may have lost some of its appetite for these shows, and not all UK winners or finalists have gone on to sustain a pop career beyond the first album. The albums are often rush-released to capitalise on the winner's fame before the fickle public moves on. These albums are often little more than cover recordings of other people's songs and it is difficult for the artist to really show what he is capable of or to build a longer-term career. Amongst the artists who have achieved success is Leona Lewis who for various reasons waited quite a long time before her album was released after she won *X Factor* in 2006. It went to the top of the download and physical album and singles sales charts and managed to stay the course running up the second highest weekly sales figures of 2007 behind Arctic Monkeys. Her fourth album was a chart hit in December 2013. Others who seem to have staying power are boy band 'JLS' who made five albums before announcing their split in April 2013, Olly Murs and Alexandra Burke. Of course the big success had been the pop phenomenon which is 'One Direction'.

One of the main drawbacks for me to these shows is that they create an expectation amongst many people that it's easy to get a break, get on television, get a million-pound record deal and be set for life. The expectation is rarely met in reality and yet even the evidence of all the one-hit wonder winners or finalists who disappear without trace does not dampen this belief. Many people now fail to realise that there is a huge amount of work, effort and time that goes into making a true career in this business. Many so-called overnight successes have, in fact, laboured away for years honing their craft until they are finally spotted. Reality television shows lead many young people to believe that they are somehow entitled to their fifteen minutes of fame, that everyone has a record in them and that it's really rather easy. Why else are so many on Facebook or You Tube plugging their own records? There isn't that much quality around and there is a danger that true talent will get lost in the noise. The need is greater than ever for an angle that will bring you to the foreground.

BRANDING OF ARTISTS

Many artists are now recognising the value in the name, the 'brand', and are actively trying to put themselves into a position where they can make some money out of that brand. They may not have followed exactly in the footsteps of The Spice Girls, but they do pick and choose the products they wish to be involved with, for example, clothing shops or ranges.

To a greater or lesser extent, a successful artist is always going to be a brand, in the sense of being a name that people recognise. The more successful the artist is, the more likely it is that the name, likeness and image will be recognised by members of the public. If they like or admire that artist's reputation, they'll want to know more about him and will buy things that tell them more about him like books, magazines and records. They'll buy products that have his name or likeness on it such as calendars, posters, T-shirts or other items of clothing. If an artist is associated with a computer game, new phone or fast car, then those items become desirable and the manufacturers of those goods pay for the association with a 'cool' artist brand. Witness also the number of perfumes being endorsed by celebrities – there are his and hers Beckham perfumes, for example. Part of this branding process involves doing merchandising deals for these products. If you have taken steps as early as you can afford to protect your brand, then you will have an easy means of stopping others from cashing in on your name without your approval.

Cross-media branding is becoming increasingly important. It has been shown that consumers are spending more time online, reading and researching as well as being entertained. The branding strategy must engage online users. The artist's official website should be dynamic and regularly updated. Some labels are using linkage of a well-known artist brand with a website hosted by the label to cement their relationship with the artist and share revenues from products bought on the website such as concert tickets, with the record label picking up a percentage of the ticket price.

It's usually a good idea to use the same name, tag-line/slogan – which could be the title of the new album or the name of the tour – and imagery and logo across all forms of marketing. This ensures a consistent message and enhances the brand. Make sure that all media carry your name and contact details. Check that any online links between sites work well and link to a website that carries a consistent message.

If you're considering linking up with other sites with a view to drawing traffic to your site and theirs, then you may agree to share revenue with that site. For example, if you link to a site which supplies mobile ringtones and customers come from that site to yours and buy your latest record, you might agree with the mobile ringtone supplier to pay them a percentage of the value of the sale as a kind of referral fee of 3–5% and vice versa.

If the name, likeness or logo is one that can be trade marked, you can apply to register a trade mark or marks. Not all names are registrable. If it's too common a name or it's descriptive of something, the Intellectual Property Office won't let you register it.

Even if you haven't got a trade mark registered, if someone tries to pass themselves off as you in order to cash in on your reputation and this results in loss or damage to you, you have the means to try to stop them. This is called an action for 'passing off'.

If your fans are looking for information about you or where to buy your records they will look under your name. They aren't usually going to start looking under the record company name. In fact, many fans may not know or care what label your records come out on as long as they can find copies of them in their record shop or online, which is partly why record companies are concerned to own, or at least control, artists' websites and domain names. A fan is going to search for the artist's name. If you wanted to find information on Katy Perry on the Internet, you would search against 'Katy Perry' rather than under her record company, Capitol Records. Record company websites have improved. At first they tended to be corporate affairs where the services and information provided was intended for other companies or businesses; now they're generally more of a magazine format where news on all the major artists on the label is brought together in one place. Some have links to specialised websites, many of which are owned and put together by the artist or his management team. These links open up many new possibilities for marketing an artist. Many now also require the artist to submit regular updates to a blog of what the artist has been up to/is listening to/what films they like etc. and will link into Twitter and social networking sites like Facebook where the artist's latest exploits will also be found.

Is branding a good idea? While I believe we can never underestimate the public's interest in the inside story and behind-the-scenes glimpses of artists, you do have to be careful to avoid overkill. To some artists the whole idea is anathema. Most artists know that they have to work on building up a name and a reputation in order to sell their records. Some, though, think that they're somehow selling out if they put their name to other products – selling their soul as it were. It's obviously a personal thing.

Some artists, particularly those boy or girl bands with a relatively short shelf life before a new favourite comes along, do embrace branding in order to make as much money as they can as quickly as they can. Others are content to limit their branding activities to tour merchandise or sponsorship deals to help support a tour that would otherwise make a loss. It all comes back to the game plan (see Chapter 2).

I've also worked with artists who take the sponsor's or merchandiser's money and put it into charitable funds rather than spending it on themselves. Some make a point of telling the public they have done this, others keep it quiet.

Is it a sell-out? I don't think it is. If it's not right for you, don't do it. However, before you come over all credible and refuse to entertain any form of branding, just remember that you're already doing it to some extent when you use your name to promote sales of your records or tickets to your gigs.

There are many artists and bands whose image doesn't easily lend itself to selling loads of posters, T-shirts and so on or whose image is not going to be user friendly for family-focused adverts – I'm thinking here of some of the Death Metal bands. If that is you then fine, don't waste time or money on it. You also don't have to have your name associated with every product that comes along. Indeed, it's probably not wise to do so, as the public will quickly tire of you. The products you choose to associate with should be selected with the overall game plan in mind. An interesting example is Alexandra Burke, winner of the X Factor in 2008. She has featured in television adverts for Sure deodorant. An interesting choice of product, some might say a little risky, but the ads also featured her latest single 'All Night Long', so that guaranteed airplay for the song and helped drive it to the top of the pop charts.

If you do decide to do merchandising deals for your name, logo or likeness, you also need to decide how far you're prepared to go in protecting that merchandise from the pirates who will inevitably come along and try to steal your market, often with inferior products. Even if you don't do merchandising deals, you may find that the pirates do. I know of artists that have decided, for example, not to do a merchandising deal for calendars, only to find that unofficial versions appear in the shops anyway.

MERCHANDISING DEALS

In its simplest form, a band is involved in merchandising when they sell tickets to their gigs. The band name attracts the fans that have bought the records and now want to see them perform live. The ticket to the gig is bought on the back of the band name. If the band's core business is performing live, then the band name is being used to sell records or other goods like T-shirts and posters. It's often live concerts which make the money, not sales of records. If the concert is well attended, then the artist may also sell plenty of merchandise. Even the most credible of artists usually has a T-shirt or poster available for sale at the gigs. If they don't offer something, it is likely some of the fans will get them from the pirates outside.

In the entertainment business, merchandising has been big business for years. People can buy the T-shirt, the football strip, the video game and the duvet cover bearing the name and image of their favourite cartoon character, football team or pop group. One Direction, Disney and Manchester United Football Club are good examples. They know that there's a lot of money to be made from maximising the use of the name and likeness.

HOW DO YOU GO ABOUT GETTING A TRADE MARK?

Before you can begin to use your name to sell merchandise outside your core business of selling records, it's essential that you have a name or logo that's easily marketable and that you have or are starting to get a reputation that people can relate to. You should think of a distinctive name and logo from the beginning. We all know how difficult it is to find a name that no one else has thought of and we saw in Chapter 1 how to check this out. The same thought must go into making your logo as distinctive as possible.

If you're going to have any chance of holding off the pirates, you need to protect your rights in your name and logo as far as possible. If you want to prevent others jumping on the bandwagon and manufacturing unauthorised merchandise to satisfy market demand, you'll need to have your own house in order.

If you are going to go for trade mark protection, you should do so early once your career has started to take off, as if you wait too long then it may be too late. It's important to get trade mark protection as early as possible. Elvis Presley's estate was not able to protect the use of the Elvis name for merchandising as a registered trade mark in the UK because it waited until ten years after his death.

The Elvis Presley Case (re Elvis Presley Trade Marks [1997] RPC 543)

In 1989, Elvis Presley Enterprises Inc, the successors to the Estate of Elvis Presley, filed UK trade mark applications for 'Elvis', 'Elvis Presley' and the signature 'Elvis A Presley'.

The UK trade mark applications were accepted by the Trade Marks Registry but were then opposed by Sid Shaw, a trader who'd been marketing Elvis memorabilia in the UK since the late 1970s under the name 'Elvisly Yours'. He opposed the registration of the marks by the Elvis Estate on the grounds, among others, that they conflicted with Sid Shaw's own prior trade mark registrations for Elvisly Yours. The Registry upheld the Estate's applications. Mr Shaw appealed to the High Court, which allowed the appeal. In a judgement which was quite critical of character and personality merchandising in general, the court decided that the public didn't care whether Elvis Presley memorabilia was approved by the Estate of Elvis Presley or not. The Estate took the case to the Court of Appeal.

The Court of Appeal refused the Estate's appeal and refused registration of all three trade marks. The court concluded that the trade marks were not in themselves distinctive and, as there was no evidence produced by the Estate of any use of the marks in the UK which might have indicated that the marks had become distinctive of the Estate of Elvis Presley in the minds of the public, there was therefore no reason at all why the trade marks should be registered.

The Wet Wet Wet Case (Bravado Merchandising Services Ltd v. Mainstream Publishing (Edinburgh) Ltd [1990] F.S.R 205)

The courts have shown that they aren't prepared to interpret the Trade Marks Act too narrowly in favour of someone who has registered a trade mark in a band name. One example is a case involving the band Wet Wet Wet. Bravado had rights in a trade mark in the name Wet Wet Wet. Bravado asked for the Scottish law equivalent of an injunction to be ordered against Mainstream to prevent them from infringing that trade mark. Mainstream were publishing and marketing a book entitled *A Sweet Little Mystery – Wet Wet Wet – the Inside Story*. Mainstream argued that they were not using 'Wet Wet Wet' in a trade mark sense, but rather that it was used to describe the subject matter of the book. They also said that they weren't suggesting in any way that it was published by Bravado and, as such, somehow 'official'. Bravado argued that if they couldn't prevent this use then it would be meaningless having the trade mark, because they couldn't then stop it being used on other merchandise relating to the band.

The court decided that the words were being used in the course of trade but refused to grant the injunction, because it said that would be interpreting the meaning of the Trade Marks Act too narrowly. If it were so interpreted, then any mention of the group name could be an infringement of the trade mark.

Starbucks (HK) Ltd (and others) v British Sky Broadcasting Group plc EWHC 3074 (Ch) (2 November 2012)

Late in 2012 the High Court in London found that the Community Trade Mark that Starbucks (HK) Limited had registered in respect of telecommunications and television broadcasting services was invalid. The case was triggered by an announcement by BSkyB that it intended to launch a new internet television service under the name 'Now TV' as sell as the website NOWTV.com and a Now TV logo. Starbucks had an existing registration of a logo in trade mark classes which included telecommunications services: webpages, computer programs and data, television broadcasting services, radio and television transmission and computer games. BSkyB counterclaimed that the registration was invalid, alternatively that it should be cancelled on grounds of non-use. BSkyB's case was that the word NOW suggested to the general public that something was instant and immediate, modern, fashionable and up-to-date. This might have gone against them because there was also evidence that NOW coupled with another word like *The Now Show*, could be a valid trademark. The Judge, Arnold, felt more important was that the word NOW was commonly used in online guides to identify the programme currently showing. The Judge found that the word NOW was not inherently distinctive for a television service and that the Community Trade Mark was invalid for the services in question. The logo had been the element that had led to the registration being allowed in the first place but now the claimant was trying to enforce the trade mark for elements of the registration that did not include this logo. This last point is an important one for those of us advising that to get a trade mark registered you should come up with a distinctive logo, as it would seem, after this case, that this does not, of itself, guarantee that your trade mark will be sufficiently distinctive and therefore a valid registration. (Source: Calleja Consulting Limited 2013)

How to apply for a trade mark

You don't have to be already rich and famous to apply to register a trade mark in your name or logo. In fact, as we saw in the Elvis case, there are dangers in waiting too long to apply for a trade mark. As soon as you can afford to, you should think about doing it. You can apply to protect your name or that of your brand worldwide, but this would be expensive. To start with, I usually advise that you apply to register the name in your home market, for example the UK for a British-based band, and then in other places where you have, or hope to gain, a market for your records and other merchandise, for example the US, Europe or Japan. You can make an EU-wide Community Trade Mark Application.

Each country has its own special rules for registration of a trade mark and, in many cases, an application to register a trade mark in one country can help you with applications in other parts of the world. For example, the rules at present allow you to backdate an application for a trade mark in the US to the date of your UK application provided you apply within six months of the UK application. So, if you apply for a UK trade mark registration on 1 July, you have until 31 December to apply in the US and still backdate it to 1 July. Just making the application itself can trigger trade mark protection; even if it takes a year or more to get a registration, the trade mark, when and if it's granted, will be backdated to the date of the application. It also gives you priority over anyone else who applies after you to register a trade mark in the same or a similar name or logo. This is, however, a specialised area and you should take advice from a trade mark lawyer or a specialist trade mark agent. Your lawyer can put you in touch with a trade mark agent and a good music lawyer should have a working knowledge of trade mark law. While you may be happy to leave all this to your manager to sort out for you, do remember that the name should be registered in your name and not that of your manager or record company.

Once you've decided the countries where you'd like to apply for a trade mark – finances permitting – you have to decide what types of product or particular goods you want to sell under the trade mark. In most countries, goods and services are split for trade mark registration purposes into classes and it's important to make sure that you cover all relevant classes of goods and as soon as possible. You can add other classes later, but then you run the risk of someone selling goods with your name in a class that you haven't protected. For example, you may have applied to register a trade mark for the class that covers records (class 9), but not the class that covers printed material such as posters (class 15). In theory, someone else could apply for a trade mark in that area, but then you get into the whole area of passing off. It's also not usually as cost-effective. You get a costs saving by applying for several classes at a time.

A registered trade mark has distinct advantages over an unregistered mark. Actions to stop infringements of registered trade marks are generally quicker and more cost-effective than when you're relying on unregistered rights. A registered trade mark puts the world on notice of your rights. A registered trade mark is also attractive to merchandising companies, as it gives them a monopoly over the goods for which the mark is registered and may therefore give the merchandising company more of an incentive to do a deal with you. See also the power of the trademark in the *Glee* case in the last chapter.

Cartier International AG & others v. British Sky Broadcasting Limited & Others [2016] EWCA Civ 658

In 2016 the Court of Appeal upheld a decision by the High Court in 2014 whereby a trademark owner can require ISPs to block access to websites selling counterfeit goods and at the ISPs cost.

This is a very important new principle in trade mark law because the ISPs themselves were not found to be guilty of doing anything wrong but the Court of Appeal decided they had to be flexible, and agreed the injunction should be granted in order to ensure that intellectual property rights are protected in the digital environment. A key threshold that must be overcome is evidence that the ISP has actual knowledge of the infringement.

This case follows the already-established principle in copyright infringing cases following *EMI Records Ltd & Others v. British Sky Broadcasting & others [2013] EHWC 379 (Ch)* where the main ISPs in the UK were ordered to block users from access to websites that facilitated the transmission of copyright-infringing material relying on s97A of the CDPS 1988.

PASSING OFF

If you haven't registered a trade mark, then, in the UK, you can try to rely on the common law right of 'passing off' in order to protect your name and reputation. Before you can do this, you'll have to prove there is goodwill in the name. This may not be the case if you're unknown and haven't yet got a reputation in the name. You have to show that someone else is trading on your reputation by passing themselves off as you, using your reputation to confuse the public that they are you or are authorised by you. As well as having this goodwill or reputation, you also have to show that this has actually caused confusion in the mind of the public resulting in damage or loss to you. For example, a band using the same name as yours, or one confusingly similar, might advertise tickets to a gig in the same town as your planned gigs. Fans might buy those tickets thinking they're coming to see you. This loses you ticket sales and might possibly damage your reputation if the other band isn't as good as you. You have to have established a reputation in the name in the particular area in question. If your name is associated with records and someone trades under the same or a very similar name in the area of clothing, where you don't have a reputation, there is less likely to be confusion in the mind of the public.

You will recall in Chapter 1 the cases of Liberty X and Blue on the issue of band names, and another famous passing-off case involved the pop group Abba.

The Abba Case (Lyngstad v. Annabas Productions Ltd [1977] FSR 62)

A company called Annabas was selling a range of T-shirts, pillowcases, badges and other goods bearing the name and photographs of the band Abba. The band didn't own the copyright in any of the photographs and Annabas had obtained permission from the copyright owners of the photographs to use them. The band had to rely on a claim for passing off. Abba lost their application for an injunction preventing the sale because they were unable to show they had an existing trade in these goods or any immediate likelihood of one being started. The Judge also went on to say that he thought that no one reading adverts for the goods or receiving those goods would reasonably imagine that the band had given their approval to the goods offered. He felt Annabas was only catering for a popular demand among teenagers for effigies of their idols. These words have been often repeated in later cases.

In contrast there is the case involving Rihanna.

Robyn Rihanna Fenty v Arcadia Group Brands Limited (t/a/ Topshop) EWHC 2310 (Ch) 31 July 2013

In March 2012, Topshop began selling a T-shirt bearing an image of the pop star Rihanna taken by an independent photographer during a video shoot for her 2011 single. Topshop had obtained a licence from the photographer to use the image on the merchandise but had no licence with Rihanna. Rihanna issued court proceedings against Topshop for passing off, that is using her image in such a way as to deceive members of the public into buying the T-shirts because they would believe she had authorised the use of her image. The Judge found that Rihanna was a style leader (as well as a famous pop star) and had considerable goodwill in the merchandising and endorsement businesses she was involved in. He also declared that because Topshop was a well-known fashion retailer and regularly made connections with celebrities (including, interestingly, Rihanna herself on other occasions) in order to promote sales Topshop was deceiving Rihanna fans into thinking that this particular T-shirt had been approved by her. This last point was the crucial one, as just using a recognisable image of a famous person is not, in itself, passing off. To be passing off, 'a false belief has to be engendered in the mind of the potential purchaser which must play a part in their decision to buy the product'. Rihanna was also able to show in her evidence that she had consciously targeted key high fashion brands to be associated with, including Armani, who had used a T-shirt with her image on it in 2011. She also had a direct endorsement relationship with high-street retailer, River Island, for whom she was designing clothes to be exclusively sold in River Island's high-street stores and was doing this for no other high-street retailer at this time. He made a distinction between designed items such as this T-shirt and the typical screen-printed tour T-shirt with the latter being less likely to be viewed as passing off. Evidence was produced by Topshop that there were many items out there featuring her image which were unauthorised but Rihanna's answer was that she tried to police them, couldn't police them all and decided to take a proportionate response, i.e. targeting the more significant infringements. The fact that the image was recognisably one from the video would suggest that this was a publicity shot, adding to the impression that it must have been authorised by her. Having found that the elements of passing off were present here the Judge also found that these sales would cause financial loss in sales to her merchandising business and represented a loss of control over her reputation in the fashion sphere. She should be the one to choose which garments were endorsed by her. Her claim succeeded. (Source: Calleja Consulting Limited 2013)

It's clear from this case that you have to establish that you already have a trade in the area in question that could be prejudiced, or that there was a reasonable likelihood of you starting such a trade. If you're seriously thinking about doing merchandising, you should do so sooner rather than later, and should be setting yourself up ready for starting such a trade (for example, by commissioning designs, talking to merchandise companies or manufacturers, applying to register your trade mark) well in advance of when you want to start business to get around some of the pitfalls highlighted in the Abba case.

The P Diddy Case (Richard Dearlove v. Sean Combs [2007] EWHC 375 (Ch))

In September 2005, a DJ called Richard Dearlove reached a settlement in his case against Sean Combs, aka Puff Daddy, aka P Diddy, to prevent him from changing his name to just 'Diddy'. Dearlove (a successful record producer) claimed he had been using the name Diddy in the UK for his DJ activities since 1992. His High Court action settled on the basis that Sean Combs agreed not to shorten his name, agreed to pay Dearlove £10,001 in lieu of damages and his legal costs estimated at £100,000. Mr Combs agreed not to advertise, offer or provide or cause/procure others to advertise, offer or provide any goods or services under or with reference to the word 'Diddy'. He also undertook to remove from the UK all materials or articles that were in his custody, power or control, the use of which would contravene this undertaking.

Unfortunately, that was not the end of the matter. In 2007, the case came back before the court because Mr Dearlove claimed Sean Combs had breached that settlement agreement. This time he was not successful as the Judge rejected his claim for an early judgement and ordered the matter to be tried at a full trial.

Material relating to Sean Combs' album *Press Play* had appeared on MySpace and YouTube and on a website www.badboyonline.com, which featured the name 'Diddy'. Six tracks on the album contained references to Sean Combs as 'Diddy'. Dearlove claimed this was promotion under the Diddy name in the UK in contravention of the settlement. While the Judge made the important observation that placing a trade mark on the Internet from a location outside the UK could constitute use of that mark in the UK, he also recognised that the fact that the lyric to one of the songs on the album contained the word 'Diddy' could also be an advertisement for goods and services in the UK (which could have breached the settlement), particularly as many artists now use lyrics to associate themselves with various goods and services. This didn't mean that every reference to a product or service in a lyric was a potential breach of someone's trade mark; it would depend on how the lyric was used and whether it was intended to promote a product or service. The reason the Judge thought this was a matter for full trial was because he could not tell without hearing all the evidence whether this material/use of lyrics was something that was within Sean Combs' control. If it was, then he could well be found in breach of the settlement.

The importance of this case is to emphasise the global nature of the Internet and how care has to be used not to infringe a person's trade mark in another country by making something available on the Internet in one country where it wouldn't be a breach, but where it could be viewed in another country where it is a problem. The test would seem to be if the consumer in the infringing country thought the advertisement or reference to the trade mark was directed at him. It also recognised that lyrics could be used to sell other products as well as help promote the artist and his new recordings, and so when deciding if someone is advertising themselves under a particular name you need to think laterally and outside what might normally be thought of as promotion, e.g. an ad or poster or celebrity interview.

There have also been cases where personalities have taken legal action over adverts that they believe play on their voice/singing style or image.

Tom Waits

Tom has a very distinctive gravelly voice and he is protective of his voice and image. He felt that a television advert for Opel cars featured a singing voice and style that was too close to his own to be a coincidence. He claimed that the car company had deliberately used a sound-alike on one of their TV ads to imply that he had participated in the marketing campaign. He sought an injunction to stop the ads and asked for an award of at least $300,000 in damages. Waits won a similar court case in Spain where Volkswagen had used a sound-alike in a TV ad. He has a track record of pursuing such instances of mis-use of his reputation. In an earlier case involving the US company Frito-Lay, he had won a $2 million court judgement, including an award of punitive damages in the sum of $500,000. This was upheld on appeal. You'd think these advertisers would learn that he means business. He is famously critical of artists who take sponsorship money off big business and so is particularly galled when his voice is used in these very same types of ads.

OTHER REMEDIES

If you can't rely on either a trade mark or the remedy of passing off, then you will have to see if there's been any infringement of copyright, for example in a design, or possibly if there's been a false description of goods that might be unlawful under the Trade Descriptions Act 1968.

CONCLUSIONS ON PROTECTING YOUR NAME

Clearly, getting registered trade mark protection is the best way to go about protecting your brand, but when you're just getting started you probably won't have the money to spend on protecting the band name. A balance has to be struck. If you're ultimately successful and haven't applied for a trade mark, you may end up kicking yourself if others cash in on your name and market unauthorised products. If you apply late you may be too late, as in the case of the Elvis Estate. On the other hand, it's often not at all certain whether an artist is ultimately going to be successful enough to justify the expense. A sensible thing to do would be to register a trade mark in just one or two classes, including records, of course, and perhaps only in one or two countries at first and then add more countries or classes as things develop.

It's also worth bearing in mind that a record company may advance you the money to make the trade mark applications. If you don't want your record company to own your trade mark, make sure the application for the registration is in your name not theirs, even if they offer to register it on your behalf.

As we've already seen in the last chapter, there's also a great deal of mileage to be had from registering your domain name. Among other things, it gives you control of the doorway to official information on you and what you have to offer. Registration is cheap and quick, but please don't forget that it will need reviewing every couple of years. One record company, who shall remain nameless, arranged for all the reminders for domain name registrations to go to one email address. The owner of that address left the company and no one seems to have thought to check the mailbox or redirect the mail. At least one domain name registration lapsed at a crucial marketing moment and had to be bought back on the open market at considerable expense.

UNAUTHORISED, UNOFFICIAL MERCHANDISE

The line of arguments that we saw being developed in the Abba case was expanded on in a case involving The Spice Girls.

The Spice Girls (Halliwell & Others v. Panini, July 1997 (Ch.D) unreported)
The Spice Girls applied for an injunction against an Italian company, Panini, who was the publisher of an unauthorised sticker book and stickers entitled 'The Fab Five'. At this time, The Spice Girls had no trade mark registrations and, in fact, it may not have helped them if they had, because Panini had been careful not to use the name 'Spice Girls' anywhere in the book or on the stickers. So The Spice Girls were trying to use the law of passing off to protect the band's image. They argued that, even though the words 'Spice Girls' were not used, the book was clearly about them. The book didn't carry a sticker that it was unauthorised so, they argued, this amounted to a misrepresentation that The Spice Girls had authorised or endorsed the book.

The Judge was not swayed by arguments that it made a difference whether the book was marked 'authorised' or 'official'. He refused to grant an injunction. As a consequence of this decision, if a company puts out an unauthorised calendar featuring pictures of an artist or band, then, provided it is made clear that it's not a calendar that has the official blessing of the band and it doesn't reproduce copyright words/lyrics or photographs without permission, that probably wouldn't be a passing off or a breach of copyright rights. The Judge in this case went further and decided that even the use of the words 'official' wouldn't have made this a case of passing off, because the product clearly indicated it was not approved by the artist. In this particular case, The Spice Girls had a trade mark application pending, but it hadn't been registered so they couldn't rely on arguing that there had been an infringement of their trade mark. This is a good example of why it's important to have a registered trade mark if you're going to try to put a stop to the sale of unauthorised goods but this case should be read alongside the more recent ones of Rihanna and Starbucks set out above.

You might be forgiven for thinking that all these cases involve millions of pounds and are only of interest to the megastars that can employ people to do all this for them. Well, it's true that it's usually only the big names that have the inclination or the money to bring cases to court, but protecting your name can start at a very low level – like preventing the pirate merchandisers from selling dodgy T-shirts or posters outside your gigs, or stopping another local band from cashing in on the hard work you've put into starting to make a name for yourself.

HOW DO YOU GO ABOUT GETTING A MERCHANDISE DEAL?

You may start off by producing a small range of T-shirts that you sell at your gigs. You can get these printed up locally, put up a temporary stall in the foyer of the venue and sell them from there. You may also sell some off your website. If it's clear that you can sell enough to make money, then you might approach a merchandising company about doing it for you on a larger scale. The merchandising company could be a big multinational company or a small independent company. You can get names of merchandising companies out of directories such as *Music Week* or online. You can also get recommendations from your mates in other bands, your lawyer, accountant or manager.

If you're starting to sell out the larger venues and are a regular on the gig circuit, merchandising companies may approach you or your booking agent. If they do, you could try them out with your concert or tour merchandise before deciding if they're right to do your retail or mail-order merchandising as well.

THE MERCHANDISING CONTRACT

If you have a registered trade mark, this will increase your appeal to a merchandiser. However, merchandise companies will still be interested in you even if you haven't got a registered trade mark if you are sufficiently well known for them to run the commercial risk of producing merchandise for sale. The merchandise company will take a view as to whether yours is the sort of image that will sell particular types of merchandise. They will know if your image will sell T-shirts or posters at gigs and if it will also sell either the same merchandise or a different range of products through retail stores.

Even quite small acts can often sell reasonable numbers of T-shirts to fans at the gigs or through mail order off their website. If there's a steady turnover, a merchandiser will be interested in doing a deal. Obviously, if you only sell two T-shirts a month, and then only to your close family, then getting a merchandise deal is going to be a non-starter. In that case, you should be looking to do it yourself. Why would you want to do this? Well, obviously, the more that you do yourself, the more of the profit you get to keep. There is, however, an awful lot of work involved in mailing out the merchandise to fulfil orders and in ensuring that you've enough products to sell at your gigs so don't take it on unless you can see it through, as failure to meet orders can have a very damaging effect on your reputation.

If things start to go only moderately well, you'll probably need to employ someone to look after that side of things for you. You'll also need to do a deal with a company to make the clothing or other products for you to your design. You'll have to be responsible for selling it either by mail order online, through selected retail outlets, such as local record stores, and at your gigs. You'll need to be able to keep a check on the quality of the product being produced, to be something of a salesman, to be able to market the goods and to distribute them. You'll need to make sure that the orders are fulfilled promptly and that the accounts are properly kept. This is quite a tall order, even if you do get to keep the lion's share of the profits. No wonder, then, that many bands find a specialist merchandising company to do this for them.

WHAT IS IN A TYPICAL MERCHANDISING DEAL?

Obviously, each merchandise deal will be different and, once again, it's important for you to use a lawyer who is used to doing these sorts of deals. There are, however, some points that are an issue in every merchandising deal.

227

Territory

You can do a one-stop, worldwide deal with one company for all your merchandise needs, or a series of deals with different companies for different types of goods. For example, you could do a deal with one company for merchandise to sell at your gigs like T-shirts, sweatshirts, caps and so on. This deal could be limited to the UK or Europe. If the company was big enough in all the major markets, you could do a worldwide deal. If they weren't, then you could do another deal for the US with a company who specialises in the US marketplace.

If we are talking about merchandise in the wider sense of marketing your name or likeness on sweet packaging, computer games or crisp packets, then you'll do your deal with the company that manufactures those goods. That deal could again be a worldwide one or one for specific countries.

If you're going to do a worldwide or multi-territory deal, make sure that your merchandise company has the resources to look after your interests properly in each country. Find out if they sub-contract the work and, if so, who to. Is the sub-contractor reliable?

Term

If you're doing a series of concerts, you could do a merchandise deal that was just linked to those dates. If you were doing a world tour with various legs, it's likely you would do a deal with one merchandise company that covered the whole tour. However, you could do a deal with one company to cover the period of the UK or European legs, and with another company or companies in other parts of the world. This isn't as common, as it's difficult to administer and police. The term of the contract would be the duration of the tour or of that particular leg of it.

If you're doing merchandise deals to sell goods in shops or by mail order, then the term is more likely to be for a fixed period of time, probably a minimum of one year and up to three years or more.

The more money the merchandising company is investing in manufacturing costs and/or up-front advances, the longer the term they're likely to want in return. The longer the term, the better their chances will be of recouping their investment.

Some merchandising deals are linked to recoupment of all or a proportion of the advance. The term of the deal runs until that happens. This can be dangerous if sales don't live up to expectations or if the merchandising company isn't as good as you would like them to be. The best thing to do with these types of deals is to have the right to get out of the deal after, say, a year by paying back the amount of money that is unrecouped. This will give you the flexibility to get out of a deal that isn't working.

Rights granted

The deal will usually be a licence of rights in your name and likeness for a particular period, not an assignment of rights. The rights granted will be the right to manufacture, reproduce and sell certain products featuring your name and/or logo. If you have a registered trade mark, you'll be required to grant a trade mark licence to the merchandising company to use the trade mark on specific goods.

The rights granted could be for particular products or for all types of merchandise. These days the trend is towards limiting the granting of rights to particular products. You could grant the right to use your name or likeness or your registered logo on T-shirts and keep back rights to all other products such as calendars, posters, caps and so on.

You might grant the right to use your band name and/or logo for some particular types of a particular product and keep rights back to other forms of the same product. For example, you could grant a licence for ordinary toys and keep back the rights to use your name on musical toys. You could then do merchandising deals for all or any of those types of toys with one or more other companies. If your music is going to be used in the musical toys, then you or your publisher will license the right to include the music for either a one-off 'buy-out' fee or for a fee and an ongoing royalty (see Chapter 4).

Record companies may do a variation on a merchandising deal with an artist to use his voice/catchphrase for downloads of sounds for mobiles. This may be included in the record deal, particularly if it's a 360-degree type of deal, but if the deal is an older type then it may not be covered and there may need to be a separate deal done.

Now that the first flush of enthusiasm for quirky mobile phone downloads has died down, there isn't the clamour there was a few years back. Now it is much more likely in an exclusive licence or recording deal that the record company will require that the artist record specific clips for such uses and will be paid usually a percentage of what the record company earns from selling those clips on to the middleman aggregator, who offers the downloads to the public via a communications company. Because there are several parties who take a 'cut' before the record company, let alone the artist, sees a share, these deals are not the lucrative earner everyone hoped they were going to be but they do provide an additional revenue source for the record companies. If instead of your voice an extract from one of your songs is used, then the aggregator should also clear the right to use the music and lyrics from the publisher, creating an additional income stream for the publisher too.

There is also an increase in record labels wanting to also act as your exclusive merchandiser or at least your partner for online sales. If you do decide to consider them as your merchandiser you should make sure they either have all the team in place in-house or have business deals in place with partners who can fulfil the supply or distribution of the goods. If you can try to have an arrangement where they have to match an offer that you already have in the marketplace, then you know you are getting a good market price as well.

Quality control

Once you've decided what goods are going to feature your name, likeness or logo, you have to make sure that the goods are of the highest possible quality. If you don't keep a tight hold on quality control, you could do potentially serious and possibly irreversible damage to the reputation of your brand. If a T-shirt featuring your name and logo falls apart, or the colours run on the first wash, then that is going to reflect very badly on you. The fan that bought the T-shirt won't care that it was another company that made it – they'll blame you and give you a reputation for selling shoddy goods.

The contract will usually say that the merchandising company must submit samples of designs for you to approve. If they're making the goods to a design you've given them, then they should make up samples to that design. Only once you're satisfied with the quality of the sample should you authorise full production to go ahead. Even then, you should have the right to inspect the product at short notice and to insist upon improvements if the quality has dropped to an unacceptable level. The contract should contain a guarantee that the product will be of at least the same quality as the sample you've approved.

It's also important that the merchandising company makes sure that what it manufactures complies with all local laws. Toys and other children's products in particular have very stringent safety standards. You may want to insist that the manufacturer takes out product liability insurance. Be careful also if the company sub-contracts any of the processes. The sub-contractor must also stick to rigid quality controls and ensure product safety, carrying insurance against any damage caused by the product.

If the design is one created for you, either by the merchandising company or a third party, make sure they assign the rights in that design to you. If you don't, you may find that the designer comes knocking on your door for more money. You may want to use the same design as the artwork for the album sleeve. As we saw in Chapter 6, you should have made sure under your record deal that you can acquire the merchandising rights in that artwork.

Methods of distribution

The rights you grant can be limited not only to certain types of products, but also to certain methods of distribution.

You might grant mail-order rights only or limit the rights to selling merchandise to retail shops or at your gigs. There are specialist companies who are good at doing tour merchandising but aren't as good at selling goods to retail shops, and vice versa. There are also specialist etailers who are expert at selling online. It is important that you find the right company for the right method of distribution.

Depending on the means of distribution, the basis on which you're paid may also change, varying from a straight royalty to a flat fee or a percentage of the net receipts. If in doubt ask for a breakdown of how the end figure is arrived at. Ask for details of who is taking what cut off the top before you see your share. If it seems high or wrong, challenge it or ask for further explanations. This is a developing area and at the moment there is no absolute right or wrong way to account – it's a business decision and can be challenged or negotiated.

Advances and guaranteed minimum payments

You may get an advance against what you're going to earn from sales of the goods. This advance is recoupable from those earnings but, as we've already seen with other types of music business deals, the advance isn't usually returnable if you don't sell enough to recoup it. One exception is if you're doing a merchandising deal for a live tour and you don't do some or all of the concerts. Then you can expect to be asked to repay some or all of the advance. Some tour agreements also say that advances are repayable in whole or in part if ticket sales at the concerts don't reach a particular level. For example, you may get a fixed sum, sometimes called the Guaranteed Minimum, that isn't repayable unless you cancel the whole tour. Then there are other payments that are made which are dependent either on you doing a particular number of big, stadium-type concerts or on you selling a minimum number of tickets over the whole concert tour. If you don't do those gigs or don't sell enough tickets, then you don't get those further payments.

There's also another catch with tour merchandise agreements, which is the one that I touched on above. The contract may say that the term continues until you've earned enough from sales of the tour merchandise to recoup either the whole advance or the Guaranteed Minimum. If you aren't certain that you'll be able to do this within a reasonable time, then you'll want to have the option to get out of this by paying back the unrecouped amount. If you don't have this option and your tour isn't a big success, then you could be stuck with the same tour merchandising company for the next tour, without the prospect of any more advances. If you can get out of it, you can try to find someone else to do a deal for the tour merchandise for the next year's tour, and may even get them to pay you another advance.

The advances could be payable in full when you sign the deal, or in a number of instalments linked to concert appearances or sales of product with, say, 25–33% of the total being payable on signature.

Royalties and licence fees

You'll usually receive a percentage of the sale price of the goods as a royalty, which will go first to recoup any advances you've already had. This percentage will either be calculated on the gross income or, more usually, on the net income after certain expenses are deducted. Deductions can include VAT or similar sale taxes, the cost of manufacture and printing of the goods, and all or some costs of their distribution and sale. With online sales there may also be a charge for things like secure credit card systems.

When you're doing a tour merchandising deal, commissions or fees are often payable to the owners of the concert venues for the right to sell merchandise on their premises. It's usual for the merchandise company to deduct this payment from the gross income. Some companies will also try to deduct other expenses, including travel and accommodation costs for their salesmen and other unspecified expenses. I'm not convinced that these should be deducted and it's a good rule with all these deductions to look at them very carefully, and to ask for a justification for the deduction if necessary.

Obviously, if you're being paid a percentage of the gross income, it will be a much smaller percentage than if it were a percentage of the net. A fee of 20–30% of gross would be equal to about 60–70% of the net income, depending on what is deducted from the gross. For example, if you had a gross income from sales of T-shirts featuring your name of £10 per T-shirt, a 20% royalty would be £2. If you had a net income of £2, then a 60% royalty based on the net income would be £1.20.

Accounting

Accounts are usually delivered for retail or mail-order deals every three or six months. Obviously, from your point of view, you'll want to be accounted to as quickly and as often as possible. You should have the right to go in and inspect the books of account regularly – at least once a year. You should also be able to go in and do a stock check from time to time.

Online sales will have similar accounting periods to mail-order deals and the same principles apply. Make sure you have the right to check the books.

Merchandising deals for tours are different. There is usually a tour accountant who will check the stock and the sales sheet on a daily basis. He will expect to be paid within a very short period of time, preferably within 24 hours of each gig or, at the very latest, within seven days.

Trade mark and copyright notices

If you have a trade mark registered, the contract should confirm that they will include a trade mark notice on each product and a copyright notice for each design.

Termination rights

As with all contracts, the merchandising contract should say in what circumstances the deal can be brought to an end. These should include a persistent failure of quality standards, failure to put the product into the marketplace by the agreed date, and other material breaches of contract, for example, if they don't account to you when they should. If the company goes bust or just stops acting as a merchandise company, you should also have the right to end the deal.

Enforcement

This could be the subject of a chapter in its own right. The contract should say who's responsible for tracking infringements of your rights. There's usually a requirement that the merchandising company reports to you any infringements of your trade mark or copyright that they come across on each product. It's as much in their interest as yours to keep pirate activities to a minimum.

There are civil and criminal remedies to stopping infringements. You can also enlist the help of local Trading Standards Authorities and HM Revenue & Customs. Often, these authorities are prepared to seize unauthorised products bearing a registered trade mark. Even without a registered trade mark, Trading Standards Authorities are sometimes prepared to rely on the Trade Descriptions Act in order to make seizures and bring prosecutions. In my own experience, the Trading Standards Authorities are an invaluable help in clearing the streets of counterfeit products. It's possible to provide HM Revenue & Customs with trade mark registration details to assist them in identifying and seizing unauthorised products entering the country at ports and airports. Indeed, following the Gowers Review additional funds were directed to local authorities for the purpose of stopping the sale of fake goods.

360-degree models
Merchandising usually forms part of the new deals being offered by record labels. These have been dealt with fully in the chapter on recording deals above, but just to recap, a record company or production company may only offer you a deal if they can get access to additional sources of income. These might be shares of publishing, shares of concert ticket revenue or often shares of merchandising or sponsorship income. For a new artist sponsorship income is likely to be quite small, but merchandising income may be significant if the artist has a growing loyal fan base and plans to tour regularly.

The record company may only want to be paid a share of the income from these other sources of money. If they do, then the percentage they want will vary from somewhere around 10% to as much as 50% – this is all negotiable. The percentage could be of the gross income but this would be dangerous for an artist because, after deducting the record company's share and the cost of making and distributing the merchandise, there may be little or no profits left. Much better would be to base the percentage on the net receipts or profits after these expenses have been repaid. Some companies are insisting that this income is shared for the life of the deal but you may want to try limiting it just until the advances have been recouped or to, say, the end of the first contract period.

In some cases, the record company will actually want to take the merchandising rights exclusively and exploit them themselves. This is to be avoided unless there is a significant financial incentive to do this. The record company then controls all the income from this source and the artist may not receive any money until all his advances – including the record advances – have been recouped. Issues like creative controls also have to be dealt with. In some cases these other income sources continue on after the end of the term of the record deal as a reducing percentage over a period of time. Again, these deals can work if the financial upside is there, but take care that you do not tie yourself for too long and for too high a percentage or you will come to really resent this years down the line.

CONCLUSIONS

- Merchandising is the use of your name and reputation to sell goods.
- Not everyone will want to do lots of merchandise deals and not everyone will be in a position to. You have to build up a name and reputation.
- Consider registering a trade mark in your name and logo.
- If you haven't got a registered trade mark but you do have a reputation, you may be able to stop people trading on your name through the laws against passing off.
- Make sure you own the copyright in any designs you commission.
- Make sure you have the right to use the design featured in your album artwork.
- Get the marketing campaign organised well in advance.
- Agree whether the press and plugging is to be done in-house or by outside agencies.
- If outsiders are doing press or promotion, try to get the record company to agree that only 50% of the cost is recoupable.
- Get approval of any photos and biographies.
- Get approval, if you can, of any television advertising campaigns for the records – particularly if your royalty will be reduced.
- Think carefully before spending a lot of money on an expensive promotional video. Will it get seen and justify its cost? Will a cheap one work for your YouTube Channel?

Chapter 9

Sponsorship

INTRODUCTION

We saw in the previous chapter how an artist protects his name by registering trade marks or through taking advantage of the laws of passing off and of copyright.

Having protected the name, your 'brand', you can choose how far to exploit that brand. You can decide to only use it to sell your records and videos and to promote your live performances. Many artists choose to do just that and don't really go outside their core area of activity at all. This is fine. No one is saying that you have to, but you may need to look at some kind of merchandising deal to bolster your income from live work. Many tours would make a loss if they weren't underwritten by merchandising deals and often by sponsorship.

Sponsorship is a kind of extension to a merchandising deal. The sponsor uses the association between you and their product to increase awareness of the product and to encourage more people to buy it. The sponsor provides sponsorship money in return for the right to trade on your importance to a particular sector of the market. For example, a sponsor of a soft drink might look for a sponsorship deal with a pop artist who would appeal to teenagers. An alcoholic drinks manufacturer, on the other hand, would want to sponsor an artist that had an appeal to over-eighteens and, in particular, those in their early twenties.

Pepsi has been a keen sponsor of artists in recent years. The Spice Girls released a track as a Pepsi single and featured that track in a Pepsi ad on television. Robbie Williams has done sponsorship deals with Lloyds Bank, for a Royal Albert Hall concert, and several deals with Smart cars, including the premiere of his film, where a fleet of Smart cars was available to ferry celebrities to the premiere. There is also the whole area where a company features a previously unreleased track which is then released as a single. Car companies are favourites for this, with Ministry of Sound releasing the track 'Jacques Your Body' which featured in the animated robotic Peugeot car advert. EMI released a vocal version of the Lloyds Bank ad featuring Sarah Cracknell and Pepsi Max has featured music written exclusively by The Black Eyed Peas. There is also the example of Alexandra Burke's track for Sure deodorant and Faithless' deal with Fiat of which more below. More recently artists like Kylie Minogue have been associated with MasterCard's sponsorship of the Brit Awards 2014 and Laura Mvula as an ambassador for the MasterCard 'Priceless' campaign.

Sponsorship deals are commonly done for concert tours. You'll often see the name of a sponsor on the ticket. For example, 'Band X sponsored by Budweiser'. When you arrive at the gig, you'll find that there are banners and posters from the sponsors. On a big tour there may be more than one sponsor. You could have a main sponsor (the title sponsor) for the tour, another for the programme and the tickets, another for the soft drinks on sale at the venue and yet another for the alcoholic drinks. Venues often restrict the extent to which they will allow outside sponsors to plaster their brands all over the venue (see Chapter 10 on Live).

Clothing companies often loan clothes for photo-shoots or live appearances in return for a suitably prominent name check. If you're lucky, you sometimes get to keep the clothes. Diesel and other similar 'youth' brands have looked at sponsorship in the past, and up-and-coming new designers or those trying to break into the UK market may be keen to do a deal. These kinds of deals are closer to what I would call endorsements than pure sponsorship. You let it be known that you support or endorse a particular product. For example, you might mention in an interview that you do all your shopping at a particular shop in fashionable Notting Hill. Suddenly, all the wannabes are queuing at the door of that shop, partly on the off-chance that you'll be in there, but also to try to copy your look. Retailers or designers may pay in goods or hard cash for these kinds of endorsements. Some artists are almost as well known for their fashion endorsements as for their music. This was a key element in the success of Rihanna's claim against Topshop as we saw in the previous chapter.

There does seem to be a bit of a backlash or tightening up of the rules on hidden endorsements. In September 2016 the US Federal Trade Commission indicated plans to regulate hidden endorsements by celebrities through blogs, selfies, Instagram and Facebook posts etc. You know, the ones that suggest a celebrity is crazy about a particular product, a pair of trainers, say, but they don't say they've been paid to post this and have been given the trainers for free. It's a difficult area because some celebrities genuinely only do praise stuff they really like, and getting paid is a bonus. But the test the Federal Trade Commission adopts for whether this is a hidden endorsement and therefore falls foul of the Advertising Code is: would it make a difference to a consumer if they knew the endorser had been paid in some way? So the idea is for greater transparency, for the blogger to say out loud they are paid to endorse the produce or for it to appear on screen or with a #ad or a #sponsored hashtag. But it's not easy because on services like Snapchat there is nowhere sensible to put the # and it is only there for a few seconds. I think we can expect more regulation in future.

HOW DO YOU FIND A SPONSOR?

There are a number of ways to get a sponsor. It's possible for a band to approach a designer or company to ask for sponsorship. The shoe company who makes Doc Martens boots has, on at least one occasion that I know of, sponsored an artist following a direct approach from the manager. Companies want to promote themselves as supporting and encouraging youth culture of which, of course, music plays a huge part. There is also the tried and trusted word-of-mouth recommendation from friends or other contacts in the business.

Sponsorship Agents

Apart from the direct approach, another means of getting a sponsorship deal is to approach a specialist agent who represents one or two big companies looking for suitable projects to sponsor, or who will act for you and go to potential sponsors on your behalf. There are lists of these agencies in the *Music Week Directory* and magazines like *Audience*. If you're sufficiently successful to have a brand that a sponsor might be interested in, they or their agents are likely to approach you or your manager direct. As with all these things, don't feel you have to grab the first thing that comes along. If you're desperate for some funding to underwrite a shortfall on a tour, then by all means do a deal, but keep it short and see how things work out before you get in too deep. Choose carefully as an ill-chosen product or sponsor can do more harm than good.

What do they charge?
If you employ an agent to find a sponsorship deal for you, then they will usually take a percentage of the deal they do for you. This percentage can vary between 5% and 15% of the gross sponsorship income. For example, if the agent brokers a deal for a drinks company to sponsor your next UK tour and the drinks company is prepared to offer £100,000 for the privilege, the agent would take between £5,000 and £15,000 of that as their fee. If the sponsorship is made up partly or wholly of goods rather than cash, the agent will expect to get their percentage in the cash equivalent of the value of those goods. So, if the drinks company were to offer £80,000 in cash and £20,000 worth of free lager to give away to your fans, then your agent on a commission of 15% would still want their £15,000 in cash.

The money is usually paid to the agent at the same time as you are paid. If you are paid in two instalments, half at the beginning of the deal and the rest when you finish the tour, then your agent would get 50% of their fee up-front and 50% when you get the balance of the money.

The agent may want to be exclusively employed as your agent for a period of time. This is usually for a minimum of a year but could be longer. During that time you wouldn't be able to use any other sponsorship agents, so you have to make sure that they are good enough first. The advantage you get from an exclusive arrangement is the incentive that the agent has to bring deals to you as opposed to anyone else. The disadvantage is that you can't go to anyone else if they don't get you particularly good deals. If you can get an agent on a non-exclusive basis, that will give you more flexibility.

If the agent gets you a deal for some tour sponsorship and that sponsor comes back to you to sponsor your next tour, then some agents insist that they should also get commission on that repeat work, even if they are no longer your exclusive agent by the time of the second tour. The logic is that they made the initial introduction and so should benefit from any follow-up. I can see this logic, but obviously other factors also play a part in you getting the follow-up offer for the next tour, such as the professional way you dealt with the first deal, the benefits that the sponsor saw that came from your efforts and your increased fame in the meantime. So, while it might be acceptable to agree to pay the agent for a short while after the end of your relationship with them, I would try to draw the line at, say, six months. This is all subject to negotiation when you take them on.

The agent could be your only agent worldwide and be solely responsible for getting you sponsorship deals around the world. As many sponsors are multi-national companies, this may not be such a bad thing, but if you think your agent doesn't have the necessary overseas connections you might just agree that they can act for you in the UK and decide to use other agents overseas.

If an agent is representing a company that comes to you with an offer of sponsorship, you wouldn't expect to have to pay him a fee for brokering the deal. In those circumstances, he should be paid by the company concerned. If he also looks to you for payment, you would be right to resist unless there were good reasons.

ETHICAL CONSIDERATIONS

No, don't worry, I'm not going to go all serious on you and talk about your moral values – well, actually, I suppose I am a bit. What I want you to think about is whether you'll accept sponsorship from any company that offers it and the more the merrier, or are you going to select who sponsors you on moral or ethical grounds?

When you decide on your game plan to look for sponsorship deals, you have to think about what effect that will have on your brand and your reputation. There is a narrow line to be drawn between using sponsorship by selected companies to enhance the brand and of being accused by fans of 'selling out'. The products you choose to be associated with must complement the image you've established for yourself. For example, if you're aiming at the teenage market, you may alienate them (or perhaps the parents who supply the pocket money) by being associated with alcohol or tobacco. On the other hand, if you cultivate a bad-boy image, you won't want to be associated with cuddly toys. The exception to this would be if your plan is to reposition yourself in the marketplace. For example, if you wanted to move out of the teen or pre-teen market, you might choose sponsors of adult products to show you're growing up. Although the recent activities of former teen stars Justin Bieber and Miley Cyrus might be seen as taking this to the extreme. You should also consider the moral sensibilities of your fans. You could alienate a large proportion of them if you had manufacturers of GM foods or a fur company as your sponsor.

There was a mixed reaction to the news that U2 were sponsoring a special customised black iPod. Some thought it was an astute, 'cool' move, while others thought it odd that a band which had been so averse to sponsorship deals was doing one at a late stage of their career.

Don't forget that the companies that you're being sponsored by will also expect things from you. They won't want you to do anything that will bring their brand into disrepute or show them up in a bad way. Bear this in mind when negotiating your sponsorship deal. You need to be careful that you keep an even balance between your and their expectations. If you feel at all uncomfortable about what you're being asked to do, then that should give you a signal either to try to change it or to pull out of the deal.

Your public is a very fickle thing. It's very difficult to know whether they will accept what you're doing as par for the course and what they expect from you. If your fans think you're selling out, then you and your press people are going to have quite a bit to do to redress the balance.

The other issues you need to think about are whether you want to be associated with companies that are involved either directly or indirectly in activities or causes that you disagree with. For example, if you're a committed vegetarian, you may not want to be involved with a company that has a subsidiary that is in the business of raising battery hens. If you have a strong aversion to anything to do with cruelty to animals or animal testing, you won't want to do a sponsorship deal with a company that had a French sister company that ran laboratories that used animals to test their products. If these things matter to you, then you need to have an ethical check made on the company to make sure that they aren't in any way involved with things that would be unacceptable to you. Remember that, although they are using their association with you to benefit their business, you are being associated with them too, and with the sort of things that they stand for.

SCOPE OF THE SPONSORSHIP DEAL

The sponsorship deal could be for a particular tour or for a series of tours. For example, it could be just for the UK or European leg of your tour or could be for the whole world tour. It could also just be for a particular project. A company could sponsor you for a particular event, for example, a one-off concert, or they could expect some ongoing personal endorsements of their product. They may want you to do personal appearances or to give private performances at their company sales conferences to rally the staff. They may want you to write and record a song especially for them that they may want to release as a promotion or as a proper commercial release. If you have an exclusive record deal, you can't do these deals unless you first get the record company's agreement to waive their exclusivity. They may agree to this if they think that the publicity will help sell lots more records, or if the sponsoring company has access to markets in parts of the world that your record company can't break into without spending a lot of money. For example, some of the soft drinks companies have a huge market in parts of South East Asia or in South America. By being associated with them in those countries, you're getting a huge amount of exposure that should help to sell lots of your records. This exposure could be much more valuable than any amount of marketing money that your record company may be prepared to put into launching you in those areas. Obviously, it makes sense in these cases for there to be a considerable degree of co-operation between what your record company is planning, what you're doing in terms of live appearances, and what the sponsor intends to do. If you can dovetail these plans, then your chances of world domination come a lot closer.

Whether it's a tour sponsorship or an individual event sponsorship, it's a reasonable rule of thumb that the more a sponsor expects from you the more you can expect to be paid.

Exclusivity

You could have only one sponsor at any given time or you could have a series of sponsors for different products. If you're only going to have one sponsor then, in return for that exclusivity, you should get more money.

If you're going to look for a number of different sponsors for different products, then take care that you don't narrow down your options too much. If you're going to have a drinks sponsor, then limit the extent of their sponsorship to alcoholic or non-alcoholic drinks, depending on what you're looking for from another sponsor. For example, if Pepsi or Coca-Cola was looking to sponsor you, you might limit their sponsorship to soft drinks. You couldn't have another soft drinks sponsor, but you could have a sponsor for alcoholic drinks. If you have a food sponsor, try to limit it to their particular product, for example, biscuits or crisps or whatever. This would leave you with lots more food products to find sponsors for. Be careful what you agree to do in return for the sponsorship money or you could find yourself in trouble.

> *The Spice Girls v. Aprila (The Spice Girls Ltd v. Aprila World Service BV [2000] (Ch))*
> An example of this is a case brought by The Spice Girls against an Italian scooter company. The Spice Girls were suing the company for payment of the balance of the monies they said they were due under a sponsorship deal that they'd done with the scooter manufacturer. The scooter manufacturer had produced a series of scooters, each in the colours that were associated with each member of The Spice Girls. For example, they'd produced a bright-orange version as the Geri Spice Scooter, Geri Halliwell being otherwise known as Ginger Spice. Geri Halliwell had, however, left the group shortly after the deal was done. The scooter company refused to pay and counter-claimed that The Spice Girls had misled them, because at the time they did the deal they knew that Geri Halliwell intended to leave the group. In February 2000, the court decided against The Spice Girls and found that they had misled the scooter company, who didn't have to pay them the balance of their sponsorship money. Furthermore, The Spice Girls were ordered to pay damages to the scooter company for the losses they had suffered.

WHAT'S IN A TYPICAL SPONSORSHIP DEAL?

The services

The first thing you have to establish is what they want you to do or what event they expect to be sponsoring. Remember to keep the scope of their sponsorship as narrow as you can without them reducing the money on offer, if you want to allow yourself the possibility of getting other sponsors.

If the sponsor expects you to do a series of things, for example, writing a new song, doing a live concert tour, making a television ad or a TV special, then make sure that you aren't over-committing yourself. By taking too much on, you may not be able to do it all properly and professionally. If you agree to do too much, you'll end up either not doing it or doing it badly. This will reflect back on you and could do you more harm than good. If you fail to deliver the goods, the sponsor could decide to sue you. It happens rarely but it is not impossible.

Exclusivity

Once you've agreed what they are going to sponsor and the product that will be associated with you, you have to decide if you're going to have one exclusive sponsor or whether you are going to give them exclusive rights for a particular product or type of product, and still have the option to take on other sponsors for other products.

243

Territory

Next, you have to decide whether the deal is a worldwide one or if it's to be limited to particular countries. You could do a deal for just the US or the Far East, depending on the type of sponsorship. For example, one company that is 'big' in that area of the world but not so well known in other parts of the world could sponsor the Far Eastern section of your tour. You could then switch to another sponsor for the US or European leg.

Creative control

If the sponsor intends to feature your name and likeness in any way in the campaign, whether on packaging, adverts or otherwise, you'll want to have prior approval of those uses. You may want to insist on or ask for a special photo-shoot with a photographer of your choosing. You could then submit to them a number of examples of photos that you like and agree that they can have final choice.

If you're writing a special song, then you ought to have some say in what it sounds like, even if the sponsor does give you a brief to work to. If you are recording a song for them that has been specifically commissioned, you'll want to know whether any particular lyric or theme is to be featured and whether you're comfortable with that. If you're being asked to record a new or special version of an existing song, or to allow a particular track to be used in the campaign, you'll need to know whether they intend to change the lyrics or music. If they do, you'll probably want some control over that and to have final approval. Bear in mind, also, that that approval should extend to any co-writers or composers of the original work, and that your publishers and record company may have to give their permission to you making the recording of the new version. You may also want to check the context in which the song is being used in case you find that offensive.

Term

You have to agree how long the deal is to last. If it's for a specific event or a tour then the sponsorship deal will run from the lead-up to the event, which could be weeks or days before the tour, and end shortly after the event or tour has been completed. The sponsor may occasionally have the right to use up printed materials or products they have already manufactured, but this wouldn't normally be for more than three to six months and they shouldn't manufacture more of the product in anticipation that the deal is about to come to an end. Obviously, during the time that they're allowed to sell off the product, any exclusivity they have ends so that you can go off and look for a new sponsor. If it's a general sponsorship deal for a particular product then you might agree that it runs for a year, perhaps with an option to extend it by mutual agreement. You would normally only agree to an extension if you got paid a further sum of money. You'll want to make sure that any remaining stocks are sold off as soon as possible at the end of the deal, as it could interfere with either the sponsorship deal for the next part of the tour, or a new sponsorship deal for the same type of product.

You should also bear in mind that the longer your name becomes associated with one company for a particular product, the more difficult it will be to get a deal with another company. For example, if the public has come to associate your name with Pepsi for soft drinks, Coca-Cola is less likely to want to sponsor you. Some of you might be saying at this point, 'I wish I had this problem.'

Banner advertising at venues

If the sponsorship is for a tour or part of a tour, the sponsors will usually want to have their name on banners in each concert arena. They may agree that these only go up in the foyer or they may want them in the concert hall itself. Many artists insist on no banners over the stage and, if the sponsor's name is being projected on to the stage backdrop, that this stops several minutes before they go on stage. Whether you want to insist on these kinds of restriction will depend on your own views as to how closely you want to be associated with the sponsor, as well as your bargaining power. I don't think it's unreasonable, though, to ask that the banners aren't so intrusive that they detract from your performance.

If your sponsorship deal involves publicity for the sponsor at the concert venue, you have to be careful that you don't run up against any restrictions within the venue itself. The venue owner may already have given the drinks concession to another company. For example, Coca-Cola may already have the right to have their soft drinks on sale at the venue to the exclusion of all other competing brands. If that is the case, the venue won't take it too well if your sponsor, Pepsi, then drapes their banners and logos about the place. That doesn't mean that you definitely won't be able to do the sponsorship deal, just that you'll have to be aware of any restrictions and make sure you don't agree to do anything in the contract that you can't put into effect on the ground. Any sponsor will want to have the opportunity to put a stand in the foyer. You shouldn't guarantee that they can do this, as there may be venue or local authority restrictions. Any permissions required and fees payable should be the sponsor's responsibility.

Meet and greets

Whatever the type of sponsorship deal you do, it's likely that the sponsor will require you to be involved in some kind of 'meet and greet' sessions. These are where the sponsors, their key customers and possibly competition winners get to meet you. This may be before or after a concert or at specially organised events. Bear in mind that a live performance can be very draining. You may not want to meet a lot of people beforehand, and afterwards you may need time to come down from the adrenaline rush of performing. Don't over-commit yourself. Some bands share the meet and greet sessions out between them. It's the job of your manager or sometimes your sponsorship agent to make sure that your sponsors don't get overeager and expect or even demand too much of you.

Freebies and promotional activities

By this, I mean things that the sponsor will expect to get for nothing as part of the sponsorship fee. They will usually want a guaranteed number of free tickets to your concerts. They will always want more than you'll want to give. There will need to be a compromise. You may offer more tickets at bigger venues and less or none at all at smaller ones.

The sponsor may want you to attend press conferences for product launches or to make personal appearances. These should always be subject to your availability and to the other professional commitments that you have. If you're on a concert tour in Europe, you don't want to find yourself committed to having to return to London for a press conference. You should also try to limit these appearances to a maximum number of days over the term of the deal.

Take care before you guarantee that you'll do a concert tour in a particular region. You may not be able to deliver this or, if you do, you may lose a lot of money. However, the sponsor may agree to underwrite all or part of such a tour if it's important to them that you perform in those parts of the world.

If the sponsor wants to feature you in adverts, they need to specify how many, whether TV or radio, and the extent to which you have to be involved. You should have rights of approval. It's unlikely that you'll be able to limit the number of times they can repeat the adverts unless you have considerable bargaining power. If you do, then you should aim to allow them a reasonable number of repeats without it getting to the stage that every time you turn on the television there you are. There's nothing more off-putting than that. The sponsor shouldn't want that either, but sometimes they need to have the brakes applied for them.

They may want regular Tweets, Facebook posts or blog entries. If so then make sure it's not an unreasonable number because you only want to do this when you have something pertinent to say. Otherwise you'll sound like an idiot.

Trade mark licences and goodwill

I discussed in the last chapter the advantages of registering a trade mark. If you have a trade mark either pending or registered in your name, or a logo, then in your sponsorship deal you'll be expected to grant a licence to your sponsor to use that trade mark. You should limit the licence to the uses covered by the sponsorship deal and the licence should end when the sponsorship deal does.

Payment

I bet you were wondering when I was going to get to this. What are you going to get paid for all of this work? The amounts can vary widely depending on what you're expected to do, the size of the company, your fame, the length of the deal and how exclusive it is. Each will have to be negotiated on a case-by-case basis. The sponsor or the agent will usually come to you with a figure for what the sponsor thinks it's worth and, after due consideration, you may want to accept that or try to push it higher. Figures of a million pounds plus for sponsorship of big-name artists are not unusual.

The sponsorship contract won't only spell out how much you'll get paid – it will also say when you will get the money. The sponsorship fee could be money alone, or cash and goods, or occasionally just goods (although in that case it's more of an endorsement deal). It's not usually recoupable or returnable. There are exceptions, though. If you break your side of the bargain, for example by not doing the tour, or if it's a case of misrepresentation as in The Spice Girls scooter case above, then the contract may say that you are required to repay some or all of the money. Or you may get sued for its return. You may also be required to return some of the money or to pay compensation if you bring the sponsor's brand into disrepute.

When you'll be paid will also usually be some kind of compromise. The sponsor will want to hold back as much of the fee as they can until they are sure you are delivering your side of the bargain. On the other hand, you'll be actively promoting the sponsor's product and you'll want to be getting some, if not all, of the sponsorship fee in the bank. At the very least, you'll want to be paid as soon as specific things have been achieved, for example, some of the money should be paid when you sign the deal, some when you start the concert tour and the balance at the end of the tour.

You should also be clear what is included in the fee. If you're doing a recording of a song you have written, remember that there will be mechanical royalties to be paid to your publisher and any co-writer (see Chapter 4). If you have an exclusive recording deal, your record company may want payment in return for releasing you from that exclusivity. If an advert is going to be put together with visual images for television, for example, a synchronisation fee will be payable to your publisher and to the publisher of any co-writer. These can be significant amounts of money. Who's going to be responsible for these fees? Are they included in the sponsorship fee so that you have to sort it out with the publishers? Or is it the sponsor's responsibility? The answer can make a considerable difference to what you end up with in payment.

You should have the right to end the deal if the sponsor breaches the payment terms or otherwise doesn't fulfil their side of the bargain.

CONCLUSIONS

- Decide on the types of product you want to be associated with.
- Either target those companies that produce those products yourself, or through an agent, or decide that you'll wait until they come to you.
- Decide if you're looking for one exclusive sponsor or a series of deals for particular products.
- Decide if you want to do a worldwide or limited country deal.
- Make sure that the services you have to provide are manageable and that you have any necessary permissions from your record and publishing companies.
- When setting the level of the fees, agree what is to be included.
- Try to get as much of the fee paid up-front as possible.

Chapter 10

Live

INTRODUCTION

The live sector is a risky business to be in, with open-air festivals at the whims of weather and the vagaries of competing events like the Olympics. There is also a worrying trend in the closure of many iconic venues such as Fabric nightclub in London which was shut down under licensing laws but re-opened after an appeal which was well-supported by the music industry. However, despite the set-backs the UK live music scene continues to be buoyant. A 2013 report on the value of music to the UK economy estimated that the live music market generated £904 million in 2015. (Source: *Measuring Music*, published by UK Music in 2016.)

The secondary ticketing market continues to give the industry significant problems. This is where tickets are diverted to resale websites where more can be earned in commission than on the direct-to-customer official sites. Some promoters, and possibly also some record labels and managers, deliberately divert tickets to resale sites which they have an interest in. There are regular calls for legislation or greater controls of this market. A Private Members Bill on Ticket Touting was brought forward by MP Sharon Hodgson in 2011 seeking to place a 10% limit on the amount of the mark-up but, despite support, it failed to make it onto the statute book. Ms Hodgson, together with fellow MP Mike Weatherley, was more successful in the area of consumer legislation where they succeeded in getting a provision in the Consumer Rights Act 2015 (CRA) requiring sellers of tickets to provide the actual seat numbers, the face value of the tickets being sold and any restrictions that the promoter may have placed on those tickets. They had hoped to also force the resale sites to disclose the name of the seller but in this they were unsuccessful. Still a small step at least in the campaign for greater transparency of these arrangements. As required by the CRA the government commissioned a report into secondary ticketing by Professor Michael Waterson who conducted an independent enquiry and produced a lengthy report in May 2016, which called for stricter enforcement of the CRA. This has been supported by industry organisations such as the Music Managers Forum. However, the Government postponed its response on the issue, citing more pressing political issues such as Brexit and a change of Prime Minister. This has muted the impact of the report somewhat but debates in Parliament continue and opposition to the practice is also getting more organised. In some respects there is an acknowledgement that it may not be possible to fully control the secondary ticketing market but that we could, perhaps, do better with the primary ticketing market and maybe make better use of technology.

Of course, a secondary ticket market can only flourish where the demand for tickets is high and is, perhaps, an inevitable by-product of the improved fortunes that the live industry has enjoyed in the past few years. There is an inherent difficulty in making the distinction between fans who will pay whatever the market demands to see their favourite acts and the rights of those who can't attend an event to sell-on their ticket as against the wholesale and cynical purchasing of tickets online specifically for the resale market and the use of 'bots' who hoover up tickets online for resale. A practice made much easier by the anonymity and ease of online trading. An amendment to the Digital Economy Bill passed in April 2017 allows the creation of a criminal offence to use bots to bypass limits on maximum ticket buys set by event organisers, and also requires resellers to provide a unique ticket reference and booking number when offering tickets for sale. Live Nation, which owns Ticketmaster and its resale sites Seatwave and GetMeIn, and EBay, which owns StubHub and other players like Viagogo, have been against greater regulation of the market, but did appear to support the ban on bots. The use of bots is already banned in the US through the Better Online Ticket Sales Act. Our legislation in 2017 follows a similar line, but did not go as far. This may be a step in the right direction but this whole area is big business and there are many other ways in which ticket touts can acquire their stock of tickets for re-sale, including contracts with venues. Clearly this is a very murky area and it would be good to have more transparency. The amendment passed on 26 April 2017 seeks greater transparency in the deals done to exploit artist and songwriter rights online. It is possible that this principle could be extended to ticket sales. (Additional reporting source: CMU Trends Report by Chris Cooke published on 19 December 2016).

There are also websites which claim to provide a more ethical service such as Twickets which allows fans to sell unwanted tickets at face value. Add-ons are also a problem, you know the kind of thing: when premium prices and postal/print charges can add between 20% and 40% of the tickets' face value.

We are it would seem naturally social animals at heart and for a good night out fans are willing to spend large sums of money on going to see artists perform live. However, a period of consolidation usually follows a rapid expansion in the number of promoters and festivals and we have seen several festivals die a quiet death or go into hibernation for a year or two. T in The Park has announced a 'break' for 2017 and Glastonbury will take its regular fallow year in 2018 for the sake of the land and the people of the surrounding towns and villages.

GETTING STARTED

When you are starting out, you'll probably get gigs in a very hand-to-mouth way. You or your manager will chase them up, probably starting in your home town with local pub dates. If you live in a town with a large student population, you might get on to the university/college circuit. Local bands are often very popular for 'freshers' or summer balls, possibly as support to other better-known acts. Getting to know the local social secretary at the university/college can help.

If you can get the local press and radio behind you, this can open up more local gigs. Don't forget college radio. If you make a fan of the station manager or a particular DJ, they'll plug not only your local dates but also those further afield. Take copies of your demo to the station and use your best selling skills to convince them they could be in at the start of a future superstar.

Once you have a local following, you can look to venture outside the area to bigger and (hopefully) better-paid gigs. A word of warning – don't even think of inviting A&R people to your gigs unless you are well rehearsed and 'tight' in your playing and command an enthusiastic local following. I've been to many gigs where the band makes the fatal error of treating it as just another session in front of their mates. They act far too casually and are under-rehearsed. If the local record company scout happens to be at that gig, he could be put off you for life, or it could set back your campaign for a record deal by several months while the damage is repaired. Don't get me wrong. I know that every act has its off day when, for whatever reason, it just doesn't come off. Scouts will take an off day into account. What they won't forgive is if you aren't acting in a professional way. You should treat every gig as a professional job and the potential one when you'll be discovered.

Try to find out who the local scouts are for the major record companies. It may be someone at the local college or radio station. Local bands that have been around for longer may be able to tell you, otherwise ask the reporter on music events at the local newspaper or find an online blogger or someone who regularly tweets about local music. Whoever the scout is, they may be looking to move into the business themselves using the discovery of a great local band as a stepping-stone. Some managers now also act as a kind of A&R outpost so don't ignore local managers either.

Doing all this is very hard work and mostly unrewarding. Some bands get to play in venues in larger towns by doing a deal with the venue owner or promoter where, in return for booking the band, they guarantee there will be a minimum number of tickets sold. If you don't sell enough tickets, you have to make up the shortfall. It pays to drum up 'rent-a-crowd' from among your local fans, friends and family. I know of bands that sell package tours – they hire a coach and sell tickets to the gig and a coach to get you there and back. This proves especially popular where the band manages to get a gig in a larger town or city. Then the trip to the gig is combined with the chance of a day out in the city for the fans at a reasonable price.

As I mentioned in Chapter 1, you might also consider entering one of the many competitions run around the country. These might be billed as 'Battle of the Bands'. Look out for adverts in the local press or the music papers like *NME* or online. These contests are often viewed as slightly cheesy, not quite a credible way to break into the business. If it gets you noticed, what's the problem? If nothing happens, then you don't have to mention you were ever involved in it, but please do be aware that there are many dubious competitions around, particularly online, which promise you a record deal or a gig supporting a 'name' artist or event. Many of these turn out to be spurious – either they are a complete scam with the organiser taking the entrance money and never delivering, or the 'prize' is worthless or accompanied by an exclusive record or management contract that no lawyer worth his salt would advise you to sign. Please check carefully. If in doubt don't enter. If the entry fee is small enough to risk it, then it might be worth it but don't expect miracles. If it looks too good to be true, it probably is.

There are also some venues that have special showcase evenings for unsigned artists or writers. The ones I know about are mostly in London, but there may well be others in a town near you – ask around. Club promoter Tony Moore has an unsigned-acts night at a pub called The Bedford in Balham which, although 'south of the river', still attracts the A&R crowd. He also has a more central venue in the Regal Rooms at The Distillery pub in Hammersmith. They are a recognised source of new band talent so are regularly checked out by the A&R scouts. The PRS occasionally supports events for artists who are either completely unsigned or have only signed a record deal. The American collection societies BMI and ASCAP also hold unsigned-artists events from time to time. See Chapter 1 on Getting Started for more ideas.

You can also try to get in on the unsigned-acts part of the UK music conferences such as Liverpool Sound City or The Great Escape in Brighton. The unsigned gigs are held in local music venues and pubs and are a magnet for A&R scouts. To be part of the unsigned section, you have to submit your demo and a brief biography to the organisers, who then have the unenviable task of wading through a vast pile of material to come up with a shortlist.

Most artists who are already signed see live concerts as an essential marketing tool. People who haven't bought your record yet may go to a gig and love what you do so much that the next day they go and buy up your entire recording output. A good review of a live gig can give your latest release very valuable publicity. Also, the current emphasis being placed on radio-friendly artists means that if your records aren't the sort that Radio 1 or 2 or other mainstream radio stations are going to play, you have little alternative than to build a fan base through live concerts. For some non-mainstream genres such as folk, blues or jazz, sales of the artist's recordings at gigs form the main part of their sales income alongside mail order or sales of CDs off their websites.

GETTING A BOOKING AGENT

The next stage on from you or your manager doing all the legwork yourselves is to get a booking agent. This will probably happen after you sign a record deal (see Chapter 3). It may, however, happen before if you've established a reputation as a good live act and have attracted the attention of local agents because they can see you're a safe bet for venues they regularly book acts for.

Do you need a booking agent? Possibly not. If your horizons are set at only playing local pub venues and/or you don't mind doing the work yourself, you probably won't need one. It's someone else that you're going to have to pay, so you want to make sure it's going to be worthwhile before you get one. Also, they aren't likely to be interested in you unless you've already established some reputation for live work so you'll probably have to be beyond the pure beginners' stage.

What you may find, though, is that certain venues are closed to you, because the venue owner only books acts brought to him by selected booking agents. Having a booking agent can also give you credibility to get into more prestigious or bigger venues, and open up the possibility of supporting bigger 'name' acts. As the booking agent is on a percentage of what you get, it's in his interests to drive a hard bargain. If the agent is any good, you should end up with a better deal than if you had negotiated it yourself. They can also be an A&R filter for record labels, tipping them off to interesting new artists they've taken on.

You might think that your manager could do the job of a booking agent. Yes, he could and in the early days probably will, but specialised booking agents are the experts in putting together larger events such as a UK or European tour of the medium to large venues and stadiums. They know all the promoters, they can get the best deals and have a better chance of getting the prime dates than you or your manager, who don't do this on a day-by-day basis. The agents also know about all the main venues you're likely to want to play, and one or two that you'll not have thought of. If the venue is outside the main concert circuit, they have the specialised expertise to negotiate a good deal for you. With everything else that's going on around a tour, you or your manager may not have the time to do this properly. It may pay to find someone who can. Getting a good agent on board can greatly increase your chances of getting good gigs at good money.

In the past couple of years we have seen several mergers in the live agency marketplace with a tendency towards larger, global companies, incorporating not only music and live gigs but also film, literary and modelling agencies. The Agency Group merged with United Talent Agency and CAA with William Morris Endeavour. Paradigm Talent Agency acquired a 50% stake in the Coda agency. Agencies are also getting involved in sponsorship companies and with ticketing agencies.

How Do You Find a Booking Agent?

You can ask your mates in the music business. Which agents do they use, which ones do they rate and which have they found to be trustworthy? Word of mouth is often a very reliable method of finding a good booking agent. Be sure that the booking agent works in the same area of music as you, otherwise he won't have the contacts in the right places to be of use to you.

Booking agents are also listed in directories such as the *Music Week Directory*. You could call local ones and try to find out which sorts of acts they regularly work with and what venues they book. Another good source of information on agents and who does what is the monthly magazine *Audience*. It also gives you music business news, including details of up-coming festivals and other music industry events.

If you have a record deal and you don't have a booking agent, it's likely that your A&R man will direct you or your manager to a good one. While obviously you should take on board their suggestions, you shouldn't blindly follow their advice. As with finding a manager, you should also ask around and arrange to meet more than one agent if you can. You should get them to come and see you perform live. Who seems the most enthusiastic? You should also ask around as to which booking agents are seen as having the most 'clout'. Your record company, accountant and lawyer should all have had experience of dealing with booking agents and can give you some guidance. If the agent who is interested in you works for a big organisation, find out if you'll be dealing with him in person or if he'll be passing you on to someone else in the organisation. Many of the 'name' agents have one or more assistants who may, in fact, do the day-to-day legwork; make sure you meet them and feel comfortable about them representing you.

If there's a good buzz or hype about you and particularly if you are signed to a record deal, booking agents will probably approach you or your manager, either direct or via the record company. If this happens, the same tips apply. Ask who else is on their books. Ask around about their reputation, honesty and reliability. Get them to meet the band and see you perform live. Make sure the agent 'gets the picture' as to what you're trying to achieve. Have they got enough time to devote to you or are they caught up with their major acts most of the time?

WRITTEN BOOKING AGENCY CONTRACT?

Some agents don't have written contracts with the artists they represent. They prefer to work on trust. They tell the artists what commission rate they take and when they expect to be paid and they leave it to the artist's tour manager to sort out things such as the riders (see below), security requirements and so on. The risk for an agent in not having a written contract isn't as great as for a manager, because the agent is probably only booking one tour at a time and will have sorted out in advance his commission on that tour. He has no interest in ongoing record or publishing royalties, and probably not in merchandising or sponsorship income. That said, even though some agents don't bother with written contracts, most booking agents like to have a contract to keep things clear and to give them some certainty so that they can plan what's to happen in the future. Indeed, since the introduction of employment agency regulations reputable agencies may feel it is appropriate to put their terms in writing

THE CONDUCT OF EMPLOYMENT AGENCIES AND EMPLOYMENT BUSINESS REGULATIONS 2003

These regulations apply to all kinds of employment agencies who charge a fee to the people they get work for and that includes actors, musicians, singers, dancers and other performers as well as songwriters, authors, directors, those involved in the creative aspects of film and theatre productions, models and professional sports people. The rationale behind the regulations is to ensure that the client knows the terms on which he is doing business with the agent and what the fees will be. The regulations seek to ensure that the client cannot be made to suffer a penalty if he terminates the agency contract, nor require the client to take other services provided by the agency. The terms of business have to be given to clients in writing and can't afterwards be changed without the clients' agreement. A separate client account must now be kept and regular statements provided.

Also, in a nod in the direction of health and safety issues, the regulations require the agents to consider the suitability of the client for the job in question, e.g. not putting forward someone as a trapeze artist who can't stand heights or has no training for the job. On the other hand, they also require the client to inform the agent if he becomes aware of any reasons why he is not suitable for the job.

The terms on which the agent is employed by the hirer – the circus owner looking for the trapeze artist – must also be clearly stated and written down in one document. The regulations also place an obligation on the agent to ensure that the client has all the necessary permits/union membership etc. necessary for the job in question.

If the agent wants the right to deduct his fee from the fees for the job, he has to have specifically agreed that with the client in the engagement agreement. For this reason, if no other, it is in an agent's interests to have written agreements with his artists. Agents can be sued in a civil court if they breach the regulations.

Craig Joseph v. Jason Spiller [2009] EWHC 1152 (QB) (22 May 2009))

In 2009, a case came to court which involved a dispute between a band and a booking agency over contract terms and in particular the clause which required the artist to use the same agent for any subsequent re-engagement within a twelve-month period by the same venue/promoter originally booked by the agent (the 're-engagement' clause). These clauses are often contentious and here the Judge accepted the argument that the re-engagement clause could not form part of the contract between them as it did not comply with these regulations. The grounds for reaching this conclusion were that Regulation 14(2) provides that, where 'possible', all the terms of a work-seeker's agreement must be included in a single document and copies of the relevant document or documents must be supplied to the work-seeker. In this case, there were two documents, namely the basic artist agreement form itself and the terms and conditions made available on the website via a hyperlink. Thus, it would have been 'possible' to include these in one document but this was not done. Nor were copies supplied. This case highlights a difficulty which could well arise with the now often-used tactic of referring to terms and conditions in a separate document via a hyperlink.

What is in a Booking Agency Contract?

In many ways, the booking agency contract is similar to a management contract (see Chapter 2). There are several parts of the contract that are common to all booking agency contracts.

Exclusivity

The booking agent will be looking for an exclusive arrangement. He won't want to be competing for your work with other agents. The arrangement with the booking agent sits alongside the management agreement. Indeed, the manager may be very involved in the appointment of the booking agent. The management contract will usually give the artist the right to approve the identity of any booking agent. The manager looks after all other aspects of touring other than the actual booking of the concerts. There is danger of an overlap in the commission arrangements. The artist doesn't want to be paying a booking agent and the manager out of his gross income. The management contract will usually say that the manager takes his commission after any commission to a booking agent has been deducted. The management contract will usually give the artist approval over the terms on which the agent is appointed, particularly if he wants to charge more than the industry norm of 10–15%. The booking agent's fee should be deducted from the gross income first, and the manager's commission should be calculated on the net amount that's left after the agent's commission and any other deductions agreed in the management contract have been taken off.

Territory

The contract could be a worldwide one or it could be for a specific territory, for example North America. If it's a worldwide deal, then it's possible that the booking agent will want to use local sub-agents in some territories. For example, the booking agent may have his own offices in the UK and Europe, but be linked with another company or individual in the US. Until the recent influx of US agencies into the UK market, there was a kind of gentleman's agreement that agents did not try to poach acts in their respective territories, but the gloves are now off with the result that most deals are now offered on a world-wide basis. This doesn't mean to say you HAVE to appoint the same agent worldwide but that is likely to be the first option presented to you by the bigger agencies.

You may want to have the right to approve the identity of any sub-agents. Any sub-agent's fees should come out of the booking agent's fee and not be payable by you.

If it's a worldwide deal, you will want to be satisfied that the booking agent has the necessary contacts himself or through established sub-agents to do a good job in all countries where you are likely to want to perform live. It's no good appointing a UK booking agent worldwide when he can do a great job in the UK but hasn't a clue how to deal with promoters or venues in other parts of the world.

Term

The length of the term can vary considerably. It could be for a particular tour, for example the UK Arena tour. In that case, the contract will end after the last date of that tour. You are then free to do a deal for the next tour or for the

US leg of the same tour with another agent, as long as it doesn't interfere with the UK booking agent's rights.

More usual is an open-ended term, continuing until one party gives the other notice to end the arrangement. The usual notice period is a minimum of three months. There may also be an agreement that notice can't take effect during a tour, or that the agent gets commission on the whole of a tour they have set up, even if the arrangements with them are terminated before the tour is finished. This is only fair, because tour arrangements often have to be set up months in advance.

Many booking agents are looking for the certainty of a fixed-term contract. This could be as short as a year, but terms of three to five years aren't unusual. Obviously, from your viewpoint, the longer you're committed to one booking agent, the more need there is for a contract that puts definite obligations on the booking agent to try to get work for you. The contract should also contain a get-out if it's not working out, because the booking agent can't get any work, or is otherwise falling down on the job.

The booking agent's duties

As we saw with management contracts, the agency contract often doesn't set out in any great detail what the booking agent will do. The agent's duties are usually expressed in very general terms. There should at least be some kind of obligation on the agent to try to get work for you. After all, that's his job. If there's a fixed-term contract and if you're ready to do gigs and your agent can't or won't get you any work, then you should have the option to go to another agent.

On the other hand, if the agent does get you work, you should have the right to decide whether you actually want to do the work. The contract will probably give you the right to turn down offers of work if you do so on reasonable grounds. For example, if the booking agent gets you three dates in the North of England and a fourth a day later in Torquay, it might be reasonable to say that you can't reasonably get yourself and your gear from one end of the country to the other in that time. Or, if you did, it wouldn't be cost-effective once you take into account the travel costs in getting there. If, however, your booking agent has got you work which you turn down for no good reason, you can't then say that the agent hasn't done his job. Most good agents will try to iron out these kinds of things before presenting the details of the gigs to you for approval.

Your duties

You will usually have to agree to refer all offers for live work that come to you to your booking agent. Because of the exclusive arrangements, you mustn't act as your own booking agent. You will also usually agree to keep your booking agent aware of your plans. For example, if the plan is to release the new album in September, you'll be expecting to do live dates to help promote that release. You'll need to tell the agent at the beginning of the year so that he can begin to outline a tour in consultation with you and your manager. Many of the bigger venues are booked up months, if not years, in advance for key dates, and the earlier the agent is told of the plans the sooner he can start to take options on the key venues and dates. These provisional bookings are confirmed when the details of the tour are firmed up. If you're tying a tour in with the release of your album, the dates won't probably be finally confirmed until the approximate delivery date for the album is known. That said, it doesn't always work to plan. If the recording overruns, then the delivery date will shift and could have an impact on the tour dates. However, gigs at big venues are usually set up for a few months after the album release and as an integral part of the promotion surrounding that release. Tours also have to try to tie in with any plans to release the album overseas. A wise artist manager will have the agent in the discussion around the marketing plans for the album release.

You'll usually agree to use your best efforts to do the dates that the booking agent has booked and which you have agreed to do. Obviously, illnesses do occur, and sometimes tours or particular concert dates are cancelled at short notice due to this. It's possible to take out insurance against having to cancel a tour, or one or more dates, if illness or accident affects one or more band members. These insurance policies aren't cheap, but, if the artist gets laryngitis halfway through a world tour or, as happened with Oasis, three band members were involved in a car crash causing the cancellation or postponement of some US dates, it is comforting to know that insurance will cover any losses. Kanye West cancelled the remaining 21 dates of his 2016 tour and was hospitalised for a time shortly after his wife, Kim was the victim of a robbery. Insurance policies can also be taken out to cover dates that have to be cancelled because not enough tickets have been sold. These are, of course, very expensive and are probably only worth it for big stadium dates. If you've got yourself a decent manager, you shouldn't have to worry about whether the necessary insurance is in place, as he, or the tour manager, will do this for you.

Insurance policies can also be taken out to cover things like bad weather on open-air gigs. The owner of the site that hosts the Glastonbury Festival described in the press how he'd been offered insurance cover against bad weather, but hadn't taken it up because the premium was too high. Given the number of years that the site turns into a giant mud bath, it probably is too high a cost especially as the mud has now almost become a part of the experience for the stoic British festival-going public.

You can get insurance cover for most things at a price. I remember a situation when a member of a band was spending a year living outside the UK for tax reasons. The rules at the time allowed you to return to the UK for a given number of days in that year. The band was doing a world tour, which included some dates in the UK. The last of these dates fell on the last day that this band member would have been entitled to be in the UK and not lose the tax advantages. The concert was due to finish at 10.30 p.m., which meant that with a helicopter standing by he should have been out of the country in time. If he wasn't, he would lose significant amounts of tax savings, so an insurance policy was taken out to cover him against that happening. Everything was going very well until the band got a little too enthusiastic in the number of encores, and it was getting nearer to 11 p.m. when they finally left the stage. A very swift dash to the helicopter followed and, luckily, our man was just away and out of UK air space in time.

Gary Marlow v. Exile Productions ([2003] EWHC 2631)
But don't think you can always be protected against cancellation or no-show. Van Morrison's service company, Exile, got into trouble in 2003 when it was ordered by a court to pay Gary Marlow, the owner of the Crown Hotel in Marlborough, £40,000 in damages. Mr Marlow had booked Van Morrison to appear at his hotel and was also the promoter of the gig. There was a written contract which, according to Exile, gave them a prior right of approval of all advertising and promotional materials, i.e. it would seem Van Morrison wanted to keep it relatively low profile. But the contract also said Mr Marlow should do his best to promote the show. Mr Marlow mentioned the intended appearance of Van Morrison in answer to some enquiries from the press. As a result, Exile decided Van Morrison would not perform, arguing that this interview breached its right of approval over publicity. However, the Judge decided that it was the nature of a promoter's contract to promote and if the artist wanted to place restrictions on that promotion these had to be clear, unambiguous and not contradictory. This contract was not drafted in this way so Exile was found to have wrongfully prevented Van Morrison from performing and had to pay up.

Michael Jackson

When Michael Jackson collapsed and died shortly before beginning a residency of fifty dates at the O2 in London in 2009 his physician, Dr Conrad Murray, was subsequently found guilty of involuntary manslaughter and given a two-year jail sentence. Jackson's family brought a $1.5 million damages claim against the promoters of that tour, AEG, who had employed Murray. The family argued unsuccessfully that the company was to blame for hiring someone who was not fit or competent to do the job he was hired to do. It is believed that the parlous financial position that Murray was in made him keen to hang on to his job and perhaps more susceptible to provide the prescription drugs that Jackson wanted. However, the jury found that AEG did not have a responsibility to look into Murray's personal life and reasonable for AEG to assume that he was competent to perform the tasks he was hired for in a responsible way. He had had no malpractice claims against him. The jury found that AEG was not liable but Jackson's mother, Katherine, has since filed an appeal against the decision.

The fee

What is the agent paid? His fee is usually a percentage of the gross income from an artist's live appearances. It will include the appearance fee and also any benefits that you receive in kind as opposed to in cash. For example, the payment you get for a particular contract could be made up of a £10,000 appearance fee plus a car provided by the tour or venue promoter, or free travel or hotel accommodation. The agent will usually want to add the value of the car, the travel, the accommodation and so on to the gross income in working out his fee. It's here, of course, that you can see the value of a tour accountant. One of his many jobs will be to see that a proper value has been placed on these non-monetary items.

The fee is usually between 10% and 15% of the gross income. If you're paid £10,000 in appearance fees and a car worth £10,000, then your booking agent will receive 10–15% of £20,000 (i.e. £2–3,000). The agent will negotiate with the promoter or with the venue direct, and will usually agree that the promoter or venue pays him his fee direct, with the balance being paid through to you. There may be a deposit paid which the agent may well hold as security for his fee. Once it's clear that there are sufficient ticket sales to mean that date won't make a loss, the booking agent may well agree to release that deposit to you, less his agency fee, although, as we saw above, the new regulations mean that he will have to get your written approval in order to deduct his fee from these monies and he has to keep the fees in a separate client account. Or the agent may negotiate guaranteed minimum payments from the venue or promoter, which aren't returnable, even if insufficient tickets are sold to make the date viable. The booking agent will usually insist on being paid for any work that has been contracted for or substantially negotiated during the term of the agency contract. For example, you may contract to a forty-date tour through a particular agent and then move on to another agent for the rest of the dates or for the next tour. While you may be free to do this, you will still have to pay the first booking agent for the work he did in putting the original forty-date tour together. Sometimes the agent will limit his commission to concert dates that you do within six months of the end of the term of his contract. This could be a little hard on the agent. If the artist is doing a world tour, it's likely that that could run well beyond six months. If the agent has done the work in setting up the tour, there are strong arguments for saying that he should be paid for that work. As it's unlikely that you will have to pay any other booking agent for that same tour, you aren't going to get a double-hit for fees. If the booking agent has done an all-right job and the contract isn't being disputed, or hasn't been brought to an end because the booking agent is in breach of contract, this position is a reasonable one to take. Often, if your agent leaves one company to go to another one and you move with him, he agrees to pay some of his fees to the old agency in return for taking you with him.

Accounting

The booking agent will usually want to collect the money and deduct his commission before paying the balance through to you.

You'll want to make sure that the money is paid into a separate client bank account. You'll need to see detailed statements of what has been received, from where and how the commission is calculated. You'll want the balance to be paid through quickly and will need to have the right to carry out an audit of the booking agent's books and records to make sure you've received amounts properly due.

This is particularly important where some payments may be received up-front in the form of deposits from the venues, or as guaranteed sums regardless of the number of tickets sold. The deposit may be returnable in some circumstances. One of the jobs of the tour accountant is to keep track of all these arrangements as well as keeping a close eye on any sums paid in cash on the night. These deposits do not automatically have to sit in the separate account under the agency regulations so you might want to specify in your agreement that they should.

The balance due to you should be paid through at the end of each gig, but that may not be possible, in which case it should be at least weekly. Sometimes payment may come at monthly intervals if the arrangements are particularly complex or involve overseas tax issues. If you aren't going to be paid on the night and payment is to be delayed, then a rough outline – called a settlement sheet – should be prepared at the end of each gig and given to you or the tour accountant within three days to check.

Assignment and key-man provisions

You need to establish who is going to be your agent – your key contact at the booking agency. The larger the booking agency, the more important it is to get this sorted out. There's nothing worse than signing up to an agency thinking that you're going to be dealt with by one of the hot-shots, only to discover that he has passed it to a junior with no experience or clout.

If you can, you should get a right in the contract to terminate it if that key-man isn't available to you as your agent. Obviously, a good agent is going to be working for more than one artist and is going to be in great demand. You can't therefore expect him to be there for you every minute of the day. But when it comes to putting together a big tour, whether you're the headline or support act, you need to know that the agent is there for you to lend his experience and bargaining skills to sorting out the details. The agency isn't going to be very happy about agreeing to key-man clauses in the contract. If a particularly good agent wants to go off to another agency, or wants to set up on his own account, that puts him in a very good bargaining position. You can terminate the contract if the agent leaves and then move to his new agency if you want to. The agent can use the fact that you could terminate to negotiate better terms for him if he's to stay with the agency or better settlement terms if he still wants to leave. If the agency does agree to a key-man clause, then it will probably say that the right to terminate only arises when the agent is consistently not around for thirty days or more. They will also usually exclude periods when the agent is genuinely ill or on holiday.

If the agent plans to sell up or sell on the contract to another company, or wants to buy into a bigger company, you should have the right to refuse to be tied to these arrangements unless the agent first gets your approval.

Finally, the contract should give you the right to terminate the term of the contract if the agent is insolvent or breaches his obligations, for example, if he doesn't pay the balance of the ticket money when he should and he fails to correct this within a reasonable time of you putting him on notice that he should.

PROMOTERS

A promoter is responsible for booking artists to perform live at particular venues. This could be one man promoting a single venue or a multi-million-pound multinational corporation owning the right to promote a whole raft of large and small venues such as Live Nation or AEG.

WHAT DO PROMOTERS DO?

Promoters are responsible for securing the venue and for selling the tickets. The promoter may be the venue owner himself, or it may be a separate company which has an arrangement with a particular venue. This arrangement may be exclusive or non-exclusive. The promoter may deal direct with the artist or his manager or he may negotiate through a booking agent. Promoters make their money on their margins. They are the risk takers. If they own the venue, then they want to cover their costs and make a profit. If they just deal with a venue, they make their money on the difference between what they have to pay through to the venue and what they have to pay to the artist/booking agent after allowing for their own expenses. The promoter may also control the sales concessions at the venues, for example for selling food, drink or merchandise. The promoter may charge for the rental of these concessions and/or take a percentage of the takings.

A promoter may promote just one venue or perhaps a festival or a series of venues. There are promoters who operate nationwide, but also those who operate only in particular parts of the UK.

Once the dates are pencilled in, the promoter will want an agreement committing the artist to do these dates and laying out the terms on which they will perform.

Naturally, these sorts of arrangements are only likely to affect the main artists on the bill – the top billing or headline acts. A supporting artist will have little or no say on the terms of the deal with the promoter. The promoter may agree a fee with the headline act and it's up to that act to agree a deal with the supporting act as to the terms on which they will appear on the bill.

Some promoters are also branching out into controlling other ancillary income streams not historically within a promoter's remit, such as merchandising.

What's in a Promoter's Contract?

Your obligations

The contract will set out what concerts you will do, when and where. The contract could spell out the length of time you are required to perform. For example, it may say that you're expected to do one 'set' (performance) of at least forty minutes' duration. For smaller venues, it may say that you're expected to do two forty-minute sets with a break in between.

Promoter's obligations

The promoter will agree to provide at least the venue, ticket sales facilities and basic door, stage and backstage security arrangements. Thereafter, it's down to the individual arrangements agreed in each contract. The promoter may agree to supply certain equipment and personnel, for example, a particular sound desk or sound engineer. If the dates include any overseas gigs, then any personnel they supply should be provided with all necessary permits, including work permits for overseas dates or for overseas personnel working in the UK.

The promoter will also usually be required to provide an agreed level of back-stage amenities in the form of dressing rooms, toilets and meeting or VIP areas.

It's also usually the responsibility of the promoter to provide insurance cover against injury or death caused to members of the public. This is called public liability insurance. It's vital to ensure that this cover is in place. Obviously, it will be the manager's job to check this once there is a manager on board, but a member of the public can get injured in the early days as well, so you should think about this. Unfortunately, accidents do happen at live gigs; people do fall or get caught up in the crush at the front of the stage. If there isn't insurance in place, the person injured could look to you for compensation. If anyone is employed to do any construction work, for example for the stage or lighting rig, then those sub-contractors should also carry insurance or, once again, responsibility could fall back on you. There was an unfortunate spate of concert-related deaths and serious injuries in recent years, beginning with the deaths of nine music fans at the Roskilde Festival in Denmark in 2000, followed by the deaths of twenty-one clubbers in Chicago and hundreds of deaths at the Rhode Island Club where a fireworks display as part of the band Great White's set led to disaster. An accident involving one of the trucks carrying concert equipment for George Michael forced the singer to cancel a show in Prague. In Atlanta, opening artist Ray Lavender and Akon band members had completed their sound checks and left the stage when the canopy suddenly caved in. In the UK, incidents like these have led to greater insistence on health and safety issues and to the setting up of the Safety Focus Group as an offshoot of the International Live Music Conference in 2001. The International Centre for Crowd Management and Security Studies (founded in 2000) is housed at Buckinghamshire New University. ICCMSS provides research to help improve safety at events and the University runs a number of specialist courses on safety and event management. It is currently endorsed by the Security Industry Authority (SIA). Noise levels form a key point of the Health and Safety Rules which have to be complied with. This is a very specialised area where experts are usually called in to advise, particularly for outdoor events.

The Licensing Act

The Licensing Act which became law in 2003 and began to have an impact in 2005 brought about major changes to how venues are licensed. The focus was on health and safety and public order issues and it was a radical overhaul of the UK licensing system. One major change is that venues that put on live music regularly needed a premises licence from the local authority, whereas before they did not need an entertainment licence for one or two musicians performing together. The exceptions for occasional events and purely acoustic sets were maintained, but there was concern for the impact of the changes on the live music scene and this led to the launch of the Government-supported Live Music Forum, whose remit includes the evaluation of the impact of the Licensing Act and the promotion of the performance of live music generally. Its report in mid-2007 recommended making exceptions from the need for licensing for acoustic sets or for venues where live music was incidental to the main event. They also suggested an exemption for small venues holding fewer than a hundred people. A major review of the workings of the Act produced a report late in 2010 entitled 'Rebalancing the Licensing Act'. This resulted in a rethink and The Live Music Act officially came into effect on 1 October 2012. It removed the requirement for venues with an alcohol licence to purchase an additional licence for hosting a performance of live music for small venues.

It also removed the Local Authority licensing requirements for:

- amplified live music between 8 a.m. and 11 p.m. before audiences of no more than 200 people on premises authorised to sell alcohol for consumption on the premises;
- amplified live music between 8 a.m. and 11 p.m. before audiences of no more than 200 people in workplaces not otherwise licensed under the 2003 Act (or licensed only for the provision of late-night refreshment); and
- unamplified live music between 8 a.m. and 11 p.m. in all venues.
- There is no longer an audience limit for performances of unamplified live music.

In April 2015, new provisions were introduced within the Act to increase audience thresholds for amplified live music performance to 500. At the same time the Government also deregulated recorded music for 'on-licensed' premises when they have an audience of at least 500.

In July 2012 superstars Bruce Springsteen and Paul McCartney had the plug pulled on them by the organisers of Hard Rock Calling, Live Nation, to a barrage of complaints from fans. Bruce Springsteen was already half an hour over the 10.30 curfew when he called McCartney onstage to do two numbers with him. The microphones were silenced before they could thank the audience and they had to leave in silence. The problem is that Hyde Park is near a number of residential areas and growing numbers of complaints caused them to slash the number of concerts and crowd limits. Ultimately Live Nation withdrew from promoting concerts in Hyde Park and AEG Live replaced them.

The Private Security Industry (Licences) Regulations 2004
As if this weren't enough additional red tape, regulations intended to protect against unscrupulous bouncers or doormen were also introduced in 2004. The Private Security Industry (Licences) Regulations 2004 require all door supervisors and security staff to be licensed and to display an identifying licence at all times. The application requires them to declare any criminal convictions or cautions. There are separate regulations and licences required by those supervising these activities. Private security firms who provide security for pubs, clubs and the like must also be licensed.

Artist riders

Anyone who's seen the spoof film about the music business *Spinal Tap* will know about the occasionally ridiculous artist riders. These are the lists of specific requirements that the artists have for their comfort and entertainment backstage. Only black jellybeans and sandwiches cut in circles will do! I've seen some very strange riders in my time. One was twelve pages of very detailed menu requirements, including very specific types of cereal and drinks that can only be bought in the US. As this was a European tour that was pretty unreasonable and changes had to be negotiated and substitutes found. Other riders specify only a crate of good whisky and five crates of beer. Well, it is rock 'n' roll. Some artists take their own caterers with them, or will only use a caterer that they know is familiar with their particular requirements. Some riders are there for a very good reason. For example, an artist may be a vegan or vegetarian, or allergic to particular food. I've also seen riders that insist that all hotel rooms have hypo-allergenic bedding and pillows.

It's usual to leave the negotiation of the details between the manager or the tour manager and the promoter. It's not usually cost-effective to get your lawyer involved in this. The riders do form part of the contract, so the promoter has to make sure that the requirements are reasonable, affordable and obtainable. If they don't comply and the omissions are sufficiently serious, this could be a breach of contract. Even if the omissions are more minor in nature, it can cause major grief with the artist, which is the last thing a promoter wants just before the artist goes out on stage.

Fees

You and your booking agent are dependent on the promoter for ticket sales and income. You'll want to be sure that you're guaranteed a certain level of income. If you're already an established artist, you may be able to get a Guaranteed Minimum included in the contract. This guarantees you will be paid this amount, regardless of whether the promoter sells enough tickets. This is where the promoter takes the risk. They have to get the level of the Guaranteed Minimum right, because they'll have to pay it even if they don't sell a single ticket.

Over and above any Guaranteed Minimum sum, you might receive a fixed percentage of the promoter's net receipts. For example, if the Guaranteed Minimum is £10,000 and, after the promoter has paid out certain agreed expenses, you are entitled to 10% of the net receipts, then if the net ticket sales are £100,000 you will only get the Guaranteed Minimum. If the net receipts are £250,000, then 10% is worth £25,000. After deducting the Guaranteed Minimum of £10,000, you are now due another £15,000. The tour accountant will have to check very carefully that the expenses that the promoter can deduct are reasonable and that the percentage you receive of the net monies represents a reasonable return. The alternative is that you receive a further fixed payment dependent on levels of ticket sales. For example, it could be agreed that you get a Guaranteed Minimum of £10,000 plus, if ticket sales exceed £25,000, you receive another £15,000. With this type of payment arrangement, you must assess how realistic it is that ticket sales will be high enough so that you have a reasonable chance of receiving further payments.

Payment and accounting
The contract should set out when any Guaranteed Minimum payment is to be made. Usually at least half of it should be paid up-front and the rest on the night of the first of the concerts.

The balance of any payments should be made on the night of each gig or possibly at the end of a particular leg of a tour or end of each week of a tour.

It's important that you or your tour accountant (if you have one) has access to the box-office tills and receipts on the night of the concert and ideally all ticket stubs should be kept for at least three months afterwards in case they need to be checked by an accountant. Further payments under the merchandising deal may be dependent on a given number of people being at each concert. The ticket stubs and any head count on the night will prove the number of people at a particular date, so access to this information and proof could be very important. With the increase in the number of tickets sold as mobile barcodes, the tour accountant/tour manager/you now has to make sure there is a record of all online payments too. Receipts for any expense that the promoter is allowed to deduct should also be scrutinised and kept for later checking. Only allowable expenses should be deducted.

Other income
The promoter or the venue owner may have done deals with catering companies or drink suppliers. The contract should set out whether or not you should get any share of the profits from these sources. For example, the venue may have a deal with Coca-Cola that they are the official suppliers of soft drinks to the venue. An artist that commands a very loyal following of fans who will ensure

that his concerts are a sell-out can only be of benefit to Coca-Cola in the considerable number of soft drinks it will sell at those concerts. If you have sufficient bargaining power, you can insist on sharing some of the money that Coca-Cola pays to the promoter or venue for the right to be the exclusive supplier.

The sale of merchandise can be an important source of income for you. The promoter/venue may make a charge for the right to set up merchandising stalls at the venue. Your merchandising deal will cover whether the merchandising company is allowed to deduct some or all of this charge from the gross income before you receive your percentage.

Restrictions

The contract should insist that the promoter stops anyone from recording the performances, unless of course a live recording or film of the concert is being made. Your record contract will probably say something about you not allowing anyone to make a recording of your performance. While it's very difficult to prevent a bootlegger unofficially and unlawfully recording the performance, you can show the right spirit by putting this requirement in the contract with the promoter. This will demonstrate that you don't condone this sort of activity. If you do intend to make a film of the performance, perhaps to make a video or for a live webcast or television broadcast, the contract should make sure that the promoter will allow access to the venue for the recording at no extra charge. You also need to be sure that the audience knows they will be filmed and for what purpose. Signs at all entrances usually spell this out. It's impossible to stop people recording part of the act on their mobile phones and putting it online immediately after the show. This is unfortunate because the quality is often very poor. If it is too poor or damaging to the artist you can request that the ISP take it down as an unauthorised recording. Or you can have a marketing strategy which makes official footage available on selected websites or the artist's own site or makes DVDs or videos available for purchase through services like LoveLive.

Each venue has its own restrictions on parking and when the stage crew can gain access to load equipment in or out. Any particular stipulations or restrictions should be set out in a rider or schedule to the contract. In residential areas, there may be severe restrictions on how late the artist can play and there may be an early curfew on when the crew can load the equipment back out. They may have to come back the next morning. If so, you need to ensure the equipment is kept securely and that it's insured against loss or damage. If it's a nationwide tour, the tour manager will need to know these restrictions well in advance. It wouldn't be funny if you had a date in Scarborough on the Friday night and your equipment was still in Torquay because the crew couldn't get in to load out the equipment after Thursday's Torquay gig until seven o'clock the next morning. Here again, a good tour manager is worth his weight in gold.

An important part of protecting your brand is to ensure that there are no sales of unauthorised merchandise inside or outside the venue. It's easier for a promoter to control illegal merchandise inside the venue, but he may say he has no control over what happens outside. In that case, you should try to make sure that the venue and the promoter co-operate with Trading Standards officers or other personnel who are trying to stop unauthorised or pirate merchandise. In practice, however, the promoter will say it's not his problem.

GETTING FUNDING FOR LIVE WORK

Funding for a tour can come from a number of different places. At the lowest level, where you're just starting out and doing local gigs, you can expect to be paid little or nothing over and above some petrol money and a few free pints of beer. As you progress, you may get a small percentage of the ticket sales and may make some money from sales of T-shirts or recordings of your performances that you sell at the gigs. There probably won't be much in the way of profits after the cost of hiring a PA and paying for transport.

It is possible to make a decent living from live gigs if you can keep your costs down, play decent-sized venues, and have a loyal following of fans, but it's very hard work.

Once you're signed to a record deal, bigger venues may open up to you. A booking agent may come on the scene and get you slots as support bands or lower-down-the-order gigs at summer festivals. Money can be made from merchandise sales or from tour sponsorship. However, it's likely that you won't make a big profit on live work until you've achieved quite a degree of success and fame as a recording artist. Even then, you may barely break even if you have an expensive live set with lots of special effects and a cast of thousands. If your live set is kept very simple, without loads of backing singers or a live orchestra, then you stand a better chance of making money. But it's important to balance cutting expenses back to a minimum against the risk that the show is a disappointment to the fans, which would be counter-productive.

Tour Support

Most artists need the support of their record company to get them out on the road, at least in the early days. The record company will sometimes agree to put this in the record contract but, even if it's not specifically in the contract, it's usually in the record company's interests for you to be out touring and promoting your new album. Indeed, if it's a 360-degree model deal the record company has a financial interest in building up your fan base for live gigs. If you can only do this initially by making a loss (the shortfall), then the record company may come to your rescue and underwrite this shortfall. This is usually called tour support.

Tour support is usually 100% recoupable from royalties from record sales. This is, however, negotiable and if you have enough bargaining power could be reduced to 50% recoupable, with the remainder being treated as a non-recoupable marketing expense of the record company. Sometimes, if the tour support is for a tour in a particular part of the world, for example Japan, then you could agree that the tour support is only recouped from Japanese record sales. In the current climate, however, just getting some tour support may be an uphill struggle and if it has to be 100% recoupable many artists will accept that as the price for the support.

In addition to making up any shortfall, the record company may pay a 'buy-on' fee. This is the fee payable to the headline artist on a tour or to their record company for the privilege of being allowed to support them. For some new artists, the association with a more established name gives them an opening to a much wider potential audience, as well as the chance to perform in bigger venues. For the headline act, this is an additional source of income, reducing the amount of tour support they'll need from their record company. Buy-on fees for large venues and for concerts by big-name artists can run to tens of thousands of pounds. It's one of the reasons why you'll often see a big-name artist being supported by another smaller act who's on the same label. That way the costs are kept in the family.

How much tour support will you need?
Before you can go to your record company to ask for tour support, you need to have an idea how much you'll need.

First, you'll need to get someone to prepare a tour budget. This could be your manager or your regular accountant or bookkeeper. However, when doing a bigger tour, either as headline or support, consider getting a specialist tour accountant on board. The tour accountant could be someone at the regular accountancy firm, or one recommended by them, or by friends. Your A&R contact or manager can suggest people, and possibly also your lawyer. Most importantly, the tour accountant must be honest, must understand how tour promoting works, and be brave enough to tackle unscrupulous promoters about to run off with the cash midway through the gig.

The outline budget will make guesstimates of income and expenditure. As details such as any Guaranteed Minimum, any buy-on fees, merchandise advances and so on become known, they are factored in. The number of musicians and how elaborate the stage set or lighting effects will be will all affect the tour budget.

Once you have a good idea of the likely profit (or perhaps loss), an outline draft budget is prepared which your manager then takes to your record company to negotiate the level of tour support. It's important, therefore, that you don't make wild guesses and are as accurate as you can be as to what you're likely to need.

The record company will usually set a maximum amount that it will pay to underwrite the shortfall. For example, the draft budget may show a tour loss of £18,000. The record company checks the figures and makes its own assessment of how valuable it will be to it in record sales if the tour goes ahead. It may decide that one or two dates should be dropped, or that some of the costs could be saved. It will set a limit on how much it will pay. In this case, after some adjustments, it may say that it will pay up to £16,000 in tour support. You and your manager have to see if savings can be made. If the tour then goes ahead and it does better than expected and only loses £15,000, then the record company underwrites a £15,000 shortfall not a £16,000 one. The actual amount it will pay (up to that maximum) is determined by details of the actual costs which you or your tour accountant or tour manager supplies after the end of the tour with supporting invoices and receipts. If the tour does worse than expected and makes a £17,000 loss, then the record company is still only obliged to pay £16,000, and may insist that you pick up the rest of the bill yourself.

So it's important to get the figure for the anticipated shortfall as realistic as possible.

The record company will usually agree to pay part of the tour support up-front. This means that the essential personnel can be paid some of what is due to them and essential equipment can be hired. You then have to juggle who gets paid along the way, and who has to wait until the final instalment comes in from the record company.

Even if there is something in your record contract about tour support, it's unlikely that all the details will be included and it is usual to set out these detailed arrangements in a side agreement to the main record contract. Copies of all side agreements should be kept together with the record contract. If you're reviewing the accounting statements or are considering doing an audit, you need to have details of all the arrangements you've reached about what amounts are or aren't recoupable and from what sales. Unless the side agreement is very simple, a lawyer should review it before it is signed.

OTHER ISSUES

There are some other things that have to be taken into account when planning a tour.

Tax planning

Your accountant should advise you whether there are any tax advantages to you in putting your touring services through a limited company and, if so, whether that should be a UK-based or offshore company. They may suggest a limited liability partnership if you are a band. The LLP structure is frequently used by professional partnerships such as firms of accountants and lawyers, but it is a structure that can also have its uses for bands in appropriate circumstances.

If your accountant does advise use of a limited company or LLP, a service agreement should be put in place between you and that company or between the band and the LLP. The contract with any promoter will then be with the limited company or LLP.

In some countries, there is an obligation to pay tax in that country on earnings from live work undertaken there. The promoter may have to deduct the tax before he hands the money over. In that case, the contract with the promoter must make sure that the promoter has to hand over to the relevant tax authorities the sums he has withheld. In countries where there are reciprocal tax treaties in place, it's possible to claim exemption from some of these taxes or you may be able to reclaim some or all of the amounts withheld. The promoter should be obliged to do all the necessary paperwork and to supply you with any forms you may need to complete to show the country in which you or your service company is based and pays tax and the local tax authorities should either confirm exemption from tax on the income or provide a certificate of how much tax has been withheld so this can be offset against UK income for tax purposes.

Obviously, everyone's tax circumstances are different and these are only very general comments. Nothing will substitute for proper, professional tax planning and advice. Such planning should be done as far ahead as possible. Rule changes in the US makes specialist accountancy advice essential before you leave the UK. And of course the knock-on effects of Brexit on cross-European touring are as yet unclear so specialist advice is vital on matters like withholding tax and visas. Visas, where required, must be applied for well in advance and the cost of them factored into the touring budget. There are specialised agencies that can help with this.

Publicising the tour

This is the joint responsibility of you and the promoter. Your record company also has a vested interest and will want to co-ordinate its own marketing efforts with the tour dates. For example, if the label had planned a poster campaign in particular towns in the UK, it may decide to target those towns where you're doing live dates. The tour posters may also give information on when your latest record is to be released. The promoter or the venue will publish adverts in the music and local press listing forthcoming tours. Your press officer and the internal press office at your record company will get to work placing the information in the press, getting interviews and personal appearances for you to promote the tour. You'll be expected to mention it in interviews with the press or on radio or TV. If you see an artist start to raise his profile and appear on talk shows, it is almost always because he's got something to promote.

Your record company has to be careful not to overstep the mark. A few years ago there was a spate of legal actions brought by Camden Council against the senior executives of Sony and BMG in an attempt to curb illegal fly-posting. Camden Council took the unusual step of using anti-social behaviour orders (ASBOs) on the executives after accusing the companies they led of saving money on legitimate poster sites by putting up posters for albums and gigs on any available space, including shop hoardings and pillar boxes. Service of the orders meant that the court had the power to order jail sentences of up to five years (in extreme cases) if the executives did not stop the practice. The ASBOs were seen as a last resort when prosecutions and requests to stop fly-posting had failed. They seem to have had some measure of success as the executives reached compromises with the council to avoid a continuance of the orders and promised not to commission any more illegal fly-posting.

Of course, the Internet is now an indispensable part of the promotion for any artist. The Other were the first to use SMS text messages to fans to alert them as to the whereabouts of the next 'secret' gig. Twitter and IM replaced SMS as a means of helping fans keep up to speed on your plans, as well as your artist website, your YouTube or Facebook sites and Instagram photos of everything from your breakfast through to the dressing room or stage sound check at your latest gig. The Q&A video App on Twitter was used to help drive single 'Shout Out To My Ex' by Little Mix to number 1. Moments is another of their tools (a kind of curated life story) which is being used by artists to involve their fans and followers directly, for example, the story of the week of release of a track. Links to SoundCloud, Deezer or Spotify can be embedded into a Moment story, too. Viral marketing also uses databases of information to target fans. The record company's or artist's website, possibly with a link to the promoter's site or that of the venue, can offer the possibility of ordering tickets online and maybe offering competitions to win tickets or to meet the artist or at a pre- or post-show 'meet and greet'. Artist and record company websites fulfil a vital role in promoting the tour or selling tickets online. The fan club can also be invaluable in publicising a tour. The regular newsletter or blog sent out to fans can give details of forthcoming live events and where tickets can be bought. Sometimes the fan club does a deal with the promoter and/or a travel company to offer special travel, accommodation and ticket packages at a reduced rate to fan club members. The fan club has to be careful not to offer things that it can't deliver. For example, members of the Boyzone fan club were apparently offered special top-of-the-range seats at Boyzone concerts as part of a special package. It seems that the promoters didn't deliver the expected good seats, leading (apparently) to a demand for the return of monies. Such bad experiences can have a very negative effect on the fan base and their support for the artist.

Even unofficial fan sites can prove a valuable means by which the word is spread about a forthcoming tour or album. If you read a few, you'll see that they are often ahead of the game when it comes to spreading news, although you do have to sort the facts from the speculative gossip.

OTHER PERSONNEL

Tour manager
Depending on the size of the tour and your degree of success, you may appoint a tour manager to work alongside your manager in organising the day-to-day

details of the tour. Tour managers go out on the tour and handle all crises as they come up. They are generally paid a weekly fixed fee and receive free travel and accommodation and probably a fixed daily sum for expenses. Good ones are worth their weight in gold.

Sound and lighting engineers

How your music sounds and how you look on stage is crucial to the success of your live performances. Most bands learn at an early stage the importance of having their own sound engineer and not relying on some stranger in a strange venue. As soon as they can afford it, some bands will bring them along, as well as their own lighting engineer as the venues get bigger or if a fantastic light show is a key element of the stage show. Both of these will probably be on a daily or weekly rate with free accommodation and travel and daily expenses.

Backing band and session musicians

Backing musicians and singers may have to be engaged for the tour. These could be a whole band if you're a solo artist or supplemental to the core band members, e.g. a horn or strings section or extra backing singers. There are many different types of arrangements that can be reached with regular band members. They can be on an annual retainer or on a small, daily-based retainer for when they aren't needed and a higher fee when they have work to do at rehearsals, at personal appearances, interviews and during the tour. When they aren't needed, they could be on a first-call basis, which means they have to drop everything to make themselves available for you. Or they may be completely free to do other work but on the understanding that if you call for them and they aren't available you'll get someone else. You can only afford to do that if they are replaceable. If they are crucial to your 'sound', then you would be better advised to put them on a retainer on a first-call basis.

Other non-regular members of the band will generally be engaged on a daily or weekly rate plus free accommodation and travel and daily expenses. Additional fees may be payable to regular or non-regular members for other promotional work, such as appearing in a video, for a live TV or radio performance, or a webcast to promote the tour. The fee that they are paid could include any of these extra activities and fees. It's important that you agree a 'buy-out' of all rights on the musicians' or vocalists' performances, whether they are your regular band members or not. If they are Musicians' Union or Equity members there

278

will be minimum rates for the work you want them to do and rules on what can be bought out in the way of rights and what will be the subject of further repeat fees. If you don't buy out the rights you may get into difficulties if you then go ahead and do a TV or video deal for performances including those of the session musicians or singers. You may believe you've cleared all rights and say as much in the contract. If, in fact, you haven't, then the musician or vocalist or their union can come out of the woodwork at the most unhelpful moment. In the light of the recent successful claims by session musicians years after the event (see the chapters on publishing and band arrangements), it would also be advisable to get a written confirmation that they have no interest in the songs they are performing.

All these personnel should be given written agreements specifying their fee, when it will be paid and what you expect to get by way of services and rights in return.

You should consider whether personnel, whether or not regular members of the team, should enter into confidentiality agreements. These make it clear that they have to keep confidential anything that they find out about you from being on the road with you. These agreements are intended to head off people selling salacious stories and pictures to the press. If, however, they are regular band members, then it could be counter-productive, because they could get upset at what they might see as you not trusting them, but if they have no intention of selling their stories then they shouldn't really have an issue. For more on the issue of privacy, see Chapter 12.

The importance of getting things clear in contracts with musicians is borne out by a case involving Elvis Costello.

The Elvis Costello Case

Elvis Costello employed Mr Thomas as a musician to perform on his European tour as part of his band. Mr Thomas was also going to do the US tour, but under a separate contract. Costello employed Mr Thomas through his service company, Elvis Costello Limited. The tour had breaks in it between countries in Europe when Mr Thomas's services were not required. Mr Thomas took a seven-day break between the UK and US tours and put in a claim for payment. When he didn't get paid, he applied to the court to wind up/liquidate Costello's company for insolvency, i.e. being unable to pay its debts when they fell due. The court declined to do that, but did order that Mr Thomas be paid on the basis that the court decided it was part of the European tour.

CONCLUSIONS

- If you are already a successful live and recording artist, consider new partners like promoters for your music industry deals.
- Evaluate so-called 360-degree models carefully – they can work if you do your sums right.
- Get yourself a good agent.
- Get adequate insurance.
- Tie touring in with your record company's marketing plans.
- Use the Internet and other forms of viral marketing to advertise forthcoming tours.

Chapter 11

Band Arrangements

INTRODUCTION

The solo artists and songwriters among you may want to skip this chapter, but if you co-write or plan any kind of recording collaboration it would be worth you reading it to see some of the potential problems.

It may seem very negative to talk about problems before you have released a record or even got a deal. But that's exactly when you should be looking at the things that cause friction within bands. If you address these at the beginning when everything is going well, it will be much easier and cause less tension. If you wait to raise these issues until you've been on the road non-stop for six months and can't stand the sight of each other, then, believe me, it will seriously strain, if not destroy, the relationship.

WHO OWNS THE BAND NAME?

Ownership

As we saw in Chapter 1, choosing the right name is vital, but, once you've decided on a band name and have done what you can to check that you have the right to use it, you have to decide who owns that name.

The record company won't normally expect to own the band name. There are exceptions, particularly in the field of manufactured bands or ones where the record company thinks up the name and concept and hires in people to perform. In such cases, they might have a very good argument to say that they should own the name, but this then forms part of the deal. Some production companies also insist on having the right to hire and fire members of a band. Maybe if it is an entirely manufactured band this is acceptable but not, I think, if the band comes to the label already formed.

What the record company will expect you to do is to confirm that you have the right to use the name and that they have the exclusive right to use it in connection with the recordings you make under the record contract and a non-exclusive right after the contract ends.

Music publishers will also want the exclusive right to use the name in connection with exploitation of your songs during the term of the publishing contract and a non-exclusive right after the end of the term. You don't want to give exclusive rights for all uses of the name to any one company, for example your record company, as that would mean that you couldn't then use your name to sell merchandise or do a sponsorship deal.

Who within the band owns the name?

It is essential that you sort this out at the beginning. I also firmly believe that you should put what you have agreed in writing. But I realise that I'm probably whistling in the wind. I tell every band about to sign a deal that they should have a band agreement. They usually nod and say that they understand why they should have one, but most of them never do anything about it. But bear in mind that if it isn't spelt out in an agreement no band member can use the name without the agreement of the others. Recent court cases around band names and trademarks include ones involving The Animals, Wishbone Ash and Hawkwind.

It doesn't have to be a terribly formal document – although I would advise that a proper band agreement drawn up by a lawyer would be best. Even if you don't go for that, it would be better than nothing to write down what you've all agreed and sign it and then keep it in a safe place. You may think that this is over the top and a bit unnecessary, but if you can't prove who owns the band name you can get the very unedifying spectacle of two or more band members arguing over who has the right to use the name and possibly ending up with none of them being able to do so.

Holly Johnson, former lead singer with the band Frankie Goes To Hollywood, is another who was trying to claim sole right to use the name. For such a relatively short-lived band, this one sure does seem to have generated quite a bit of litigation.

Frankie Goes To Hollywood Case

Holly Johnson tried to register a trade mark in FRANKIE GOES TO HOLLYWOOD for goods and services including music, video and recording goods, entertainment, clothing and other merchandise. He was opposed by the other members of the band, Peter Gill, Mark O'Toole, Paul Rutherford and Brian Nash. The Registrar decided that the goodwill in the name was owned by the band as a whole which had accrued from the point that recording and performance started and no agreement regarding ownership of that goodwill had been made at the outset. If only Mr Johnson were allowed to use the trade mark then this would be a misrepresentation and result in damage to the other members. He decided this was the case even though Mr Johnson was the better known of the former band members. Mr Johnson had acknowledged there was a partnership and it was a fact that he had not established any goodwill in that name before he was a member of that partnership. So as soon as they started recording together as members of the partnership goodwill began to accrue to that partnership. In an echo back to the cases of Liberty X and Blue, the Registrar found that even after sixteen years of inactivity there was still residual goodwill to protect. They still sold records and there was other evidence that they still have goodwill – one example was the fact that an episode of the TV series *Friends* featured a character wearing a 'Frankie Says Relax' T-shirt. So Mr Johnson's application failed.

It can happen that just one or two members of the band own the band name, for example where they form the core of the band and the others aren't permanent members. A band may be made up of a core of the vocalist and the lead guitarist who do most of the writing, and a rhythm section of bassist and drummer on a wage and not signed to the record contract. The core members may not want to share ownership of the band name with the other two unless and until they become full-time permanent band members. But as the Frankie case highlights it is essential that this fact is recorded at the outset.

It's more common to agree that all members of the band own the band name. More sophisticated band agreements could set out who gets to use the name if the band splits up. You may decide that, in that case, none of you could carry on using the name or that those who carry on performing together as a band can continue to use the band name and that the one who leaves can't. Then you get problems if two or more members leave and set up another band. There is no simple solution and it's something that you should talk over with your lawyer, as they will have some suggestions that you may want to adopt.

That said, you may not, in fact, get any say in what happens to the band name if the band splits up, because the record contract may well decide the issue for you. The contract might say that the record company has final say over who can continue to use the band name. This may seem unfair but, if you think about it, the record company has invested a lot of time and money in building up the name and the reputation in that name through its marketing efforts. It won't want to risk losing control of that if one or more members of the band leave and, as a result, no one can continue to use the name. You may get a chance to say no to this at the time the record deal is negotiated if you already have a band agreement in place or, as usual, if you have a lot of bargaining power. If the record company does decide who gets to use the band name, then you have to think about whether the other band members should be paid some kind of compensation for the loss of the right to use the name. As is made clear by the Frankie Goes To Hollywood case above, it's possible that, either under the terms of the partnership/band agreement or by the operation of the Partnership Act 1890, the band name will be treated as an asset of the partnership that forms part of its 'goodwill'. There are formulas that accountants can use to work out how much that goodwill is worth. If, for example, the partnership is dissolved because the band splits up and the vocalist continues as a solo artist, then the others could have the value of their share of the goodwill in the name calculated and paid to them as part of the settlement between the band members. It's quite a difficult and delicate question and needs to be treated carefully. This is another good reason why you should sort it out at the beginning before any tensions (or pretensions) get in the way.

BAND STRUCTURES

You can decide on the ownership of the name and things like how the income is to be divided between you, but before your lawyer can put what you've agreed into a legal document you also need to decide what legal form the arrangements between you are going to take. There is no simple answer as to which is best. Each band's needs are going to be different and you have to look at each on its own merits. It's important that you involve both your lawyer and your accountant in this question, as your lawyer will be looking to protect you from a legal viewpoint and your accountant will be looking at the financial and tax implications for you of the different types of agreement. Your accountant will know your personal circumstances and will be able to advise whether one type of structure works better than another for you.

The two main types of arrangement are a limited company and a partnership. There is also a subspecies called the limited liability partnership which is a kind of hybrid of the two with features of a partnership, such as joint liability for partnership debts, but with some limitation on the extent of an individual partner's liability to third parties. This structure has been adopted by at least one label I know of and is common amongst professional partnerships such as law firms and accountants. Ask your accountant if it could work for your band.

If you decide that the band should be a partnership, then the band agreement will usually take the form of a partnership deed. This is like a legal contract that sets out how the partnership is going to operate on a day-by-day basis and puts in writing what has been agreed about the band name, the split of earnings and so on. If you decide to become a limited company, then you'll probably be advised to have a shareholders' agreement, which does the same thing essentially as a partnership deed, but also deals with what happens to your shares in the company if the band splits up or one or more members leave. At the risk of confusing things even more, it's also possible for the band to take the form of a partnership or a limited company, and for the individual members to decide to set up their own company to provide their services to the band through a company. I'll go into this in more detail below.

LIMITED COMPANY

A few years ago, accountants regularly advised bands to set up a limited company for some or all of the band's services in the entertainment business. There were good tax reasons for doing so, especially the tax year out, which was only available to employees and not to self-employed individuals or partners in a partnership. This particular tax loophole has now been closed and the tax advantages have been considerably reduced. The reasons now for setting up a limited company are more complex and you're going to have to take specialist advice from your accountant and lawyer.

The main advantages are: you can spread your income (for example, a large advance) over a number of years and therefore not have it all taxed in the year in which you get it; it may be a more tax-efficient way of distributing income to band members; and it might protect you from legal actions because anyone bringing such an action would have to sue the company in the first instance.

Also, if a lot of the band's income is going to be earned overseas, an offshore company may be used to avoid paying UK tax until you decide you need to have access to the money in the UK, but here again any schemes to avoid or reduce tax liabilities can come under scrutiny even if perfectly legitimate. Don't forget the flack that Gary Barlow got in the press for what were at the time apparently legitimate tax schemes to reduce his tax bill, later successful challenged by HMRC.

Among the main disadvantages are that there are more rules governing what companies can and can't do, accounts have to be published so members of the public could find out how much you earn (although there are exemptions that allow small companies to file abbreviated accounts) and there are also higher administration charges with a limited company.

Obviously, the sooner you get advice and decide on the band structure the better. If you leave it too late and try to put the structure in place after you've already entered into contracts, things get much more complicated. If you've already done a record deal as individuals and you then decide you're going to have a limited company, the record deals would have to be 'novated' (i.e. renewed) in the name of the company. Also, if you've already received some money as an individual, this might jeopardise a scheme to take money out of the country or may result in HMRC deciding you should be taxed as individuals, regardless of the existence of the limited company.

On a more basic level, if you decide halfway through the negotiation of a record or publishing deal to change the structure, the business affairs person at the record or publishing company isn't going to find this very funny, as they'll have to redraft the contract to deal with the new structure. I was recently told an hour before a record contract was about to be signed with a major record company that the deal was to be done through a limited company. The record contract was with the individual. When I rang the record company's lawyer to let him know, he was in despair. Ten people were meeting in an hour to get this contract signed – we had no time to change it. So we went through a fiction that the deal was signed, drank the champagne and had the photos taken. Then we lawyers went away to turn it into a deal with the limited company so that it could actually be signed and the signing advance paid.

If you do decide on a limited company, bear in mind that you'll have to pay to get the company set up, to have the name that you want (assuming that name is available) and you'll have to pay the annual running costs.

The band members (or possibly their service companies if they have them) will be the shareholders and you'll have to agree how many shares each member is going to have. This will probably be an equal number but need not be. Day-to-day decisions on the running of a limited company generally require a 50%-plus majority. If it's a two-member band and each has 50% of the shares, then each can block a decision by the other. Major decisions of the company generally require a 75%-plus majority. So, if you have a four-member band with equal shareholdings, one member could block major changes but three could gang up on the fourth to push through day-to-day decisions. To get around the problems that this could bring, the band is usually advised to put a shareholders' agreement in place which will govern how day-to-day matters are to be dealt with. Major decisions could require unanimous agreement, otherwise three out of four band members could vote through a major change against the wishes of the fourth. The shareholders' agreement will also deal with what is to happen if a member wants to leave. It will usually require that they resign as an officer of the company and that they first offer their shares to the other band members. If a value for the shares can't be agreed, an accountant is usually brought in as an arbitrator to decide the matter.

PARTNERSHIP

This is the main alternative structure for bands at present without the limited liability option but that may change if limited liability partnerships gain further ground. The band members are in partnership together for the particular venture of being a band. All partners are treated equally and profits and losses are shared by all. You'll usually be advised to put a partnership agreement in writing. That agreement will decide how the venture is going to be run on a day-to-day basis, whether all partners are equal (or whether some are more equal than others) and what is to happen to the band name if the partnership is dissolved. It will record whether anyone has put any money (or goods, such as equipment) into the partnership and, if so, whether this is intended to be working capital of the business or a loan, and whether the equipment has been gifted to the partnership or is still owned by one member and is on loan to the band. Does each band member own the equipment he uses, for example a drum kit or a guitar? What if it was bought with band advances – does that make it joint property? What about the vocalist who has no equipment other than a microphone or two? Does he share ownership of other equipment with other band members? The partnership deed should deal with these things.

A partnership agreement can also deal with the question of who is entitled to what shares of the songs, the publishing advances and income. This is a very tricky subject and a very emotive one, which is why I say that it should be dealt with at the beginning of the relationship before money starts to be earned from the songs (see Chapter 4 on publishing deals).

Even if you don't have a written agreement, there can still be a partnership. The taxman will look at the reality of how you work together and how things like the band income are dealt with.

SERVICE AGREEMENTS

Regardless of the structure in place for the band, it's possible for an individual band member to have his own company, which we often call a service company. This service company is exclusively entitled to some or all of the individual's services. The service company can then enter into the record or publishing deal, hold shares in the band's company or an interest in the partnership. Record and publishing companies are used to these arrangements and are usually happy to incorporate them into their contractual arrangements, especially if they are told at an early stage. They will usually want the individual to sign an agreement, called an inducement letter, to confirm that the service company is entitled to his services and agreeing that if the service company drops out of the picture for any reason then the individual will abide by the contract personally.

A service company is usually set up for tax reasons but HMRC looks closely at service companies, as they are often used as a device to add weight to an individual claiming that he is self-employed and not an employee.

This issue sometimes comes up when an artist engages musicians for a particular tour or to record an album. The musicians may want to be treated as self-employed. The musicians' contracts have to be very carefully drawn up to establish the existence of a self-employed relationship. This is definitely one for the lawyers.

BAND INCOME

Whatever structure you put in place, you have to decide what is to happen to the income.

Record, video, touring, merchandise and sponsorship income is usually shared between all band members. As we've seen, there are exceptions where a band consists of one or two core members who are signed up to the record or publishing deal and the other members are employed to work alongside these. In such cases, these 'employed' members are usually either put on a retainer or a weekly wage, or they are employed as session musicians. Session musicians are only paid when they work but, as they aren't usually signed up exclusively, they are free to work for others (see Chapter 5).

While most disputes usually arise in the area of songwriting income, this doesn't mean that arguments never arise in relation to recording income or indeed sometimes both.

The Cure Case (Tolhurst v. Smith and Others [1994] EMLR 508)

Laurence Tolhurst was the former drummer and co-founder of the band The Cure, who was asked to leave the band in 1989. He sued the lead singer of the band, Robert Smith, and the record company for damages arising out of deals done in 1986. Tolhurst argued that the record deal done with Fiction Records Limited in 1986 gave Smith the lion's share of the recording income and left Tolhurst with 'the crumbs'. He asked the court to confirm that there was a partnership in place and to order Smith to account to him for 50% of all profits receivable under the 1986 agreement. He also argued that he had been forced to enter into the 1986 agreement by undue influence exerted by the record company and its owner, Chris Parry. He said that Mr Parry and Fiction Records should account to him for all their profit under the 1986 deal after an allowance for their skill and labour on the basis that the contracts were unenforceable.

The case turned into a character attack on Tolhurst as allegations were made that his contribution to the band's success had declined as a result of his drinking problems. Part of Tolhurst's case was that he hadn't been given enough information about the 1986 deal before he signed it and that he hadn't had independent legal advice. Once again, we see the familiar themes emerging. Tolhurst argued that the deal should be set aside and that the court should order an account of all record income to determine how much he was actually entitled to.

The Judge dismissed his claim and said that the question of undue influence didn't arise because, although the record company would have been in a position to exercise undue influence, the terms offered were not obviously bad. In fact, the Judge said that he thought that Tolhurst was lucky to have been offered these arrangements at all in the circumstances, and found that he hadn't signed the 1986 agreement under undue influence. The fact that Tolhurst hadn't had independent legal advice didn't affect the court's decision, because the deal was not a bad one. The Judge also decided that there was no partnership in place in respect of the 1986 agreement, as Smith and Tolhurst had, in fact, come to a different arrangement on what was to happen to the income.

Disputes often arise in relation to songwriting income. There's no problem if all members of the band contribute equally to the songwriting process. Then the income from songwriting should be split equally. This is, however, relatively rare. Much more common is the situation where only one or two members of the band write all the songs. This can give rise to two possible sources of resentment. Those who write the songs could come to resent sharing advances or royalties with the non-writing members of the band. Or, if the songwriters don't share the income, this then gives rise to resentment from the non-writers, who miss out on a potentially lucrative form of income.

Plastic Bertrand

In July 2010, another blast from the past appeared and disabused fans of a long-held belief. Plastic Bertrand, the French New Wave artist who had a hit in the 1970s with 'Ca plane pour moi' (It's Gliding for Me), was revealed as not, in fact, being the singer on the record. The vocalist was, it turns out, the producer of the record, Lou Deprijck, and Plastic (as he is known to his fans) had only lip-synched to the record. This emerged in a Belgian court case, which was the result of Deprijck's attempts for recognition both in respect of the original recording and a 2006 remix by Deprijck. A musicologist confirmed the voice was the same on both recordings. But the emergence of this piece of deception was a by-product of a dispute between Deprijck and AMC, which is Plastic Bertrand's record label, over who has the right to license the rights to advertising agencies which was still a very lucrative business even after all these years. The outcome of the case was not known at the time of writing this but sadly listening to the track will never be quite the same again.

Of course, leaving aside these tensions, there may also be arguments about who actually wrote what. As we saw in the Kemp case, members of Spandau Ballet brought a case against Gary Kemp arguing that they were entitled to a share in the publishing income as co-writers of the music on the songs they recorded. They were largely unsuccessful, but there will be other arguments as to how much band members actually contribute to the creative process by the way in which they interpret or perform the song. If the contribution is a genuine one, then they should be credited as a co-writer, but is their contribution the same as that of the main writers? If not, what is the value of their contribution?

What do you do if only one member of the band writes the songs, a publishing advance comes in, and the band is broke? Just imagine the tensions that could then occur if the songwriter takes the publishing advance and doesn't share it with the other band members. Even if he agrees to share the advance equally with the others, what will happen when the advances are recouped and publishing royalties start to come through? Should the royalties then go to the songwriter or continue to be divided equally? There isn't one answer to this, as it's so personal to the individuals concerned but you only have to look at one or two cases to realise how important it is to try to sort this out.

Here are three examples of ways in which I have seen bands deal with this issue. There are many more possibilities. One band I know had an arrangement where one member controlled all the songwriting and took all the publishing income. When this began to cause tensions, he volunteered to share percentages of his publishing income from some songs with the other band members. I've also heard the story, which may be a myth, that the members of rock band Queen had an agreement where they got to be the writer of the songs to be released as singles in turn. If true, this is very democratic, but doesn't really deal with the problem if some of the band members are weaker songwriters and don't write such successful songs as others in the band. A third way of dealing with it is to share the advances and royalties equally until the advances have been recouped. After that, each band member has his own account with the publisher and the income from each writer's contribution to the songs would then be paid into his own account.

Three very different solutions to a very difficult issue. Whatever works for you should be written down as soon as possible. If circumstances change, review the arrangements and see if it would be fair to change them.

The Status Quo Case (Lancaster v. Handle Artists Management Ltd [2008] EWCA Civ 1111 (22 April))

This case stresses the importance of being clear in any settlement about what your intentions are. Mr Lancaster, a former member of the group Status Quo, tried to argue that a settlement he had entered into some twenty years before to end earlier litigation had not had the effect of preventing him from claiming a share of certain royalties because those royalties were not in people's minds at the time the settlement was entered into, they had been forgotten. It seems to have been accepted that that may well be true but that the wording of the settlement was wide enough to operate as a 'clean break' in respect of all money claims.

ACCOUNTING AND TAX

One of the main things that can cause problems with a band is tax and VAT. In both cases, bands often don't keep enough money back to pay the bills. HMRC has very heavy powers to impose penalties on you. They are often one of the main creditors forcing a winding up of a limited company and they can and will make you bankrupt. Even if they give you time to pay, there will be financial penalties and interest to pay.

Your accountant will advise you how much should be kept to one side for tax, and if he's doing your books for you he'll be able to tell you what to expect to have to pay the VAT man. He'll also probably advise you to keep all your receipts. He can then sort out which ones you can legitimately recharge as business expenses against tax. If you haven't kept them, there is no proof. So do yourself a favour – get a cardboard box and get into the habit of throwing all your receipts into it. If you were more organised, you could have a file divided into the months of the year and put the receipts in the relevant month. This makes life a lot easier for you or your bookkeeper/accountant when it comes to doing the accounts.

You'll need a band bank account and, unless your accountant is doing all the books for you, you'll need a basic accounting system. This could be a simple computer spreadsheet. In it you'd keep a record of the income you received, where it was from and what your expenses were for doing that work. So, if you did a gig in March you'd record how much you received and how much it cost you to do the gig (and don't forget to keep receipts for all your expenses).

LEAVING MEMBER PROVISIONS

These are the clauses in recording or publishing agreements with bands that deal with what happens if one or more members of a band leave or the band disbands totally before the contract is over. The record or publishing company naturally wants to try to prevent this happening. They've invested a lot of money in supporting the band, making records or videos and in promoting them around the world. The last thing they want is a band falling apart on them. But, of course, no words in a contract are going to keep a band together if one or more of them has decided to call it a day. Individuals develop personally and creatively, and not necessarily in the same direction. One member of the band may get married and have children and not want to spend as much time on the road. Or they may change their artistic style, which might be more suited to a solo career than to being a member of a band. Of course, there is also the possibility that the band members will grow to hate the sight of each other after years on the road, or that the band just comes to the end of what it can do creatively. With so much money resting on building the reputation of an artist, when a split happens, the record or publishing company may well want to be able to try to salvage what they can of their investment. They will want to have the option to pick up the rights in any new projects that the songwriters or artists go into without having to compete in the open market. The record company will also want to try to have the right to continue to use the name of the band that they've invested a lot of money in building up as a brand.

Record and publishing companies will also want to have the option to pick and choose who they continue the deal with (sometimes called the Remaining Members) and who they drop. For example, if the drummer leaves the band the record company will want the right to continue with the remaining members of the band on the basis that they continue to perform and record as a band. They will also want to have a contract with any replacement drummer, who may be put on the same terms as the remaining members or may be on a retainer basis.

If the whole band splits up, the record or publishing company will want the option to do new contracts with each individual member. A publisher might only do new contracts with those they know are songwriters who will probably go on to do other things. A record company may decide only to continue their deal with the lead vocalist or other main focus of the band, guessing that they will team up with other artists to form another band or will have a solo career.

There's usually a system built into the contract that gives the record or publishing company a breathing space while they try to work out what they're going to do. The record contract will usually give the company the option to call for a leaving member to deliver to them demo recordings of what he would do as a solo artist or with his new band. They will usually provide studio time for him to make these demos. The contract may also require the remaining members of the band to demo new tracks, with or without a replacement member, to see if the company think there is a future for the band, or if they should drop them now. The record or publishing company may know immediately whether they want to continue with a leaving member or any or all of the remaining members and may come to a quick decision. Don't hold your breath, though – they will probably take the maximum time they have under the contract in order to look at their options.

Once demo recordings have been delivered to the record or publishing company, they usually have a month or two to decide what to do. In that time, both the leaving member and the remaining members of the band are in limbo. The term of the contract is usually suspended in the meantime.

A record company may decide to take up an option on the leaving member's new project, but not that of the remaining members, or vice versa. They may also decide to take up their option on the remaining members. They may decide to abandon both to their fate.

For the leaving member or remaining members who are dropped from the contract, that is the end of their obligations to the record or publishing company.

They don't have to repay to the company their share of any unrecouped balance on the account. However, their share of royalties from recordings made or songs written by them up to the time of the decision to drop them will continue to be applied to recoup the unrecouped balance. The dropped artist or songwriter won't see royalties from those recordings or songs until that advance has been fully repaid in the normal way. For example, let's assume that there is an unrecouped balance on the record account of £100,000 and that the record company continues with three remaining members and drops a fourth (leaving) member. Let's also assume that the band shares advances and royalties equally. The leaving member's share of the debt and of the royalties will be 25%. The leaving member's 25% share of royalties from recordings made while he was a member of the band will go to recoup £25,000 of the unrecouped £100,000 debt. After that's happened, 25% of any further royalties from those recordings will be paid through to the leaving member. If the record company continues with the remaining members and pays them further advances, the leaving member's share of royalties doesn't get used to recoup those additional advances as he won't have received any share of them. His debt is fixed at the time he is dropped from the contract by the record company, or at least it should be. This is something your lawyer has to deal with when he negotiates the contract.

The situation with the remaining members whose contracts continue is slightly more complicated. Their 75% of the royalties from those old recordings goes to recoup their 75% share of the unrecouped balance (£75,000 in our example). Their share of anything else that's earned from the old recordings first goes to recoup any new advances they have received and only when both the old account and the new account are recouped will they be paid any royalties. It also works the other way around. The royalties from their new recordings go first to recoup the new advances. Any surplus goes to recoup their 75% share of the old debt. Only when both accounts are recouped will they see royalties from the new recordings.

If the contract continues with any remaining members, or if a new contract is issued to the leaving member, the record or publishing company will want to continue to have the same rights to the leaving member and/or remaining members as it had under the original recording or publishing contracts. There are, however, one or two parts of the contract that it likes to try to change. The record company may try to change the minimum recording commitment from an album to one or more singles, the rationale being that, until the record company knows how the new line-up will perform in the marketplace, it doesn't want to risk committing to make an album. You should hold out for an album commitment, even if it releases a couple of singles first. The record label will also usually want options to future albums. This could either be for the number of albums left under the original deal, or for that number plus one or two more. This should be agreed at the time the record deal is originally negotiated, when you'll have more bargaining power. There's no guarantee that the record company will want to negotiate this with you in the middle of a leaving member/band split situation. The record royalties are usually the same as under the old agreement, but may go back to the rate that applied in the first contract period so, if you've received an increase in your royalty based either on record sales or because it's later in the contract, it might go back to the rate before the increase took effect. The advances are usually a fraction of the advance that you would have got for that contract period. For example, if you were a four-piece band and one of you left and you would have been entitled to £100,000 for the next album, then the remaining three members might expect to be entitled to £75,000. This isn't, however, a foregone conclusion. Your lawyer will have to fight for it on your behalf.

Because an artist walks away from the unrecouped debt and has a chance to start again, many are actually crossing their fingers and hoping they'll be dropped. This is a fairly short-term response, though, because it will all depend on whether they can get into a new deal. It's certainly no reason to split up a band in the hope that you'll get dropped.

There are leaving member clauses that have special arrangements. There may be different rules on recoupment, or different levels of new advances, depending on which member of the band leaves and how 'key' he is seen to be to the proceedings. They may feel that the lead vocalist/front man should command a larger advance and more preferential terms if he leaves than, say, the bassist. They may even say that they're only interested in leaving member rights for the key people. As you can imagine, these sorts of provisions can be very disruptive and, if it's the band's first deal, such arrangements ought really to be avoided, both from the record company's viewpoint and the band's. At this early stage, no one knows who is going to turn out to be the star. Who'd have thought the Genesis drummer, Phil Collins, would turn out to be an excellent lead vocalist and very successful solo artist?

Different arrangements can also occur with publishing deals. For example, one of the four writer-performers in the band may be a prolific writer for adverts or jingles in addition to his work for the band. In these circumstances, it's possible for all four members to have separate accounts and to initially receive an equal share of the advances. It only really works if each writer earns an equal share of the income, as that goes first to recoup the total band advances. After that, if this writer earns significantly more from his work as a jingles writer, his income from that source is only credited to his account. At the next accounting date, he will then receive a correspondingly larger royalty cheque. The Minimum Commitment may have to change in publishing deals after someone leaves. If one songwriter previously wrote 25% of an album and the others 75% and after a split both are expected to deliver 100% of an album each, then there is going to be a problem. So, in leaving member clauses in publishing deals your lawyer will usually try to reduce the Minimum Commitment to an achievable level.

WHAT HAPPENS TO A BAND'S ASSETS ON A SPLIT?

If there is a partnership or band agreement, then that will say what happens to the band's assets if the band splits up or one or more members leave.

If there's no written or verbal agreement that you can prove between the band members and if they're in a partnership, then the Partnership Act 1890 will govern what happens. Essentially, the partnership is dissolved unless all partners elect that it can continue. If agreement can't be reached on a fair way of dealing with the assets, then the partnership is dissolved and the assets have to be realised (i.e. sold) and the proceeds divided equally between the partners. If agreement can't be reached on whether something such as the goodwill and reputation in the band name should be given a value and, if so, what value, the matter is usually referred to an accountant acting as an arbitrator. The way, if at all, that the record company deals with the name in the recording agreement may help determine if it has a value.

If the band was not a partnership but had shares in a limited company, then the shareholders' agreement and/or the Memorandum and Articles of Association of the company will say what is to happen. Usually, the remaining members would want to have the right to require the leaving member to resign from any office as director or company secretary and also to sell his shares. The arrangements would normally give the remaining members the right to buy those shares back at a certain price or in accordance with a fixed formula. Or it may require the shares to be valued by an independent accountant. Tax questions could arise here, so everyone should take advice from an accountant or a tax lawyer if a split occurs. In the absence of written arrangements, there is a danger that the company could become unworkable. If the leaving member is a director or a company secretary and he hasn't been guilty of any wrongdoing, then without a written agreement it won't be easy to remove him from office. If he has service contracts, employment advice should be sought before terminating those arrangements. Without an agreement, you can't easily get shareholders to sell their shares and, depending on the size of their shareholding, they could block votes requiring a 75%-plus majority or, indeed, those requiring a simple 50%-plus majority if it's a two-man band or two or more members out of a four-piece band have left.

Once agreement has been reached as to what to do with the band's assets, this should be recorded in a settlement agreement, which should be drawn up by a lawyer. This is particularly important for matters such as rights to band names or copyrights.

The partnership or band agreement should be very clear as to who owns what and who has brought what into the deal. For example, if one of the band members has a Transit van that he allows the band to use, then that should be noted. A band member could also have put money into the band to keep it going. This is either a loan to the band, with or without interest, or, more practically, it's a gift for the use of the partnership that they may or may not be allowed to get back an equivalent sum if they leave. It's also usual for the leaving band member to take with him any band equipment that he particularly uses. This is fair, unless one person has the use of a lot of expensive equipment, which was paid for out of band advances. In that case, you would expect the equipment to be valued and for each remaining band member to either get equipment to that value, or be paid his share of its value by the leaving member who is going to take the equipment away.

If a band name is genuinely closely associated with one individual, then it may be fair to say that that individual should be allowed to continue to use the name after the band splits. But, as it may well have been all the band members that will have helped to make the name successful, the person using the name after a band splits up should consider compensating the others. If a figure can't be agreed, it can be referred to an accountant to value it. In many cases, however, the name dies with the end of the band.

Each band member should continue to be responsible for his share of the record or publishing company unrecouped balance. Once the old accounts are recouped, the individual band members should be entitled to their agreed share of any royalties. This will usually be covered by the record or publishing deal.

It's also wise to decide whether the band members have to unanimously agree before something can be done with the material that they created together, or if it's going to be a majority decision. For example, a few years after a band splits, the record company wants to put out a Greatest Hits album. The record contract may give the band approval over whether the record company can do this. The band agreement or settlement should say whether all the band members have to agree or not. The democratic thing would be to say yes, they should. The practical thing would be to say that it has to be a majority decision, so that one person couldn't hold a gun to the heads of the others or their record company. The same situation arises with approvals of the use of material in adverts or film. My own view is that it should be a decision of all band members where this is practically possible but that, if the band has split up and one or more have gone out of the business and aren't easily contactable, then the decision of the remaining members who are in contact should prevail.

If no agreement can be reached, the parties are headed almost inevitably towards litigation and the courts. Even though the reform of the legal system in England and Wales now places considerable emphasis on conciliation and alternative dispute resolution (ADR), we still occasionally see the largely unedifying spectacle of bands fighting it out in court. An example of what happens if things are not dealt with clearly enough is the Busted case.

James Bourne v. Brandon Davis

Between December 2000 and October 2001, James Bourne, Matthew Sergeant, Kiley Fitzgerald and Owen Doyle composed and performed songs together as an early line-up of the band Busted. There was no written agreement but the Judge accepted that there was a partnership at will, just as we saw in the Frankie Goes To Hollywood case above. This line-up split in 2001 and James Bourne and Matthew Sergeant joined up with Charlie Simpson to form the new Busted line-up. In March 2002, this line-up signed a record deal with Universal-Island Records. As part of that deal James Bourne assigned all his performing rights in the earlier recordings to Universal-Island. This is quite common. This line-up was very successful and continued until January 2005 when it again split up and James Bourne went on to form a new group called Son of Dork. In August 2005, he did a new record deal with Mercury Records and again assigned his performing rights in performances of his before the date of the contract.

In 2005, Brandon Davis issued a nine-track CD featuring performances of the original line-up made in a hotel in 2001. Immediately James Bourne, Mercury Records and Universal-Island issued proceedings for an injunction alleging infringement of Mr Bourne's performance rights and passing off by using the name Busted in relation to these recordings. The court ordered an immediate injunction in September 2005. In October 2005, Mr Doyle, from the original line-up, purported to sell to Mr Davis all the consents necessary in respect of his performances and to assign to him the copyright and performer's property rights and other rights in connection with those recordings. Mr Davis argued that this agreement had the effect of assigning all the performers' property rights of all four on the basis that it was partnership property and he as a partner could deal with it and binds all his partners. The Judge accepted that all performers' property rights could become partnership property. It would not be necessary for there to be a formal agreement to give effect to this. Where Mr Davis's claim failed was because he had waited too long after the split to do anything. Four years was too long a gap to claim that Mr Doyle was acting in the ordinary course of their partnership to sell the property rights of the partnership. Nor could it be seen as part of the winding up of the partnership. But even if they were partnership property the Judge decided they were still held by the individuals who retained a beneficial interest so the partnership did not have exclusive rights to dispose of the rights. At best they could argue that the rights should be applied for the benefit of the partnership not of the individuals. So James Bourne was within his rights to grant his individual performer's rights to the record companies; Mr Davis did not have the right to the performer's rights because he knew Mr Doyle didn't have Mr Bourne's authority for the assignment and in any event for something like this the consent of all four members would have been required under the Copyright Act (s 191 A(4)).

The main lesson to be learned from this somewhat complex legal case is that to avoid any doubt it is best to deal, in writing, with partnership arrangements and rights such as performer's rights as well as copyright in either the band agreements or in a settlement after a split to be clear what everyone's rights are. And as a further twist, in late 2016 the group got back together again and recorded another album which they subsequently toured.

CONCLUSIONS

- Decide on a good name for the band and protect it as far as you can.
- Decide on a band structure and put a written agreement in place.
- Decide who is going to be allowed to use the name if you split up.
- Make sure any leaving member clauses in your contracts are fair.
- Decide these things at the outset while you're still friends.

Chapter 12

Moral Rights and the Privacy of the Individual

INTRODUCTION

Moral rights have their origins in well-established European principles of law aimed at protecting creative types and ensuring their works are treated with respect. These are also called *droit moral*. In this chapter I'm only going to give an overview of these rights and of where they can be used. There are many books on the subject if you want to read into this further, e.g. *Copinger & Skone James on Copyright*, written by Nicholas Caddick (QC), Gillian Davies and Gwilym Harbottle. The revised 17th edition was published by Sweet & Maxwell in 2016 and has a section on UK moral rights.

Moral rights are separate from copyright. In some circumstances, you can keep your moral rights when you've had to assign your copyright to someone else.

In mainland Europe, it has long been felt that an artist's rights to receive financial reward for the use of his work can be adequately protected by the copyright laws, but the integrity of the work itself deserves separate protection. Hence the development of a separate *droit moral*. The UK legal tradition treats economic rights as more important than those of artistic integrity. Why doesn't the UK value the integrity of creative works, you may well ask. It's not that we don't give them a value. It's a question of emphasis and the answer lies in the cultural differences between the UK and the rest of Europe and in the different legal histories.

The European principles of moral rights were included in the major international legal convention on intellectual property, the Berne Convention (it first appeared in the 1925 Rome Treaty) and, in particular, the 1948 Brussels Revision of the Berne Convention. Article 6 [bis] of the 1948 Brussels Revision to the Berne Convention contains two basic moral rights: the right to be identified as an author of a work and the right not to have that work distorted, mutilated or otherwise altered in a manner which could be prejudicial to the author's honour or reputation.

The UK lagged a long way behind and, indeed, the fact that we didn't incorporate these two basic moral rights into UK law meant that for many years the UK was unable to fully comply with the Berne Convention.

As the UK became more integrated into Europe, it became clear that we were out of step not only in not fully complying with the Berne Convention but also in not giving sufficient weight to these rights. The general principles of harmonisation, which govern the operation of the European Union, meant that the UK had to come in line on these moral rights. As we will see, it did so, but in a peculiarly British fashion.

The 1988 Copyright Designs & Patents Act was the first UK statute that effectively incorporated all the principal moral rights. There had been limited moral rights in the 1956 Copyright Act but the 1988 Act was the one that brought the UK in line with Europe and enabled us to comply with the provisions of the Berne Convention. Since 1 February 2006, performers also have the legal right to be identified as the performer and to object to derogatory treatment of their recorded or broadcast performances. This was introduced by the Performances (Moral Rights, etc.) Regulations 2006.

The moral rights aren't linked to who owns the copyright in the work in question. They may be the same person, but not necessarily. For example, you could assign your rights to the copyright in a musical work to a music publisher, but as the author of the work in question you could retain your moral rights. In fact, in law you can't assign moral rights, they remain with you or your beneficiaries on your death. This is intended to protect you from unscrupulous people who may want you to assign your moral rights alongside your copyright, more of this later.

If you and your fellow band members co-write a musical work together, then you each have these moral rights independent of each other. Just because one of you has decided to abandon his moral rights doesn't mean that the rest of you have to.

In reality, the 1988 Act merely put into law what had previously been dealt with in contracts. The crucial difference was that in a contract you can only bind your contracting partner, whereas with moral rights you can enforce them against third parties who were not party to the contract. For example, you may have a clause in your contract that says you have to be credited as the composer of the music. If your publishing company forgets to do this, it's a breach of contract and you can sue them. If, however, the works are licensed by your record label for inclusion on a compilation album and the compilation company doesn't credit you, then unless you have your moral rights you can't take action because the contract is between the compilation company and your record label and not with you. If you have your moral rights, you can take action against the compilation company for breach of your moral right to be identified as the author, whether or not your record label wants to take any action.

WHAT ARE THESE RIGHTS?

There are four moral rights, but only three of them are likely to affect you. These three rights only exist in respect of copyright works (*ss.178 and 1(2) CDPA*). If a work is out of copyright, then you don't have moral rights in relation to it.

THE RIGHT OF PATERNITY

The first moral right is the right to be properly identified as the author of the work or as the performer when the performer's performance is broadcast or when a recording of his performance is communicated to the public (*s.77 CDPA*). This is also known as the paternity right.

The right is owned by the author of a copyright literary, dramatic, musical or artistic work, and the performer in relation to his performances. So, as a composer or lyricist of original songs, you would have the right to be identified as having written the words or composed the music and, as a performer, your name or stage name or the name of your group should also be identified in a manner likely to be noticed by the audience for your performance.

It's also possible that you'll have moral rights in the artwork used for the packaging of your records if you were the person who created that work (see Chapter 5 on artwork). You'll notice, though, that the owners of the sound recording copyright don't have moral rights in that sound recording.

The right exists in relation to a musical work and lyrics when that work is exploited in one of five ways:

1. When the work is commercially published; this includes not only sheet music but also in sound recordings or as soundtracks to films.
2. The issue to the public of copies of the work in the form of sound recordings.
3. The showing in public of a film, the soundtrack of which includes the work.
4. The issue to the public of copies of a film, the soundtrack of which includes the work. Remember that the definition of 'film' will include DVD.
5. If a work has been adapted and the adaptation is exploited in one of the above ways, then you have the right to be identified as the author of the work that has been adapted. If the arrangement itself is capable of copyright protection, then the author of the adaptation may also have a right to be identified as its author.

There is also a moral right to be identified as the performer when that work is broadcast or a recording of it is communicated to the public, but there are exceptions. The requirement that the performer must be identified does not apply when it's not reasonably practicable and it also doesn't apply when the performance is given for reasons relating to advertising or news reporting. Otherwise the poor DJs would be in danger of breaching your moral rights every time they irritatingly didn't give you a name check after playing your record on the radio. There is no guidance at present as to whether it would be taken as being 'not reasonably practicable' to name all the performers on a recording. Common sense suggests that a failure to give the group's or performer's name or stage name would be a breach unless it was inadvertent but it would not be practicable to name every performer, including session players. In the light of recent cases, it may be prudent in session musicians' agreements to specifically waive the moral rights to be identified.

If you have moral rights in the artistic work (the artwork), that right comes into effect when that work is exploited in one of the following ways:

1. If the work is published commercially.
2. If it is exhibited in public.
3. If a visual image of it is broadcast or otherwise made available to the public.
4. If a film including a visual image of the work is shown in public or copies of the film (which will include DVDs) are issued to the public.

Section 77(7) of the 1988 Act sets out details of how the author is to be identified. One example is that the author of the musical or artistic work must be identified on each copy. This is logical: you wouldn't want a record company to be able to get around the right by identifying you on the first, say, one hundred copies issued and not on any of the rest.

Assertion of the right

There is, however, one very big 'but' here. In order to be able to rely on the paternity right, you have to have first asserted that right. You may have noticed on the inside cover of books published since 1988 that there is a statement along the lines of 'the right of [author's name] to be identified as the author of this work has been asserted in accordance with sections 77 and 78 of the Copyright, Designs and Patents Act 1988'. This is the book publishing world's way of asserting the author's right of paternity. If you write a song and don't want to have the right to be identified as the author, then you just don't assert your moral right of paternity and you don't insist of having a credit clause in your contracts. But why wouldn't you want to be identified?

If you do want to be identified, then you can assert your right generally – as in the statement above – or in respect of any particular act. For example, you could assert your right to be identified as the author of the musical work in the sound recording, but not if that sound recording is then included in a film. Again, you may wonder why anyone would make the distinction. You can choose to assert your rights in the document in which you assign any copyright in the work, for example in an exclusive music publishing deal where you have to assign your rights for a period of time (see Chapter 4), or you can do it by some other written means that brings your assertion to the attention of someone. They are then responsible if they breach your right. The problem with this is that it's only binding on those people to whose attention the assertion of rights is brought. For example, you could put in a written document that you asserted your right of paternity, but if that document was then put away in a drawer you wouldn't have brought it to anyone's attention and so couldn't rely on your moral right later if someone failed to identify you as the author of the work. Putting it in the assignment document is the best way of ensuring that anyone who later takes any interest in the work assigned will have notice of your assertion of your paternity rights.

If the musical work has been jointly written, for example by all members of a band, then each is responsible for asserting his own right of paternity. One band member can't take it upon himself to assert it on behalf of the others.

There are a number of exceptions which are set out in *s.79 CDPA*. The most important one for you is likely to be the fact that, if the copyright is one that you created as an employee, your employer and anyone acquiring rights from you doesn't have to identify you as the author of that work. So, for example, if you wrote a jingle as part of your job as an employee of an advertising company, then, unless there was anything in your contract that said your employer had to give you a credit, he wouldn't have to do so and you wouldn't be able to rely on any moral right of paternity.

THE INTEGRITY RIGHT

The second moral right is the right of an author of a work, or a performer in a broadcast on a recording which is then communicated to the public, not to have that work subjected to derogatory treatment (i.e. to have someone treat your work in a way that reflects badly on the work and, indirectly, on you) (*s.80 CDPA*). This is sometimes called the integrity right. The right is owned by the author of a copyright literary, dramatic, musical or artistic work, by the director of a copyright film (which includes DVD) and by a performer in relation to a broadcast of his performance or where a recording of his performance is communicated to the public. Once again, the right only applies in relation to a work that is in copyright and it doesn't apply to sound recordings.

The right has several hurdles to it. First, you have to establish that the work has been subjected to some form of treatment, i.e. that it has been added to, or parts have been deleted, or the work has been altered or adapted in some way. Something has to have been done to it. This can be as little as changing one note or one word of the lyrics. It isn't a treatment of a work if all you do is put it in an unchanged form in a context that reflects badly on its author. For example, if someone uses your song as part of a soundtrack for a porn video, that of itself isn't a treatment of the work for the purpose of your moral rights. Nor is it a treatment if someone just changes the key or the register of the music.

In a case involving George Michael, the court was asked to consider the question of what was a treatment (*Morrison Leahy Music v. Lightbond, 1993 EMLR 144*). Someone had put together a megamix of George Michael's tracks using 'snatches' from five songs. They had also slightly altered the lyrics. The court decided that this was definitely a treatment.

Once you've established that there has been some form of treatment, you then have to show that that treatment was derogatory. For these purposes, that means a distortion or mutilation or something that is prejudicial to your honour or reputation.

When you've established both these points, you then have to look at whether the treatment has been subjected to a particular type of use. In the case of a literary or musical work, the integrity right is infringed by:

1. Publishing it commercially.
2. Performing it in public, broadcasting it or otherwise making it available to the public.
3. Issuing copies to the public of a film or sound recording of, or including, a derogatory treatment of the work.

In the case of an artistic work, the treatment has to have been used in one of the following ways:

1. By publishing it commercially.
2. By exhibiting it publicly.
3. By broadcasting or including in a service which makes available to the public a visual image of a derogatory treatment of the work.
4. By showing in public a film including a visual image of a derogatory treatment of a work or issuing to the public copies of such a film.

In the case of a film (which includes DVD), the integrity right is infringed by a person who shows in public or includes in a cable programme service a derogatory treatment of a film or who issues to the public copies of a derogatory treatment of the film. In the case of a performance, it's the broadcast of the work or where a recording of a performance is communicated to the public. These rights also apply to online or digital reproduction via the Internet.

FALSE ATTRIBUTION

The third right is an extension of a right that existed under the previous Copyright Act of 1956. It is the right not to have a work falsely attributed to you. This would happen if someone says that a piece of music is written by you or that you directed a particular film and that isn't in fact the case. This false attribution needn't be in writing – it can be verbal. It also needn't be expressed – it can be implied. So someone could suggest on a television programme that you were the author of a particular piece of music when you weren't, or could imply that you were without coming straight out and saying so. In many ways, it is the mirror image of the right of paternity.

If there has been a false attribution, then it has to be applied to a work that has been used in one of the following ways before it can be said to be an infringement of this moral right:

1. If a person issues to the public copies of a literary, dramatic or artistic work or a film in which there is a false attribution. So, for example, if the credits wrongly identify you as the author of the music, this could be an infringement of your moral right.
2. If a person exhibits in public an artistic work, or a copy of an artistic work, in or on which there is a false attribution.
3. If, in the case of a literary, dramatic or musical work, a person performs the work in public, broadcasts it or otherwise makes it available to the public, saying wrongly that it is the work of a particular person or, in the case of a film, shows it in public, broadcasts it or makes it available to the public as being directed by someone who had not in fact directed it.
4. Material issued to the public or displayed in public, which contains a false attribution in relation to any of the above acts, is also an infringement. This could catch publicity posters for films, or adverts in magazines for a book, or the false credit on the packaging for a recording of a piece of music.

There are also rights against those who indirectly infringe this right. The rights extend to making available over the Internet or making digital online copies of the works.

PRIVACY OF PHOTOGRAPHS

The final moral right is the right to privacy in any photographs that you commission (*s.85 CDPA*). This is intended to protect against unauthorised use by newspapers and such like of private photographs that you have commissioned. When you're starting out in the business, this right may not be of immediate practical interest to you. There's always the motto that there's no such thing as bad publicity. However, later in life, when you're a megastar seeking to protect your privacy at all costs, you may remember this right and use it against unscrupulous photographers keen to sell their soul and your life to the tabloids. This right can be used alongside the privacy and confidentiality rights that are being developed by the courts implementing the Human Rights Act, as we will see later in this chapter.

OWNERSHIP OF RIGHTS

As I've already said, the moral rights belong to authors – to composers of musical works and writers of lyrics intended to be spoken or sung with music and to performers on sound recordings or broadcasts of their performances. A record producer may have moral rights but not as the producer but because he may have also performed on the record or contributed to the writing of the words or music (see Chapter 5). The owner of the sound recording doesn't have any moral rights.

The real beauty of these rights is that they are rights of the author or performer, who can't be made to assign them. A songwriter may have been required to assign the copyright in his words and music to a publisher as part of a publishing deal (see Chapter 4), but he can't be made to assign his moral rights. If he retains his moral rights, then he is in a position to take legal action against someone infringing those rights, even if the publishing company wants to take no action.

There are, of course, difficulties with the moral right of paternity, as you would have to show that you had the right, that it had been infringed and that you had asserted the right in such a way that the person infringing it had notice of the assertion. If your assertion was in an assignment document and was general in nature, you could take action against the assignee of the rights and against anyone else taking an interest in the rights subsequently. This could help you take action for infringement of your paternity right against your publisher or one of his sub-publishers, but not so easily against someone who was acting unlawfully.

The other moral rights do not have to first be asserted.

DURATION OF RIGHTS

The paternity and integrity rights last for as long as copyright exists in the work in question. The same applies to the right of privacy in commissioned photographs and films (s.86(1) CDPA). After a person's death, the right to take action for infringement passes to whomever he specifically directs. This can be more than one person. The right against false attribution lasts until twenty years after the person's death. If there is an infringement after his death, then his personal representatives can take action. It's not a criminal offence to infringe moral rights but, if proven, you have the right to seek injunctions and/or damages. Most importantly, you can exercise a degree of control over what's being done with your work.

THE CATCH

There is, though, one other big problem with these rights. You'll recall that the two main moral rights were fully introduced into UK law in 1988 in order to enable the UK to fully comply with the requirements of the Berne Convention. The Convention said that the laws of signatory countries ought to contain the author's moral rights. There was, however, nothing in the Convention that prevented a country incorporating the rights into its laws but then making concessions to other economic interests. This is exactly what happened in the UK. It arose largely as a result of intensive lobbying by the powerful record and publishing interests in this country. It is also a result of the longstanding laissez-faire tradition that we spoke of earlier. In the UK, we still favour economic interests over author's rights. So what happened was that, having included the rights in the 1988 Act, the Act then went on to say that the author could elect to waive his rights, to agree not to assert the right of paternity or to enforce any of the other rights. The waiver must be in writing and signed by the person giving up the right. The waiver can be for a specific work, for works within a specific description or works generally. It can apply to existing and future works, can be conditional or unconditional and can be revocable. The same points also apply to the moral rights of performers.

What was the consequence of this waiver provision? I'm sure you can guess. As soon as the industry realised these rights could be waived, all contracts were changed to include as standard a waiver of these rights in the widest possible terms. Clauses were included which provided for an absolute, unconditional and irrevocable waiver of any and all moral rights of whatever kind in relation to all existing or future works. They even put them in record contracts where there was initially little or no chance of the right existing in the first place.

Conclusions

So why bother discussing these rights if you're going to have to waive them anyway? Once again, it comes down to bargaining power. If creative controls are important to you, then you could try to insist on not having to waive them. If you're forced to waive your moral rights, then try to only waive them against uses of your works by properly authorised people. Try to retain the right to enforce your moral rights against unlawful users of your works and infringers of your rights.

If you're made to waive your rights, your lawyer will then usually use that as a lever to try to get some of the benefits of the rights through the back door. It helps us to negotiate more favourable credit clauses for you and to cover what happens if you aren't properly credited. We rely on the integrity right to get you contractual consents as to what can or can't be done with your work. For example, that your words and music can't be changed without your consent.

PRIVACY OF THE INDIVIDUAL

I've been talking in this book about how you can capitalise on your fame and fortune – but there is another side to the coin. What rights does a famous person have to prevent others from cashing in on his fame and intruding into his private life? Can celebrities protect their privacy? What happens if the press gets too intrusive?

There are two opposing schools of thought at work here. On the one hand, you could argue that personalities have worked hard to create their fame, why shouldn't they be able to benefit from the results of this hard work and control what others do with that celebrity? On the other hand, some consider that the fame of a personality is created by the public – it is society at large that decides whether or not an individual is famous or not, so their name and image should belong to the public.

The courts of different countries adopt different approaches. In the US, it's much easier to protect your personality and the publicity associated with it. In the UK, the courts have, for over half a century, adopted the approach that if you choose to go into an arena where you get fame and maybe fortune, then your name and reputation is a matter of public interest and public property.

The cases on the laws of passing off that we discussed earlier clearly show that the courts are not overly keen on assisting famous personalities to clear the market of 'unofficial' merchandise (see Chapter 8). So, if there is no trade mark or copyright infringement and no breach of the Trade Descriptions Act, what can you do? Well, in the UK, a law has been developed which gives celebrities and others in the public eye the possibility of a much broader protection, indeed a right of privacy, based on the law of confidence. At its heart are Articles 8 and 10 of the European Convention on Human Rights. Article 8 is the right to respect for privacy for private and family life, home and correspondence and Article 10 the right to freedom of expression. As you can easily see, there are bound to be occasions on which the two contradict one another. The Convention was incorporated into English law by the Human Rights Act 1998 which became law in the UK in 2000. The law has developed from there through a series of cases. Here is a selection of some of those cases:

An early case with indications for how this area of law would develop was that involving the racing driver Eddie Irvine.

The Eddie Irvine Case (Irvine and Another v. Talksport Limited, Chancery Division, 13 March 2002)

The case gave some hope that the courts were starting to acknowledge that there is a commercial value in the name and image of a well-known individual, which the individual is entitled to protect.

Talksport produced a limited-run advert with a doctored picture of Eddie Irvine showing him seeming to hold a radio, not a mobile phone, in his ear with a 'tag' line that suggested he supported a particular sport radio station.

Irvine brought an action for damages for passing off and argued that he had a substantial reputation and goodwill and that the defendant had created a false message that a not insignificant section of the public would take to mean that Irvine had endorsed the radio station. The radio station argued that there was no freestanding right to character exploitation enjoyable exclusively by a celebrity, and a passing-off claim couldn't be based on an allegation of false endorsement.

The court agreed with Irvine and held that an action for passing off could be based on false product endorsement. The Judge recognised the fact that it was common for famous people to exploit their names and images by way of endorsement in today's brand-conscious age, not only in their own field of expertise, but a wider field also. It was right, therefore, for valuable reputation to be protected from unauthorised use by other parties. The fact that the brochure had only had a limited distribution was not relevant. Even if the damage done may be negligible in direct money terms, the court accepted that potential long-term damage could be considerable.

The Michael Douglas Case (Michael Douglas, Catherine Zeta-Jones, Northern & Shell Limited v. Hello! Ltd [2001] EMLR 199)
This involved a claim by actor Michael Douglas and the publishers of *OK!* magazine that *Hello!* breached his privacy by secretly photographing his wedding to Catherine Zeta-Jones and publishing the photographs ahead of the exclusive that had been given to *OK!*

Three Judges reviewed the history of the developing law of confidence, not privacy, and the effect, if any, of the introduction of the Human Rights Act. They considered the acceptance of a right to appropriate protection of one's personal privacy as an extension of the law of confidence – placing a fundamental value on personal autonomy. The court declined to expand on a new right of privacy saying that Mr Douglas and *OK!* had sufficient protection under existing laws of confidence.

The earlier CA case of *Kaye v. Robertson* was not followed on the basis that the law had moved on to develop a law of privacy without the need for first establishing the relationship of confidentiality, which sometimes had to be done very artificially.

On balance, they decided Mr Douglas had a right to privacy, even though he had waived that right by agreeing a deal for publication of photographs of the event in question, his wedding.

The legal saga continued with £14,500 damages being later awarded to Mr Douglas and Ms Zeta-Jones and just over £1 million to *OK!* for the commercial damage.

Hello! then announced it would appeal the amount of damages awarded and the decision of the House of Lords in May 2005 was that, whilst Douglas and Zeta-Jones were entitled to damages for breach of their right of privacy, *OK!* was not also entitled to damages. This was both a significant blow to *OK!*, which had anticipated £1m in damages and the bulk of its legal costs, and one that has created a huge hole in the case law, which was thought to protect a magazine from a 'spoiler' story run by a rival. It seemed that protection is not available under the privacy or confidentiality laws in those circumstances. Unless there is an appeal to the European Court, this would seem to be the end of this particular saga but we can expect more cases in this area as magazines seek to establish the extent of what they can or cannot protect in terms of exclusives.

The courts have shown more of a tendency to grant injunctions in the area of privacy than, for example, libel. This fact, together with the hope of celebrities for an improvement in their right to privacy from intrusive paparazzi and tabloid reporters, has led to several new cases in this area.

The Footballer Case (A v. B & C (2002) EMLR 21)
A footballer wanted to prevent the publication of kiss-and-tell stories by getting an injunction against a newspaper. The court said it had to balance the interests of the individual against freedom of speech and decide whether there was a public interest to be served in allowing publication. It decided that, on balance, it wouldn't prevent publication.

This case seemed to make it clear that at this stage in the development of the law nearly all intrusions on privacy were to be dealt with in the area of breach of confidence. This seemed to be a move away from the Douglas case, which clearly wished to establish a separate law of privacy. By having to rely on the law of confidence, it would be necessary for celebrities to show that the information was obtained in confidential circumstances. The case also seemed to show the court's sympathies tipping in favour of freedom of the press, while stressing the need for a balancing act between privacy of the individual and the public interest. By that, I don't mean that just because it's a piece of juicy news that it's in the public interest, but that public figures have to accept that their activities do, in some circumstances, make it in the public's interest that they be written about, whether they like it or not.

This approach seems to have been followed in other cases brought by celebrities.

The Jamie Theakston Case (Theakston v. MGN Ltd [2002] QBD EMLR 22)
Another celebrity caught, as it were, with his trousers down was the TV presenter and actor Jamie Theakston, who visited a brothel and was photographed by one of the women there, who then threatened to sell her story to the press, apparently because he failed to pay for services rendered. Theakston sought an injunction to stop her. The court applied the rules on confidence and decided that the woman owed him no duty to keep the matter secret and that the public interest was served by a story that he had visited this place. They also ruled, though, that that interest didn't go so far as photographs, and made an order preventing the publication of the photographs.

The Naomi Campbell Case (Campbell v. MGN Ltd [2004] UK HL 22)
One of the first of the privacy cases to come to trial after the implementation of the Human Rights Act was one brought by the supermodel Naomi Campbell against the *Daily Mirror*. The *Mirror* intended to publish details of Ms Campbell's drug addiction. She sought an injunction to prevent them. The court decided that, while there was a public interest in knowing of her addiction (she had, apparently, previously proclaimed an anti-drugs stance), this didn't extend to details of her therapy with Narcotics Anonymous. It granted her an injunction for breach of confidentiality, but awarded the very low sum of £3,500 in damages – a signal it was thought that the court didn't think much of her behaviour. The Judge went so far as to say, 'I'm satisfied that she lied on oath.' This was a clear case where the damage caused by the publicity surrounding the case and her evidence in court may well have outweighed that caused by the original article. Appeals took the case right to the House of Lords where in May 2004 the original decision was upheld by the Law Lords on a 3 to 2 majority decision. The case has become a benchmark case establishing that there could be a new cause of action for 'misuse of private information'.

In the case of *Re S (A Child) [2005] 1 AC 593*, the court laid down some guidelines for how to reconcile the apparently contradictory provisions of Articles 8 and 10 of the Human Rights Act. Lord Steyn laid down four propositions that could be derived from the Naomi Campbell case. 'First, neither article has as such precedence over the other. Secondly, where the values under the two articles are in conflict, an intense focus on the comparative importance of the specific rights being claimed in the individual case is necessary. Thirdly, the justification for interfering with or restricting each right must be taken into account. Finally, the proportionality test must be applied to each. For convenience I will call this the "ultimate balancing test".' By an 'intense focus', the Judge meant that the court must consider all the facts, looking at each piece of information separately and by reference to the overall context. The way in which this has been applied in practice has been demonstrated by a number of subsequent cases.

Sebastian Coe Case (Reported in the Guardian *in June 2004)*
Shortly after the House of Lords decision in the Naomi Campbell case, Sebastian Coe brought a High Court action seeking an injunction against a newspaper publishing details of his mistress's abortion. As this was private medical information, which the courts had declared suitable for protection in Ms Campbell's case, he might have expected to succeed but he did not.

> *Sara Cox v. the* Sunday People *newspaper (Reported in the* Guardian *on 9 June 2005)*
> DJ Sara Cox sued the *Sunday People* newspaper after it published nude shots of her and her husband, John Carter, on their honeymoon whilst relaxing on a private beach. The action was settled with an award of £50,000 in damages.

> *Elizabeth Jagger Case (Reported in* The Times *on 10 March 2005)*
> Elizabeth Jagger brought a claim for an injunction in the High Court to prevent further publication of CCTV footage of her 'heavy petting' near the doorway of a nightclub with her then boyfriend, Calum Best. The Judge said she had a right to privacy and that when balanced against public interest he thought it came down firmly on the side of privacy in this case.

As in many other areas of English law, much can depend on the individual judge who hears the case. A 2006 case involving a Canadian musician applied the guidelines set out in *Re S (A Child)* to draw some conclusions as to where to draw the line between the need for privacy and the desirability of a free press.

> *Niema Ash v. Loreena McKennitt ([2006] EWCA Civ 1714, published 14 December 2006)*
> Although perhaps not a household name here, Ms McKennitt was a very successful Canadian folk singer who toured internationally. In 2005, a friend (or perhaps more correctly former friend) of hers, Niema Ash, published a book she had written entitled *Travels with Loreena McKennitt: My Life as a Friend*. Ms McKennitt claimed that the book contained a great deal of personal and private information about her life which she was entitled to keep private. Ms McKennitt was someone who took pains to protect her reputation and privacy. She was relying on the duty of confidence to keep private and business affairs private. She succeeded in this claim first time round but Ms Ash appealed.
>
> The Court of Appeal decision is useful to lawyers because it summarised the state of the law of privacy and confidence. As we have already seen, English law does not contain a specific right to sue for invasion of privacy so the cases have to be brought as breaches of confidence. That area of law also encompasses the provisions of the Human Rights Act but in ways that are not always comfortable. A balance has to be drawn between the right of an individual not to have his private information misused as against the right of freedom of expression. In addition, the court has to consider whether the individual complaining of misuse of private information had a reasonable expectation of privacy. This

latter requirement is behind some of the inconsistent decisions above. The Judges some-times find that the claimant's own behaviour has led to them foregoing this expectation of privacy. An example might be if a film star used his family to promote an image of a happy family man; he might then have given up his right to expect to prevent others from publishing pictures of him with his family.

Ms McKennitt passed the first hurdle in that the Court of Appeal Judges found that the majority of the information was of a personal nature that did fall within the category of private information. They declared it was necessary to consider each passage separately to decide 1) if the reasonable expectation of privacy had been passed and 2) whether there were any 'limiting factors' to be applied, such as that the material was in the public domain, or that it was in the public interest to disclose the information. The Court also felt that there could be a category of information which did not warrant protection because it was 'banal, trivial or anodyne'. Ms Ash had, rather ingeniously, argued that it could not be private to Ms McKennitt because she had shared the same experiences. But the Judges rejected this line of argument. They found that the book wasn't about Ms Ash's experi-ences but those of Ms McKennitt and so was not being used as an expression of her personal experiences.

The Judges also decided that in this case merely because Ms McKennitt sought publicity for herself she hadn't lost all right to protect herself against publicity that she didn't like. We will see later that more recent cases have developed this idea of a lack of protection where the complainant has himself put information of a similar kind in the public domain.

So, having decided this was private information that she was entitled to protect, the Court of Appeal then had to decide if that right was outweighed by the right of freedom of expression.

The Judges found here that the freedom of expression didn't automatically outweigh the right of privacy. Each case has to be looked at in detail. In this case, they found that Ms Ash did not have her own story to tell, only that of Ms McKennitt and just because it had, as it were, come into the public domain by being told to Ms Ash by Ms McKennitt did not mean Ms McKennitt had lost her expectation that that information would be kept private. It might I think have been different if Ms McKennitt had already given a 'warts and all' interview to a newspaper.

Ms Ash thought that she had the right to expose what she saw as Ms McKennitt's hypocrisy in the difference between her public and private life. The Judges disagreed that there were any special circumstances that would justify the revealing of that private infor-mation. A charge of hypocrisy alone was not enough of a reason. And in any event they found on the facts that Ms McKennitt was not, in fact, a hypocrite.

On the other hand, the Court also made clear that there was no automatic right to a private life by a person in the public eye, but that in some circumstances there were areas of their lives that they were entitled to keep private. Special circumstances would need in future to be shown if, for example, the private life of a football player were to be made public without his consent. Special circumstances would be matters that fell within the area of political or public debate and would not therefore normally apply to the private lives of individuals, even politicians and those in the public eye.

The case was also important because it established that there was a reasonable expectation of privacy in relation to false allegations, untrue, distorted or misleading information. This meant you could in effect bring a case for 'false privacy', i.e. the publication of material which, if it were true, would constitute misuse of private information. Recently, Angelina Jolie and Brad Pitt successfully sued the publishers of the *News of The World* for invasion of false privacy over an untrue claim that they were separating.

Exactly a week later, the Court of Appeal handed down its judgement in the appeal by Associated Newspapers to be permitted to publish extracts from the Prince of Wales' private journals.

Associated Newspapers Ltd v. HRH Prince of Wales ([2006] Ch 57 CA)
In some respects, this case looks to be obvious, but it nevertheless ended up in the Court of Appeal. This is probably a reflection of the amount of money newspapers can make from stories of a revealing nature, as well as the fact that this is a still developing area of law where the press perhaps sensed a chance to gain some ground in the privacy versus press freedom battle.

Prince Charles kept handwritten journals (eight in total) containing his impressions and views in the course of his overseas visits in the period between 1993 and 1999. An employee of the Prince's provided copies of the journals to the *Mail on Sunday* who published substantial extracts relating to a visit to Hong Kong in 1993, including comments which were disparaging of certain Chinese dignitaries he had met. Her actions were a breach of her employment contract. Prince Charles sued her on two grounds, breach of copyright and breach of confidence. On the breach of confidence case, the issues were essentially the same as in Ms McKennitt's case outlined above. Was the press freedom of expression enough justification to override the Prince's right to privacy in his private life?

The court which first heard the case thought it did not and gave judgement to the Prince. The newspaper appealed.

Once again the Court of Appeal Judges outlined the state of the current laws of confidence and in this case also discussed the extent to which the employee was in a position of confidence such as to fairly and reasonably recognise that the information was private.

Once again there was the question of the balance of interests to be weighed, but in addition the Court of Appeal felt they had to consider how this weighed up when you also took into account that the information had been obtained as a result of a breach of a confidential relationship based on a contract – here an employment contract. The newspaper argued that there was a public interest in the publication of the journals.

In this case, both the fact that the employee had a contract which contained a clause obliging the employee to keep the contents of the journal confidential and the balance in favour of even the heir to the throne having a right to keep his thoughts private fell in the Prince's favour. No one is so famous that they lost all right to a private life.

Max Mosley Case (Max Mosley v. News Group Newspapers Ltd [2008] EWHC 1777 (QB) 24 July 2008)

In a case which neatly summarises just that point, Max Mosley sued for breach of confidence and/or the unauthorised disclosure of personal information, in breach of his right to privacy under Article 8 of the European Convention on Human Rights. The basis of the claim was that the content of the published material was inherently private in nature consisting as it did of sadomasochistic and some sexual activities, and also that there had been a pre-existing relationship of confidentiality between the participants. Articles in the *News of the World* had claimed that Mosley was involved in Nazi orgies and on the *NOW* website there was video footage of the activities in question. It was Mr Mosley's case that they had all taken part in the activities on the understanding that they would be private and that none of them would reveal what had taken place. The Judge was told that there is a fairly tight-knit community of S&M activists on 'the scene' and that it is an unwritten rule that people are trusted not to reveal what has gone on. Mr Mosley alleged against the woman in question (known as 'Woman E') that she breached that trust and that the journalist concerned must have appreciated that she was doing so. Mr Mosley claimed exemplary damages. The *News of the World*'s case was that Mr Mosley had no expectation of privacy in relation to the information concerning the events, and alternatively that even if he did his right to privacy was outweighed by a greater public interest in disclosure such that the newspaper's right to freedom of expression under Article 10 of the Convention should prevail. The newspaper argued that the public had an interest in knowing of the newspaper's and/or Woman E's allegation that the party involved Nazi or concentration camp role-play and that, because of his role as President of the FIA, the public had a right to know that Mr Mosley was committing offences such as assault occasioning actual bodily harm and brothel-keeping.

Mr Justice Eady said it was clear that the claim was partly founded, as in *McKennitt v Ash* (above), upon 'old-fashioned breach of confidence'. He reviewed the case law and reiterated the principles laid down in *Re S (A Child)* and acknowledged that the law of 'old-fashioned breach of confidence' had been extended in recent years under the stimulus of the Human Rights Act.

Applying those principles to the particular circumstances of this case, it was necessary to examine the facts closely and to decide whether (assuming a reasonable expectation of privacy had been established) some countervailing consideration of public interest might be said to justify any intrusion which has taken place. In other words, was the intrusion proportionate? Was it necessary to reveal every detail? And was it necessary to secretly record the goings on? Was secret recording itself an infringement of human rights? More specifically, as was acknowledged in the Naomi Campbell case, there could be a genuine public interest in the disclosure or the existence of a sexual relationship, but the addition of salacious details or intimate photographs could be disproportionate and unacceptable.

The initial footage had been shown on the *NOW* website under a lurid headline and it had attracted over 1.4 million viewings before the *NOW* agreed to take it down and not reinstate it without first giving Mosley 24 hours' notice. When the *NOW* later gave that notice, Mosley tried to get an injunction but failed because, in effect, it had been so widely disseminated that the injunction would have made little practical difference. The Judge, Justice Eady, again said that whilst there was no legitimate public interest to be served by the additional disclosure the footage was so widely available that the 'dam has effectively burst'.

At the full trial of the matter, the Judge found as a question of fact that there was no Nazi theme to the activities. He also found that there was a duty of confidence owed to Mosley by Woman E who had revealed the activities to the press and made the secret recording. The Judge also rejected the public interest defence on the basis that there was no evidence of criminality or a Nazi theme at the party to justify either the intrusion of secret filming or subsequent publication. There was no question of a sexual offence being committed since everything was consensual. He thought that the disclosure and the secret filming was not proportionate and was not justified as being in the public interest.

Perhaps the most interesting part of the case from a legal point of view is the value that the Judge placed on the damages he awarded to Mr Mosley. It was acknowledged by the Judge that Mr Mosley's life had been, in effect, ruined, but said that exemplary damages were not appropriate in claims of infringement of privacy. He agreed that Mr Mosley was entitled to 'adequate financial remedy' for the purpose of acknowledging the infringement and compensating, to some extent, for injury to feelings, the embarrassment and distress caused. The Judge said that no amount of damages could fully compensate Mr Mosley for the damage done. Taking into account that what could be achieved by a monetary award in such circumstances was limited and that any award must be proportionate and avoid the appearance of arbitrariness, the Judge came to the conclusion that the right award was £60,000. Although it does not seem much for a ruined life, it was record damages for a privacy case where until then the damages had been fairly low. The expense of defending a legal action may still be enough to prevent editors from over-stepping the mark but this measure of damages is nevertheless not so high that if they are sued the damages awarded would not cripple most newspapers. Some newspaper editors still feel that the case went too far and effectively put many activities of a sexual nature undertaken in private amongst consenting adults out of bounds for publication.

However, it is still the case that if there had been a Nazi element or if there had been criminality then the Judge may well have concluded that the exposure of these activities was proportionate and justified.

Since the trial, Mr Mosley has campaigned, so far unsuccessfully, for a change to the law to require that 24 hours' notice is given before information is published. As he had discovered to his own cost, once privacy has been breached it is lost forever. Damages are not always sufficient compensation.

What has also now to be considered is the extent to which an individual can lose the court's protection where they have put information about themselves in the public domain. Many lawyers who in the past would have focused on litigation to protect the privacy of their celebrity clients are now working instead on educating them as to what it is appropriate to post on their websites, Twitter feeds or Instagram accounts if they are to retain the hope of protecting their privacy if it is later breached.

In the case of *The Author of a Blog v. Times Newspapers Ltd [2009] EWHC 1358 (QB)* a serving police officer had been writing and publishing a blog with his views on policing. *The Times* worked out who he was and the author sought an injunction to prevent them publishing his identity. The blogger argued that the newspaper was under a duty of confidence not to reveal his identity and that he had a reasonable expectation of privacy in respect of the information that he was the author. The argument that *The Times* had a duty of confidentiality seems to me a tenuous one and Mr Justice Eady, again, decided that just because he'd written the blog didn't mean *The Times* had any duty of confidence to him or that he had a reasonable expectation of privacy as blogging was a public activity. He also said that even if the expectation of privacy had been found to exist it would be likely to be outweighed by a countervailing public interest that a police officer had been making these communications. This fact would assist the public in assessing the value of the opinions he was expressing and in concluding whether it was suitable for serving police officers to communicate such matters publicly.

SOCIAL NETWORKING SITES

The vast amount of information now published on social networking sites has the potential to impact generally on what the court will give protection to. If someone comes to the court seeking protection of their privacy but their own pages on Facebook contain all sorts of lurid stories about what they get up to in their private lives, there is a good chance that the court will take that into consideration, particularly when deciding whether to grant an injunction.

It has also been established in a high-profile case involving Sally Bercow (the wife of the Speaker of the House of Commons) that a Tweet can be defamatory. Bercow was sued by Lord McAlpine after she falsely accused him by implication of being 'a paedophile who was guilty of sexually abusing boys living in care'. She Tweeted 'Why is McAlpine trending?' followed by *innocent face*. Ms Bercow denied the Tweet meant that, or that it meant anything defamatory of the claimant but lost her case. The principle that if you repeat a defamatory allegation made by another it is treated as if you had made the allegation yourself was found to apply after she followed up on a BBC *Newsnight* programme in which McAlpine wasn't named but various allegations were made which were wrongly directed online at Lord McAlpine.

The Defamation Act came into force on 1 January 2014. It has brought in a higher test for bringing a defamation claim. You now have to show that there is a likelihood of 'serious harm to reputation'. There is also a statutory public interest defence. But alongside these it also created a new defence for website operators who host things like message boards, comments sections and probably social media (although that is not clear). Up until now website operators have been liable alongside the person posting the defamatory material and could only escape liability by taking down the offending material as soon as possible. Regulations published under the Act are trying to address the problem of anonymous postings of defamatory content. Now, if a website operator receives a complaint and it wishes to rely on the new defence it must contact the anonymous poster and ask them to provide their name and address. It they do not respond then the material must be taken down. If they respond giving their name and address and confirming that they object to the material being removed then the website operator can leave the material on the website but not be liable for it. The complainant can apply to a court for the website operator to release the name and address therefore making it easier for the complainant to sue.

CONFIDENTIALITY AGREEMENTS

If a confidential relationship does exist (for example, between a celebrity and his housekeeper, driver or bodyguard), then it's important that there is a confidentiality agreement put in place. This will make the extent of the confidentiality clear and confirm that such matters will remain confidential and will add a claim for breach of contract to that of confidence.

HARASSMENT ACTIONS

Apart from seeking court orders in the civil courts for injunctions, celebrities can, and do, seek the involvement of the police to prevent the activities of paparazzi and reporters whose activities border on that of stalking. They rely on legislation introduced in the 1990s to prevent private individuals from being hounded or stalked. If the police can be persuaded to get involved, they can be very effective in 'moving on' recalcitrant members of the press. If they won't, then private criminal actions are possible, although such cases rarely come to trial as the celebrity would have to give evidence and many are reluctant to do so. Whether it's a police or private criminal case, the court is going to want to see detailed evidence of the extent of the harassment, so private detectives are often hired to produce photographs of the paparazzi hounding the celebrity, and his private security staff are often called upon to produce detailed statements of the extent of the harassment. Many of these paparazzi are freelance and make their money from selling stories and photos to the highest bidder. 'Exclusives' can net them tens of thousands of pounds in syndication rights worldwide. No wonder they are keen, and no wonder that many celebrities are forced either into almost total isolation in the UK or to move overseas, France and the US being particular favourites, where the privacy laws are stronger.

CONCLUSIONS

- Try to retain your moral rights if you can.
- Assert your right to be identified as an author of a work early and as widely as you can.
- If you have to waive your moral rights, use this to get improved creative controls in the contract.
- Put confidentiality agreements in place with those who work closest with you.
- Consider harassment actions if intrusion becomes too much.
- Before embarking on privacy/breach of confidence actions, consider whether the potential bad publicity of a trial could outweigh any advantages gained.
- Be careful what you say about yourself on social networking sites as this could undermine any later claim you may make for protection from the court for your privacy.

Chapter 13

Sampling and Plagiarism

INTRODUCTION

Sampling and plagiarism are two sides of the same problem. Plagiarism is the taking of someone else's ideas and passing them off as your own. Sampling is essentially the same thing, but the subtle difference between them is that to be guilty of plagiarism you need to show that someone had access to your material and that it was not just coincidence that it sounds very similar to your work. Sampling is always only a deliberate act. The person doing the sampling deliberately takes part of someone's work and then, possibly after manipulating it, includes it in their own work. Both sampling and plagiarism are infringements of copyright (*ss.16–21 CDPA*). If you sample the actual sound itself by copying the digital recording, this is an infringement of the sound recording copyright. If you don't actually make a copy of the sound recording copyright, you could take the piece of music that you're interested in using and get someone to replay it, to re-perform it in an identical way. This is still sampling, but it would then only be an infringement of the musical copyright in the music and the literary copyright in any words used.

Is sampling theft? Many people argue that all cultural evolution is based on taking bits of existing popular culture and adapting and changing them. They argue that all new musical genres 'borrow' or are influenced by earlier ones. R&B

from gospel, and rock 'n' roll from R&B and so on. Those that believe this think that clamping down on sampling stifles this growth. They would be in favour of the removal of all restrictions on using parts of someone else's copyright.

This is all very well, but if you were to take this to its logical conclusion then no one would be able to protect their work, music would be devalued and people wouldn't be able to make a living from their work. Surely that's likely to lead to less creativity rather than more? I believe that it's wrong to deliberately take someone else's work without their permission, without paying them anything for it and without giving them proper credit.

HOW MUCH IS A SAMPLE?

Although sampling has been around since the 1960s, there's still an awful lot of confusion about what is a sample. A lot of people think that just because they've only sampled a couple of notes or a few seconds of someone else's work they haven't sampled it at all. That simply isn't true. What the 1988 Copyright Act says is that there has to have been copying of a 'substantial part' *(s.16(3) (a) CDPA)*. It's a question of the quality of the part sampled and not the quantity.

There are a number of cases where the courts have considered what is a 'substantial part'.

Colonel Bogey Case (Hawkes & Son Limited v. Paramount Film Service Limited [1934] 1 Ch 593)

In the case of Hawkes & Son, Paramount had included the sound of the 'Colonel Bogey' military march in a newsreel. They used twenty-eight bars of music lasting about twenty seconds. The question was whether twenty seconds out of a four-minute piece was a substantial part. The music performed by the band made up the main theme of the march. The court clearly looked at the quality of what had been copied as well as the quantity and found that an infringement of copyright had taken place. Judge Slesser said, 'Though it may be that it was not very prolonged in its reproduction, it is clearly, in my view, a substantial, a vital, and an essential part which is there reproduced.'

The Beloved Case (Hyperion Records Limited v. Warner Music (UK) Ltd 1991)

So, could something shorter than twenty seconds constitute a sample?

The band The Beloved sampled eight seconds of a recording of a piece called 'O Euchari'. The sample was repeated several times in The Beloved's track 'The Sun Rising'.

The sound recording of a performance by Emily Van Evera of the work had been sampled. Hyperion owned the rights in that sound recording and sued. At a preliminary hearing, the Judge gave his opinion that an eight-second sample was not too brief to constitute a substantial part. He wanted the matter to go to a full hearing. However, as happens with so many sampling cases, Hyperion settled out of court and permission to use the sound recording sample was given retrospectively.

The 'Macarena' Case

A claim was brought by Produce Records Limited that the dance hit 'Macarena', which had been released by BMG Records, infringed the copyright in a sound recording by The Farm called 'Higher and Higher'. The sample consisted of a short sound made by the vocalist Paula David, which Produce alleged had been used or 'looped' throughout 'Macarena'.

Because so few sampling cases get to court, a lot rested on this case. If it went to a full court hearing and the court confirmed that such a short sample could constitute a substantial part, this would be a firm ruling that could be relied on in later disputes. After such a judgement, it would be very difficult to rely on the widely held view that three seconds is the minimum amount necessary to constitute a substantial part. It was more important as a potential guideline for samplers than it was for BMG to win this particular case. A decision that the part sampled didn't constitute a substantial part would mean success for the record company, but it wouldn't necessarily have given any guidance on what is a substantial part. Each subsequent sampling case would continue to be decided on a case-by-case basis. On the other hand, if the case had gone against BMG and such a short sample had been said to be a substantial part, then BMG would have lost this particular case, but all record companies would also have lost the argument that such a small sample couldn't constitute an infringement of copyright. BMG settled out of court on terms that remain confidential. Possibly the potential downside was too great.

The question also comes up from time to time as to whether you can sample a rhythm or a drumbeat. I would argue that you can if it can be shown to be original and distinctive and if a substantial part has been copied. There are, of course, only so many rhythms in popular music and many drum and bass lines used currently are, in fact, the same as have been used in earlier works. This is particularly true in the area of reggae music. Inevitably, there is going to be duplication.

Perhaps some of the most interesting cases to emerge in the last two years have been in the US and not therefore of direct bearing on our rights in the UK. However, they may indicate a general direction that Judges here might also be minded to follow. Perhaps the most high profile was that of *Pharrell Williams, Robin Thicke and Ti v. Bridgeport Music Inc et al*. In April 2015 a US jury found that the 2013 song 'Blurred Lines' copied parts of Marvin Gaye's 'Got To Give It Up' without permission. The claimants were awarded nearly $7.4 million (later slightly reduced to $5.3 million) and ordered to pay over 50% of songwriting and publishing revenues. The verdict is interesting because the jury appear to have been persuaded of the similarity of the two works by the style and feel, rather than a strict application of copyright law. The case is currently under appeal, and at the heart of that appeal is the argument that the judge and jury should have considered sheet music rather than listening to samples of the two songs. There are concerns in the music industry that songwriters will be punished for being 'inspired' by other songs.

The size of the award appears to have had an immediate impact, with a string of recent high-profile songwriting/copyright infringement claims hitting the courts, including early stages of an alleged $20 million claim involving Ed Sheeran's 'Photograph', which was settled out of court in April 2017 for an undisclosed amount. A case brought by the estate of deceased Spirit guitarist Randy Wolfe, alleging that the members of Led Zeppelin had copied 'Taurus' by Spirit in their famous work 'Stairway To Heaven', was thrown out by an LA court. In contrast to the 'Blurred Lines' case the jury was not allowed to hear the original recordings of 'Stairway to Heaven' and 'Taurus' in determining their verdict. Instead, they heard an expert perform both songs based on the original sheet music. The result here led to arguments that frivolous or opportunist litigation and litigators should be subject to further restrictions. In the US even those who win rarely recover their legal costs and Led Zeppelin were said to have incurred nearly $1 million in legal fees to clear their name in a case some say should never have been brought.

HOW DO YOU CLEAR A SAMPLE?

If it's clear that you've sampled someone else's work, then this is an infringement of their copyright – unless you get their permission to copy and reproduce their work. If you don't, they could sue you for damages for the copyright infringement and also for an injunction stopping you from continuing to use that sample. As you can imagine, record companies aren't very happy about having an artist who samples material from others and doesn't get their permission. It's very expensive for the record company if there's an injunction and it has to recall all the copies of the single or album and remove the offending sample before re-cutting, re-mastering and reissuing the record. In fact, if it's too expensive it may not bother redoing it and just kill the single or album. That isn't a good result for an artist, so it's best to get permission to use any samples. This is called 'clearing' samples.

Most record contracts, whether they're exclusive recording agreements or licences, will have a clause in them that says the artist guarantees that all samples are cleared before the recording is delivered to them. This makes it clear that it is the artist's responsibility. This is only fair if the artist put the sample in there in the first place. But bear in mind that producers and remixers also have the opportunity to introduce samples into the recording at various stages in the process. Their contract should make them responsible for clearing any samples that they introduce. Sometimes it's the record company that has the idea that including a particular sample will turn a good song into a great monster hit. If the record company is encouraging you to include a sample, then it has to take responsibility for clearing it, possibly as an additional recording cost. That cost may or may not be recoupable, depending on the contract.

In a case on this point, the Judge (Terence Etherton QC) seemed to have had sympathy for the defendant.

The Walmsley Case (Richard Walmsley v. Acid Jazz Records Limited, Chancery Division 2000)

Walmsley had recorded a track that contained two sound recording samples. The track was licensed to Acid Jazz and the contract required Acid Jazz to pay royalties to Walmsley. Walmsley gave a warranty that the copyright in the track was free from any third-party claims. Why he signed such an agreement is unknown, but as we will see part of the explanation may be that he didn't pay much attention to it. Acid Jazz refused to pay any royalties, even though the track was a chart success. Acid Jazz said the track had given rise to a number of disputes and that it had had to pay out monies in settlement. It said that it was relying on its warranty, which it said Walmsley had breached. Walmsley's evidence was that he'd told Acid Jazz at the time of the agreement and subsequently of the samples, and had been told by Acid Jazz that no licences were required and, if any were to be sought, Acid Jazz would do it.

The Judge found that Acid Jazz owed the royalties to Walmsley and, although Walmsley was in breach of contract, Acid Jazz was not permitted under equitable principles to rely on it because it had had full knowledge of the true position from the outset.

With some types of music, particularly in the dance, electronic and hip-hop arenas, the record company is fully aware that there will be samples and will often help to clear them. This can be an advantage, as they can use their greater resources and clout to pull favours and get things cleared quickly. This clout can have its downsides. If you're a small, struggling independent label that asks to clear a sample, the person whose work is sampled is less likely to ask for large amounts of money than if you are Universal or Sony for example.

When Should You Seek Permission?

Ideally, you should try to get clearance before you've recorded the sample. Then, if you don't get permission, you haven't wasted recording costs and time. In reality, this won't usually be possible. It can take time to track down the owners of the work sampled to find out who you have to ask for permission. Even once you find them they may take their time in getting back to you. You may then have to negotiate terms for the clearance. In the meantime, you can't get on with finishing the recording of that track. This could hold up delivery of the record and its eventual release. Also, you're going to need a recording of what the sampled work is going to sound like in your version of it, even if it's only a demo. In practice, therefore, the clearance process takes place after the recording has been made or during the recording process. Sometimes it's left until the record has been delivered. I think this is too late to start the clearance process. Some feelers should have been put out beforehand, at least to find out who owns it and to get an idea of whether they're likely to give you a problem.

Most record contracts and licences will say that delivery of a recording hasn't taken place until evidence has been produced (usually in the form of clearance letters or agreements) that all samples have been cleared. If you haven't used any samples, they will want you to give a warranty (a sort of guarantee) to that effect. Until delivery has taken place, it's unlikely that you'll get any advances due to be paid on delivery (see Chapter 3). Nor will time start to run for your record to be released and the marketing plan won't be put into action. Therefore, the sooner samples are cleared the better.

Some people say that they are willing to take a risk that the use of a sample won't be spotted. They think that, if it's sufficiently obscure or hidden in the track, the sample won't be discovered. Well, it's just possible that you could get away with it if it is a limited edition, low-key release. For example, if you are only going to press up 1,000 CDs of the record for release on your own small label, then you might be lucky. Even if it is spotted, the copyright owner of the sample may not bother to take any legal action because the amounts involved and the legal costs and hassle of suing you wouldn't warrant it. But what happens if a bigger record company licenses your track in and gives it a big marketing push? Or if you make it a big success in your own right and find you're licensing it to loads of different compilations? Or it is picked up to be used in an advert or a soundtrack of a film? If you haven't cleared the sample and you are found out, you'll end up with a big problem on your hands, because now the copyright owner of the sampled work has an incentive for taking you to court. The record company that has licensed the track from you may get sued by the sample owner. The record company will in turn usually have an indemnity from you. This means that, if they are sued, they can make you responsible for the damages and costs involved because you've breached your warranty that there were no uncleared samples in the recording. By lying to them you may also have irretrievably damaged your relationship with that label for the future. Is it worth the risk? That is for you to judge. It is also much easier with the Internet to find tracks which might once have been obscure, low-key releases. Whilst this has its advantages it also has significant disadvantages if you were hoping to keep your track low key. Personally, I really don't think it's worth the risk and I have seen many deals come unstuck through issues arising from uncleared samples. At the very least tell the record company about the samples as early as possible and enlist their help to clear them.

Where Do You Go To Clear Samples?

If you are trying to clear samples, who do you go to for clearance? If you've sampled the actual sound recording, you need to seek permission from the owner of the original sound recording, although they may have passed it on to someone else by licence or assignment of rights. You can start by looking at the recording that you sampled it from. It should have a copyright notice on it that will say who was the copyright owner at that time, for example '© Sony Music Entertainment 2016'. So your first point of call would be Sony. They should be able to tell you if they still own the rights. If you don't want to show your hand too soon, you might want to do this through your lawyer on a 'no names' basis.

You must allow yourself plenty of time. The first thing you should be trying to achieve is an agreement from them in principle to the use of the sample. Some artists won't allow their works to be sampled under any circumstances, so it's best to know this as early as possible. Once you've got the agreement in principle, then you can negotiate the terms. This can also take time, but you should know fairly early on whether they are going to ask for a ludicrous amount for the clearance, which will make it uneconomical for the sample to be used. Remember that as well as clearing the use of the sound recording sample, you have to clear the use of the underlying music and, if appropriate, words.

The owner of the copyright in the words and music may be the songwriter credited on the sampled recording. It's quite possible, though, that the songwriter may have assigned or licensed his rights to a music publisher. So you'll have to look at whether a publisher is credited and go to them to see if they still own or control the rights. They may only do so for part of the world or they may have passed the rights on or back to the original writer. The PRS for Music database should contain details of who claims to own or control the publishing rights. This would be a good starting point if you're a member of PRS. If the title or the songwriter's name is a common one, for example John Smith, then the database is going to throw up a lot of names. Try to narrow down the search by supplying as much detail as you can.

The importance of clearing samples with the correct party is highlighted in the following case.

The Ludlow Case (Ludlow Music Inc v. (1) Robert P. Williams, (2) Guy Chambers, (3) EMI Music Publishing Limited, (4) BMG Music Publishing Limited, Chancery Division, 2000)
Ludlow published the song 'I'm The Way'. Robbie Williams and Guy Chambers co-wrote 'Jesus in A Camper Van', which was published by EMI and BMG.

Because two lines of 'Jesus' resembled 'I'm The Way', Mr Williams approached Ludlow to acknowledge the resemblance and to agree that Ludlow would be a co-publisher. Ludlow wanted 50% – Williams and Chambers offered 10%. Ludlow refused and, just as the album containing the track was to be released, repeated their demand. EMI registered Ludlow as having a 50% share in the lyrics, i.e. 25% of the whole song. Ludlow then brought a claim for 100% of the copyright and of the income and sought an injunction.

The Judge found there had been an infringement of copyright, but thought it was borderline. He gave his opinion that what the defendants had offered was generous, but left it to another court to determine the amount of damages. He also decided that, on balance, Ludlow's conduct had been oppressive, governed by money and that they had gone along with things and had seemed to have been agreeing to things up to the last minute before release. He refused an injunction at summary judgement. An injunction was granted at the final hearing, so future pressings of that album could not contain this offending track without reaching an accommodation with Ludlow.

What sometimes happens is that it's possible to clear the underlying words and music but not the sound recording. If you're adamant that you have to use that sample, then you can try to get it reproduced almost identically by having it replayed or recreated. Then you haven't sampled the original sound recording, so you only have to clear the underlying music/words. Of course, if you do a very good job of it and it sounds identical to the original, it may not be believed that you've replayed it and you might still be threatened with legal action. Then you may need independent evidence from, for example, the studio engineer that you didn't use the sample sound recording and probably a musicologist's report.

I was once involved in a case where this happened. The client sampled part of a sound recording, asked for permission, which was denied, so set about replaying the sample to recreate the sound. He even went to the trouble of pre-empting the problem by getting a specialist report from a musicologist to confirm that he hadn't used the original sound recording but had replayed it. Nevertheless, the owner of the original sound recording wasn't convinced and threatened to sue my client's record company, who had released the track. Using a right it had under its record contract with my client, the record company 'froze' the royalties that would otherwise have been payable to my client on the track in question until there was an outcome to the dispute. The money stayed 'frozen' for over a year and, as it was a substantial amount, my client was understandably very frustrated. Ah, but I hear you say, it serves him right for copying someone else's work. Well, before you get all high and mighty, just make sure that no one can ever accuse you of sampling or plagiarism.

How Much Does It Cost?

This is always a question of negotiation. It will depend on how important the track is that you've sampled and how crucial it is to you that you use it. There is no set list of fees.

Record companies will usually clear sound recording copyrights for an up-front sum, sometimes with a further amount when you sell a certain number of records. For example, £1,500 up-front and another £1,500 when you've sold 10,000 copies of the record that includes the sample. This usually comes out of the artist's royalty, but may be shared with the record company if it really wants to keep the sample in or keep its artist happy.

Publishers of sampled works may clear rights for a one-off fee or a fee and a further sum based on the number of records sold. More likely, however, is that they will want a percentage of the publishing income on the track. In effect, the publisher of the sampled work is saying that their writer should be treated as a co-writer on the new work and receive a co-writer's share of the income. That share could be as much as 100% if a substantial use has been made of their work. If the use is less substantial then a lower percentage may be agreed.

As we saw with the Ludlow case above, claims for 50% or more of a song may be claimed even if a relatively small percentage is sampled – it's a copyright infringement and the owner of the sampled works is entitled to be compensated. If it's a blatant offence, the court will be asked to award additional damages.

If you're going to do a lot of sampling in your work and are going to end up having to give away some or all of your publishing on certain tracks, do bear in mind that this may make it very difficult for you to fulfil your song-writing commitment to your publisher – make sure you take this into account when setting the original level of that commitment.

What Happens If You Don't Clear Something?

If a sample isn't cleared and a dispute arises, your record company may suspend payment to you until the dispute is resolved. There may be a limit on how long it can suspend payment, but this could be a year or more. PRS for Music also has the right to suspend any payments of publishing income and has a disputes procedure that has to be followed. They won't directly intervene to resolve a dispute, but can sometimes be used as an arbitrator.

Failure to clear samples in good time could result in an injunction preventing distribution of copies of your record, or an order that they be brought back from the distributors and destroyed. You could also be sued for damages for the copyright infringement (ss.96–110 CDPA).

However, it's not all bad. Not all copyright owners sue or want payment when their work is sampled, some are content with a name check. The earlier you ask permission and the more respectful you are, the more likely you are to get clearance to use it.

PLAGIARISM

For the purposes of this chapter, when I'm talking about plagiarism as opposed to sampling, I'm talking about a situation where someone takes another's work and copies it, passing it off as his own work. There are, as we saw above, potential overlaps with the situation where you replay a sound sampled from another's work. But what I'm describing here are cases where a songwriter has claimed that another songwriter has stolen or copied his work; where the similarities between two pieces of work are so striking that you would have to believe the one was copied from the other. As we will see from the cases below, once you've established similarities between two pieces of work the crucial test is whether the person being accused of plagiarising the work has had access to the other work. It's possible to unconsciously copy something or indeed to arrive at a very similar-sounding piece of work purely by chance.

The John Brett Case
In the late 1980s, songwriter John Brett accused the composer, Lord Andrew Lloyd Webber, of copying two songs written by him in Lloyd Webber's musical *Phantom of the Opera*. Although there were similarities between the pieces, Lloyd Webber was able to show that he had written the song first. He produced evidence that it had been performed in mid-1985, whereas Mr Brett's evidence suggested that he had not sent demo recordings of his songs to his solicitor until a month later. His claim failed.

The Ray Repp Case
In another case involving Lord Lloyd Webber, a songwriter called Ray Repp brought a legal action in New York accusing Lloyd Webber of plagiarism. Mr Repp claimed that Lloyd Webber had stolen a passage from his song 'Till You' and had used it, again, in *Phantom of the Opera*. Once again, Lloyd Webber was cleared, and afterwards made a passionate statement condemning the increase in cases alleging plagiarism. He blamed the lawyers and people with an eye to the main chance. He said there were too many people around who thought it was worth a chance, because record companies would rather settle than fight potentially damaging court cases. I understand that his office returns unopened all unsolicited demo CDs sent to him. The same policy is, I believe, adopted by other well-known songwriters who wish to avoid any such claims.

The Francis Day and Hunter Case (Francis Day & Hunter v. Bron [1963] Ch 587)
This case is an early one in this area that set out a number of guidelines for what constitutes plagiarism. In this case, it was argued that eight bars of the chorus of a song entitled 'In A Little Spanish Town' had been copied in the song 'Why'. The Judge found a number of similarities between the two works but decided that copying (i.e. plagiarism)

had not been proved. It went to the Court of Appeal. That court also agreed that copying had not been proved, but took the opportunity to consider the subject of copying generally. The Appeal Court Judges said that you had to establish that there was a definite connection between the two works, or at the very least to show that the writer accused of copying had had access to the work of the other.

The 'Chariots of Fire' Case ([1993] EMLR 306)
The film *Chariots of Fire* and the music written for it has also been the subject of a number of court cases.

The songwriter Logarides had written a piece for television called 'City Of Violets'. He claimed that the songwriter Vangelis had copied four crucial notes from 'City Of Violets' when writing his theme tune for the film *Chariots of Fire*. Logarides said that, consciously or unconsciously, Vangelis had infringed his copyright. The court decided that there was insufficient similarity between the works for there to have been an infringement. This ruled out the argument that Vangelis had unconsciously copied it, because it wasn't similar enough. The evidence that was produced to show that Vangelis had had access to the work was also not very strong, although the court thought that it was possible that Vangelis had heard the song 'City Of Violets'. Logarides was not able to prove that Vangelis had actually had access to his work.

The Beyoncé Case
In 2005, songwriter Jennifer Armour brought a lawsuit against Beyoncé Knowles claiming that Beyoncé's 2003 hit 'Baby Boy' included lyrics from Armour's song 'Got A Bit Of Love For You'. Armour brought evidence to show that Beyoncé's record label had had access to her song as it had been sent to them by her former manager. She also said that representatives of Beyoncé's collaborator on the song, Sean Paul, had also been sent a copy. Whether or not Beyoncé had ever heard Armour's song did not have to be decided in the end because the case failed at the first hurdle. When the two songs were compared side by side the court came to the conclusion the two songs were 'substantially dissimilar' and therefore there was no copyright infringement to complain about.

But it isn't always deliberate. It seems that it is perfectly possible for a songwriter to copy another's work unconsciously. I have a client who was unaware that he had copied a snippet from the Don McLean song 'Vincent' until it was pointed out to him and the same thing happened in 2004 to Scottish band Belle and Sebastian. Apparently, a track on a single by the band to be released in June 2004 entitled 'Wrapped Up In Books' was very similar to a hit single by

Sir Cliff Richard entitled 'In The Country' written by his backing band, The Shadows. Belle and Sebastian were seemingly oblivious to the similarity until it was pointed out to them by friends. They decided the best thing to do was to come clean before the single was released and approached the publishers of The Shadows' song, Carlin Music, with an offer of 20% of the publishing on the 'Wrapped Up In Books' song. Luckily for them this was accepted by Carlin. Contrast this with the Ludlow case above and take care that you approach the correct people for permission.

SOUND-ALIKES AND PARODY

A sound-alike is where someone deliberately sets out to imitate a successful piece of music. It's often used by advertising agencies when they don't want to pay the price for the right to use the original of a piece of work. Instead, they commission songwriters to write a piece that is a close imitation of the original. This is an art form in itself. We have already seen in the chapter on marketing and branding the cases where Tom Waits has successfully sued advertising agencies or their clients for use of sound-alikes of his distinctive voice. Here are some further cases in this area:

The 'Chariots of Fire' Case (No. 2) (Warner Music Limited and Others v. de Wilde [1987])
In another *Chariots of Fire* case, Clarks Shoes was found to have deliberately set out to gain a financial advantage from using a piece of music that had a very close similarity with the *Chariots of Fire* theme. This was found to be blatant plagiarism, but because it was so obvious the case didn't really set any guidelines.

The Williamson Music Case (Williamson Music Limited v. The Pearson Partnership and Another [1987] FSR 97)
Another case, involving the advertising company Pearson, used a parody of the song 'There Is Nothing Like A Dame' in an advert for a coach service. The lyrics were changed but the layout of the verse and chorus was similar. The manager of the licensing division of the MCPS heard the advert and thought it sounded very like the original song 'There Is Nothing Like A Dame'. He told the publishers of the song, Chappell Music Library. Williamson Music Limited was the exclusive licensee of the song in the UK. They and the other plaintiffs complained of infringement of copyright. Williamson Music Limited retained the right of approval to all requests for a synchronisation licence in

---

relation to that song. No such consent had been given. The Judge applied the test of whether an ordinary, reasonably experienced listener would think on hearing the track that it had been copied from the other work. He granted an interim injunction on the basis that Williamson Music had established that there was a case to answer, but it seems he was of the opinion that there had been infringement of the music but not of the words.

It seems that the test for whether something is a parody that is allowable and one that infringes copyright is that, in the case of the former, the parody has to only conjure up the idea of the original – it becomes an infringement if it uses a substantial part of the original.

Parody is defined by the OED as being: 'an imitation of the style of a particular writer, artist, or genre with deliberate exaggeration for comic effect'. As part of the implementation of the Hargreaves recommendations, the Government has passed legislation to introduce such an exception into UK law as part of the 'fair dealing exceptions'. The new law came into force in April 2014 and provides that 'Copyright in a copyright work is not infringed by any fair dealing with the work for the purposes of caricature, parody or pastiche'. Also 'To the extent that the term of a contract purports to restrict or prevent the doing of any act which would otherwise be permitted under this section, that term is unenforceable', i.e that you cannot contract out. Caricature, parody and pastiche are not defined and by placing it in the area of fair dealing the general principles such as the amount used, whether it was necessary, the economic effect on the original, the amount of work that went into the parody etc. will apply. The move has not been welcomed by rights owners who feel that it is unnecessary and the thin end of the wedge, but it looks like it is with us to stay and may well open up a series of test cases until its scope is more clearly defined.

SESSION MUSICIANS' CLAIMS

In recent years there has been a spate of claims by session musicians, sometimes many years after the original session took place, that they were not properly paid for the work they had done. These cases point out the importance of ensuring that the agreement with the session musician covers not only their performances as a musician or vocalist but also their interest, if any, in the underlying musical composition.

It was thought that the Kemp case that we looked at in Chapter 4 represented the legal position in the UK that band or session members did not have any interest in a song if they merely interpreted or played what the songwriter directed them to.

However, this position was challenged in the Bluebells case in 2002, upheld on appeal in 2003.

Beckingham (aka Valentino) v. Hodgens and others – [2003] All ER (D) 247 (Feb)
Session player Bobby Valentino was hired to perform a violin part in a song written by Bluebells member Robert Hodgens and already recorded by the band. The Judge accepted Valentino's claim that he had been given a free hand to create the violin part, whereas Hodgens had claimed that he had told him what to play and had even played it to him on the guitar. Now clearly one could argue that this case just turned on the facts that the Judge just preferred Valentino's version of events. This alone therefore would not have opened the floodgates and the 50% interest in the song that the Judge awarded to Valentino would have been seen as a one-off.

What made this case stand out was the manner in which the Judge side-stepped the issue of why it had taken Valentino so long to make his claim – a delay of over fifteen years. Usually that would have been enough to successfully argue that the claim was time barred. In what appears to have been an attempt by the Judge to find in favour of Valentino, the Judge decided that the correct interpretation of the situation was that Valentino had originally granted a licence to use his contribution to the song for free; that he was entitled to revoke this licence at will, and that he had done so when the song was re-released fifteen years later and went on to be a big hit. Valentino was awarded his share of royalties from 1993 when he could be said to have revoked his licence. It was important that Valentino was not seeking any share of income prior to 1993 when he put Hodgens on notice that he was asserting a claim.

Now this interpretation of the situation really stresses the need for clarity in your session agreements, but it also may have given others the idea that they could bring claims many years after the event – some more serious than others – including claims to record royalties from the school choir who performed free of charge in the original recording of Pink Floyd's 'Another Brick In the Wall' to a threatened claim against Rod Stewart by Ray Jackson, the mandolin player on Rod's recording of 'Maggie May'. It culminated in an April 2005 decision in a case brought by session singer Clare Torry against the writers and publishers of Pink Floyd of hit song 'The Great Gig in the Sky' off the *Dark Side of the Moon* album.

The Pink Floyd Case

Ms Clare Torry was a session vocalist paid £30 to perform on the track 'The Great Gig in the Sky' and was given a credit for her performance. Some thirty years later, she brought a claim, in a similar fashion to the Bobby Valentino case (above), for a 50% interest in the song. The case settled out-of-court for what is rumoured to be a substantial cash payment and since 2005 all issues of the track show her as a co-writer alongside Richard Wright. The catalyst for the publisher EMI and the writers in Pink Floyd to reach a settlement may have been because the Judge had indicated that he was convinced by Ms Torry's claim that she had employed a special wailing technique, recorded in a series of sessions and effectively helped to compose the song. The parallels with the Bluebells case are obvious.

Pink Floyd were themselves in court in 2010 successfully arguing that a clause in their contracts which prevented their record label, EMI, from releasing individual tracks from their 'concept' albums without their consent could extend to making individual tracks available online on sites like iTunes.

Finally, of course, there is the case concerning the song 'Whiter Shade of Pale' which we looked at in detail in Chapter 4 and which seems to confirm this trend towards favouring the claimant even many years after the event.

CONCLUSIONS

- If you sample someone's work, you'll have to get permission to use both the sound recording copyright and the copyright in the underlying music and/or lyrics.
- Put the process of clearing samples in hand as early as possible.
- If there is any chance of an uncleared sample being found and legal action taken, don't take the risk, clear it or remove it.
- If you can't clear the sound recording copyright, then see if you can replay the sounds to sound like the original and clear the rights only in the underlying music/lyrics.
- If you copy another's work and pass it off as your own, then you're guilty of plagiarism, unless you can show that the similarity was completely coincidental and that there was no way that you could have heard the work you're accused of copying.

Chapter 14

Piracy

INTRODUCTION

Piracy is still a huge, worldwide problem when it comes to illegal copies of CDs. The worst offenders in the area of physical pirate copies are Eastern European and Far Eastern countries, including Taiwan, Bulgaria, the Ukraine and Pakistan, with weak copyright laws and little or no means of enforcement, although Taiwan is beginning to recognise it has to do something. Countries in which piracy is rife also export these illegal records into the UK. Despite the existence of over hundreds of legal music services piracy remains largely unchecked and seems largely to be treated as unstoppable when it comes to CDs already in the marketplace. There does not seem to be enough of a groundswell of consistent support from Government to tackle piracy. The Digital Economy Act has been stuck in the starting gates for years, with arguments raging on about who should be responsible for the cost of enforcement notices for online infringers. The focus has shifted to engaging with the major online players like Google, YouTube and iTunes to provide a legal, licensed source of music, and the rapid growth of online streaming of music (as opposed to downloads or physical) copies has somewhat shifted the focus from piracy to how to get paid for online streaming, making service providers responsible for illegal content on their sites and bringing unlicensed sites into the licenced fold.

Record company trade bodies, like the UK's BPI, the IFPI and the US body RIAA, first tackled both physical and Internet piracy by legal actions against pirates and illegal file-sharers winning the support of the court for orders to force ISPs to disclose the identities of individuals distributing multiple music files illegally on peer-to-peer networks. The individuals faced claims for compensation for copyright infringement and legal costs. But when it became clear that this was an expensive and time-consuming method of bringing pressure to bear they also began to exert political pressure on the ISPs to take action alongside the anti-piracy organisations such as the IFPI to battle illegal downloads of music. Bad publicity when schoolgirls were charged for copying files meant that the industry also wasn't winning the battle for hearts and minds and switched some of its efforts to educating people that what they were doing was wrong. This education process continues.

The Gowers Review recommended that ISPs adhere to the industry practice for data sharing to allow people who illegally download or indeed upload to be identified and targeted. The ISPs were very reluctant to move away from their stance that they were just the conduit and could not be held responsible for content on the websites they hosted. As we saw above the appeal in the Scarlet v SABAM case struck a blow in support of this stance. When they did not comply voluntarily, the then Labour Government announced the intention to introduce legislation to force them to do so and to allow the barring of users from Internet access if they are found guilty of illegal downloading on three separate occasions. After a prolonged process of lobbying and political manoeuvrings, the Digital Economy Act became law. The premise behind the Act is that the ISPs and the content owners would work together to identify and issue letters of warning to users found to be illegally downloading music content. If the warnings are not heeded, then the Act provides that technical measures could be introduced in graduated stages to reduce the quality of or even in the final resort to bar access of an infringing user to the Internet. As is often the case with legislation, the devil is in the detail and key elements of the process are to be regulated by a Code of Practice drawn up by Ofcom, which would be subject to parliamentary approval. Consultations around the drafting of the Code revealed that it is likely that the bulk of the cost of issuing the warning letters will fall on the content owners (a 75:25 split of costs between owners and ISPs seems likely). The implementation process has been further slowed by a successful application by BT and TalkTalk for a High Court Judicial Review of the process by which the Act came into law to see if there had been sufficient scrutiny and debate. The case concluded in April 2011 with failure for BT and TalkTalk. They appealed but also lost that appeal in March 2012. So whilst the Act is law it is not effective until there have been statutory instruments setting out in this Code of Conduct who is responsible for the costs of enforcement action and the mechanism for sending out the warning letters. Ofcom had drafted the necessary regulations by the end of 2103 but they have now been stalled by the Treasury which is concerned the proposed distribution of the costs involved will not work and wants a rethink. This has pushed back the implementation until 2017. But at the moment the website blocking has not been implemented and is the subject of further consultation by Ofcom.

There were some key victories in the courts against online large-scale pirates, the most high profile of which was the successful action against the owners of 'The Pirate Bay' (Fredrik Neij and Sunde Kolmisoppi). The Pirate Bay was one of the world's largest file-sharing services online, using the BitTorrent protocol to make it possible for users to connect with each other and exchange digital content including music, film and computer games, through file-sharing. Neij and Kolmisoppi (along with two others) were charged with complicity to commit crimes in violation of the Swedish Copyright Act. They were found guilty in 2009 of facilitating mass copyright infringement and were sentenced to one-year prison terms. They were also held jointly liable for damages of approximately i3.3 million. Their appeal against this verdict was thrown out by the Swedish Supreme Court in November 2010 which upheld the original decision, whilst at the same time reducing the prison sentences on three of the four owners but increasing the damages awarded to approximately i5million. The Court refused the right to appeal further in February 2012.

Meanwhile several entertainment companies brought private claims within the Swedish court proceedings for damages for copyright infringement. In the UK various record companies including three of the major labels in the UK at the time (EMI Records, Sony Music Entertainment and Warner) applied for an injunction against the six main UK ISPS requiring them to take measures to block or impede access by their customers to The Pirate Bay. In this we see an echo of the Scarlet v. SABAM case that we dealt with in an earlier chapter. In this case they were successful as against five of the six ISPs who were ordered to block access to the Internet protocol address of The Pirate Bay.

Having been blocked from further appeals in the Swedish Courts Neij and Kolmisoppi applied to the European Court of Human Rights on the basis that they could not be responsible for how people used The Pirate Bay, whose original purpose had been (they claimed) merely to facilitate the exchange of data on the Internet. They relied on Article 10 of the Human Rights Act that they had a right to freedom of expression. But the European Court of Human Rights was having no truck with this and declared their application inadmissible. The balance of interests between the protection of the rights of copyright holders and the right of the individual to facilitate the sharing of information came down firmly on the side of protecting the rights of copyright holders by a wide margin (Source: *The Reporter*).

The problem is that the website continues to operate by switching owners and/or locations, moving its main domain from country to country sometimes two or three times a week as shut-down orders follow it around (which highlights the difficulty of enforcing anti-piracy measures against companies based in territories where the laws and enforcement may not be as effective, or indeed where ownership and location can change seemingly overnight. As at 18 December 2013 it had returned to the .se domain, i.e. Sweden, but we have no doubt not heard the end of this saga.

In February 2013 in a case brought by EMI Records Ltd (on their own behalf and representing the other members of BPI and PPL) brought an action against British Sky Broadcasting Ltd and the other main ISPs operating in the UK seeking an injunction blocking access to three more peer-to-peer file-sharing websites KAT, H33T and Fenopy all of which also used the BitTorrent protocol. The injunction was successful but the practical effect of such orders is doubtful when owners can move domain or country so easily or set up under a different name tomorrow. The case is, however, useful from a legal perspective for the detailed way in which the Judge Mr Arnold considered the various matters to be decided in some detail, giving some guidance for future legal actions. The case also interestingly revealed that blocking sites was reasonably successful.

In 2013 the City of London Police (Intellectual Property Crime Unit) launched an initiative called 'Operation Creative' which resulted in the suspension of forty websites by the domain name registrars which had been shown to be providing unauthorised access to copyrighted content. Interestingly *The Times* reported that the Unit was also going for the commercial jugular by working with the advertising industry to turn off their advertising revenue by removing ads from well-known brands off these sites.

But it's not just online that steps have been taken – legal actions continue against pirates of physical copies too.

R v. Malone

In March 2007, it was reported that the Airdrie Sheriff Court in Scotland had jailed George Malone, who had built up a black market operation selling thousands of fake DVDs and CDs. He admitted producing the illegal copies and selling them at industrial estates across west central Scotland. He was sentenced to nine months in prison and his assets were seized.

DRM is effectively a dead letter and the focus has shifted to providing ways to legitimise and monetise downloads.

WHAT IS PIRACY?

Piracy is theft. It is the reproduction of someone's copyright without their approval and generally on a commercial scale.

There are three different types of pirate records.

Counterfeit recordings

These are copies of CDs, cassettes or vinyl records that also copy the packaging, artwork and graphics. For example, someone gets hold of a master recording and uses it to make copies of it, which they then pass off as the original. They don't usually care what the sound quality is like, or even if the CD will play at all. They just want to make them look as much like the original as possible so that they take your money and you don't find out until you get home that it's a pirated copy. The trade marks and logos of the original copyright owners are also copied to make them look as much as possible like the originals. This is an infringement of the trade mark, which could give rise to a legal action in its own right (see Chapter 8). Of course, if you're buying these CDs from a market stall at a fraction of the usual retail price, you've only yourself to blame if they turn out to be dodgy copies.

Pirate recordings

Whilst this can, of course, be either copying in physical form (i.e. CDs) or in digital form, whatever form it takes it is basically the same thing: the unauthorised duplication of an original sound recording. The pirate takes a master recording and copies it without the permission of the original copyright owner. This could be done in an almost commercial fashion or be just you or me illegally downloading (i.e. copying or duplicating) a track we find on an online website. The sound quality is usually as good as the original on physical copies but not always on online copies where there are sometimes issues around compression of the sound. Pirate recordings have different packaging and the trade marks and logos of the original copyright owners aren't usually on the record or packaging in its physical form. In some cases, this is done in order to undermine the market for the original by putting out a pirate copy first. This used to happen a lot in the dance sector of the industry. So-called 'white label' copies of a new single were released to the press and to DJs for review in advance of its commercial release. They were called white labels because, in their vinyl form, they had a white label, which says they aren't for commercial use. Unscrupulous characters then copied that recording and put it on their own compilation record without getting permission and without paying anything for it. This undermined the legitimate market for that single. Of course, in the digital online world the market of the original owner of the pirated recording, as well as the performers and the songwriters, is being damaged because no one is paying them for the right to copy and distribute their work.

Pirate physical recordings are generally made in countries with little or no copyright protection and then exported to other countries. The practice is, however, spreading to other countries where the agencies in charge of anti-piracy are less effective. As we saw in the note about the Pirate Bay case above, this move to another jurisdiction can be used by online operators to bypass or evade sanction for their actions.

In rare cases, publishing rights may have been cleared and authorisation obtained from a collective body like the MCPS, but no permission has been obtained to reproduce the master sound recording. This might happen with the 'white label' dance issues referred to above. For example, if you were putting a pirate copy of a master recording on your own dance compilation, you might apply for a mechanical licence to get the right to reproduce the song on that master. This lends an air of respectability to the release and means you have one less collective body to worry about. You don't bother to get permission from the owner of the sound recording. You hope that he either doesn't get to hear about the release, or hasn't the money or the inclination to sue you for copyright infringement. In most cases, however, permission is not sought from the writers of the song, or the performers, or the owners of the copyright.

Sometimes those who are accused of illegal copying of physical copies of recordings argue that they have a valid licence to release a sound recording because of a chain of contracts going back many years. Often, in the 1960s and 70s, ownership of copyright was not properly recorded and there have been many changes of ownership down the years. In those days, it wasn't unusual for deals to be single-page, sketchy outlines that didn't make it completely clear who owned what and who could do what with the recordings. This confusion has been successfully exploited by later record companies claiming to have the right to put out recordings under some dodgy deal struck twenty years earlier. It's sometimes very difficult to prove them wrong.

The Phil Collins Case (Collins v. Imrat Handelsgesellschaft mbH [1994] W.M.L.R.108)
In the early 1990s, Phil Collins, ex-Genesis drummer turned successful solo artist, brought an action against Imrat, a record distributor, in respect of royalties for sales in Germany of a CD recording of one of his US concerts, which was made without his consent. Under German law, German nationals are entitled to stop distribution of performances made without their consent, regardless of where the performance takes place. Foreign nationals couldn't rely on this law where the performance had taken place outside Germany.

The court decided that all European Union countries should provide nationals of other European Union countries with the same degree of protection as they would have had in their own country. This has been a key decision in the tightening up of performers' rights across the EU.

Bootlegs

A bootleg is a recording of a live performance, whether it's at an actual gig or off a television, satellite, radio or Internet broadcast, which is made without permission of the performers.

You used to see shifty-looking people at gigs with half-hidden tape recorders making terribly bad recordings of the performance. With the improvements in technology and the miniaturisation of the devices, it's now easier than ever to make reasonable digital recordings.

R v. Langley
A man who was described as 'one of Europe's most notorious music pirates' who was also known as 'Mr Toad' pleaded guilty to selling bootlegged recordings of Led Zeppelin gigs. He sold illegal recordings he had made at live gigs on his Silver Rarities and Langley Masters labels. His arrest came after the BPI organised a raid on his stall at a Scottish record fair. Led Zeppelin guitarist Jimmy Page gave evidence before the Glasgow court

346

that he had not authorised the recordings, which he said were of poor quality. He also drew a distinction between fans who swapped recordings and professional bootleggers. Langley pleaded guilty to two copyright and three trade mark infringements.

R v McPhillips
In March 2011 police In Edinburgh raided the home of Paul McPhillips and found fake CDs and DVDs worth around £200,000. McPhillips had been selling bootlegs online. The scale of the operation was such that the Court felt there was no other alternative than to hand down a jail sentence of sixteen months.

HOW DO YOU SPOT A PHYSICAL COUNTERFEIT, PIRATE OR BOOTLEG RECORD?

Counterfeits

These are often on sale in markets, at car-boot sales and from street traders selling goods out of suitcases on street corners. The prices are usually 50% or less than a full-price record in the shops.

The packaging will often be of poor quality, possibly blurred print, especially when it gets to the small print. Sometimes there is a white border on the edges of the inlay card for the CD where it's been copied. These inlay cards may look genuine on the outside; it's only when you open it that you see it's a poor representation on the inside. The trade marks may be removed, smudged or partly obscured as the pirates try to get around an allegation of infringement of trade mark. The name and logo of the original record company may also be missing, blurred or obscured. There may not be a Source Identification Code. This was something introduced a few years ago to show the place of manufacture. The sound quality will often be very poor, particularly on cassettes. Copy protection devices will definitely be absent.

Bootlegs

These are often found on sale at music festivals, second-hand or 'underground' record stores and collectors' fairs. They are aiming at the die-hard fans who want to own every available recording by their favourite artist. The price is often the same or higher than the legitimate product to reflect how desirable they are to collectors and fans.

The packaging may leave off company information; there could be no catalogue numbers or proper credits. The inlay cards will often be simple colour photocopies. Bootleg CDs can be very good sound quality and difficult to tell apart from a genuine recording.

HOW CAN YOU STOP PIRACY?

It is not possible to completely prevent illegal uses of music on the Internet. Whilst BPI/RIAA and IFPI actions may deter the casual or opportunist illegal file-sharers, they will not deter the hard-line pirates. Legislation and cooperation between content owners and ISPs may add a deterrent. Copy-protection devices and DRM are now a dead letter. The commercial solution to making money for the artists, songwriters and copyright owners is to have business models that consumers are prepared to buy into (see more in Chapter 7).

However, this doesn't mean that control of illegal manufacturing plants and seizure of illegal copies has been abandoned. The underlying rights being infringed are the same whether the infringement is online or the reproduction of physical tapes or CDs.

Copyright

Pirate recordings may infringe the sound recording copyright and the rights in the music and lyrics as well as the artwork. It's an infringement of copyright to repro-duce, issue copies to the public, perform in public or include it in a cable programme (including online). These are what we call direct infringements of copyright.

Indirect infringements of copyright include importing, possessing in the course of trade, selling or exhibiting infringing copies in public and/or distributing them in the course of business (*ss.22–26 CDPA*). These are obviously aimed at the distributor or retailer. They have to know or have reason to believe that they are dealing with an infringing copy.

Moral rights

If the writer or composer of the lyrics and music isn't identified, or the work has been subjected to derogatory treatment, this may well be an infringement of moral rights if these have not been waived (see Chapter 12).

Trade marks

If the artist's or record company's trade mark name or logo is reproduced without permission of the trade mark owner, this is an infringement of the Trade Marks Act 1994.

Trade description

If the record has been misdescribed or represented as something that it is not, this may be a breach of the Trade Descriptions Act 1968.

ENFORCEMENT

First, decide who you're going to go after. Who have you got evidence against? You could try to take action against the pirate manufacturer, but this may be difficult if they're based overseas. You could decide to try to stop distributors from starting or continuing to distribute pirate records. You'll have to move fast. If nothing has been distributed, you could try to get an injunction to stop distribution taking place. If it's already been distributed, you may need court orders against the person retailing the product.

So, when you've decided who you want to target, what can you do?

Civil action

You can apply for an injunction, although you have to move quickly. You can ask the court to make an order preventing infringement of your rights. The court can make orders preventing further sale, distribution and/or import of pirated products. You'll probably also make a claim for financial damages and reimbursement of your legal costs.

Criminal action

You have to show that the defendant had reason to believe he was dealing with an infringing copy of a copyright work. The penalties are imprisonment and/ or a fine. For this kind of action, you need to involve the police, who will need to have explained to them how copyright exists in the product and how it is being breached. You also have to convince them that it's sufficiently serious for them to put resources into the case. In April 2005, the US Senate made it a criminal offence capable of a sentence of up to ten years' imprisonment for those found to be illegally copying and distributing pre-release music and films in the US. The obvious targets were those who illegally acquire films or albums by important artists before the official release date. There is no indication that the UK Government has plans to follow suit.

Private criminal prosecutions

The CDPA gives you the right to bring a private criminal prosecution (s.107 CDPA).

It also makes it possible for an officer of a company to be liable to prosecution for an offence committed by the company. This is to avoid companies slipping through the net.

If someone is found guilty of infringement, the court can order that all the offending articles are handed over and can order their destruction. I'm sure you've all seen pictures of companies like Rolex using a steamroller to crush fake copies of their watches.

Trading standards officers

These are local government officers and they can be very helpful if you get them on side. A good friend of mine is an ex-Trading Standards officer and he tells me they like nothing better than a good raid on a pirate. They usually act to enforce breaches of trade mark using powers given to them under the Trade Descriptions Act among others. They can enter premises and seize goods. Their rights also now extend to infringements of copyright. They can prosecute for offences such as fraudulently applying a trade mark and the application of a false description to goods. As part of the implementation of the recommendations of the Gowers Review of Intellectual Property, Trading Standards received an additional £5 million to assist in the fight against piracy. This was to help the officers with their new role as also enforcers of copyright infringement. Changes to the CDPA 1988 were implemented in 2007 to give them the right and authority to enter premises, seize goods and documents relating to copyright infringement as well as trade mark infringements. Because these offences are criminal ones, there is the possibility of an unlimited fine and up to ten years' imprisonment, so it is hoped this may act as a deterrent to some pirates.

ANTI-PIRACY UNITS (APU)

One APU, the Copyright Protection Unit, is run by the BPI. The National Fraud Intelligence Bureau (NFIB) has seconded a leading expert to the Unit to help the police to better understand the illegal distribution and sale of music online by organised crime gangs. Another is run by PRS on behalf of its writer and publisher members.

THE INTERNATIONAL FEDERATION OF THE PHONOGRAPHIC INDUSTRY (IFPI)

This represents the international recording industry. If you're a member of the BPI, you automatically become a member of the IFPI. It has about a hundred members in over seventy countries. It is involved in the international fight against piracy. It lobbies governments for appropriate copyright protection and helps to ensure the laws are enforced.

OTHER BODIES

Other bodies involved in the fight against piracy include:

* the Federation Against Software Theft (FAST), which was set up in 1984 to represent the software industry (both publishers and end users). It was the first organisation globally to champion the professional management of legitimate software and protect publishers' rights. It aims to reduce, restrict and/or lessen the incidence of unauthorised dealings in computer software. It works to promote the legitimate use of software and protect its members' rights through education, enforcement, lobbying and promoting standards and best practice in business;
* the Federation Against Copyright Theft (FACT), which represents film and video producers, manufacturers and distributors as well as TV and the satellite industries; and
* UKIE represents publishers of interactive software such as computer games. The National Crime Agency became operational in October 2013 and is made up of four divisions: Border Policing, Economic Crime, Organised Crime and the Child Exploitation and Online Protection Centre (CEOPC).

Chapter 15

Collection Societies

INTRODUCTION

As you know by now, copyright is the right of an individual and, in most cases, that right should be exercised as the individual decides and on his own behalf.

However, there comes a time when it makes more sense for these rights to be exercised collectively by an organisation set up to represent the interests of its members. To make doing business as easy as possible requires a one-stop service. For example, it wouldn't be commercially viable for the owners of a radio station to have to go to the copyright owners of the sound recording copyright and of the rights in the songs on each of the records that the station bosses want to play on their programmes. It would be far too time-consuming and costly. Hence the existence of collection societies which represent the interests of publishers, record companies, authors and performers. There are several of them, brief details of which are outlined below. They all have useful and informative websites which it would pay you to look at. These organisations fulfil an essential role but are not the most interesting area of the business. However, at the moment there is a lot going on in this area, much of it outside the UK. The biggest piece of legislation is The Collective Management of Copyright (EU Directive) Regulations 2016/221. The Regulations impose greater transparency and governance of collective management organisations. Because of the way in which a collective management organisation is defined, MCPS falls outside its remit but has voluntarily entered into a memorandum of understanding with the IPO.

In Germany, the collection society GEMA has been in the spotlight as the result of a court ruling that could force it to change the entire way it accounts for royalties to its members. Historically, like many societies, GEMA has collected money from performance rights and paid out a proportion to the writer and a proportion direct to the publisher. The same system applied to mechanical rights. The performing right is assigned to GEMA (just as it is with the PRS) and the publisher only has a contractual right to share in the income. Custom and practice has dictated that this money is collected by GEMA and paid out to both writer and publisher. The case brought by two authors Bruno Kramm and Stefan Ackermann ruled that there were no clear contractual rights for this to happen in this instance. Now this could have a limited impact, but if it is more widely interpreted it would mean that the publishers would have to get their share direct from the writers (which will be fraught with difficulties) or deduct it if licensing direct. It is said that the German government is considering legislation to address the problem, and on the practical level German lawyers are advising revisions to contractual arrangements to make the existing arrangements contractually binding.

Independent Music Publishers' E-Licensing (IMPEL) a collective of independent music publishers was set up to directly licence the online mechanical rights in the publishers' Anglo-American repertoire and they have appointed MCPS to license and administer these licences on their behalf. IMPEL became a limited company in January 2015 and is owned by the MPA. It subcontracts some of its administration to a company called ICE.

WHAT ARE COLLECTION SOCIETIES?

They are, in effect, organisations set up by the various categories of rights owners to administer their rights collectively as their sole, or one of their main, purposes. Their existence is envisaged by *s.116 (2) CDPA* which defines a licensing body.

On the whole, collection societies are private as opposed to state-owned bodies, but they are subject to some form of government or state supervision. In the UK, that supervision is provided for partly by the 1988 Copyright Act, which established a form of compulsory arbitration in the shape of the Copyright Tribunal, and in part by the Competition Commission (formerly the Monopolies and Mergers Commission). Overseeing the whole thing is of course the EU which does intervene or introduce pan-EU legislation when it thinks that national solutions are out-of-step or require updating, review or harmonisation.

The purpose of most collection societies is to provide a practical and economical service to enable its members to enforce and administer certain of their copyrights. These bodies make it easier for others to get licences to use copyright works. There is also certainty in that the payment for these uses will usually be at a fixed rate or one individually negotiated within certain guidelines. The idea is also that, by acting collectively, administration costs are reduced.

There are, of course, possible dangers inherent in that these collection societies are, by their nature, monopolies. It's the job of the Competition Commission to police whether that monopoly position is being abused. Public Performance Limited was the subject of a review by the Commission in 1988 and the Performing Right Society Limited came under critical review in 1996 and has since modified its rules to address some of these concerns.

BLANKET LICENCES

One of the features of collection societies is that they grant so-called blanket licences for certain rights in all the works controlled by the society for a particular purpose, for a particular period of time and at a particular rate. Anyone wishing to take advantage of these blanket licences has to take a licence for the whole catalogue. For example, the Performing Right Society Limited (PRS) can negotiate a blanket licence with radio broadcasters for the right to broadcast to the public all the works controlled by PRS. The licence is for a given period of time, say a year, and is subject to review. PRS negotiates with individual radio stations or, more likely, with their representative bodies the rate that applies to these licences. It could be a flat fee per annum or it could be linked to the revenue that the radio station earns, for example, a percentage of the advertising revenue earned by commercial radio stations, or it could be a combination of both.

Whilst the collection societies became adept at negotiating and administrating collective licensing schemes in their own countries and for non-digital means of distribution, things became more difficult for them when it came to digital uses and when they came under pressure from the European Commission to make it easier for new commercial ventures to flourish across the European Economic Area (EEA). Whilst this is a laudable aim, it takes time to get all members to agree on a course of action and on the rate to be set for centralised licensing, particularly when that involves new media and means of distribution where the people setting and negotiating the rate had little knowledge of which of these formats would have staying power and what an appropriate means of setting a rate was. For some time, they felt their way forward. The European Union thought they were being too slow in establishing cross-Europe licensing schemes and issued a report in October 2005 which urged the societies to review and reform their practices and, in particular, to 'provide for multi territorial licensing in order to create greater legal certainty for commercial uses and to foster the development of legitimate online services'. Perhaps fearing that solutions would be imposed on them from above, since the publication of this report, there have been committed attempts to reform their practices also making advances in the area of use of music online and on mobile phones. The collection societies and individual publishers are establishing schemes which will facilitate one-stop licensing across Europe. This is an attractive proposition for commercial users of music in new applications or services.

Still on the international front, PPL continues to expand its role by offering to collect income from neighbouring rights overseas on behalf of performers.

Closer to home, too, there have been rapid advances in the availability of blanket licences for online and digital uses of music. A glance at the PRS for Music website will reveal schemes for everything from DVDs to memory cards. There are still some services which do not completely fit into any of these licence categories as I found when I tried to license an online music review site which didn't quite fit. In these circumstances, details of the proposed use/turnover or profits per annum and number of tracks used have to be submitted and they give consideration for one-off uses or confirm the use is, in fact, eligible for an existing licence.

The biggest challenge that has faced the music publishers and their collection society in the last couple of years has to be the arguments over the appropriate rate to apply to online uses of music. MCPS-PRS, as it then was, reached an agreement with the major record companies and with some of the ISPs in 2006, but some ISPs, including Yahoo, refused to sign up to the deal and all ISPs and some of the major labels had issues over how to define the revenue on which they would pay the agreed rate. So the matter was referred to the Copyright Tribunal. After a very expensive and drawn-out hearing, the Tribunal ratified the terms of the settlement on rate, proposed some but not definitive guidelines for the definition of revenue, and provided for an arbitrator to be called in if final agreement on that subject could not be reached in individual cases. The agreed rate for on-demand music downloads and subscription streaming services is set at 8% of gross revenues. The rate set for interactive webcasting services is 6.6% of revenues and for non-interactive webcasting it is 5.75% of revenues. A minimum royalty 'safety net' was set.

With effect from 1 January 2013 some (but not all) Welsh rights holders, who had become discontented with how their existing collection societies, PRS and MCPS dealt with their Welsh language music repertoire, withdrew their broadcasting and televising rights from PRS and gave them instead to a new entity, Eos. Discontent was on several levels, but a key factor was the decision of PRS to alter its method of distributing broadcast revenue to Welsh language composers and rights owners resulting in a significant drop in their income. Mechanical and online rights continue to be represented by PRS for Music.

Eos tried to negotiate with the BBC who broadcasts several services in Wales including BBC Radio Cymru, BBC Radio Wales and BBC One Wales. BBC Radio Cymru is the only one which is dedicated to Welsh language music but they all require a repertoire of Welsh language music to meet the BBC's local remit. Eos began negotiations with the BBC over the terms of a blanket licence but by the end of 2012 they had failed to reach an agreement. This quickly began to affect the BBC's ability to provide a full programme service and in February 2013 it brought a reference to the Copyright Tribunal. As the full hearing would take some time the BBC applied for an interim order for the Tribunal to set a reasonable rate and terms on which the BBC could license the Eos repertoire pending the full hearing. The parties reached an interim arrangement by agreement of £10,000 per month. In May 2013 the Tribunal reviewed those arrangements and confirmed they should stay in place pending the final decision of the Tribunal. The BBC was arguing for a ceiling of £100,000 a year in licence fees for the Eos repertoire. Eos was looking for £1.5 million per annum. At the time of writing I can find no update on the current status of Eos.

The Copyright Tribunal has quite broad powers to determine what is reasonable and is required to take into account all relevant circumstances. In so doing it can look at comparable licences. It also has to make sure it does not unreasonably discriminate between licences.

The Copyright Tribunal heard arguments and decided that it was reasonable to look to the terms of the licence previously operated by the PRS for Music with the BBC as a comparative and as a starting point. Various formulas were put forward for assessing what part of the overall PRS for Music licence fee would apply to Eos repertoire. The BBC said that the appropriate licence fee was £46,000 per annum. Eos disputed the formula and methodology applied by the BBC and argued against the PRS for Music licence as being a fair basis for comparison. It felt, for example, that insufficient weight had been given to the cultural value of the Welsh language. Whilst the Tribunal did not accept that different values should be placed on different pieces of music it did make an allowance in its final calculation of the uniqueness of the Welsh language and its contribution to the diversity of culture in the UK as well as the fact that the BBC and Eos relied on one another and that the BBC might need to pay more than a pure numerical calculation. However, this would only apply to the indigenous Welsh language material controlled by Eos and not to any other element.

The final conclusion reached by the Copyright Tribunal was that a licence fee of £100,000 per annum was reasonable and ordered that the term of the licence run from 1 February 2013 to 31 December 2015. It meant that the BBC had overpaid for the first year by £20,000 as it had agreed the interim rate of £10,000 per month but the Tribunal hoped it would be pragmatic in seeking to recover this.

Regulations setting standards for collecting societies came into force on 6 April 2014 (The Copyright (Regulation of Relevant Licensing Bodies) Regulations 2014) to enable the Government to enforce minimum standards as set out in voluntary Codes of Practice introduced by the collection societies, and if these standards are not met, to impose their own set of minimum standards.

These Regulations also paved the way for the implementation of secondary legislation to allow UK extended collective licensing (ECL) schemes, which are incorporated in The Copyright and Rights in Performances (Extended Collective Licensing) Regulations 2014, and came into force in the UK on 1 October 2014. An ECL scheme is one under which a collecting society, subject to certain safeguards, is authorised to license specified copyright works on behalf of all rights holders in its sector, and not just those for whom it has specific permission to act. Collecting societies that operate ECL schemes are given enhanced powers (in being able to manage the rights of non-member rights holders), and must therefore adopt appropriate codes of practice, designed to protect rights holders.

ADMINISTRATION

A main role for the collection societies is the administration of the rights, making sure that a member's interests have been properly registered, that people using the rights have the necessary licences and have paid the negotiated rate. They collect in the monies, allocate and distribute them. The societies charge their members a fee for the administration of the rights, usually a percentage of the gross income they collect.

Sometimes a society will administer more than one right. For example, in Europe a number of the collection societies administer not only the performing rights but also the right to copy or reproduce works. In the UK, the PRS and MCPS initially combined many of their managerial and administration functions under the name of PRS for Music but MCPS is now effectively standalone and has put operation of its back-end functions out to tender to ensure it is getting the best deal for its members.

RIGHTS GRANTED

The societies either take an assignment of certain rights from their members or they have a licence from their members or act as agents for them. The terms of membership of a collection society will usually dictate what form the rights granted will take. The idea is to establish through these membership rules a clear mandate to grant licences to use certain rights. There has been less certainty than is desirable in the mandate of some of the collection societies to deal with new technologies but this is gradually resolving itself at least in the domestic market.

The collection societies usually have reciprocal arrangements with other societies so that they can protect their members worldwide. These reciprocal arrangements mean that the UK societies can represent the interests of their UK members and of foreign artists, writers and composers within the UK, with both categories of writers receiving the same treatment.

One of the main advantages of collective licensing is, of course, the greater bargaining power that you can get by being part of a big collective effort. The rates and rewards for uses of your works that the collection societies can get for you should be better than what you could get on a one-to-one basis.

OTHER COLLECTIVE BODIES

There are a number of other music business bodies that represent the interests of various parts of the business. These could be collective bargaining or interest groupings such as the Music Managers Forum (MMF), Featured Artists Coalition (FAC) and AIM (The Association of Independent Music). They also include unions like the Musicians' Union (MU) and Equity, the British Academy of Composers, Songwriters and Authors (BASCA), the Music Publishers Association

(MPA), the MCPS and the PRS (see below). What all these groupings have in common is that they act as a forum for debate and, to a greater or lesser extent, as a means of using collective bargaining power to get things for their members that as individuals they could find it very hard to achieve.

THE SOCIETIES

In the following section I'm going to briefly describe the structure and function of some of the main bodies that exist in the UK at the moment. More details can be obtained from the individual societies, most of whom also publish leaflets describing what they do for their members and their websites are, on the whole, very informative.

THE BRITISH RECORDED MUSIC INDUSTRY (BPI)

Strictly speaking, this isn't a collection society as such, but an organisation that represents the interests of UK record companies. It's a non-profit-making trade association that was set up in 1973.

The BPI is based in London and its members are UK record companies. Its 400-plus members account for around 90% of the recorded music sold in the UK. Its mandate is to 'discuss matters of common interest and represent the British record industry in negotiations with government departments, relevant unions and other interested parties and to promote the welfare and interests of the British record industry'. It has full and associate membership categories.

There is a fee to become a member of the BPI and these fees mainly fund its activities. The subscriptions for full members in 2016 are a minimum fee of £67.50 plus 5% of PPL UK distribution payments, plus VAT. BPI members have to be approved and agree to be bound by the membership rules and the Code of Conduct that the BPI maintains.

The BPI Code of Conduct deals with how the music charts are drawn up and involves the BPI investigating alleged irregularities, for example, if there is an attempt to buy up unusually large numbers of copies of a particular record in order to artificially gain a higher chart position. If the BPI finds that a member has been guilty of infringing the Code it can employ sanctions against that member, including expelling them as a member and/or imposing a fine. It is a part owner of the Official Charts Company alongside the Entertainment Retailers Association.

Because it's a trade association rather than a rights body, it doesn't take any rights from its members nor does it grant licences or otherwise administer or collect money from exploitation of rights.

The BPI provides a forum for discussion and acts for its members generally on matters in which they have a common interest. It is a founder member of the lobbying body UK Music, the umbrella organisation set up to represent the interests of the British commercial music industry. The BPI has lobbying, education and research functions; it also negotiates agreements with other groups such as music publishers, the Musicians' Union or Equity. It has an important function in protecting members' rights through anti-piracy initiatives and in promoting British music overseas. Its Anti-Piracy Unit is active in trying to reduce the amount of piracy in the UK. Its role includes taking high-profile litigation cases against pirates and giving publicity to successful seizures of pirate goods.

PHONOGRAPHIC PERFORMANCE LIMITED (PPL)

This is the record industry's licensing body. It licenses records for broadcasting and public performance, collects the revenue generated and distributes it.

It represents a large number of record companies (about 5,750), some of which, but not all, are members of the BPI, and over 45,000 performers.

The PPL is based in London and was incorporated as a company limited by guarantee in 1934.

The PPL negotiates collective agreements with broadcasters. It also protects the rights of its members and takes legal action to protect those rights. It doesn't, however, have its own anti-piracy unit or staff, but relies on its members to bring infringements to its attention.

PPL has a number of different tariffs that apply to the various uses of the music in its repertoire. These are usually payable annually. There are minimum charges and how much is paid out to the members depends on the use. The rights it administers include broadcasting, public performance, dubbing of background music (a role it took over in 1985), multi-media uses and digital diffusion rights.

PPL distributes the income it collects to the owners of the sound recordings and to the performers on the tracks who have registered their performance with PPL. It is a not-for-profit organisation so there is no fee to join. It covers its costs by charging a fee to administer the rights.

As part of the initiatives being explored for making one-stop licensing easier PPL and PRS have issued joint licences for some uses so that both master and publishing rights can be cleared under one licence. More are in the pipeline although they are of limited application such as joint licences for amateur sports clubs and small workplaces.

VIDEO PERFORMANCE LIMITED (VPL)

This is a company associated with PPL. It is the record industry's licensing body for music videos. Its members are the owners of public performance rights in music videos being publicly broadcast or made available to the public in the UK.

VPL licenses music videos for broadcasting and public performance. It applies a number of different tariffs to the different uses of the music videos.

VPL takes an assignment of its members' public performance and dubbing rights in music videos and a non-exclusive licence of the broadcasting rights.

VPL collects performing income from use of music videos but, unlike PPL, it's not obliged by law to share this income with performers, only with its record company members. There is no fee for joining as it covers its running costs by charging a fee to administer these rights.

ASSOCIATION OF INDEPENDENT MUSIC LIMITED (AIM)

This is a relatively new association, set up in 1999. Its members are drawn from the independent sector of the music business, mostly the record company side but including publishers, production companies and manufacturers. It's a non-profit-making trade organisation for independent record companies and distributors in the UK.

AIM is based in London, and acts as a forum for debate and also has a lobbying function. Its function as a trade association means that it also has a collective bargaining role.

THE PERFORMING RIGHT SOCIETY (PRS)

PRS is the UK collection society for composers, songwriters and music publishers and is charged with administering the public performance and broadcasting rights in music and lyrics.

Both music publishers and songwriters are members. It was set up in 1914 as a company limited by guarantee. It also represents almost a million foreign music copyright owners through its affiliations with overseas collecting societies.

PRS is based in London. When you become a member of PRS, you have to assign your performing right to PRS. Although members assign rights, they can reserve some categories of rights or types of use of rights in all their works and the rules do allow members to request that PRS doesn't license the performing right in a particular work, for example, if it is unlawfully sampled.

The criteria for membership by a writer is that your work is being broadcast on radio/TV, used online or performed live in concert. There is a membership fee.

The Mechanical Copyright Protection Society Limited (MCPS)

This company was set up in 1911 in order to collectively license mechanical reproduction of music, i.e. the copying of music and the synchronisation of music with visual images (see Chapter 4). MCPS, which had previously had a partnership sharing back-end and administration resources with PRS under the name PRS for Music, was bought outright by PRS in 2013. MCPS continues to operate as a separate limited company under the MCPS moniker and is responsible for the licensing of mechanical rights, but the royalty processing services are currently carried out by PRS under an agreement between itself and MCPS. This agreement is now in short-term extension whilst the MCPS puts the operation of these functions out to tender.

MCPS has both publishers and songwriters as members. Its main area of activity is the negotiating and administering of collective licence schemes.

MCPS doesn't take assignments of rights, but its membership agreement provides that the member appoints MCPS as his agent to manage and administer the mechanical copyright in the UK. It has the mandate to grant licences and collect royalties, but there are exceptions which you can retain for yourself and not grant to MCPS. There are full details on the PRS for Music website – see Membership section. It's also obliged to use its best efforts to prevent infringement of its members' rights. It can take legal action in their name and often does so.

MCPS charges its members a commission for administering the rights and collecting the royalties. You can become a writer member if your music is being broadcast on radio/TV; used online; performed live in concert or otherwise played in public, but as a writer you may not need to become an MCPS member if you are published and your publisher is a publisher member.

Acknowledgements

Thanks to Rico Calleja and *The Reporter* for the majority of my information on the law and cases and to Ben Challis for the general music law updates. Acknowledgements also to CMU, MBW and *Music Week*. To Tom Orange for additional research and to Greg Williams for his help with the typing of the manuscript.

Index